VOLUME 2

THE GOLF
MARKETING
BIBLE

ANDREW WOOD

Legendary Marketing
www.LegendaryMarketing.com
800-827-1663

© 2017 Legendary Marketing

ISBN-13: 978-1546660286
ISBN-10: 1546660283

Price: $69.95

This book is dedicated to the PGA & LPGA professionals, the unsung heroes of the golf industry. I am glad to count hundreds of them among my friends. I want to say a heartfelt thank you to them for enhancing my enjoyment of the game in every way. From my initial introduction to golf, to my early lessons on swing, etiquette, and history, a PGA professional was always close at hand and still is today!

The Golf Marketing Bible

Table of
CONTENTS

INTRODUCTION

P erhaps the most potent quote I have ever read in my life is Albert Einstein's definition of insanity. He defined insane people as: *People who do the same thing over and over again and yet expect different results!*

Nowhere is that quote truer than in the world of golf course marketing.

I never cease to be amazed by the seemingly ostrich-like mentality of some people in this business. Clubs desperately cling to the hope that even though 100 of their closest competitors have identical websites, identical email marketing and identical pricing courtesy of their favorite 3rd party tee time vendor, it will somehow bring them more business!

Clubs are putting up boring web sites and running weekly discount e-mail, competing against each other by offering deeper and deeper discounts, losing five bucks or more a player and hoping to "make it up in volume!"

My company, Legendary Marketing, is an ad agency, but is very different from a traditional ad agency. We are a PR company but are also very different from a traditional PR company. We are a web site company and a sales training company. Most important of all, we are a marketing company. That means that unlike a traditional agency that is only a cog in a wheel, Legendary Marketing can help you do everything from generating prospects to selling prospects, to building a brand and building long- term customer relationships. We do golf, real estate, and destination marketing ONLY and we do it better than anyone.

THE GOLF BUSINESS IS CHANGING—AND CHANGING FAST!

Since I wrote the first edition of this book back in 2005 the golf business has been turned upside down by many things including the 2008 recession, changes in lifestyle, the internet and the advent of third party tee time vendors. There are new rules for golf marketing. In fact, rather than rules, they are more like laws. If you break them, you will not succeed. There are plenty of courses that won't make the 36-hole cut in a tough market, which means they won't be playing at all on the weekend! That may not be you, but I urge you to read this book carefully. It is based on real marketing results from the thousands of clubs, resorts, golf schools and destinations worldwide that Legendary Marketing has helped with their marketing. Whether or not you choose to do business with my company or pass this information on to someone else for immediate action, this book contains proven strategies for golf marketing success. Ignore them at your peril!

– Andrew Wood

Marketing Legend

Crystal River, Florida

Andrew@LegendaryMarketing.com

CHAPTER ONE

The Legendary Point of View

HOW I DISCOVERED THE SECRET TO EXPONENTIAL GROWTH FOR YOUR GOLF CLUB IN—OF ALL PLACES—A KARATE SCHOOL!

I want to share a little history with you and explain how I developed a golf marketing system that NEVER FAILS. I am also going to show how you can grow your club's bottom line by at least $50,000 - $250,000 this year (significantly more if you are a large operation).

Before you tell me how poor or saturated your market is, let me say this: I don't care where your club is located, what the economy is like, or how much competition you have. The principles I will share with you for explosive growth work anywhere, anyplace, anytime!

In *The Golf Marketing Bible*, you will discover numerous strategies for success in three potent areas:

✔ How to generate substantially more leads,

✔ How to gain more money from each sale you make, and

✔ How to get golfers coming back to you again and again!

Armed with this information, you can *instantly* improve your results and quickly DOMINATE your market!

Perhaps the biggest problem you will have in applying our Legendary marketing system is that most people in the golf business don't believe in exponential growth because they have never experienced it. They have put their hearts and souls into running their clubs and have not seen growth for the last few years, perhaps even a decade so they cannot imagine generating a 200 or 300 percent increase in profits in a single year. Therefore, they don't even try.

I have been fortunate enough to enjoy such massive growth in three different ventures—actually, four counting Legendary Marketing. Each time the growth was generated the same way: by finding the most effective marketing strategies, not just copying what everyone else was doing, and then testing, tweaking, and changing every small detail of the sales and marketing operation until every single area produced maximum results. Before I disclose the secrets to achieving this kind of success at your club, let me share my life-changing experience in the karate business and how it propelled me into a career in marketing. I will also reveal the exciting discovery I made, and how it can catapult YOUR course, resort, real estate development, or teaching facility to the very top while your competition stumbles in the dark.

ALL I EVER WANTED TO BE WAS A GOLF PRO!

All I ever wanted to be was a golf pro, but one small detail held me back from a career on the Tour: lack of talent! Don't get me wrong, I'm usually a scratch player, and I worked at it for years, but I just didn't have that extra edge that a pro player needs.

As fate would have it, I gave a golf lesson to a karate instructor and soon after was accidentally thrust into a new career in the martial arts world.

Two years later, in the late 1980s, I experienced the thrill of exponential growth for the first time. I bought a small karate school in Irvine, California, with no money down. The first month, the business lost $1,000; the second month, it lost $1,000. At that point I was running my school the same way most people run their golf courses. I ran ads in the local paper which looked exactly like the ads all my competitors were running. What I didn't know then was that *all* those ads were terrible to begin with. When I copied them and made alterations, I only made them worse. I never really questioned if there was a better way. I was, as Henry David Thoreau so aptly put it, "Living a life of quiet desperation!" Sure, the phone rang occasionally or someone walked in with a coupon, but the weeks came and went with little real progress and zero profits.

Finally, I sat down with a yellow pad and began some serious soul searching. First, I asked myself what I was doing wrong. Second, and perhaps most important, I wondered what I was going to do about it. The simple act of writing questions down on paper can bring amazing clarity. I quickly realized (surprise, surprise) that the first thing I needed was paying customers. I also realized that since the phone wasn't ringing, my ads were not working.

Please understand what kind of Quantum Leap thinking was going on at this point. Most business owners or managers don't ever think like that. Instead, they are more likely to subscribe to the Professor Slutsky theory.

THE PROFESSOR SLUTSKY THEORY

For those of you not familiar with the good Professor Slutsky's work, allow me to digress a moment. The noted professor did pioneer work with frogs. He started his experiments with a perfectly healthy frog. He yelled "Jump" until the frog moved. He then measured the leap. Then, under anesthesia (in the most humane way possible), he amputated one of the frog's front legs and repeated the "jump" experiment. After measuring again, he amputated the frog's other front leg, yelled "Jump" and measured the leaps, which, as you can guess, were decreasing in length. The frog's back left leg was cut off and again the professor yelled "Jump." The frog's wobbly attempt was duly measured, whereupon the final leg was removed. The professor yelled "Jump" once more but the frog did not respond. Professor Slutsky concluded that, "after amputation of all four legs...the frog became deaf."

I mention this story because whenever marketing doesn't work, most business owners immediately point to the medium rather than the marketing itself. The newspaper doesn't work, TV doesn't work, radio doesn't work, and the website doesn't work and social media is just worthless hype! Rarely if ever do they consider the simple fact that *their* marketing is at fault!

EUREKA!

I came to that exact realization one December morning in late 1987. What followed was a decision that changed my life forever. After acknowledging that I didn't *really* know the first thing about marketing, I rushed to the local bookstore and bought all eight of their marketing books. The first was David Ogilvy's classic *Ogilvy on Advertising*. I was amazed to learn how changing a simple headline could produce a 500 percent increase in response...how adding a picture of scissors next to a coupon could increase redemption by up to 35 percent...how reverse type (white letters on black) sharply decreases readership, and so on. Before I finished the second book, I ordered *twenty more books!* I was like a man possessed...highlighting, underlining, and taking notes for 30 straight days. All through the Christmas holiday I soaked up marketing information like a sponge.

Up until then all the ads that I had seen for karate schools were pictures of people flying through the air and kicking somebody in the face. What I didn't realize was that 80 percent of the world gravitates towards the negative. So when most people looked at these ads, they saw themselves as the one getting kicked! Instead of running in to sign up for karate, most ran the other way!

After reading the books, I designed some new ads. I began putting pictures of smiling women and children in the ads. I listed the benefits and changed the headlines to *Build Your Child's Confidence* and *Build Your Self-Esteem*. I changed the whole focus of my advertising to let people know that the martial arts were fun!

BINGO!

The phone rang off the hook. I signed up 30 new students in a single month as opposed to the five I typically signed up! I was ecstatic but realized there was still work to be done. If I could get such a massive increase in response just by studying the gurus of marketing, perhaps I could capitalize on these leads even more by improving my sales skills. I purchased tapes from the likes of Dale Carnegie, Tom Hopkins, Joe Girard, and Zig Ziglar. Suddenly, instead of closing two out of ten leads, I was closing eight out of ten and it didn't cost me a dime more to do it!

Next, I turned my attention to customer retention, newsletters, thank-you cards, and follow up. I adopted the tactics I found in books like Carl Sewall's *Customers for Life*. By the end of the year, customers were staying an average of six months instead of three!

Imagine what it could do for your income
if all of your players played your course twice
as often as they do now!

NATIONWIDE FRANCHISE FROM SCRATCH IN JUST SIX YEARS!

At 27 years of age, in my second year in business, I walked out of a 1,250 square foot karate school in a suburban strip mall with $128,000 in my pocket—a net gain of $121,000 over my previous year's income. And this was in the 1980s when you could buy a new Taylor Made Tour Burner driver for $115!

Six years later, I had 156 franchise schools, plus 275 affiliates nationwide and was making millions.

Lots of people built martial arts empires based on teaching styles and reputation. I did it solely on the RESULTS of my *marketing system*. I did it by creating a system that could be duplicated. Regardless of teaching style or location, a school owner could connect the dots and be guaranteed a predictable result for his time, money, and effort.

Here's what specific, proven, tested systems look like for karate schools:

- ✔ Do this specific promotion (Kids' Ninja Birthday) and you will get 15–20 leads.

- ✔ Run this ad (He Never Cleaned His Room Until I Took Him to Karate) in the local paper's family section and you will get 18–20 calls.

- ✔ Follow this script (Phone Script 101) when the prospects call and 16 of them will agree to visit for a trial lesson.

- ✔ Follow this exact process when the prospect shows up (from greeting to sign up and everything in between) and 12 of the 16 people will sign up for lessons.

- ✔ Of the 12 people that sign up, follow this procedure (Upgrade 101) and eight of them will upgrade to a $3,000 program in the first six weeks.

Bottom line? If you followed the program, there was very little chance of failure. Each component had been tried, tested, and measured so the results were within a tight range, completely predictable across the country regardless of city, state, facility, or style. Because it worked and because it was structured in a step-by- step manner that anyone could follow with little effort, it was hugely successful! You can do the same thing with your golf marketing.

LEVERAGE, SYSTEMIZE, SUCCEED!

The success I enjoyed in the karate business and am enjoying in the golf business all goes back to that one simple premise. Start with a solid marketing strategy and then test to find the marketing techniques that work best. You can then leverage each aspect of your marketing plan by just a few percent and turn it into a system that can be repeated again and again. This process can have a cumulative result of *hundreds of thousands of dollars in a single season*. That means leveraging the power of every single ad, every single promotion, coupon, postcard, sales letter, and phone script. Follow this strategy and you can leverage your income exponentially anywhere, anytime, under any market conditions.

Think about it...

The ads that generate leads for your club whether online or offline cost the same to run whether they pull five responses or 500. The billboard on the highway is the same cost to rent each month whether people drive past it without a glance or hang an instant U-turn and head straight for your parking lot!

It costs you the same salary whether your outing or membership director converts two leads out of 10 or seven leads out of 10.

And it costs the same for the employees at the counter whether you sell a player a $45 green fee or a $2,800 membership, so you might as well MAXIMIZE every single aspect of your marketing!

TACTICS VS. STRATEGY

Most golf clubs, resorts, and real estate developments are run on a tactical basis, not a strategic one. Budgets are made and ads are run, but strategy and tactics rarely change from year to year. Clubs run the same type of ads, mail the same type of coupons, and resolve to do a better job of collecting e-mails and using the Internet. Whoosh… another mediocre year goes by.

But it doesn't have to be this way! In a very short time, YOU CAN DOMINATE YOUR MARKET. What it takes is a commitment to change and the use of proven systems.

Consider this...

Let's say that you have 1,000 e-mail addresses of golfers in your area and every time you send a blast it drives ten rounds to your club at an average fee of $50. What would happen if you simply doubled the size of your e-mail list? This isn't exactly rocket science.

If you double the size of your e-mail database, you will double your results, meaning every blast will now bring in 20 rounds. Now imagine what would happen to your bottom line if you tripled or quadrupled the size of your e-mail database.

Exponential growth, that's what!

Five thousand e-mails would drive 50 rounds or $2,500 as opposed to the $500 in revenue you presently generate from 1,000 names! And that's not just once—it's each and every time you do a blast!

Legendary Marketing provides a great resource for this www.LegendaryLeadGeneration.com

Let me give you a real-world example...

One client recently built an e-mail list of over 8,000 names in less than a month when there was a foot of snow on the ground. (He also got them to answer 20 questions about their playing habits!) How many names did your e-mail list grow this month? While most clubs would have been ecstatic capturing that much player data in a year, let alone a month, this club went a step better.

He entered his data in our data alliance, increasing his reach twofold. (The alliance lets you use twice as many of our names as you put in.) Now he will start the new season with access to 24,000 names, addresses, and e-mails of golfers in his market...up significantly from last year's total of almost none.

Let's assume he only gets 100 players to respond to each e- mail and he mails offers just twice a month. That's 200 players times $50 which is $10,000 a month, times seven months for a total of $70,000. And let's say each player spends an average of $20 on cart fees, beer, and balls. That adds another $28,000 worth of income for a grand total of $98,000 in income from just his e-mail marketing alone. Best of all, the promotion cost him nothing! That's an ROI (return on investment) so great that my meager math skills simply can't calculate it!

But exponential growth is not just about your e-mail marketing. It's about major improvement in your print ads, sales letters, brochures, web site, follow-up, and even the way you answer the phone.

Let's take another example...

Most courses spend X amount of their budget on coupons or ads of some kind. Suppose the ad demanded a response and that the club tracked the results. Let's even say that the response was good and 50 players brought in the ad. What most clubs do at that point is think, "Great, that worked, let's file it away for next year." What they should do is go back and TEST. Try a stronger headline, a different offer, or a different approach. A simple change in the wording can increase response by 500 percent! Think about it... instead of 50 players, an ad could generate 250 players. And that applies to every ad, every mailer, every postcard! If you could increase response just 10 percent from each one, imagine what it would add to your bottom line!

A direct mail piece (which still works amazingly well) can produce staggeringly different results based on the call to action alone. For example, a golf real estate company produced a $200,000, 40-page direct mail brochure. Though it had lots of pretty pictures, it had no subheads to draw the reader into the copy and no captions under the pictures. So it had already broken two of the most basic laws of direct mail marketing. But it got worse. The only call to action was a bounce-back card. You know, one of those postage-paid deals that worked great in the 1980s before the advent of the Internet. What did the bounce-back card offer the reader? A video tour of the property? An invitation for an on-site visit? An invitation for the sales staff to call the prospect to answer some questions? NO. It offered the prospect another 40-page puff piece left over from the previous year's unsuccessful campaign. Exciting, huh?

A direct call to action on the last page could have turned this loser into a winner, increasing response exponentially. But the brochure looked nice so everyone okayed it without any thought as to what they wanted the prospect to do next! Amazing? Not really. Most golf marketing is awful when it comes to obeying the basic rules of response-driven marketing. A few simple changes to the offer could have made the difference between a meager 0.3 percent response and a 2.5 percent response...between 300 leads and 7,000 leads!

Don't stop me now; I'm on a roll...

Take those bland "Dear John Doe" follow-up letters or emails that golf operations send to real estate leads, former resort guests, and potential event clients. They cost the same in printing and postage or email list rental whether they generate 0.1 percent or 3 percent response. And that goes for however many of these things are sent out from your club! We're talking tens of thousands of dollars here.

APPLY THESE STRATEGIES TO THE GOLF OUTING BUSINESS

Why send out 100 corporate-speak letters or emails to past tournament directors (some of whom might be dead) hoping that 20 of them book again this year? How about trying a completely NEW STRATEGY that none of your competitors will even dream of? Start with a telemarketing campaign to expand your database. Follow it up with an aggressive direct mail campaign and or once a month. Sounds retro I know but it works great and none of your competitors will be doing this! You could bring in 15 more events this year at an average of $10,000 an event! There's another $150,000 to fatten your bottom line.

Imagine for a moment that your tournament database was 500 current names instead of 100 dusty names that haven't been checked in five years. If you contacted an additional 400 prospects in the next 30 days—I mean actually talked to the people who are going to hold a tournament in your market this year—how much more business would it mean for you? Double, triple, perhaps ten times more business!

Using just such a telemarketing approach, we generated 467 leads in Orlando; 375 in Denver; 480 in Westchester County, New York; and plenty more in other areas. Our in-house telemarketing staff makes over 4,000 calls and builds a database of prospects in your area including charities, large corporations, and fraternal organizations. How many courses have the time or personnel to do that in-house? Probably none! But how many outings would you have to book from a list of 400 prospects to make this type or service worth its weight in gold?

Let's just say you book 20 more outings this year. What percentage of growth would that mean for your outing business— 20 percent, 50 percent, or perhaps even 100 percent? That's my whole point. A simple change in strategy and a simple reallocation of funds could exponentially increase your outing business!

I haven't even touched on the different ways you can package your outings *without discounting* to bring in droves of additional business. For example, several of our clients out-marketed all their competitors last year by offering a $25 tee gift to every player who played in an outing. Instead of discounting their green fees to match others in the area, they changed the rules by offering more value. The tournament organizer looked like a hero by giving every player a gift. The course wins, too, because the gifts were closeouts that cost only $2 each. A classic win-win situation and a dramatic increase in outing business! That's the power of exponential marketing. By adding 400 more prospects to your database, contacting them more regularly, and making slight changes in the outing package, the results could easily increase outing revenues by $100,000 or more!

HOW TO CREATE A STRONG MARKETING SYSTEM

Establish your desired results. Each system should have a clear, concise statement of the result the system is intended to accomplish.

Diagram the system. The system should be presented in a diagram showing the sequence of events and how they relate to each other.

Describe clear benchmarks. Each action should be identified in sequence so that benchmarks or intermediate goals are created and that the process is clear and unmistakable to anyone who will perform the work.

Assign accountabilities. Accountability must be assigned for each system and the overall system. Accountability should be identified by position, not by person. People come and go...accountability does not!

Determine the timing. Set specific timelines for each bench- mark and document them.

Identify required resources. Every system requires resources such as staffing, postage, supplies, and information. A detailed list of the specific resources and quantities must be provided.

Quantify the system. How will you know you are getting the results you want? You need quantification to give you that objective view.

Establish standards. A good system sets the standards for performance and behavior of the staff operating it. Standards are most easily stated regarding quantity, quality, and behavior.

Document the system. It's not a system until it's documented! You cannot expect people to follow a system that is not documented.

Train in system usage. Both management and staff must be trained in the proper use of the systems *so that EVERY lead is handled in a seamless, consistent, and systematic manner.*

The rest of this book will explain all you need to know to implement such a marketing system, from measurement to benchmarking to marketing methods.

SUMMARY

Superior results come only from better marketing and better follow up. You can achieve better marketing by testing and improving each aspect of your approach. By improving many aspects of your marketing 1–10 percent, you will create MUCH better results overall. Don't expect to do what everyone else does and get better results! Remember that Einstein roughly said that you're crazy to expect new results when you do the same thing over and over!

The best way to ensure that follow up on your new, improved marketing is done consistently and professionally is to systemize it. If you make sure that every person is contacted the same way, the same number of times, and is sent the same follow-up materials, nothing will slip through the cracks. Sales will increase and so will your income.

Make no mistake; following a system in the short term takes more work. There are more steps to follow and more reporting is necessary. Ultimately, however, systems create *less work* as you become *more efficient* and make *more money*. You'll soon wonder how you ever got by without them! Using systems is actually easier than just doing what strikes you as right at the time.

CHAPTER TWO

Don't Fall for These Marketing Myths

O ne of the major reasons that most clubs don't market effectively is that they are under the influence of marketing myths. Who knows how these misleading ideas got started, but many of them have been around for decades. So, before you start any marketing program, you first need to "clear the decks" of these marketing misconceptions.

In this chapter, you will discover:

✔ The secrets of successful golf marketing (an overview; later chapters will provide the details)

✔ What the biggest myths in marketing really are

✔ Why long copy works better than short copy

✔ Why if everyone likes your ad it is probably worthless

✔ How to avoid being seduced by the law of large numbers

✔ Why copying your competitors is a bad idea

To introduce you to the concepts in this critically important chapter I'd like you to read the following letter I sent to my clients.

How a man drowning in debt can change your entire perspective about golf marketing... And dramatically increase <u>Your Club's</u> PROFITS!

Dear Reader:

If spelling, proper punctuation and grammer mattered at all in the REAL world of marketing, I'd be pushing a shopping cart up 5th Avenue with a sign around my neck saying,

"Will Work For Food!"

Instead, despite my lack of formal English skills, I have written 14 books, made millions for myself in three different industries and generated many millions more for my clients! (Some of my clients are already up 33% this year! The ones who listen and act!)

So why then are people in the golf business so caught up in "proper" punctuation, typestyles, logos and image in their clubs' marketing efforts, rather than RESULTS?

Why do they want short copy that ends neatly at the bottom of every page even though long ragged copy like what you are reading now is proven to be more effective in generating response?

Why do they want, glossy ads, lavishly expensive brochures and National Geographic-like photography?

Why do they insist on politically correct copy that polarizes no one and at the same time MOTIVATES no one to ACTION?

I'll tell you why...because the people making the marketing decisions at most clubs don't have to meet payroll out of <u>their</u> own wallets, that's why! *(Add to this the fact that most of them don't know much about marketing and you're really in trouble!)*

They have never had a 2nd and 3rd mortgage on their family's home at the same time! They have never had an additional 121,527 dollars and 58 cents, spread over five different credit cards to keep the kids in private school and to stop the payroll checks from bouncing!

If they had, they would quickly throw out the BS that passes for conventional marketing wisdom in the golf industry! And they would stop 95% of their existing marketing DEAD IN ITS TRACKS! Especially if designed by a traditional ad agency!

Instead, they would target ONLY those people they KNOW for a FACT are their true target market.

Then they would start trying to squeeze every single ounce of response from every single penny they spent reaching ONLY that market!

And they would measure it so meticulously that they would know to the penny what every single promotion produced in terms of leads, conversions and profits!

They would trash the $20,000 image brochures, $10,000 print ads and flashy websites packed full of beautiful pictures and unreadable reverse type that SIMPLY DON'T INCREASE YOUR BUSINESS!

Instead, they would go back to the REAL basics of GREAT MARKETING. Sound Marketing that will make you Millions!

I learned the REAL BASICS OF MARKETING SUCCESS a long time ago because the very food that my family was going to eat depended on my next direct marketing campaign! The lists I choose, the words I crafted, the offers I devised, the calls to actions, the testimonials and P.S. I wrote brought checks in the mail. Checks that were rushed to the bank in a never ending game of beating the bounce charges!

As I got better at targeting my TRUE market and writing headlines and copy, the checks increased until finally I hit pay dirt with a single 8-page letter. That letter, mailed many times brought in over 4 million dollars in three years with a profit margin so huge, even I am embarrassed to tell you!

So how does that information help your club make more money?

It helps you if you PAY ATTENTION to RESULTS not personal preference, image or what others (your manager, boss, owner, ad agency, spouse, etc.) expect you to do because that's what everyone else is doing in the Golf Industry.

It helps you if you stop wasting your money on worthless print ads, expensive brochures and worthless image conscious websites and instead turn your attention to finding targeted prospects and making paper sales pitches to the people who are most likely to respond to your offer. **Let me repeat that, a paper sales presentation** (or web presentation). That means they have a beginning, a middle, an end, a call to action, testimonials and an irresistible offer or Unique Selling Proposition. (See Chapter 8 for more on your USP.)

Here's The Formula for REAL Golf Marketing Success in a Nutshell:

Pick a target list of people who you think are REAL prospects. That means they play a lot of golf right now! Then use your website, landing pages or telemarketing to qualify them as REAL prospects.

Market DIRECTLY to no one, but them! NO ONE!

Send them a sales pitch! Anything else is a TOTAL waste of Money! A real sales pitch on why they should show up at your club's door!

Get them to respond to something, anything that gets them to put their hands up and say "YES I'm interested!"

Follow up on the sale pitch with multiple invites to visit. Get them in front of you!

Sell them a tee time, a lesson, a room or a lot with a carefully scripted presentation.

Ask for referrals and upsell!

By the way, I spelled *grammar* incorrectly at the beginning of this letter to make my point about spelling and grammar and just so someone could complain about it! (If you're worried about my spelling, you're not focusing on your marketing enough!)

Andrew Wood

Marketing Legend

(At least in his own mind!)

P.S. If you think your clientele is too rich, too smart, or too sophisticated for this type of direct approach you are wrong! Very wrong and you are losing millions in the process!!!

P.P.S. By the way, I am not saying you should not have a brochure, it just shouldn't look anything like the one you have! And yes print ads can be a part of your marketing but not the 99.9% you see in the golf magazine on your desk! They are KILLING trees without getting any response.

UNDERSTANDING WHY MOST GOLF MARKETING FAILS

Before I get into the "meat" of how to massively improve the effectiveness of your marketing, it's important to take time to debunk some of the common myths about marketing. This is a

VERY IMPORTANT step because, on your journey to marketing success, managers, owners, spouses, board members, golf pros, and cooks WILL QUESTION YOU AT EVERY TURN. They will question your strategy. They'll tell you that you must do this and that because that is what your competitors are doing. They'll beg you to discount, disagree with your long copy, and advise you on graphics, colors, and media at every opportunity.

**There is no place for myth
or personal prejudice in a comprehensive,
results-driven, marketing system.**

Most opinions are WRONG!

Everyone has an opinion about marketing. Rarely, however, are those opinions based on facts. Instead, they are almost always based on personal preferences for colors or styles, or based on myths that have been handed down for decades from others and repeated so many times that they are now WRONGLY considered to be FACT by 99 percent of people. Most important, since the people judging your marketing are rarely the same people as those you are trying to attract, their opinions on anything are worthless! Worthless because their opinions are based not on marketing science but are based on their own social, economic, and psychological preferences, NOT those of the people you are trying to attract!

Unless you are willing to drop your personal preferences and debunk years of marketing misinformation in favor of proven marketing science, you cannot accomplish your goals of achieving Legendary Marketing at your course.

The following pages include the biggest myths and inhibitors to marketing success. READ THEM, understand them, believe them and take them as gospel. Share them with your owner, boss, manager, spouse, or whomever else is most likely to sabotage your efforts. Get them to understand the science of EFFECTIVE marketing before you attempt to market, so that everyone is on the same page, moving in the same direction.

AN ESSENTIAL CRASH COURSE IN MARKETING MYTHS

1. People don't read anymore. MYTH! The biggest myth in marketing is that *people don't read anymore* or at least they won't read lots of copy. The truth is, in fact, the opposite. In almost every case, long copy will out-pull short copy. The key factor is INTEREST. If people don't care about golf, they won't read anything, long or short. If prospects are interested in what you have to offer, and if you provide information in a compelling fashion, they will read it. The more you tell them, the more they'll trust you and the more interested they'll get in your offer.

Send me a magazine on horses, and I'll pass it to my wife without glancing at a single page. Send me a magazine on cars, and I'll give it a quick flip through. Send me a magazine on sports cars, and it will get a little more of my attention as I flip through every page, scanning for something that catches my eye. But send me a magazine on Ferraris, and I will take it to bed with me and read it cover-to-cover, word by word, every article and every relevant ad. The difference in how I read these different magazines is my level of interest in the subject matter. If I am interested in a topic, I want to know as much as possible. If I am not interested, I don't want to know anything. Your customers are no different. They will pay attention to what interests them and will ignore what does not! They want more of what interests them and less of what does not!

This very week as proof my best performing article among many, across many different platforms including Facebook, LinkedIn and email was four pages long!

2. The more people who like your ad, the better your ad or website! MYTH! Design your marketing to create response, not to please your owner, your members, or your wife!

Graphic designers are not marketers! In fact, in many cases, they have the opposite effect!

Web designers are not marketers!

And, if the truth be told, most ad agencies are not marketers! A nice way of explaining this is that most ad agencies are bored with simple approaches that work. Or, they are so busy that they tend to produce generic ads. A more cynical way of explaining the failure of many ads produced by ad agencies is that the agencies are more interested in competing for awards and inflating their egos with their clever designs than they are in making money for their clients.

Recently I gave three important presentations to large potential accounts. In each case, several of the people in the room did not play golf, and most had minimal "real" marketing experience! If you want to estimate what marketing will appeal to your audience— golfers—you should have your prospects judge it. That's what focus groups and market research are about. (Research with small numbers has problems, too, but at least it's a start.)

No matter what people say about being "open-minded," they (as we all do) judge you on their preconceived notions about marketing and with their personal preferences for design, text, and style. They may know something; they may know nothing—but make no mistake about it, 99 percent of the time they judge your work based on what they like, or think they know about marketing, not on what will actually work!

The key to great marketing is not to design ads, websites, and mail campaigns that people like. It is to design marketing that motivates targeted prospects to take the action you want.

Your target market is a very tiny percentage of the entire population. Your ideal prospects are a certain age, have certain hobbies, wants, needs, and passions. If the people who make marketing decisions are not avid golfers, they cannot possibly understand the emotional connection that a good ad will have with an avid golfer any more than I can understand why my wife enjoys mucking out horse stables and riding the beasts. (I was once given some very sound advice which I will share now. Never take up a hobby in which the main party eats while you sleep!) Nor unless they have exceptional marketing experience are they qualified to provide any useful input on the ads in question—*but they will anyway!*

Some of the best golf marketing my company has ever produced has never seen the light of day because it does not meet the criteria of the person paying the bills. I call it the Everyone-Loves-My-Ad Syndrome!

Just because everyone loves your ad doesn't mean that the phone will ring or that people will buy your lessons or come to your course.

You should design ads and websites specifically for the people who you think will buy.

You should test different ads and headlines based on *response*. It doesn't matter whether you like the ad, your wife likes the ad or anyone on your staff likes the ad. What matters is whether or not the people you want to buy respond to the ad.

I once designed an ad for a well-known manufacturer of graphite shafts. At the time it was quite simply the best ad I had ever designed. With all due modesty, first, let me tell you that I understand golf advertising better than just about anyone on the planet. Second, I backed up my knowledge with abundant and irrefutable research on what people look for when they buy a golf club. Third, I designed an eye-catching ad that showed the product in use, had a sub-box that highlighted the product, and copy that would have golfers foaming at the mouth in anticipation of owning such a club. The VP of marketing who had been in the golf business for many years loved it. So did a host of golfers with whom I had tested the ad! The new CEO, a recent Harvard graduate who *didn't* play golf, wasn't sure. He said he wasn't getting a "warm, fuzzy feeling" about it. He left the conference room, which adjoined the manufacturing plant, and entered the factory. There I watched in complete disbelief as he wandered from worker to worker, of whom 50 percent spoke no English, and the other 50 percent were suffering from the effects of too much glue sniffing and showed them the ad.

Five minutes later he returned and announced, "The boys don't get it!" **The boys didn't get it because the boys didn't play golf.** *He* didn't get it. He wanted the workers to feel good about the ad; he didn't want an ad that would work! Unfortunately, this general scenario occurs in many, many businesses. Owners, CEOs, and marketing executives who don't know the first thing about advertising, and who don't truly understand their end users, make terrible decisions based on what they like, not what the customers and prospects are looking for or will respond to!

Shoppers buy only two things: benefits and solutions. They do not buy features. They do not buy because of your logo, because your picture happens to be in the ad, or because you have been in business for 20 years. They only care about what your business or product can do for them. Is it cheaper or more reliable? Will they feel more important being a member of your club? Will they hit the ball farther, straighter, and more consistently with your golf clubs?

After my first ad for the shaft maker was rejected, I came back with another that offered information to people in the club-fitting business who were among the prime buyers of their shafts. This time the CEO turned down the idea because he feared it might generate too much interest—and clog up the company's phone system! I resigned after that one.

The shaft maker's new ad agency designed a two-page color ad containing a picture of a large tree with a hole in it, the hole supposedly made by a golf ball on its way toward a distant green. One of their golf shafts lay across the bottom of the page. There was a weak headline, which I can't recall, but it had nothing to do with the product. That was it. No reason to buy, no benefits, no testimonials! Although they had a good market and a great product, they allowed themselves to be bought out by a larger company with deeper pockets because with marketing like that you can go broke quickly!

Before you hire anyone to design an ad campaign, website or landing page, educate yourself. Read a good marketing book. Discover the real principles of marketing from a true leader in the field, not from someone who happens to run a small design company down the street and thinks they know something about marketing. Read *Ogilvy on Advertising*—Ogilvy built the biggest ad agency in the world from scratch. In its pages, you will discover many things you never knew, like why long copy ALWAYS sells better than short copy. Or get the classic book *Scientific Advertising* by Claude Hopkins, or Al Reis and Jack Trout's classic book on *Positioning*. Or one of Dr. Rick Crandall's newer books on marketing services. In books like this, you will discover that the real secrets of marketing are not what most people think they are— in fact, very often they are the opposite!

The number one goal of a good email, ad, letter, social media post, or brochure is to connect with a specifically targeted reader and motivate that reader to action.

In the case of an ad for a golf club, that means not just any reader. Not your wife who doesn't play golf, or son who is 14 and into rap music, but a targeted reader, a golfer.

Even better, you probably want a very specific type of golfer, a player of a certain age and income. Your ad should be written and designed only for him, not anyone else. What anyone but that targeted reader thinks of your copy or design does not matter one iota! In fact, if lots of unqualified people look at the ad and like it, it's an almost sure sign that the ad is not speaking to your target audience in an emotional and personal enough way to be effective. It's almost like "they" should be the only ones who get it!

3. Reaching 100,000 people is typically more effective in generating revenue than mailing to 500 people whom you know for a fact play golf and live in your market area. MYTH!

Thousands of ad salesmen make a living on seducing golf courses with large numbers. It boggles my mind when I talk to golf courses looking for 100 new members. They're running ads statewide, even nationwide, in numerous glossy magazines or web portals that total 3 million readers when they are in fact looking for 100 people willing to spend, say, $75,000 on a membership and perhaps a half a million on a home. The theory is that a certain percentage of people who read your ad will respond. That, my friend, is simply not true!

In a 100-page magazine, only a tiny fraction of the readers will ever see your full-page ad with the picture of the signature hole in a section that has 12–16 pages of similar ads featuring a fairway as green as a shamrock flanked by water so blue that an Aegean postcard would go green with envy! Maybe only 1 percent will read your smaller ad.

The same is true of people who blanket market to new homeowners—a group where, statistically, 90 percent don't play golf!

Successful marketing is, and always will be, about reaching targeted prospects.

A targeted mailing list of 5,000 prospects would be 70 percent cheaper and about 1,000 percent more effective than mass advertising in the newspaper or web portal to 100,000 people. But that small number throws people off. They think BIGGER is better. In fact, TARGETED is better! That means targeted mailings, targeted e-mails, targeted websites, and doubling or tripling the play of the people you already have as players. Targeted Facebook ads would be even better driving people to a landing page at a fraction of the cost.

If you ran a Facebook ad and got 150 names, addresses, and e-mails, you would be so far ahead of the game compared to a local newspaper ad or web portal that it's not even funny! But most people just don't get it! They think the numbers are too small. Instead, they are seduced by huge circulation numbers when they should be focused on the *quality* of the leads they get, not the *quantity!*

4. You don't want to exclude or offend anyone with your marketing. MYTH!

That's exactly what you want to do—exclude all those people who aren't good prospects, so you don't waste any more time or money chasing them. When I say offend, I don't mean you stand up and insult them. Think of it more in terms of how a Republican might react to a Democrat's comments.

For example, say you are the proud owner of an 8,000-yard, Pete Dye masterpiece with water on every hole. Your market is clearly better players.

LADIES, SISSIES, WIMPS, AND 30 HANDICAPS NEED NOT APPLY!

This might be a nice provocative headline to appeal to macho single digits like me! Sure, some ladies or higher handicappers might take offense, but the number of macho guys you excite by this headline will more than make up for the furor of a few people who are obviously NOT your true target market. In fact, if people make a fuss about your ad, you will get free publicity with the target market that matters to you!

You have to take a stand, and the more targeted your stand is to your true market, the more effective your marketing will be, even at the expense of excluding or even irritating some players.

5. If all your competitors are doing it, you have to do it too just to compete! MYTH!

You do not have to advertise in the local golf publication just because 50 of your favorite competitors do! You don't have to be on Golf Now or EZlinks just because your competitors do. In fact, it's plain stupid to do so. Nor do you need to discount because they do! The less you act like your competition, the quicker you will define your own position in the marketplace!

Those are the five big myths we come up against again and again. Don't let your marketing decisions be influenced by these dangerous beliefs.

TOP 20 REASONS WHY MOST GOLF MARKETING FAILS

In the next few pages, I'm going to save you hundreds of thousands of dollars and years of trial and error by detailing exactly why most clubs fail to reach their marketing goals. This is not subjective; this is not our opinion. It is based on over 20 years of research into the science of marketing and the analysis of several hundred golf club clients. (Some of these 20 reasons also relate to the five major myths I just covered. That's okay; this is a full list.)

Here are the top 20 reasons why clubs' marketing efforts fail. Read them, believe them and resolve not to do them!

1. They don't collect enough data (golfers' names, e-mails, and so forth).

2. They don't do enough with the data they do collect. This process works best when it's completely automated such as e-mails added automatically to your list.

3. Their websites are ineffective. They don't increase business!

4. They do not track their ad or promotional campaigns, so they have no exact way of knowing which ads or promotions were effective.

5. Their ads, email and website copy stink! They have cute headlines, pretty pictures, and impotent corporate speak copy that motivates no one into action.

6. They run campaigns that people say "look good" rather than ones that actually get the phone to ring.

7. There is no written sales process or scripting or training of the people answering the phones and in charge of memberships, outings, and banquets.

8. Follow-up to all requests is not automated or systemized, so follow- up is poor.

9. They do almost the exact same marketing as ALL their competitors; they are afraid to risk being different.

10. They have a poor seat of the pants social media strategy rather than a detailed 90-day plan.

11. They discount green fees to get more business rather than look for ways to add more value.

12. Their budgets are based on a percentage of gross or a number someone handed down from head office instead of being based on the goals they are trying to meet. In other words, the goals are pure fantasy with no consideration whatsoever of the income they need to generate.

13. They do NOTHING to set themselves CLEARLY apart from other clubs in their marketplace. Yet these clubs still say "We have the best course and great customer service"...yeah, yeah, yeah, tell it to the judge (as my kids used to say!).

14. Their service is about 80 percent worse than they think it is! They have no system in place for measuring service, and they never run extensive customer surveys so they never really know how good or BAD their service TRULY is!

15. They fail to thank their customers with letters, cards, and small gifts as is done in almost all other professional businesses.

16. They confuse "loyalty" programs with discount programs! Loyalty is earned, NOT BOUGHT!

17. They fail to outsource the things they don't do well (like social media).

18. They don't capitalize on the marketing automation that's available to help them maximize their operations the most!

19. They don't spend enough time studying or doing marketing. (You tend to get the best results from the things you focus on

20 They keep doing what they have always done because it's easier than changing to a more systematic approach that would actually work. Meanwhile, their market share is sinking faster than John Daly in quicksand.

SUMMARY

Now you have the key information why most clubs don't get where they want to go. You are ready to do things differently and get the corresponding successful result!

CHAPTER THREE

Benchmarking and Measuring Your Results

All successful marketing begins with information. But information alone is not enough. You need insight and understanding into what makes your customers and prospects tick—what motivates them, what offers they are most likely to respond to, and what is the most effective way to communicate with them. But, first, a question.

WHERE ARE YOU NOW?

You may not have a clue as to where you are now. You may have just taken over a club, you may not be privy to past information, or you might just be lousy at keeping records—most people are! No matter how good or bad your information is, you have to start somewhere. The first step to achieving marketing success for your club is clarity—knowing where you are and where you want to be!

In this chapter, you will discover:

✔ What benchmarking is

✔ How to benchmark yourself

✔ Your strategic indicators

✔ How to measure your marketing results

✔ How to measure your status

We will start by benchmarking where you are now. Benchmarking is a process where you compare yourself to others. The simplest comparisons are to your direct competitors. However, benchmarking can be much more than that. You should also be comparing yourself to the best. And, by the best, I mean more than other golf courses. For instance, you should compare your restaurant to the best restaurants in town. You might study Disney World to determine what kind of entertainment experience your golfers want. And, you might compare your pro shop to Nordstrom or some other store that is known for great customer service.

Benchmarking is done in three stages:

Find tangible numbers about your current performance.

Measure intangibles like how you stack up to your competitors.

Take stock of your resources and programs you already have in place.

The benchmarking process we employ is very detailed. There are many worksheets and we constantly tweak them to make the data more useful (and, therefore, more valuable). I urge you to put in the work necessary to measure your real strengths and weaknesses.

To give you a brief idea of what's involved, use the following scales to rate your club and your competitors' clubs on the following scales:

1 = Lowest; 10 = Highest

How good is your course layout? 1 2 3 4 5 6 7 8 9 10

How good is your course conditioning? 1 2 3 4 5 6 7 8 9 10

How well known is your course 1 2 3 4 5 6 7 8 9 10 in the area?

How do you compare against your competition in general?	1	2	3	4	5	6	7	8	9	10
How do you compare against your biggest competitor?	1	2	3	4	5	6	7	8	9	10
How do you compare against your second biggest competitor?	1	2	3	4	5	6	7	8	9	10
How do you compare against your third biggest competitor?	1	2	3	4	5	6	7	8	9	10
How well trained are your staff?	1	2	3	4	5	6	7	8	9	10
How loyal are your customers?	1	2	3	4	5	6	7	8	9	10

Finding out where you are now and where you want to be is an interesting, challenging, and eye-opening experience. Once you have completed these steps, you will have a far better understanding of how to measure important tangible and intangible data so that you can maximize your marketing efforts. Please take the time to do this.

The following pages contain a brief phone survey for benchmarking a daily-fee club against other local courses. If you're a membership club, you can easily modify or add questions to collect the appropriate data.

DAILY-FEE CLUB PHONE SURVEY

Hello, this is Mary from Legendary Research, am I speaking to (name)? Great.

How are you today, (name)?

That's good, (name). The reason for my call is …

How often do you play a month?	1 2 3 4 5 6 7 8 9 10
How often do you play our course?	1 2 3 4 5 6 7 8 9 10

On a scale of 1 to 10, how would you rate (course), where 1 is the lowest, least favorable rating and 10 is the highest, most favorable rating:

Staff   1 2 3 4 5 6 7 8 9 10

Overall friendliness & service of our staff?   1 2 3 4 5 6 7 8 9 10

The bag staff?   1 2 3 4 5 6 7 8 9 10

The pro shop staff?   1 2 3 4 5 6 7 8 9 10

The starter?   1 2 3 4 5 6 7 8 9 10

The ranger?   1 2 3 4 5 6 7 8 9 10

The beer cart?   1 2 3 4 5 6 7 8 9 10

The restaurant staff?   1 2 3 4 5 6 7 8 9 10

Conditions

The condition of the range?   1 2 3 4 5 6 7 8 9 10

The condition of the range balls?   1 2 3 4 5 6 7 8 9 10

The overall condition of the course?   1 2 3 4 5 6 7 8 9 10

The condition of the greens?   1 2 3 4 5 6 7 8 9 10

The speed of the greens?   1 2 3 4 5 6 7 8 9 10

The condition of the fairways?   1 2 3 4 5 6 7 8 9 10

The condition of the traps?   1 2 3 4 5 6 7 8 9 10

The pace of play?   1 2 3 4 5 6 7 8 9 10

How do you like the layout?   1 2 3 4 5 6 7 8 9 10

How difficult is the course?   1 2 3 4 5 6 7 8 9 10
(where 1 = not at all difficult and 10 = one of the most difficult)

Which three other courses in the area do you typically play?

Course #1 _____

How does (your course) rate overall against them? Not as good, about the same, better?

How would you rate the value you received for your green fee (where 1 = not at all a good value, and 10 = an exceptional value)

1   2   3   4   5   6   7   8   9   10

What do you like best about the facility? What three things should they do to make your experience better? _____

Course #2 _____

How does (your course) rate overall against them? Not as good, about the same, better?

How would you rate the value you received for your green fee (where 1 = not at all a good value, and 10 = an exceptional value)

1   2   3   4   5   6   7   8   9   10

What do you like best about the facility? What three things should they do to make your experience better? _____

Course #3 _____

How does (your course) rate overall against them? Not as good, about the same, better?

How would you rate the value you received for your green fee (where 1 = not at all a good value, and 10 = an exceptional value)

1   2   3   4   5   6   7   8   9   10

What do you like best about the facility? What three things should they do to make your experience better?_____

MEASURING YOUR MARKETING RESULTS

Most club managers and owners would have a lot of empathy for the founder of Wrigley's gum, William Wrigley, Jr. At one time, Wrigley's was one of the largest advertisers in the world. One day a young reporter asked Wrigley if the huge amount of money he spent on advertising was a waste of money. He replied:

> Young man, I am sure that 50 percent of the money I spend on advertising is a total waste. The problem is, I'm not sure which half it is!

Things have come a long way since then. Today, every aspect of your marketing is trackable and accountable, but only if the proper system is followed.

You want your marketing to produce more leads and better- quality leads. This can only be accomplished if you meticulously track the results from each email, social media ad, direct mail piece, mailing list, billboard, and print or banner ad campaign. The results will help you to spend your marketing dollars where they are most effective.

Using paper systems, your website and various analytics you will be able to track and quantify all of your marketing efforts. This will lead to your making smarter decisions about your marketing, resulting in a dramatic increase in your return on investment.

THE IMPORTANCE OF MEASURING RESULTS

Legendary Marketing was recently asked to consult on a major golf real estate project. The client had just fired their "high falutin'" ad agency that happened to be one of the hottest shops around. The agency was well known for producing high-gloss, award-winning ads and collateral materials. Unfortunately, winning awards doesn't produce sales.

When we asked the client about the exact results of their previous campaign, they looked at us with a straight face and told us it simply hadn't worked. So we pressed further: "Of the $900,000 you spent on advertising last year, how many leads came from each of the magazines or websites and from each of the ads you ran?" The blank looks and nervous glances spoke volumes. It turns out their agency didn't use any tracking codes! So the client spent nearly $1 million but couldn't tell us if their meager response came from the *New York Times*, *Atlanta Magazine*, or the *Traverse City Record a blog or banner ad*!

How could this happen?

Simple. It's a lot easier to design pretty campaigns and talk about building an image than it is to put your company on the line and deliver the goods! If you start tracking all of your campaigns, you will quickly see what works and what doesn't. Unfortunately, very few people ever quantify their marketing efforts in detail.

Key questions

- ✔ What is your conversion rate of leads-to-customers? That is, of 100 people who call or visit your facility, how many buy?

- ✔ How much do they buy?

- ✔ What does it cost you to get a new customer? (That includes ads, phone calls, follow-up letters, commissions, and YOUR TIME!)

- ✔ How long does it normally take to turn a lead into a customer? How many times do you contact them?

- ✔ Do you have a written, structured process by which this process occurs?

- ✔ How could you shorten this time?

By taking the time to answer these questions, you can quickly spot holes in your marketing plan and find ways to maximize your response. The more you measure, the better your marketing will become!

WHAT YOU MUST TRACK

You MUST set up systems to track every single ad, e-mail blast, postcard, and promotion that you run.

You must have a tracking system so that you know

your exact response to everything.

It's the only way to calculate your ROI (return on investment) and MAXIMIZE your marketing.

For example, we did an e-blast for Innisbrook Resort in Florida. The blast cost $1,500 and generated $28,000 of room-night revenue. We know this because the blast was set up with a unique contact point on the website and an 800-number that only appeared on that blast. Thirty days after the campaign, we were sure about the return on investment and whether we should use that list again.

List performance and ad performance

List and ad performance can be measured by the number of responses generated by the offer, publication, and timing.

Website and landing page performance

Web performance can be measured by factors like number of visitors, amount of data collected, tee times booked, and product sales.

E-blast performance

E-blast performance can be measured by the number of opens, the number of click-throughs, and the number of people signing up or taking advantage of a specific offer.

We have tracked the success of our in-house e-mail lists for generating golf real estate leads on a cost-per-lead basis. In other words, rather than charging a lump sum to do a massive e-blast, we will charge the client only when a real lead is generated. (I know of no one in the golf real estate business willing to put their performance on the line like that. We similarly guarantee other responses from our e-mail blasts for rounds, memberships, and so on.)

MEASURING CUSTOMER SATISFACTION

All the marketing in the world is not going to help you in the long run if you fail to meet or exceed customer expectations. Customer satisfaction should be tracked regularly using surveys:

✔ At the counter

✔ At the 1st tee

✔ Off the 18th green

✔ Online

✔ In the mail

✔ On the phone

(See also the chapter on Customer Service.)

TELE-RESEARCH AND MEMBER SATISFACTION PROGRAMS

Have you ever been contacted by phone and asked to evaluate your golf experience? Probably not. A third-party phone call like this to a recent player is by far your most effective tool in gauging customer satisfaction. The customer is far more likely to be open and honest with a third party.

Tele-research can also answer important marketing questions like why some people buy memberships or golf homes, and others don't, or why some people support every club event and others never show up. The answers to these and similar questions can have a dramatic effect on the success of your club's marketing efforts and customer loyalty.

Tele-research programs will give you fresh insight into exactly what you should be doing to attract and satisfy your current and prospective members. Members and prospective members will speak more freely to a third party about topics like:

✔ Why they play or *don't* play your club more often

✔ What they are looking for in a club

✔ What they like and, more importantly, what they don't like about your club, your people, and your offerings

✔ Why they joined or bought somewhere else

Armed with these findings, you can enhance your marketing, your offers, your pricing, and your sales presentation to gain a competitive edge. You'll also increase member retention by offering exactly the types of products and services members want.

You can, of course, do an online survey as well. Faster cheaper and easier to do but you will never get the same insight than from actually talking to your customers.

SUMMARY

Benchmarking helps you compare yourself to the best and set goals for your performance. Then you must track and measure all your marketing results. It is critical to your long-term marketing success that you know exactly what your response is to each and every method you employ. Only then can you tweak your strategy and put every dollar where it is most likely to generate a profitable return every time!

CHAPTER FOUR

Defining Your Market

What types of people make up your customer base?

What motivates them to play or join your club?

Few clubs ever take the time to answer these critical questions in any detail. (Which is good news for you!) Once you have answered these questions, you will be in an excellent position to redirect your advertising and promotional efforts, refine your sales methods, and tailor your marketing to the specific segments most likely to respond. This will give you a significant advantage in your marketplace.

The more specific your target audience, the more effective your marketing will be. This is one of the hardest concepts for most people to grasp. After all, don't you want all the business you can get? The answer is: No!

For example, let's say you have a very long and tough Pete Dye-designed course. Do you want to attract beginners and weekend duffers? If so, you are destined for six-hour rounds at the expense of angering your avid golf customers.

You should instead pinpoint your best customers so that you can target market to them. It's no surprise that seniors respond differently than business golfers. Social players respond differently than serious players. Women respond differently than men, and so on. The more you can segment your market into key groups; the higher your response rates will be!

In this chapter, you will discover:

✔ Who your perfect customer is, including demographics and psychographics

✔ How large your potential market is

✔ Where your most likely customers are located

✔ How your customers segment into various target markets

✔ How to uncover hidden geographic patterns that affect your club

Be sure to complete the worksheet included in this chapter to nail down your best markets. By doing so, you'll be that much closer to increasing players or memberships, driving more play and boosting sales and profits!

DEFINING YOUR PERFECT CUSTOMER

Back when I taught karate for a living, Darren Willard was the most perfect client I ever had. He was an athletic nine-year-old boy with a photographic memory and a penchant for learning. He took private lessons, came to all the tournaments, and his parents ALWAYS paid on time. They supported all the promotional events, referred their friends, and constantly made glowing comments instead of complaining.

Ah, if only there were more Darren Willards in the world! The good news is that there are, but you have to find them.

Can you describe the qualities of a perfect customer at your club?

You probably immediately thought of someone at your club. That's great because the first step in finding perfect customers is understanding what they look like. These are the people who:

- ✔ Pay full green fees

- ✔ Bring guests

- ✔ Buy from the pro shop

- ✔ Take lessons

- ✔ Attend special events

- ✔ Play in tournaments

- ✔ Spend money in the bar and restaurant

These are your very best customers... the type of people you need more of. They're your "A" clients, the top 20 percent from which you derive most of your income. With more players like this... well, you wouldn't need more players!

Think of 20 people at your club who fit your description of a perfect member, player, or homeowner:

- ✔ What is their age?

- ✔ What is their income?

- ✔ What do they do for a living?

- ✔ Where do they live? Ten, twenty, thirty miles away, or more?

- ✔ What do they read?

✔ What kind of player are they—avid, social, business?

✔ What exactly are the qualities of a perfect customer for you?

Do this exercise with your staff (use the worksheet on the opposite page) and try to come up with 20–50 people who seem to be the perfect clients. Take a look at their profiles because from now on these are the only type of clients you want to attract!

SEGMENT YOUR CUSTOMERS

The basic universe of golfers includes males and females between the ages of 7 and 80—not very limited! To be effective with your marketing you need to segment clearly definable groups.

Why do people play golf?

Golf experienced explosive growth between the 1970s and the year 2000. Expansive television coverage and a few superstars by the names of Palmer, Nicklaus, and Woods played a key role in generating interest in the masses.

The number of people who now play golf in the USA is stagnant at around 26 million. When Legendary Marketing asked a cross section of golfers why they played, we received a wide variety of answers.

Let's categorize some of the more commonly expressed reasons so you can see what percentage of your market falls into each category.

✔ **The addict.** Loves to practice, play, compete, gamble.

✔ **Fitness.** Enjoys the moderate level of exercise.

✔ **Outdoors experience.** Likes the open air.

✔ **Social.** Likes meeting new friends or prefers the type of friends one makes on the course.

✔ **Retirement Leisure.** Occupies one's retirement.

- ✔ **Business.** Combines business with pleasure. Golf is practically a necessity for the modern executive.

- ✔ **The fad golfer.** Watched on TV and decided to "give it a try."

- ✔ **Junior golfers.** Kids like fun; parents like safety.

- ✔ **Female golfers.** A growing group.

Each of these segments may be represented in your customer base. Although many people fall neatly into one of these categories, you must relate to each person as an individual and understand what makes him or her tick. It will make a huge difference between a high customer retention rate with maximum profits versus high attrition rate and minimum profits.

Now, let's take a closer look at each group.

The addict

The die-hard, addicted golfer is ready to try anything that might improve his game. Golf is a way of life, a crucial part of his psychological make up. Without it, he feels incomplete and unfulfilled. It's not unusual for him to relate to everything regarding the sport.

The addict practices hard before and after rounds. He studies golf periodicals and instruction books, and frequently equipment specifications. Putters and drivers are the most commonly discarded former friends! The addict is a good customer and will be among your most loyal and supportive allies, but is likely to expect the same devotion from you. He or she is not necessarily a low handicap golfer.

The light exercise fan or seeker of outdoor experiences

The golfers or would-be golfers who play for exercise or a love of the open air should not be ignored. The inherent beauty and attraction of the game turns many of these people into serious golfers or even addicts!

The social golfer

The person seeking social contact through golf may want to make new friends, meet members of the opposite sex, or spend more leisure time with a spouse or significant other who is already a golfer. The social golfer can develop into a more frequent player.

The retired golfer

People are living longer and staying active in their retirement years. This rapidly growing group is turning to golf as a form of recreation, exercise, and social opportunity. In fact, about 40 percent of all rounds are played by seniors.

Most seniors are on fixed incomes and are very concerned about their financial well-being. They are cautious with their money and always looking for bargains. Be very mindful of this when you market packages and specials aimed at this group. Seniors shop around and compare prices. You will need to be competitive to attract their business.

The senior golfer is often set in his ways. He doesn't want to change what he has for breakfast, his daily routine, his budgeted expenditures, and his backswing! Don't be discouraged by these peculiarities. Seniors comprise one of the largest groups of golfers and play more frequently than most. Their flexible schedules present you with a golden opportunity to drive more mid-week play.

The business golfer

This golfer is in a hurry, expects results, and demands value and an adequate return on his investment. He is usually constrained by time and will appreciate (more than most) flexibility in scheduling, prime tee times, and so on. Are you providing the business golfer the right setting for business deals?

The fad golfer

This individual may have become intrigued with the sport in any number of ways. Boredom with a current hobby may have set in. A change in lifestyle may have occurred. The precise reason need not concern you. The important fact is that you now have an opportunity to sell your services to this person.

Fad golfers usually don't stick around very long, but it doesn't necessarily follow that a student who seeks you out after watching a tour event on TV will quit. Some of them who enjoy the experience may eventually become dedicated players. You can also count on them to be an excellent source of referrals.

The junior golfer

Kids love to try anything that is new to them, anything their peer group is involved in, and anything that is fun. Additionally, parents often seek an activity for their children that is safe and enduring.

When you direct your marketing efforts to this group, emphasize the fun aspect to the kids and the safe, responsible aspect to the parents (who pay the fees!). Friends and playmates of youngsters in your program will often enroll too. With a little encouragement from you, these friends will, in turn, bring their friends and the cycle will continue. Summer programs can generate extra income.

The female golfer

Women comprise the largest, and possibly most significant, emerging golf market. Women represent all categories described in this module... addicts, businesswomen, and so on. Presently most are interested in the exercise and social aspects of golf. (Mixed foursomes are becoming more and more popular.) Nevertheless, the competitive instinct is a factor and can be easily observed in women's club tournaments and team play.

It's important to take into account this large and growing sector of the golf population when researching your area. The number of women who play and take lessons will only continue to grow.

OTHER POTENTIAL MARKET SEGMENTS

Other potential market segments include:

- ✔ League players

- ✔ Locals

- ✔ Out-of-town visitors

- ✔ Summer/Winter members

- ✔ Hotel customers

- ✔ Guests of major employers

- ✔ Students and faculty

The segments and motivations discussed in this chapter are by no means comprehensive. Take a look around to see how many of your customers fit these profiles. Knowing who your best customers are and understanding them is enormously valuable in aiming your marketing efforts accurately and effectively. When you have a better understanding of what motivates people to come to your club, you'll do a better job of attracting them.

USE YOUR WEB SITE TO DEFINE YOUR MARKET

The online survey is by far the most important and effective tool you can use to define and segment your market. You can learn more about a player and his playing habits in two minutes than your competitors will learn in a lifetime. What's more, your website can use marketing automation to follow up throughout the year with targeted promotions sent exactly to those people most likely to respond, based solely on their answers to these questions. Online surveys can be as simple or extensive as you wish. The sample below is a from a very extensive survey that has had great success. With technology, you can build a unique player history over time. Below is a list of the data that is collected and its use.

ONLINE SURVEY TO DEFINE AND SEGMENT YOUR MARKET

First Name (Allows for personalized e-mails and postal follow up)

Last Name

Address / City / State/Prov. / Zip/Postal Code

Phone (Tele survey)

E-mail (E-mail marketing)

What is the name of your company/ business?

Handicap

Does your spouse/partner play?

What is your age?

What is your approximate annual income?

Are you a member of a club? If Yes, which one? (A yes answer tells you a lot about them based on the club)

How many times do you play per month? (Tells you how avid and therefore how important they are to you)

When do you usually play? (Indicates preference)

Which course open to the public do you play most often? (Indicates what they will spend and also allows you to cherry pick your competitors one by one by preprogramming different offers to convert players from other clubs to yours)

Which other course do you play?

What is your favorite course in your State or Province? (Use this data to trade with other courses)

How often do you play at (your course)? (How often do they play your course)

About how far do you live from (your course)? (Helps define your primary trading area)

Which other affiliated course have you played?

In season, what do you typically pay to play golf? (Important question lets you determine what price point they are most likely to respond to)

How much per year do you think you spend on green fees?

Do you normally play as a team?

Do you ever participate in golf outings?

What are the names of the charity and corporate events you play in?

Which outings do you usually play in?

What month and where are those outing usually held?

How many lessons do you take a year?

Have you ever been to a golf school? If YES, which was the best you have attended?

Would you like information on our junior clinics and kids summer camps?

What brand of driver do you use?

What brand of irons do you use?

What model putter do you use?

What ball do you typically play?

How many golf shirts do you typically buy in a year?

What is your favorite brand of golf shirt?

What would you expect to pay for a golf shirt?

How much do you typically spend a year on clubs and equipment?

How many golf vacations do you take per year?

Where do you typically go on golf vacations? (Check all that apply)

Would you like membership information on our exciting Club Max program?

YOUR PRIMARY MARKET

Your potential market

Consider a few general statistics.

In any given market, approximately 10 percent of the population in your immediate area will have some interest in playing or learning to play golf. A much smaller percentage, about 4 percent, are avid golfers who play more than 20 rounds a year. Using a population base of 100,000, that means the potential market of golfers in your area is no more than 10,000 (travelers excluded). The avid market would be around 4,000 people.

- ✔ How many clubs in your area are fighting for a slice of your market?

- ✔ How many players already belong to private clubs?

- ✔ How many are still up for grabs?

- ✔ How many single players made up your total number of rounds last year?

Your primary market

Your primary market is the key area from which most of your customers will come. At a typical club, that market falls inside a 30-mile radius. At some, it may be as far as 100 miles. Within your primary market, you could identify several key groups. You might also have two or three secondary markets, particularly if you have both a local and out-of-town base.

Do your homework

Buy a giant County street map and place a dot or pin representing the address of each player or member. Then draw a ring around your location just outside the largest concentration of players. This will give you a clear indication of your primary trading area.

If you take the time and effort to do this, you will likely uncover some interesting patterns. You will find small clusters of players residing in particular developments or zip codes.

Travel patterns

You'd be surprised at how often a river or major freeway stops people moving in a particular direction. In other words, people may drive 50 miles to your club from the West but only 15 miles from the East. In this case, you will want to target more of your marketing to those players in zip codes to the West of your club.

Sometimes people don't like to cross state lines, county boundaries, or even city limits. A club located on a city's edge might draw very few members from another city just two miles away, yet members from the same city will gladly travel across town to join. Busy intersections and rush hour traffic can either work for or against your club's location. Identifying patterns like these can help you focus your efforts on zip codes most likely to produce results.

SUMMARY

Few clubs truly know who their market really is and thus waste untold millions marketing to people who will never visit their clubs. A small amount of time and effort spent researching your market will pay huge dividends. The more accurately you can define your "Perfect Customer" and the different segments of players to whom your club appeals, the quicker you can tweak your message. Tailoring your message to just the right type of player will deliver greater response from your marketing. Some simple market research using your website and a map

CHAPTER FIVE

Legendary Budgeting

Marketing plans don't run on air. You need a plan in place to match your goals to the your marketing budget. A great many clubs dream about selling 50 lots with a $20,000 budget or 100 memberships for $15,000. Or they want a 20 percent increase in rounds with a budget that's based on five percent of last year's miserable gross!

You cannot increase business by spending less on marketing, although you don't always have to spend more to get the results you want. Often it's just a case of spending where the response is greatest and NOT spending it where there is no direct and tangible return.

You cannot set a marketing budget based on a percentage of your gross or net. You cannot set a marketing budget based on what your competition does. (Forget industry averages; there are none.) The only way you can set the right marketing budget is to reverse engineer exactly what you want to happen.

The step-by-step process outlined in this module will allow you to look at budgeting and meeting goals in a powerful new way. A way that directly connects everything you do in the name of marketing to a specific and tangible result at the counter.

In this chapter, you will discover:

- ✔ Why most marketing budgets make NO sense

- ✔ How to design the perfect budget that will increase your business

- ✔ How to make every single dollar pay for itself

- ✔ How to calculate your ROI on every campaign

- ✔ How changing your ratios can quickly boost response from your existing budget

MATCH THE BUDGET TO YOUR GOALS, NOT THE OTHER WAY AROUND

Here's the perfect way to discover your marketing budget. If you want to sell 100 memberships, you cannot do it by arbitrarily picking a number for your marketing budget. You have to think in terms of the answer to the following question: How many leads must you generate to sell 100 memberships?

To answer that question, you need to know what percentage of leads your membership director closes.

If the membership director only sells one out of five prospects, that means you need to generate 500 leads to sell 100 memberships.

So how many leads does your $4,000 glossy ad bring in...seven or eight? Not enough. Perhaps you should look at direct mail. At a 1 percent rate of response you will need to send 50,000 letters to generate 500 leads; at a 2 percent response rate, it's 25,000 letters, envelopes, stamps, and time. Let's say it comes to $25,000 or a dollar apiece when all is said and done.

This is $10,000 more than the proposed budget, and you still have no idea if the membership director can actually sell! All you have done so far is generate the number of leads needed to sell 100 memberships. However, this is a step taken only by about 0.1 percent of courses.

We're not saying you have to spend more, just that you need a realistic plan. Measure the cost of every piece of marketing you do to generate leads. Then know how well your lead conversion process works.

BUDGET PLANNING WORKSHEET

Before you can set a realistic marketing budget, you must establish your closing ratio. Only then can you come up with a budget number. You may find this a difficult exercise, but without benchmarking, you can NEVER maximize your marketing dollars.

> **WARNING:** Before you start, you should know up front
> that you may not like the answers you come up with.
> That's because for the first time you will have a TRUE
> picture of how many leads you REALLY need and what
> you have to spend to reach your marketing goals.

Most clubs exaggerate their true closing ratios. They remember all the successes and quickly forget the failures. Very few close more than two out of every ten leads. Even the world's best salespeople don't get more than eight out of ten *(If you can close eight out of ten leads, call our office at once; I have a great job waiting for you!).*

Back in the real world, if you don't know what your closing ratio is I suggest you consider one out of ten as a starting point. Two out of ten is probably better than average, at least in membership sales. Outing and banquets could be quite a bit higher, but it pays to err on the side of caution. Golf real estate sales are often based on one in 500 leads! When in doubt, make an educated guess. Even that is better than mindlessly spending money hoping you are getting a return.

Fill out the following worksheet, and you'll have something to start with.

BUDGETING WORKSHEET

Your Market

How big is your club's potential market? (It might be 10% of the area's population. But if you are talking avid golfers, you are down to about 4%.) _____

What percentage of that market are "ideal" prospects? _____

What percentage of your potential market do you reach with your current marketing plan? _____

MARKETING DATA

Memberships

How many total membership inquiries did you get last year? (Phone, Internet, referral, walk-ins, e-mail, etc.) _____

How many of them bought memberships? _____

Membership closing ratio (Example: 100 inquires, 10 sold would have a closing ratio 1 in 10. 200 leads would be needed to sell 20 memberships, 400 leads to sell 40 memberships, and so on.) _____

This year's goal for number of memberships? _____

Number of membership leads needed to meet goals based on the above closing ratio? _____

How many membership leads do you expect from member
referrals? _____

At what cost? (gifts, etc.) $ _____

How many membership leads do you expect from your web
site? _____

Proportionate cost? (i.e., 25% of web site cost) $ _____

How many membership leads do you expect from mailing
to past inquiries? _____

What exactly will this cost?

Postcard $ _____

Brochure $ _____

Letter $ _____

Envelope $ _____

Postage & Mailing $ _____

Design/Creative $ _____

TOTAL $ _____

*Add up the total number of membership leads. Is it enough to meet your goals? If yes,
move to the next area.*

*If not, include another tactic to increase the number of leads such as our A-Z Guide to
Highly Effective Membership Marketing.*

Outings

How many total outing inquiries did you get last year?
(phone, Internet, referral, walk ins, e-mail, etc.)   _____

How many of them booked outings?   _____

Closing ratio?   _____

This year's goal for number of outings?   _____

Number of outing leads needed to meet goals based on the
above closing ratio?   _____

How many outing leads do you expect from repeat
business?   _____

How many outing leads do you expect from referrals?   _____

At what cost? (gifts, etc.) $ _____

How many outing leads do you expect from your web site?   _____

Proportionate cost? (i.e., 25% of web site cost) $ _____

How many outing leads do you expect from mailing to past
customers?   _____

What exactly will this cost?

Postcard $ _____

Brochure $ _____

Letter $ _____

Envelope $ _____

Postage & Mailing $ _____

Design/Creative $ _____

TOTAL $ _____

Add up the total number of outing leads. Is it enough to meet you goals? If yes, move to next section. If not, include another tactic to increase the number of outing leads. (This could be the Legendary Marketing: Golf Outing Sales and Marketing Manual)

Banquets

How many total banquet inquiries did you get last year?
(phone, Internet, referral, walk ins, e-mail, etc.) _____

How many of them booked banquets? _____

Closing ratio? _____

This year's goal? _____

Number of banquet leads needed to meet goals based on
the above closing ratio? _____

How many banquet leads do you expect from repeat
business? _____

How many banquet leads do you expect from referrals? _____

At what cost? (gifts, etc.) $ _____

How many banquet leads do you expect from your web site? _____

Proportionate cost? (i.e., 25% of web site cost) $ _____

How many banquet leads do you expect from mailing to past customers? _____

What exactly will this cost?

Postcard $ _____

Brochure $ _____

Letter $ _____

Envelope $ _____

Postage & Mailing $ _____

Design/Creative $ _____

TOTAL $ _____

Add up the total number of banquet leads.

Is it enough to meet you goals? If yes, move to next section. If not include other tactics to increase the number of banquet leads.

Tee Time Bookings

How many people who call the shop actually book tee times? _____

How many people who visit your web site book tee times? _____

How often do your existing customers play your course in a year?

Examples: 11,000 players 1 time 4,000 players 2 times, 230 players 3 times, 120 players 4 times, 87 players 5 times - and so on _____

Average number of times a golfer plays your club? _____

Total number of rounds divided by number of individual players? _____

Based on the average number of times a golfer plays, how many players do you need to attract to your club this year to meet your financial goals? _____

MARKETING EXPENSES

Newspaper Ads

Annual newspaper ad cost? $ _____

Number of coupons/offers redeemed? _____

Dollar value of this business? $ _____

ROI $ _____

Magazine Ads

Annual magazine ad cost? $ _____

Number of coupons/offers redeemed? _____

Dollar value of this business? $ _____

ROI $ _____

Billboards

Cost of billboards? $ _____

Dollar value of this business? $ _____

ROI $ _____

Postcards

Cost of postcards? $ _____

Dollar value of this business? $ _____

ROI $ _____

Tee Time Bookings

Cost of sales letters $ _____

Dollar value of this business? $ _____

ROI $ _____

Rack Cards

Cost of rack cards? $ _____

Dollar value of this business? $ _____

ROI $ _____

Direct Mail Campaigns

Cost of direct mail campaign #1? $ _____

Dollar value of this business? $ _____

ROI $ _____

Cost of direct mail campaign #2? $ _____

Dollar value of this business? $ _____

ROI $ _____

Cost of direct mail campaign #3? $ _____

Dollar value of this business? $ _____

ROI $ _____

Add up the totals. Is this enough leads to meet your green fee goals? If yes, move to next step. If not, add other tactics to generate enough leads.

Email Marketing (use the following for any email you sent out to generate leads or drive play)

E-newsletter # and name

Date   _____

Opens   _____

Click-throughs (CTO (click-to-open ratio) is most
important)   _____

Bookings, inquiries   _____

E-blast promotion # and name

Date   _____

Offer   _____

Opens   _____

Click-throughs (CTO)   _____

Bookings, inquiries _____

NOTE: Collateral costs from brochures, creative, etc. should be divided by campaign. For example, 10,000 brochures cost a total of $7,000 (including printing, shipping and creative). Each time you use one for membership it costs 70 cents.

Using your data

Based on adding up the numbers on the worksheet from all of the typical marketing you do for your club, are you going to generate enough leads to meet your goals in each category?

Take a look at how many leads you are short in each category and increase your budget to match the anticipated response needed. (Or, increase your efficiency!)

For example, printing and mailing a postcard to a list of 10,000 golfers might cost $5,000. The anticipated response might be .5 percent if it's lead generation for membership.

That's generating 50 leads at a cost of $200 per lead. If you close one out of 10 leads for a $5,000 membership, you will have made $25,000. A very good ROI. If you close two out of ten, you will have made $50,000.

If you are just looking for daily play, the response will need to be much higher. This depends a great deal on the offer. Let's say you rent an email list for $2000 and say you get a 2.5 percent response on a strong offer that would give you 250 leads at $40 a round. That would generate $10,000, another great ROI.

HOW TO PRODUCE MORE LEADS

Here are four ways to generate more leads:

✔ **Increase your closing ratio.** Easy to say, but it takes a commitment to training or an investment in developing better scripts and systems.

- ✔ **Increase the amount of money you generate from existing customers.** A no-brainer. Details on this will follow.

- ✔ **Increase the number of referrals you generate.** Another no-brainer.

- ✔ **Increase the amount of marketing you do.** There are many ways you can spend your existing marketing budget more effectively. Nevertheless, most clubs do not have a marketing budget in line with the number of leads they must generate to achieve their goals.

The most important aspect of your budgeting is actually outside the "budget" itself. It's finding methods that work most cost effectively. Armed with data that directly correlates money spent and money made, it's easy to justify increasing your marketing budget by ten, twenty, or even a hundred thousand dollars. It's also the reason why nearly all successful marketers use direct response advertising.

SUMMARY

Don't set your marketing budget based on an arbitrary number like five percent of gross. Set your marketing budget for the year based on performance. Base your budget on the financial goals you want to reach, not on a percentage of last year's income or some mythical number that someone in management happens to conjure up. Then work to make your performance more efficient, so you exceed your marketing goals.

CHAPTER SIX

Perfect Pricing

F ew clubs take the time to determining exactly what their products and services are, what they could be, and what they intend to charge for them. Yet pricing is the area of marketing that offers the quickest and easiest way to dramatically increase your income in a very short period of time; therefore, it's one of the most exciting concepts.

There are only three ways to make more money, assuming your overhead is fixed.

- ✔ Attract a more new business

- ✔ Charge higher prices

- ✔ Get existing customers to buy more often

Many in the golf business look to others, their competitors, members, or boards to dictate pricing policy with little thought as to the long-term effect of these decisions. Perfect pricing is all about maximizing revenue. It's about making your product appealing to the largest segment of your particular market while leaving little or no money on the table. It is about creating a value proposition in your customer's mind.

The biggest mistake most clubs make is to underprice their green fees, joining fees, or membership dues. With excess capacity and competition in many areas, the temptation is to discount your fees. Don't get caught in that trap! By using the material in this book on setting yourself apart (your USP), and by adding value and service, you won't have to discount. Your goal should be to differentiate, not discount! That said, there will be times when special pricing is useful in order to maximize response to your marketing effort or to take into account different seasons and changes in your local market conditions.

In this chapter, you will discover:

✔ Why discounting is dangerous for all but one type of course

✔ When it's okay to discount

✔ How to discount without destroying your price point

✔ The most logical way to set your prices

✔ How to increase transactional business

✔ How to package for greater profits

RUSSIAN ROULETTE—PLAYING THE DISCOUNT GREEN FEE GAME!

Too many clubs think that the only way to react to their competitors is to cut prices. In the low-price game, there is only one winner - the company that can sell at the lowest possible price. People who shop only by price have no loyalty. As soon as another course in town lowers prices, they switch and play somewhere else! In the retail business, low-cost stores like Woolworth's, Ridgeway, and Montgomery Ward are already gone even though their prices were low! Many of the rest are dying a long, slow death.

In the car business, Kia has won the low-price game at the expense of Yugo, Lada, Daewoo, and a host of other car companies you already don't remember! (Even Kia had problems and was bailed out of bankruptcy by Hyundai purchasing it.) You only have to look at the jokes about low price to know that's not where you want to be:

How do you double the price of a used Yugo?
Fill it with gas!

Now let's look at the top end of the car market: Ferrari, Porsche, Mercedes, Aston Martin, Maserati, Lamborghini, Rolls, Bentley, and the list goes on and on. Lots and lots of companies are not only surviving but, even in bad economies, enjoying some of their best years ever!!!

How can this be?

Because they are not selling on price! They are selling luxury, speed, sex, dependability, prestige, and other tangible and intangible concepts.

Now, back to golf...

Think about why you are in business. You shouldn't operate like an assembly line, pushing as many golfers through your course (or lessons) as possible. Instead, develop a value philosophy. (See the chapters on USP, Customer Service, and Experience.) How much is it worth to a golfer to be greeted by name? For staff to be sincerely happy to see him? Think of the service you receive at a fine restaurant. People can buy food in thousands of places but are willing to pay more for great ambiance and service. Everyone wants to feel special. If you can do that for *your* customers, you can be their favorite upscale course.

In any discount war there can only be one winner, usually the business with the deepest pockets. When you're competing by discounting, you are overemphasizing price. Other intangibles like service and building relationships with customers are ignored. The more price becomes the focus of your club's marketing efforts, the less attention any other factor gets, and price soon becomes the only dimension on which you are judged. Instead, look for other ways to get an edge over your discounting competitors—like service, ambiance, tournament history, great greens, food, follow up, quality, design, and fun.

By not focusing on factors that would differentiate you in your marketplace, you become a commodity judged solely on price. Discounting is easy! Being creative, REALLY increasing service, and building relationships are not! It takes time; it takes effort, it takes work! (A great deal of relationship building can be automated nowadays with your website.)

Discounting works fine; in fact, it is a great strategy if...

✔ You have lower costs than all of your competitors. Is your club is paid for?!

✔ You have a much larger database of customers than your competitors.

✔ You have a back-end strategy that will allow you to up-sell something else to your golfers once they've been to your course. A resort might give away golf to sell rooms. Myrtle Beach has been doing this for years! A real estate development may give away golf to sell lots or homes.

✔ You have much deeper pockets than your competitors and can wait a few years before you need to see a profit.

Obviously, I don't recommend discounting!

Before considering jumping into the discount game, do the math

First of all, your odds of long-term success are low. For instance, in the Orlando and West Palm Beach markets, several clubs have closed in the past year and several more are about to. All were discounting heavily. Most were the lowest price in town.

There is usually only one winner in a discount war! If you are not absolutely certain it will be you, forget it!

Second, consider this, 100 clients at $25 are the same as 50 clients at $50, or 25 clients at $100. It's a lot easier to give great service to 25 golfers than to 100 and you make the same money with less wear and tear on the course. Is there another option that might net you the same profit other than discounting?

Third, have you exhausted all the possible positions and marketing strategies that would give you an edge in your marketplace without discounting? Like adding service, value, ambiance, and follow up! (See the chapters on USP, Service, and Creating a Legendary Experience.)

When is it okay to discount?

You can sometimes use cunning and guile to make your offer appear at least as good, albeit different, without discounting. For example, offer a two-for-one green fee at your regular rate but make the second round only usable in less popular time slots. You keep your price integrity in that the customer still paid the same 50 bucks like he always did. You may think I am splitting hairs but I assure you there is a significant psychological difference between paying $50 and getting a second round free or paying $25 twice. It's a difference that can have a huge effect on your club's future.

As you can tell, I'm against the growing practice in the golf industry of discounting yourself out of business, i.e., you log 40,000 rounds and lose $200,000 in the process. Discounting frequently destroys your club's price integrity in the marketplace. The $100 club only has to offer a $50 rate a few times before it's not regarded by the golfing public as a $100 club anymore.

Here are a few additional times when discounting is acceptable:

✔ Off-season you can discount without fear of destroying your price integrity. Everyone knows that golf in Florida and Arizona is cheap in July and August.

✔ You can discount when you have a legitimate reason for offering lower prices that are credible to your customer— like the greens have just been punched or it's cart path only!

✔ You can discount all you like if your positioning is to be the lowest price, highest volume club in town. Someone has to be the cheapest and as long as you can survive and make a profit taking this stand, so be it!

✔ You can discount anytime if you are making the money up-selling something else like rooms or real estate! But remember, one day the real estate will run out!

Do NOT get caught in the vicious circle of discounting just because the course down the street dropped their rate ten bucks! It's a suckers' game and one you cannot win unless being a low- priced course is your positioning—and even then you need low debt, low overhead, and deep pockets just to play the discounting game!

HOW TO COMPETE WITH DISCOUNTERS THROUGH VALUE-ADDED PRICING & PACKAGING

Before you even consider resorting to discounting, work on as many combinations of value-added pricing as possible.

The best way to compete with cheaper clubs is to offer clearly superior value. You charge more, but you're worth it for your kind of golfers. Note that you're not trying to appeal to everyone. You must have a clear position and communicate your advantages to your segment of the marketplace (for more, see the USP chapter).

Offer premiums rather than discounting

It is far better to hold your price integrity and "bribe" your customers with a free gift than to get caught in the downward spiral of discounting. Depending on your area and price point, some offers will undoubtedly work better than others. Track them all and see what works best.

- ✔ Free cart

- ✔ Free range balls

- ✔ Free lessons

- ✔ A dozen balls

- ✔ Free glove

- ✔ Golf cap

- ✔ Golf instructional video

- ✔ Free lunch

- ✔ Free dinner

- ✔ Free guest

(See the Promotions chapter for other ideas.)

Before jumping on eBay to sell your tee times to the "lowest bidder" consider your options. Get your staff involved; brainstorm for ideas.

The millionaire and the plumber

There is an old story about a millionaire who wakes up in the middle of the night to find his toilet overflowing and water seeping down the hallway. He goes to the phone and calls the first plumber in the book who offers 24-hour service. Fifteen minutes later the plumber arrives and is escorted straight to the offending bathroom. After quickly surveying the scene, he grabs a large wrench from his tool kit and slams it down on top of the pipe just behind the overflowing unit. With that, a loud gurgling sound is emitted and the water quickly disappears down the pipe and returns to its original level. The millionaire, amazed, thanks the man and asks for the bill. At once, the plumber says $500.

"That's outrageous," says the millionaire, "you just pulled that out of the air. All you did was hit that pipe with a wrench; it only took two minutes. I want an itemized bill."

"Certainly," says the plumber, reaching into his overalls for a pen and scribbling on a tattered invoice.

Emergency plumbing service itemized bill: "$5 for hitting the pipe with the wrench. $495 for the 20 years of training and experience that taught me where to hit it! Total $500."

The moral of the story, of course, is that you are selling value. If you market correctly, you can reap the type of rewards you truly deserve. Maybe you can raise your green fees and offer a bad- weather discount. That way, people pay more for a great day. Or if you're selling lessons you could offer a handicap reduction package for a fixed price. Wouldn't some people pay $1000 to cut five strokes off their game? Or a club can offer a "lesson" round with the pro for three times the green fee and split with the pro.

PRICING YOUR PRODUCTS AND SERVICES

In order to run a successful business, you must be able to price your products or service so that you can make a fair profit after expenses. There are a lot of different ways to do this. At my seminars, I am amazed that when I ask attendees why their courses charge the green fees they do, nobody ever seems to come up with what I would consider the right answer. I usually get answers like "That's what my market will bear" or, "That's what everybody else is charging." These answers *are* the way most courses (or pros) set their prices, but they are not the *best* way. You cannot ignore the fact of what your market will bear, or what other people may be doing in your market. But you should not let these considerations be the deciding factors in determining your prices.

How much do you want to make?

Most course owners are so focused on what everyone else is doing that they never stop to think what they should be doing to run their businesses the way they prefer. They are letting others dictate their terms for them.

The first thing you should determine before asking the question, "How much should I charge for my product or service?" is, "How much money do I want to make?" Now, *this* is an interesting question. Instead of focusing the discussion on what everyone else in town is doing, let's start at the most important place, your place! What do you want to have happen? What do you want to earn?

Let's suppose, just for argument's sake, that you want to gross $2,000,000 a year. There are lots of different ways you can arrive at making that income. For instance, that's 100 rounds a day at $100 a round for 200 days a year. And that doesn't count banquets, food, and other income.

You should also consider the stress and hassle factors of dealing with an increasing number of employees and golfers. The lower your price, theoretically the higher your volume, but also the more maintenance and the employees you need. The higher your price, the more limited your market, but also the fewer employees you will need to offer superior service. (See the Budgeting chapter for more information on backwards-based budgeting.)

You set your own prices

Why do some golf pros charge $200 an hour and others $30? Why do some attorneys charge $100 an hour and others $500? Why do some accountants charge $40 an hour and others $200? Why do some stores sell a cotton dress at $40 and others at $400? In my seminars, whether the group is club owners or golf pros, I often make a point of asking what three or four of my audience charge. Let's say that a group of golf pros answered that they charge $40, 50, and 80 dollars an hour for lessons. My next question goes to the low man on the totem pole.

"Are you good at teaching?" I will ask.

"Yes," he will reply.

"Do you think then that Mr. Golf Pro over here charging $80 an hour is twice as good a teacher as you are?"

"No, I don't," he will reply.

"Then why is he making twice as much money as you?" Sometimes he will answer that it's the club, the area or some other factor, but for the most part, regardless of industry or profession, the dominant reason why one professional can charge more than another boils down to this: **That's what they decide to charge!**

WHEN TO RAISE PRICES

Raise your prices!

Through proper service, pricing and packaging, it's possible to significantly increase your income in a very short period of time by raising prices and offering extra value. This situation is made all the easier by the fact that most courses, golf schools, and resorts charge far less than they are worth! After all, how long did it take you to gain the knowledge you now have? To build your course? To maintain it? Now spend some time to find the golfers who will appreciate what you offer—and will pay for it! (Part of the secret is to target the right type of players for your club, not just anyone who swings!)

There are two times to raise your prices. The first and most obvious time is when you are too busy or approaching capacity at your present price. This is the good old law of supply and demand. If you are at capacity and don't get too greedy, it surely will work. And it will give you more money and more time to plan your expansion.

The second time is when you want to differentiate yourself from others in your area or industry. The prices you charge relate to your quality and status in most golfers' minds. Find out what perceptions exist in your area for golf. Where are the price breaks in the minds of your prospects and clients? At what point does a high-end value become expensive? At what point does a low price encourage a perception of low quality? Where is the middle ground and what can you do to move to one end or the other?

How to raise dues

Many clubs are deathly afraid of raising prices for fear of losing what they already have but rarely does this fear translate into a mass exodus, unless there are other problems. Members may bitch and complain, but few who were not going to leave anyway will quit if the cost of dues goes up 5 or 10 percent. (My club doubled its dues last year and hardly anyone blinked!) Most people will simply accept price increases and after a couple of weeks of discussing the club's shortcomings around the bar will go back to daily life. Even if a dozen people leave, the extra fees will still reap greater rewards, but let's look at how to soften the blow.

One way is a letter simply outlining where the operating costs have increased, or the proposed improvements you plan to make with the additional revenue. When people think they understand your motives, they tend to be more accepting of increases.

Another way I have used successfully is to invite members to pay their current rate for a year or in some cases more as long at they pay in full before a certain date, that is, lock in last year's rate by paying for next year in full by November 30th. Or take double advantage and pay for two years now!

There are of course more creative ways like this one from Todd Smith. One of the great rewards of dealing with thousands of clubs around the world is the feedback and ideas that you get from clients. Todd's creative letter to sell annual memberships not only grabbed my attention but also delighted everyone at my office.

He sent a letter to his annual pass holders, as usual, asking them to renew but instead of the usual 10 percent discount for acting before November 30th, he came up with a much more clever idea. The headline says it all.

Join Before November 30th And If It Snows On Christmas Day, Your Membership Is Free!

Now here is the clever bit; he took out insurance against it snowing which cost him just 8 percent of the annual membership! (To avoid all controversy, it had to snow a certain amount and be documented by the National Weather Center in the Moline, Illinois facility!) BRILLIANT!

INCREASING THE SIZE OF THE AVERAGE TRANSACTION

It's not even necessary to raise prices in order to make far greater profits. In some cases, it's just about increasing the average sale. Your player pays a $65 green fee. You hand him back a ONE-DAY-ONLY gift certificate worth $10 off any shirt in the shop. For convenience, let's say the average shirt is marked $40 and you paid $20 for it. If you sell four shirts typically on a Saturday, you make $80 profit. With the gift certificate, you sell 15 and make $150 profit.

How to raise big money instantly

Do you have a low-end course and need $100,000 for course improvements? Simply offer ten lifetime memberships at $15,000 instead of your yearly $1800. Have a higher-end course? Sell five lifetime membership at $50,000 and you just raised $250,000 without going to the bank! It sounds simplistic because it is, but it works if you package the deal right.

GETTING CUSTOMERS TO BUY MORE OFTEN

Let's say your most profitable source of business is daily fee players. If you had good data, you would know how many rounds each player at your club played last year. This data is a very important tool in helping you price your rounds. Surveys also help you by telling you how many rounds a player plays and at what other courses.

Let's say I played 15 times at $50 per round. The first time I stand in front of you at your golf shop counter this year, you sell me a $1,000 pass to play 20 times or even 30 times. Your income from me has increased at the very least by 25 percent and that's without counting carts, beer, and balls! A single sale to me could easily result in 50 percent greater revenue on the first day of the season if it is a custom package that appeals to my needs—my needs as an individual player. And therein lies another great and often overlooked truth— you build a successful business one sale at a time.

MEMBERSHIP FEES—TO BE OR NOT TO BE?

Another common practice among clubs trying to sell memberships is to discontinue the joining fee! In the majority of cases, this is a big mistake! Instead of doing away with the $5000 joining fee they should instead send out a mailing with a $5,000 check towards joining enclosed. You may think I'm splitting hairs but the difference between the two strategies in customer perception is often staggering.

REFER FOR A FEE

If you are constantly asked for a service you cannot or don't want to provide, set up a network of other clubs in your area and charge a referral fee or a booking fee of 10 or 15 percent for sending the business to them. This works very well when you are doing a good job of booking outside events, wedding and banquets. Why not develop a relationship with a competitor and hand your extra business off to them for a 15% booking fee instead of just telling the customer you are booked? I have one client that made an extra $20,000 last year by doing exactly this, booking events at other courses on days where he was already booked!

KEEP TESTING PRICES AND PACKAGING

Test, test, test and keep testing offers, bonuses and value-added promotions to increase the number of players who come and the average spent by your players. If you do 40,000 rounds, and the average spend is $6, an increase of just 10 percent will result in $24,000 more in income. And remember—golfers are already your customers. It costs you nothing to collect the extra revenue.

A NOTE ON PRICING PHILOSOPHY

When running price promotions, you must sit down and consider how you can use the promotion to make more money, not just increase traffic. If you discount, how will you make a fair profit margin back? Can you expect to make it up by selling additional full-priced items? Will you lower the perceived value of your memberships, rounds, and so on?

When it comes to packaging and pricing, it's very, very important that you don't get caught up in the trap of doing what you've always done. Because if you do what you've always done, you'll get what you always got. Don't follow the herd in your industry. Set prices based on what you want to make and the value you are willing to offer. Consider the multitude of different packages and prices you could offer to get where you want to go. Then narrow your offerings down to no more than three clear options at one time.

SUMMARY

In general, I recommend that you not price discount except in very controlled circumstances. For instance, in the offseason. Or offering free weekday rounds with weekend promotions. An ideal promotion will increase your income without cheapening you in the long term. Look for ways to add value to your memberships, daily play, and outings, so that you are not reducing the dollars you take in. Involve your vendors in special events and discounts. Create so many interesting goings on at your club that people always feel they received more value and entertainment than they paid for.

CHAPTER SEVEN

Developing a Legendary USP (Unique Selling Proposition)

How important is a USP? So important that without a great one your golf business will always be an "also-ran."

The Unique Selling Proposition (USP) was first described more than 50 years ago in the classic book by Rosser Reeves, *Reality in Advertising*. While given much lip service, the concept of USP is seldom understood or operationalized well. Reeves said that your USP must meet three criteria to be complete and powerful:

✔ It must say to your consumer, "Buy this, and you will receive this specific benefit."

✔ Your USP must be one that your competition does not, or cannot, offer.

✔ It must be strong enough to attract new customers to you. Your USP is the basis for your marketing and advertising efforts.

It is your unique advantage you use to sell your club, your lessons, outings, and so forth. Your USP should be so strong and memorable that it will both distinguish you from other clubs *and* attract new business. It should also be memorable enough to generate word of mouth to drive referrals. Some select courses have obvious and powerful USPs:

Augusta—the Masters course; Saint Andrews— the home of golf; or Pebble Beach—unique coastal beauty. Since your course is likely to be among the 99 percent that are less famous than the few like Augusta, you'll need to work harder to develop your USP.

In this chapter, you will discover:

✔ Why your USP is so important to lower your costs and increase your income

✔ Why most courses have no USP

✔ How to develop possible USPs

✔ How to gather input for your USP development

✔ Formulas for possible USPs

✔ Sample USPs

✔ How to test your USP for effectiveness

✔ How to best use your USP

LEGENDARY USP

No matter who you are or where your course is located, your club's reputation precedes you in your market. The more positive and solid your reputation for whatever your unique selling proposition is, the easier it will be for you get players, members, students, or outings. More players will seek you out, pay you more money, and happily refer you to others.

While some clubs have taken decades to build their legacies and reputations, others have done it much faster. In today's world of the Internet, direct mail, and targeted magazines for every audience, the opportunity to build a reputation quickly has never been greater. The challenge is to accurately define your unique selling proposition (USP)— the essence of what your club offers that is superior and unique.

DON'T BE A "ME-TOO" CLUB

Most managers have never heard of a USP. And while a select few instinctively emphasize their uniqueness, *most clubs have done nothing to set themselves apart in the marketplace.* Except for custom pictures, you could take one of these clubs' names out of their ads and replace it with a competitor's and the ad would be just as accurate.

The importance of accepting this challenge to differentiate yourself from your competition is that without a USP you can waste millions of dollars marketing the features of your golf club—features that every other club also has, or that no one cares about. You will be another me-too club with 18 holes, a pro shop, and a driving range.

By taking the USP challenge, you will, with a few words and concepts, set yourself apart from all of your competition. You will find yourself more focused and your message more on target while attracting a far greater number of the right type of players for you.

Let me give you a clear example of what I mean. Pebble Beach sells a once-in-a-lifetime experience, not a round of golf! Using some non-golf examples, a Kia dealer and a Rolls-Royce dealer both sell cars, but they are hardly in the same business. A Kia dealer sells transportation; a Rolls dealer sells luxury. A Timex dealer sells watches that tell time; a Rolex dealer sells jewelry and status.

Most clubs don't have a USP, and therefore they don't ever build a strong marketing program on a secure foundation. Instead, they bounce from idea to idea without a consistent theme. In fact, I've had clients who proudly showed me the twenty different ads they had run over the last five years—each touting something different! This approach wastes lots of time, lots of money, and a great deal of effort!

For your club to attract the maximum number of prime clients in your market, you must determine exactly whom you are trying to reach and what message from you will resonate with them. Then you must shape your club's performance to deliver this unique experience.

"RESTRICTING" YOUR MARKET

You might argue that if you focus your club on one USP, you will limit your market, but, that, my friends, is the very idea. *You focus your market on the people who value the one thing your club can do best.* Then you harp on it for all you are worth and develop your own niche market within a much broader category.

It turns out that this new focus doesn't limit you as much as it attracts more play. Your USP also produces a tag line on your business card, a slogan on the bottom of your ads, and is attached to your name like a double-barreled surname (the club where the pros play; the hardest course in town; the club for family play; the highest-rated course in town; the most water; the most exclusive, and so on).

Without a position around which to build your marketing, you are just another commodity that no one thinks is special! With a strong USP, you lower your marketing costs, increase word of mouth, focus your efforts to do a better job for your golfers, and increase your income.

What comes to mind when you hear Domino's Pizza? "Domino's delivers in 30 minutes or less." That was their unique selling proposition, and it fueled one of the most rapid business success stories ever. Domino's wasn't really selling pizza, what they were selling was fast delivery. There are hundreds of different chains around the country that sell pizza. But when you think of Domino's, you think of their 30-minute delivery guarantee. You might be interested to know that those ads haven't run in over three decades, ever since a driver was killed trying to get his pizza delivered on time. Yet the 30-minutes-or-less perception remains because that 30- minute USP was so strong!

The same is true in the shipping business. There's UPS, the USPS, DHL, and a host of other services that claim to get your package delivered directly to your customer, across the country, overnight. But when you absolutely, positively must have it there overnight, whom would you use? If you said the Post Office, move to the back of the class! (They lose 100,000 packages a day!) If you absolutely, positively must have it there overnight, the only company to use is FedEx. That perception has survived even through their name change from Federal Express. They have a legendary reputation for fast and reliable delivery and practically own the word "overnight." You must do the same—own a concept in your marketplace that defines what your club is all about. This will attract people to you like a magnet!

USP DRIVES INCOME AND OPPORTUNITIES

Why can Doral or Pebble Beach get plenty of players to pay several hundred dollars a round? Because they are among the world's best courses you say? While Pebble boasts spectacular oceanfront scenery, if the truth be known, Doral is a pretty average golf course, yet they can still command almost $300 a round. Why? Because it's the "Blue Monster" that's why! Because they have water on 14 holes and some very clever guy early on dubbed it "The Blue Monster!"— despite the fact that the water isn't a real hazard on more than half the holes!

It doesn't matter! Doral has done a brilliant job of getting people to believe that when in Miami, it's the place to play and stay. Sure they had some help from the PGA Tour, but there are plenty of second-rate courses that host PGA events that you or I would never dream of playing, let alone paying $300 to play! Think Eagle Trace— that has lots of water, was home to the PGA Tour's Honda Classic for many years, yet stands for nothing. You see my point. Despite the fact that they host a PGA Tour event, no one is going to pay $300 to play there!

WORLD'S LEADING TEACHER?

Marketing is not merely having a great layout or teaching talent! You need to **own** a key thought in a player's mind so that when he picks up the phone to call three buddies to play this weekend, he's already thinking about your course!

Who is the world's leading expert on the "short game?" Tiger

Woods—he's pretty good? Jack Nicklaus—he's got the wins to back up almost any claim, but, no, bunker shots and chipping were never Jack's strong suit. Perhaps it would be a really great player like Moe Norman was, who never played the Tour because he didn't like all the publicity? No, I think not. In fact, the person generally regarded as the world's leading expert on the short game is an ex-NASA scientist who rarely if ever breaks eighty!

Does that bother you? It bothers many of my PGA friends, but it shouldn't because Dave Peltz is first and foremost a master marketer and that is what it's all about.

Marketing! Selling your uniqueness!

How did Dave Peltz, an amateur enthusiast for many decades, with no particular talent for the game, became the world's leading expert on the short game?

Dave Peltz did several very interesting things to build his Unique Selling Proposition:

- ✔ He used his NASA background to gain credibility for his golf theories.

- ✔ He wrote a book—always a great start to building credibility.

- ✔ He noticed that while there were plenty of swing gurus pushing a method, no one seemed to be focusing on the area of the game that offered the greatest potential return in terms of score, the short game!

- ✔ He told everyone who would listen that he was the world's new short-game expert and that he—unlike others—had approached the problem scientifically!

- ✔ He wrote magazine articles on his theory.

Bingo! Dave Peltz, a 50-something ex-NASA employee with no teaching credentials, no tour players winning majors in his stable (when he started), and no personal playing history out-marketed 50,000 other golf instructors because of his superior USP.

SOME USP EXAMPLES

Let's look at some more examples by studying the USPs of two of the top equipment companies. To see what kind of job they are doing, take a simple test to see if you can match the companies' USPs with their names.

What company's equipment is:

For Those Who Want To Play Their Best!
The Number One Ball In Golf!

If you answered Ping and Titleist, kudos to you, and to the companies as well—their marketing stayed in your mind (and in a great percentage of other players' minds).

Interestingly enough, *Ping For Those Who Want to Play Their Best!* is a good slogan, but not a USP! Originally Ping had some technological differences which they could use to back up a claim that they improved your game (differential weighting, heel-toe weighting, and so on). However, they've lost that uniqueness. Because their slogan was catchy, it is still useful; but everyone wants to play their best, so it is not a good USP.

Titleist, The Number One Ball In Golf!
Simple and tough to argue with!

Now tell me what does Yonex stand for... quick... come on... Okay, they did have a little run about 20 years ago with a graphite- headed driver, but now what? What have they done for me lately?

For most of the last decade, Yonex had one thing going for them—the world's undisputed best left-handed golfer. (Kudos to Mike Weir, but I'm talking Phil here!) I spent almost a year trying to convince them that their USP should be *"The world's best left-handed golf clubs."* Statistically, 10 percent of the 27 million people who play golf are left handed. (In Canada, a greater percentage of the population is left-handed, but I digress.) No one in the world had ever claimed to be the world's best left-handed golf clubs, so the position was open!

AN OPEN UNIQUE SELLING PROPOSITION in this over-crowded marketing world!!!!!

This is a serious marketing opportunity!!! But the wise people of Yonex thought that .000000001 percent share, or whatever they have of the right-handed market, was better than total DOMINATION of the left-handed market!! They just couldn't see pigeonholing their market like that!!!

Why be the undisputed leader in a US market of 3 million left-handers, and a worldwide market of 30 million or so, when instead you can be a nobody in the worldwide market of 150 million right- handers?

Okay, so you get the idea. Let's get back to talking about *your* club and *your* marketing.

WHAT DO YOU WANT YOUR CLUB'S REPUTATION TO SAY?

The first step in building a legendary reputation in your community is to determine how you want people in the marketplace to perceive your club. Your USP will be the basis for getting your marketing message across and building your reputation. It will be what they remember about you and pass on to others. It will be the foundation on which all your marketing is based, from your website to your customer-service training!

If you have a strong and memorable position in golfers' minds, it will carry over into other areas. They will also think you are good in other ways.

In contrast, if you try to advertise your club as all things to all people, they will think you're a "Jack of all trades and a master of none." A strong USP doesn't limit you; it opens up your options!

Throughout this discussion, I will continually emphasize that you must pick one USP and stick to it. However, if you have distinctly different audiences, it *is* possible to have different USPs for each audience. For instance, individual golfers are a different audience than members or outing planners. Your members may be most interested in the status of the club as a place to bring business associates. Day players may be most interested in a challenging (or nonchallenging!) course. And outing buyers may be most interested in price, or doing minimum work while looking good for their bosses! If you know your submarkets, you *may* develop different USPs aimed at each group. Of course, they should not be contradictory.

HOW TO DEVELOP YOUR USP

There are several factors to consider when designing your USP. The best way to start is to gather input from your staff and golfers. If possible, get your staff together and ask them as a group to come up with individual words or phrases that define your club. Make a list of at least 10 to 20 keywords or statements. Do the same thing with your customers, either in a group (like the board) or individually. You could even send out a quick e-mail to members asking them what they think the best thing about your club is. Ways to ask about a USP include phrases like:

- ✔ Our members tell us that what they like best about us is.

- ✔ We are the only course in our area that does.

- ✔ We are the best course/club because

- ✔ The thing we are proudest of is.

- ✔ We're better than anyone else at.

- ✔ The thing people remember us for is.

- ✔ The most unusual thing about us is.

If you heard people talking behind your back about your club, what strengths of yours would you want them to be mentioning?

What is it about your course that people use to describe you (the quality of the course, the history, the status, the exclusivity, the value, the pricing, the attentive customer service, the scenery, the ambiance)? Specifically, what is it that your club does better than anybody else, or what is it that you have to offer that no one else can offer?

Try to avoid generic answers like quality or value. You can't be everything to everyone. You should, therefore, select one main perception that you want to convey in your marketplace, and back it up with a couple of subsidiary points.

Take some time to carefully consider the questions and write down your answers. Even "silly" answers can sometimes stimulate useful material. For instance, if your club has a nickname it may suggest a USP (like the Blue Demon).

Normally, the answers to these questions will involve your golf course. But they could also involve your people, your general location, your price or value, your service, your clubhouse, your restaurant, and so on.

After you have collected information, develop variations and combinations and narrow the list down to three or four of the very best possibilities. Once they have been defined, these answers should be synthesized into a possible defining statement. This may take you a while, and that's okay. This is much too important a decision to rush, but make sure you follow through and come up with just a single sentence, preferably one that offers a clear benefit to the customer.

Focus on one key trait!

Let's take the golf pro as an example. Is a golf professional in the golf business, the service business, the entertainment business, the retail business, the instructional business, or something else? Your answer to this question can have a serious impact on marketing decisions, customer perceptions, customer satisfaction, and your reputation.

At a typical country club, the golf pro may be in all of the above businesses, but sales and marketing decisions must be based on a single underlying philosophy. No one since Tommy Armour (several decades ago) has had a reputation as a great champion and also as a great teacher. It's equally tough to have great member service and play a lot of golf. You can't play a tough guy and a comic at the same time, just ask Sylvester Stallone. Every movie in which he didn't put up his dukes or didn't blow up half the world flopped!

Cadillac keeps trying to make smaller and cheaper cars and loses millions in the process every time! Remember the Catera? Don't worry; neither does anybody else despite a $100-million ad campaign! Cadillac means big and luxurious, not small and sporty. They would have had better results if they sold their smaller sports cars under another brand, a strategy Toyota used very successfully with Lexus for the opposite reason. I mean, who in their right mind was going to buy an $80,000 Toyota? The Toyota branding of inexpensive and reliable was too strong.

Speaking of branding. Lately, some of the discussion about these USP issues has also been in terms of *branding*. You brand your club, and so forth. Another concept closely related to USP is *positioning*. Positioning focuses a bit more on you compared to the competition, not on your uniqueness. For our purposes here, however, both positioning and branding mean the same thing as USP.

You will only be remembered in one key area, with perhaps a couple of sub-thoughts at most. Once you choose that area, you must use it as your central focus in making future decisions. This means focusing on one particular area and spending less time and effort on others.

It's very important that you decide what your image should be in the golf community. If you try to be everything to everybody, it won't work. And once you have developed your reputation label, it's nearly impossible to shed it. Good or bad, your reputation ultimately will depend on a few words, so choose the statement that represents your club wisely for it will stick with you for a long time.

MORE USP EXAMPLES

Cleveland makes fine irons and, I am sure, great woods, but when I think "Cleveland," what comes to mind? Putters? No. Wedges! Great wedges! Wedges that PGA Tour players use! Cleveland built its reputation on wedges and parlayed it into something more, but without their success and recognition for wedges, they were just another second-tier company. Their positioning as the maker of the best wedges gave them the leg up that they needed.

Let me give you a personal example: I am the world's leading authority on golf marketing. There are several reasons that I can make that statement and not blush:

- ✔ I wrote the only book in the world on how to market golf on the Internet. (And, obviously, I've written this book.)
- ✔ I have delivered more than 100 full-day seminars on golf marketing for the PGA, the Golf Course Owners Association, Club Managers Association, and others.
- ✔ I have written a book on how to make money teaching golf.
- ✔ I have over 20 years experience in marketing.
- ✔ I have hundreds of testimonials from people who will back up my statement that I am, in fact, the world's foremost authority on golf marketing—or at least the best person they know.
- ✔ I have a track record of success on which to draw with a very diverse range of hundreds of golf clients.
- ✔ I am a scratch player with a passion for the game, so I can talk your language.
- ✔ Most importantly, no one else has claimed this position; therefore, on top of everything else, I win by default!

My company could do marketing work for lots of other types of businesses, but we don't. We just do golf, and because of that focus and commitment, our business has grown 800 percent in two years!

Common (though faulty) wisdom will tell you that a market of everyone is better than a market of just one type of client. Common wisdom is wrong! The same is true for your club. The more clearly you define what you're all about, even at the exclusion of some types of players, the quicker your marketing will pay dividends.

"Central Florida's Best Greens"

Here's an example of one of the USPs we developed and how we came up with it.

Stoneybrook West is not the best golf course in Orlando by a long shot; it doesn't have the best holes, has little or no elevation, and is surrounded by homes. That is not to say it's a bad golf course; it's just that it's a lot like every other golf course in Orlando. We needed an edge. After brainstorming with the client, we came up with a list out of which we crafted the statement "Orlando's Best Greens." We later modified this to "Central Florida's Best Greens." This has worked out very well for several reasons.

- ✔ People from out of town want to have good greens above anything else, so it helped attract out-of-town play.

- ✔ Since we made the claim "Orlando's Best Greens," media (including the *Orlando Sentinal* and two local golf magazines) all chose to use that as headlines for articles they wrote about the course (which is nice)!

- ✔ No one else claimed to have the "Best Greens" so we were first in the market to do so, making it very hard for anyone else to take that title away from us.

"Michigan's Most Beautiful Resort"

Garland Resort in Northern Michigan had plenty to shout about with four great courses, natural beauty, cross-country skiing, and a host of other activities, but nothing was pulling the marketing message together. We solved the problem by designating Garland as Michigan's Most

Beautiful Resort! Everyone enjoys beauty whether it's golfers, riders, skiers, diners, meeting planners, or families!

SOME COMPONENTS OF USPS

Here are some other ideas to get your creative juices flowing.

Preempting the truth for your USP

While it's better if the USP you design is something nobody else can claim, it's not essential. You can choose to highlight some aspect of your club that your competitors may also possess but have failed to exploit. By being first, you lay claim to the particular benefit that you're promoting. Jack Trout and Al Ries, the originators of the term positioning, call this "preempting the truth."

Miller Brewing Company built its business on 'lite beer,' but they didn't invent the category. Coors did that more than a decade earlier. But Coors failed to position its beer as a light beer and lost out to Miller (who exploited the position to the tune of hundreds of millions). You don't have to invent it; you merely have to claim it!

Back when courses like Pine Hill or Pine Barrens in New Jersey were both among the best public courses in the world, either could have been positioned as "The Second Best Course in New Jersey, But the Best One You Can Actually Play!" (You don't even have to claim to be best to have a great USP.)

Standing out from the crowd

Let's say that you are one of ten daily-fee courses in town. You have a typical 18-hole, par-72 golf course. It's better than some, not as good as others. How are you going to make your mark?

First, look at what your competitors are doing—what do they specialize in? Take a look at their websites, brochures, print ads, Yellow Pages ads, and any other literature you can find to determine what positions they are claiming. Fortunately for you, in most cases, there will be nothing significant! However, their random claims may give you a few ideas and help you spot their weaknesses.

Have you got a great skins game Friday afternoons? I know several courses whose success is due to the number of players who show up on specific days to play in games. Encouraging such games can turn a mediocre course into a winner! **"Home of the best games in town!"**

Is your course amenable to a fast-paced round? **"Play in under 4 hours or your money back!"** That's a bold statement, but I'll tell you what—I'd pay an extra $10 to get that guarantee. With the right course, proper instructions to the players upon check in, and a good ranger program, it can be done! If you took over four hours to play a round in Scotland—and that's without the aid of a cart—they'd hang you from a lamppost!

When I lived in Southern California, I used to ski in Big Bear where I had the choice of two resorts. Both were more or less on the same mountain, and one was ten dollars a day more than the other was. Where would you ski? I skied Snow Summit, the more expensive of the two.

Why? Because they limited ticket sales and had a 10-minute lift- line guarantee! If you were not on a lift in 10 minutes, they gave you a ticket for another day free! It never happened. The two or three times I tried the cheaper place, Bear Mountain, I waited as long as 30 minutes to get up the mountain—NO THANKS!

Think about the free publicity you could get, **"Just say NO to 4-hour rounds!"** Think T-shirts, *Golf Digest* reporters at your door, and a big pat on the back from the USGA. You could run different types of speed tournaments and marathons. Or charge people on slow days by how long they spend out on the course! In fact, the promotion possibilities are endless.

Does this exclude certain people from playing your course? YES, SLOW PLAYERS, players who eat up your daylight, and upset the 20 groups behind them!! GOOD RIDDANCE!! The extra space and publicity will more than make up for the loss of Bernard Langer disciples who play slower than wounded snails!

Okay, I'm on a roll. Let's say your course is the worst of the ten aforementioned competitors. What then? *Don't* market the course as your key feature! Market something else. When the new GM of the New Jersey Nets basketball team took over in the mid-Nineties, he had on his hands the very worst team in the NBA. Not only did they have a terrible winning record, but the players had bad attitudes, and the few fans who did show up hated them! So how did the new GM manage to go from a stadium that was not even half full to selling out every game in just a few months—while the team continued to play as badly as ever?

Brilliance, that's how! Brilliance and a change in his Unique Selling Proposition. He stopped trying to sell his team. It was pointless— the Nets were terrible, and everyone knew it! He couldn't change the team play without some serious personnel changes and time to work on things. But he could change the USP and turn the team into a profitable business instead of a money pit. Instead of marketing *his* team, he started to market the stars of the opposition teams!

Come see Michael Jordan and the Chicago Bulls!
Shaq and The LA Lakers!
Larry Bird and the Celtics!

In his favor was the fact that many of the stars he was promoting were nearing the ends of their careers, so he added some of that into the mix. *"This might be your last chance to see Jordan play in New Jersey!"*

He bundled the good games into packages of five, tripled the ticket prices for those games and threw in all the mediocre games for free. He sold out the stadium in a matter of weeks while the Nets continued their mediocre play. But it didn't matter—he was no longer selling his team. He was instead selling the superstars on the *opposing teams* as the reason to come to the game.

Brilliant!

Your USP doesn't have to relate to your course

So, what can we do to help the worst course in town in our earlier example come up with a USP? Change the focus from golf to something else. Here are a few extreme examples to stimulate your thinking.

Consider the USP "An Ordinary Course Where We Treat You Like Royalty." How can you treat customers like royalty when you only charge $25 a round? How about offering a free car wash while golfers play! That's a nice touch that saves the player time and fifteen bucks, while it only costs you two guys on minimum wage! Picture this: a guy wakes up thinking, where should I play today? Umm...well, the car needs washing, let's go to YOUR CLUB!!!

Here's another idea. Turn the 19th hole into a haven of golf memorabilia, like a theme restaurant. Then people will bring their friends just to look at all the cool stuff you have on the walls. (This can be done fairly cheaply.)

Make your 19th hole the best place in town to hang out after a round. Satellite TVs, free salsa and chips, a waitress with large..., well, you get the idea!

I know some country clubs that make it on the strength of their junior swim team! Anything that makes you outstanding can make you a winner.

TESTING YOUR USP

Like other parts of your marketing, your USP can be tested. You can use focus groups to compare different USPs. You can use surveys. You can test headlines in e-mails using different USPs. You can test USPs as direct mail or advertising headlines. Just don't fall in love with the first clever idea someone comes up with. As famous advertising man David Ogilvy used to say, you don't want your ads to win awards for creativity; you want them to make you money!

YOUR USP STRENGTHENS YOUR MARKETING MESSAGE

With a USP in mind, your logo, ads, website, brochures, and other marketing material can all be designed in a very cohesive manner. This is called integrated marketing, where your different pieces reinforce a consistent marketing message and convince, rather than confuse, the customer.

All too often, course owners bounce from one message to the next, hoping in vain to be everything to everyone. It doesn't work. Once you have decided to be a tough course for serious players, don't shoot for women and seniors—stay focused. Develop your campaigns around strong images. Use strong colors that carry the feel of your USP throughout everything you do!

Confused prospects do not make good customers because confusion causes doubt. Doubt leads to fear of making a poor decision, and fear leads to paralysis or procrastination. Use your USP as a roadmap for your marketing materials. When completing any new marketing tool, ask yourself the following simple questions.

Are the graphics and copy congruent with your message?

A client recently brought me a marketing piece in which he claimed in his copy to offer both the finest and the cheapest service in town. But you cannot be the cheapest and the best. People simply won't buy that concept. They have been preconditioned to believe that the best of anything is always more expensive. The cheapest may offer good value, but you hurt your credibility, never to regain it if you also try to claim that you are the best! The best is never the cheapest. On the other side, words claiming that you are the best club in town would not be supported by printed material that was cheap looking.

Does it enhance your position in the minds of your

customers?

Check if each marketing effort stands out and brands your course's name clearly and uniquely in the minds of your prospective customers. If it's only as good as anyone else's effort, don't do it.

Stand out and be bold—or save your money and invest it in bonds!

Is your delivery consistent?

With your marketing materials in complete harmony and building on your USP, the next question to ask yourself is how consistent you are in delivering your message. In many cases, business owners develop a winning concept and then become bored with it, thinking that others must surely have tired of the concept as well. So they move on to a different and far less effective concept, just as the other one was taking root in the public consciousness.

In my golf consulting, I frequently design ads for clients that they instantly proclaim to be the most effective they have ever used. Eight weeks later, they are back on the phone asking me to design a new one, even through the original one is still pulling far better than anything else they have ever done. I ask them why they want a new ad.

They tell me because everyone has seen it already. Good ads can go on working indefinitely. Sure, you might rest them for a few weeks and then bring them out again, or perhaps change the picture, keeping the copy much the same, but the fact remains that a good ad will work far longer than most people have the patience to keep running it!

Consistency is the key to building a long-term image that allows you to dominate your marketplace. Most great marketing campaigns last for years, even decades, as has the Marlboro cowboy, the Energizer Bunny, the twins in Wrigley's Double Mint Gum ads, and Budweiser, the King of Beers.

I'm sure that in your town you can think of at least one particular business that has made an impression on you just because they are so consistent, even if their marketing is consistently bad. The Crazy Greek Mattress Shop, the car dealer who always wears a ten-gallon hat on late-night TV, or the attorney who pitches injury law with a cast on his leg. Consistency is no substitute for great marketing, but great marketing done with consistency will produce the best results of all.

SUMMARY

Trying to be everything to everyone is a sure way NOT to conquer your market. You must decide on what your core business is and build a unique selling proposition around what you do best. To define your USP, you must answer at least two questions:

✔ What is the word or statement you want to "own" in the minds of your customers?

✔ What one thing do you do better than anyone else around?

Once you have answered these questions and decided on a USP, you must stay focused and use your position as a guide to both marketing issues and business decisions.

You must make your marketing congruent with your USP message, so it builds and grows in the minds of your customers. Finally, you must remain consistent *within* your marketing message. Resist the temptation to change for change's sake. Once you find a good marketing message, ride it for all it's worth, over and over again.

CHAPTER EIGHT

Building Your Club's Opt-In E-mail List

YOU CAN BUILD YOUR OPT-IN LIST TO 10,000 NAMES OR MORE IN 90 DAYS OR LESS

The last chapter showed you how important e-mail can be for your marketing. If you want to make money online, the key is to quickly build an opt-in e-mail list (where every member of your list has specifically requested to hear from you). This is directly opposite from those who choose to try to "spam" their way to riches. Spamming is when you send to e-mail lists of people who have not contacted you or have not registered to receive your offers. In addition to your own list, there are many e-mail lists of golfers who have indicated their interest in receiving golf offers (these golfers have "opted-in"). You can rent these lists. Then when people respond to your e-mail and sign in at your site, they become part of your own list.

In this chapter, you will discover:

✔ Why spam is evil

✔ Why opt-in lists are okay to send to

✔ How to set list criteria

✔ 48 ways to build your opt-in list

E-MAIL SPAM

I know you get spammed. Everyone does. Personally, I receive around 50 or so a day. Of these e-mails, selling whatever products or services they have to offer, I delete most of them without opening them, yet they keep on coming. They are usually (though not always) poorly written and full of extremely hyped messages. I get ads for dolls, cars, credit cards, merchant accounts, golf, vacations, and more. I won't even talk about the worst stuff which is sent out. One piece after another has to be deleted, and it just keeps coming.

Why so much spam e-mail?

If everyone is deleting it, then why do spammers keep sending it? It's simple. Although the response rates are extremely low, they still do get customers. Their financial cost in sending it is almost nothing, so it's looked upon as a good advertising vehicle. Some sales are better than nothing, right? Wrong. In all of the offers to send bulk e-mails for you, you never receive the full story.

What happens after you send bulk e-mail?

When you send bulk e-mail spam, you run big risks. If complaints are received—and they will be—your access to the web could be cut off. You are presumed guilty and must prove that the people who complain opted-in to your list. You could lose your local

Internet Service Provider, your websites, your e-mail addresses, and more. Your server will cancel your account.

This doesn't even cover your reputation or the legal ramifications of sending unsolicited bulk e-mail. Currently, several states have laws on the books or in the works which can fine you $500 or more for each piece of bulk e-mail you send without a prior business relationship.

Bulk e-mail just isn't worth the problems. If you have considered using bulk e-mail, don't do it. There are so many other more effective ways to market your course on the Internet that it's not necessary to take the risks that go with spam.

What should you do?

I can tell you in one sentence what you should do instead of bulk e-mail. You should start building your own opt-in e-mail list today. E-mail marketing is effective. That's why so many people are using it. It can produce steady sales for your business.

BUILDING YOUR E-MAIL LIST—48 WAYS TO GET THOUSANDS OF SUBSCRIBERS FOR YOUR COURSE'S DATABASE

Your goal should be to build an e-mail list of at least 10,000 potential players if you are in a major market. If you are a resort or have more than 18 holes, 20,000 is your initial goal. Done right, this will slash your future marketing costs and keep your course full.

While no e-mail will be better than a TRUE opt-in at your club's own website, here are some strategies we have used with various clients to build their e-mail lists. For each of these approaches, we invite the golfer to opt in and make it clear that we will stay in touch with them.

I get hundreds of calls a year from people that have great products, books, manuals, Info products, course, apps, golf courses, retail stores and assorted business ideas. I get calls every week from clubs that want more tee times, resorts that want more room nights and private clubs that want more members!

The first question I ask is always is the same one;

"How big is your email list?"

If they don't have one, whatever world beating product or idea they think they have, is dead in the water until they do. Great ideas, the "better mousetrap" will fight its' way to the top one out of every 10,000 times. The rest of the time an average product, sent to a good list, with a decent offer will win. In fact "He with biggest database wins," has always been my rallying cry. That's why I have devoted twenty-five years of my life to lead generation, or in its basic form, list building.

Facebook Fans are Great But...

Over the last few years I have become an expert in building large Facebook fan followings, but with Facebook, you are always at their mercy, you don't own the page, they do!

They can kick you off, change their algorithm so no one sees your posts or make seeing them cost prohibitive! They have come a long ways from a free "forum" and will keep finding new ways to charge, to drive shareholder value! Not that I don't like Facebook I do, it's just you have no control over what they may decide to do.

Being Ranked Highly On Google Is Great But ...

I am lucky to have an incredible SEO expert on my team by Google is even more fickle than Facebook and can destroy months of work with a single algorithm change that sends you from the top of the search engines to the dungeon! You don't own your SEO position Google does and what Google giveth Google can taketh away!

The same goes for Google ads, in fact, I haven't personally used them in years as I find Google far too draconian with their stupid rules.

Your Only Guarantee

No the only way to guarantee your long-term income and success is to build an email database and even though it may sound retro, a snail mail database as well!

The Internet is littered with the wrecks of businesses that based their model on things that simply went away from Google rankings to print ads or MySpace!

There Are Only Three Ways to Grow a Business

1. Increase the number of customers

2. Increase their incremental spend

3. Increase their frequency of purchase

That's it folks that is all there is, and number one and number three are directly related to the quality and quality of your list!

Increase Your List Size and You Dramatically Increase Your Business

I started my golf industry business from zero in the front room of my house and quickly built a list of 10,000 (today it's 76,000). I took many long nights, and lots of Heineken as I handcrafted it from scratch but, it turned out to be a multi-million-dollar list!

In addition to growing my own lists, I have helped over 2,000 clients in a multitude of different businesses rapidly grow their email database often with amazing results.

o   I have helped hundreds of businesses go from zero to over a thousand in less than a month. Some from Zero to 10,000 in a month!

o   One grew from a few thousand to over 60,000 in a single year, with an increase in income over 1.4 million dollars in the process.

o   Another went from zero to a million names in less than a year, seriously a million, names starting from scratch in less than a year!

The good news is most businesses need nothing like that amount to do well, in fact, many can generate a million dollar business on just a few thousand names, but they have to be the right names. I will share with you every way I have used successfully to rapidly grow lists that in turn, you can mine for millions!

Why You Should Go To Ridiculous Length to Target Your Market and Hand Craft Your Prospect List...

If You Actually Want an Astonishing Response to Your Marketing!

There is an old saying that "close only counts in horseshoes and hand grenades." Nowhere is that more true than in picking the right people on which to target your marketing and **spend your hard earned money, in the hope of earning a profitable return!**

This is information that few people want.

Few people want it because it involves work, painstaking, mind numbingly, boring WORK!

Everyone wants the quick and easy solution, so they buy giant directories or mailing lists of magazine subscribers, new homeowners or dubious "prospect" names from third party email vendors.

All of these solutions are a start but that's all they are, **most are suited only for starting to building a list of REAL PROSPECTS** not for actually making a direct sale. Those that try to circumvent this FACT are always disappointed.

This year I bought two large email blasts from two different vendors in the golf industry.

One of 75,000 e-mails generated just 103, opt-ins

Another of 50,000 emails just 90 and the guy e-mailed the list three times and said he added another 20,000 names to help get the numbers up!

The offer? A free round of golf, at a $150 a round resort! Trust me, in the golf business the offer doesn't get any better than that. Conclusion while both list where from credible companies they were barely above junk quality.

The success of all the campaigns I described in the introduction and in fact, almost all "LEGENDARY" campaigns, goes back first and foremost to spending a great deal of time and effort in defining your target market and building a great prospect list.

500% Greater Response from 10% of the Mailing List

Back when I was selling business manuals and tapes in the karate business, I had a mailing list of 12,000 plus karate schools: 1148 of that 12,000 had made a purchase with my company in year one. We called that our A-list (our response list) and always mailed it first when we had a new product.

Despite the FACT that every one of the 12,000 should have been a prospect for almost anything we had to sell, that list of 1148 proven buyers outsold the other 10,852 names by 500% or more, every single time we tested until, in the end, we cut the other 10,858 completely!

Our market, like it or NOT was 1148 people. We grew the business quickly by finding products and services to sell to those 1148 people and still managed to make a multi-million dollar business out of it!

The e-Mail World

Things are no different in the email world, I have 76,000 people on my golf industry list, but 4,000 people account for well over 80% of the sales!

Multi-Million Dollar Marketing Advice Below

Here is a thought, instead of spending $2,000 to do an e-blast to a list of 100,000 people who you think, because of a single criterion or two might buy your product or service, spend $500 on building a GREAT list of QUALIFIED prospects FIRST. **People who are willing to put their hands in the air and be counted,** then email those 500 people, multiple times.

The response will be a thousand percent greater, and you won't spend a dime more that you have budgeted in the first place. In fact, you'll spend a great deal less!

Now that is still a hard concept for most people to grasp because almost everyone is seduced by the law of large numbers. 100,000 people seeing your ad does not guarantee any success! In fact, it does not even guarantee a phone call!

The First Secret to Massive Response From Your Marketing, No Matter What Your Business or Product, Is to pay attention to List Quality, Not Just List Quantity!

The techniques I am about to share with you are simple and powerful techniques, but most people won't do them.

Why?

Because they take a good deal of time, effort and in some cases even talent.

Very often the skill, experience, and judgment of a senior player in your organization (most likely you) is needed to make a good decision about who EXACTLY is an ideal prospect for inclusion on your list. Not some frontline kid with the ink still wet on his AA degree or a temp service employee.

As **Voltaire** so eloquently said, "There is nothing common, about common sense!"

Target Your Prospects Precisely

The first key to any marketing success is focus.

Specifically, who are you going to sell your products and services to?

Plan your attack carefully, focus only on those people who are most likely to do business with you and don't forget to focus on the people YOU want to do business with.

Many companies miss this critical piece of marketing advice. Do business with the right people, not just the people who want to do business. Use the 80\20 rule going in.

Set a Written Criteria for Prospect Qualification and Inclusion on Your Target List

First, decide on the criteria you are going to use to judge a prospects worth. This is critical so you can weed out the suspects early on and focus ALL of your time money and efforts only on qualified prospects.

For example:

If you are selling golf real estate and wanted to build a list, the prospect might have to answer these questions in order to make it onto the list:

- o What price range are you looking at?

- o What type of home, by size or type?

- o When are you looking to move?

- o Will the home be retirement, 2nd home or investment property?

If the prospect is looking for the price and property type you offer and wants to move in say the next 12 months, you have real prospect on your hands. If the person is looking for California Beach front for

$125,000 you have daydreamer!

For my golf business products, buyers are 85% male and usually over 40 years old. Typically a Golf course owner, manager or PGA professional.

In the martial arts business, they were black belt instructors, 98% males between 20-45 year of age.

The Reasons for Inclusion or Exclusion Can be Far Less Tangible

When building target lists for our website product, we stay away from large hotel chains. Not that we would not like to do business with them, it's just that the sales and review process is too painful (SLOW) so instead, we focus out efforts on private resorts. At private resorts, you usually find that a single person, not a committee of twelve, is making the buying decision.

You can qualify based on revenue, area, employees, competitors, clients, corporate structure, profession, age, income and so on but whatever you choose, go ahead and write down what your criteria is going to be. **Describe in as much detail as possible your ideal prospect!**

Here is another example of criteria:

In building targeted lists to go after in the golf industry:

Clubs that are not run by a large management company (usually too hard to deal with) not run by committee (also hard to deal with) have at least 18 holes, a green fee of over $50, (and therefore, a reasonable ad budget) and are not in immediate competition with one of our existing clients. It also helps if their playing season is longer than five months.

We tend to make far more sales to men than women, partly that's the industry.

Most of the decision makers are over 45 years old

These are some, although not all, of the criteria we use in building a list and at least in the golf industry all of that information is usually readily available online by looking at the club's website.

Clarity Will Increase Sales

The clearer you are on specifically who your target market is the more effective you can be in writing your sales copy, which of course results in far higher sales.

Here are some key questions to consider when defining your list criteria:

- o   How old is your best prospect?

- o   Male or female?

- o   Family, married or single?

- o   Kids or no kids?

- o   Where do they live geographically? Country, state, county, zip?

- o   What language do they speak?

- o   What magazines, websites and blogs do they read?

- o   What are their hobbies?

- o   What other businesses like YOURS might they be Facebook friends with?

- o   What other products like YOURS might they have bought?

- o   What is their income?

- o   What is their education level?

- o   **What are their wants, needs, problems?**

- o   Weight, health, money, job security, traffic, marketing, copywriting, sales, leads, prestige?

o When you pick a problem to solve, expand it as best you can?

When you start making sales narrow down your predicated criteria for real criteria. Keep narrowing your focus towards the highest performing segments of your lists!

Now let's build us a million-dollar list. I am going to start with the simplest and most cost-effective ways to grow your list and work up from there.

1. Start Your Quest for a Great List by Getting A Decent CRM System

Nothing is more important to your long-term success than your database so we want to keep all that data in one place using a CRM or customer relationship management system. There are hundreds of programs that will do the job, we have our own high-tech one, but there are plenty of others to choose from like Salesforce or Zoho.

If you don't have a good one (an excel spreadsheet is not good) start with www.Zoho.com because it's free and it's easy to use. It will keep track of all your emails, snail mails and phone numbers. If you have any phone follow up, it will also provide sales funnel so all your leads get tracked to their logical conclusion. Depending on your shopping cart it can even dump your sales in there as well.

Yes, it's a pain to type all this stuff up but the time and money this will save you, in the long run, is amazing.

Back up your list off your computer weekly.

Print out a hard copy monthly and file it just in case of a double disaster! Trust me unless you make a real effort to keep all your data in one place you will lose thousands in future sales as lists get lost or corrupted!

2. Start at Home - Look in Your Personal e-mail Address Book

Start in the simplest place by handing picking family, friends, client's, x-client's co-workers and prospects from your existing personal address list. Export all who may be interested in what products and services you are going to offer into your list server and CRM.

Then ask family, friends, co-workers and employees to suggest and invite people from their personal databases.

Hopefully, you already have your first handful of emails from the friends and family program ☺

3. Make Your Business Card an Opt-in Promotion

Use the space on the back of your business card to make an opt-in offer, people who met you in person are far more likely to respond. Few people do this but it a very simple, cheap and high converting way to generate high-quality leads. Be sure and mention in when you hand over your card.

"Joe if you look on the back of the card you can get a free copy of my special report on maximizing sales which I think you will enjoy."

Equally, you can use the back of your card for an opt-in discount or free trial lesson, anything that gets them to go to your landing page and register.

4. Use Old Business Cards to Hand Craft Your Prospect List

Don't forget to go back and look for old paper copies of names and addresses you may also have in diaries or in filing cabinets. Remember snail mail and phone numbers can still be a huge asset, so don't overlook typing them into your database, **even if you THINK you may never use them!**

Open your desk drawer, check your wallet, look in the top pocket of your blazer, you see all those business cards from the people you met at trade shows, industry events, a party or just the local bar? Some of these people are great prospects and need to be added to your list. But, let's face it, if you were ever going to type them up, you would have done it already, so give them to someone else, find a college kid, a virtual assistant or call a temp but get them on your list!

People you have met in person are far more likely, perhaps a hundred times more likely to pay attention to your sales message!

5. Harvest Prospects from The Internet by Hand

The web is by far the quickest and easiest way to build a hand-crafted list although gone are the easy days when you could you use a program like List Grabber, Address Grabber, Web Bandit or a host of others and do it in a matter of hours rather than weeks!

1998 I was looking to get out of the martial arts business and do something else, but I wanted to keep the income coming in while I figured out what to do next.

The answer was Martial Arts Business.com. I built a nice but simple site. Began populating it with relevant content and set out building an e-mail list from scratch.

I spent several weeks tracking down every website I could find that was involved in martial arts. Once there I simply clicked on the contact us page or looked for the info at the bottom of the page and copied down their contact e-mail. At the same time I begged or bought lists, the few online vendors had, of school owners and eventually came up with just over 10,000 emails.

I sent the list a free content rich newsletter and kept sending it every week. Now in the purest sense, I was sending them spam, I had not asked their permission to be opted in. Back then of course spam was far less of a problem that it is today and I had very few complaints, those that did not want my info simply unsubscribed. There were maybe 3-4 people total that I remember being irate!

I was sending a relevant newsletter to a very specific business group.

Within a few weeks, the site which was a monthly subscription base model was doing $10,000 a month and eventually got over $20,000!

When I first started Legendary Marketing, we decided to go after golf courses as one of our main target markets. I went online every night and handcrafted a list of prospects of courses state by state. I had a list of criteria that I wanted to match based on the club's green fees, who ran the club, whether I could find a contact NAME on the site and how many of the features we were promoting, were missing from their existing website.

While I'd say the number of people who opted out was larger than in the karate business it was still an insignificant number especially compared to the number of people who were willingly opting in when other people passed the newsletters around. Again technically unsolicited but with an easy and visible unsubscribe I had very few problems. The newsletter grew my business rapidly!

I repeat I was sending a very relevant newsletter to a very specific business group.

It was a long, arduous task but rather than entrust it to a college kid, I did it myself, every night for almost an entire Heineken-hazed month!

It's that important!

And because I hand picked the target lists, lists of REAL prospects, we started picking up new clients and selling products immediately!

That campaign and almost every campaign we have targeted for a decade resulted in a 3% sell through ratio, per 100, targeted prospects. With an average spend of over $10,000 and a life of over five years. We are talking a seriously large return on investment.

These days it's far more difficult to do this although you are, under the CanSPAM spam act allowed to send one solicitation to ask someone to receive your e-mails. In a business-to-business situation, this still can still work to jumpstart your online efforts although you have to be very careful.

WARNING: It takes VERY FEW complaints to your ISP provider to get your site shut down!

KEY THOUGHT: I was sending a relevant newsletter to a very specific business group to whom my newsletter should be interesting!

That's why it's best to use all of your offline marketing to drive people to your site and build your opt-in list quickly!

That's also why you need a great e-newsletter full of relevant content so people read it, opt-in and pass it on to others!

Include articles on how to use your products or services to better their lives. Back it up with histories of other customers that have succeeded with your ideas. Include articles that demonstrate your superior expertise and knowledge of your industry. And most of all use unique and personalized stories that they can't get anywhere else! Put your company's personality into your newsletter so it stands out from the others!

You can't just send out promos for your products and services you must engage, entertain, interact with and connect with your reader!

You should also opt-in your list in very small doses or 50-250 or fewer names at a time. That way you can manage any complaints or tweak your content based on response.

I still harvest emails several times a year, and it's still very effective as long as you follow my guidelines.

6. Sign Up For Other Peoples Newsletters and Reverse Engineer a List

Depending on your product signing up for multiple emails may be great way to reverse engineer a list and a lot less hassle than the mining on Facebook.

For example, if you have product or service you want to sell to Realtors sign up for every realtor's e-list in your area you will get back an email just like this.

THANK YOU VERY MUCH!

Best of all technically you now have a legitimate business relationship since you signed up for their newsletter. In fact, I have had a few funny exchanges when people they ask to unsubscribe via email and I send back an email that says I have taken you off my list, but I will continue to look forward to your newsletter.

Which almost always promotes a re-subscribe or an apology. ☺

7. Set Your Main Company Website Up Correctly For Optimum Data Collection

If you are in the info marketing business, it's very possible that you have lots of specific landing pages and might not even have a company page. But if you do have a company page it must be set up with the number one purpose of data collection in mind.

Most are not!

Remember, each person has different hot buttons that will make them act to fill out your opt-in form some will like info others contests. Most websites, because they are designed by web people or design people, NOT MARKETERS, miss the boat by employing only one way to collect email names and that's usually buried at the bottom of the page where no one sees it!

Make your data collection front and center of every page lead generation is the number one job or your website, everything else is secondary. Once you have their name, you will have multiple opportunities to sell them something! It may even make sense to build your opt-in into the header or footer design so it shows up on every page automatically!

8. Use Opt-in Ads Throughout Your Website or Blog to Collect data

While most people understand the value of having an opt-in on their home page few people offer opt-in opportunities on multiple pages or even on every page. Not everyone reaches your website via the home page nor do most people go through a site in a logical manner as they would do a brochure or a magazine. Instead, they jump around to the pages that interest them. Therefore, you must utilize banner ads, button and data caption devices throughout your site not just on the home page.

Different pages within your site may call for different opt-in opportunities based on content! You can even place data collection ads in the middle of your content rather than on the edges or your design.

Don't overlook the opportunity to do this via a text link in the actual copy.

9. Use Your Blog Comments

To leave a comment on most blogs, you have to register and that means you get their email! Encourage people to give you their thoughts and opinion's on your blog. The more people you get to respond the more emails you pick up.

Design some content for the sole purpose of getting people to opt in and comment!

✔ Ask provocative questions.

✔ Ask people's opinion "What do you think?"

✔ Post a top ten list and ask people what you missed?

✔ Do a Yes /No Poll

✔ Take a stand on a controversial issue

✔ Ask for help

✔ Respond to comments

10. Use Your Hover Ad to Collect Data

Hover ads are a special type of pop-up ads created using Dynamic HTML, Java-script and similar web browser technologies. Because they do not scroll with the webpage, they appear to "hover" over the page, usually obscuring the content.

Hover ads have a 330% higher click through rate than traditional banner or button ads so it only makes sense to use them to promote data collection!

As well as the primary page you can also use hover ads to pop up on specific pages as people surf your site so the offer is relevant to content on the page they have chosen to be on. Matching specific offers to specific content and serving it up with a hover ad will greatly increase yours sign ups.

Hover ads should be changed out regularly to keep them fresh I usually change mine ever 4-6 weeks.

Many of my clients use hover ads to promote specific events or sales which of course is fine but in the long run you will always do better keeping an opt in promotion there most of the time!

11. Make Your Brochures & Info a Download

Another simple way to increase data collection from your website is to offer brochures, checklists or product specs as opt-in downloads. Even though all this information is readily available on the website through the main menu, we generate hundreds of extra leads a month for our client, Treetops Resort by offering their brochures as a PDF download. Some people would rather print it out or share the PDF with others whatever the reason it's an easy way to collect extra data.

12. Use Your Facebook Cover Photo as a Billboard To Promote Data Collection

Another simple yet little-used tool is to use your Facebook cover photo to promote an opt-in action by focusing the visitor's entire attention on your Free download offer. You can change the button that shows up in that spot on your Facebook page to sign up now or download now and link directly to your website.

13. Use Facebook Pay Per Click Ads and Boosted Posts to Build Your Lists

The very best reason to use Facebook is not to generate a large number of fans, keep top of the mind awareness or build your brand it is to build your mailing list.

Facebook ads and boosted posts are the fastest, cheapest most targeted way on the planet to boost your lists others than harvesting them yourself. You can target a geographical area, interests, demographics, professions and affiliations.

At World's Best Golf Destinations I went from zero to 56,000 fans and 700,000 emails spending just $5,000.

At Golf Operator Magazine I went from O-20,000 fans and 76,000 emails spending $2,000.

Recently I started trading classic cars and built a local Facebook fan base of over 600 men, aged 40-65, within a 25-mile radius, of Lecanto, Florida who had muscle cars, vintages cars or classic cars in their Facebook profile for about $180.

I spend some of the money getting likes.

Some of it boosting posts I hope people will share and get me more likes.

Some of it on direct attempt to sell product

But 80% of it on getting people to opt-in to my mailing list.

Remember Facebook fans are not yours opt-in emails are!

14. Use Google Ads

Google are so hard to work with that I usually don't!

The conversations I have had with their people as to why my perfectly legitimate best-selling books websites are not worthy of being advertised on Google is mind-boggling.

For my best selling sales book, Selling-Out Sell Everyone, a 500-page masterpiece of great sales techniques selling in hardback for just $39.95!

Google rep: "You can't tell people you are going to increase their sales by buying your sales book.

AW: OH, It's a sales book what do you suggest I tell them instead that it will decrease their sales?

Google rep: I can't tell what to do just what you can't do!

I won't bore you with the rest because it went round and round like that with every one of my products in turn.

I thought maybe it was me and had one of my staff try again a few months later, but no they are just content Nazi's. It's really pretty scary the power they have!

None the less if you can deal with the hassle (I personally can't) and you are selling a product that promises virtually nothing it's worth a try. Obviously, there are people who do it successfully, I have not and therefore am not qualified to offer advice on the subject.

Try Perry Marshall

15. Use Slide Share to Build Your Lists

I have found Slide Share, which is owned by LinkedIn to be an excellent tool for building lists and connecting with new people. Put together a short slide show, PowerPoint presentation with an opt-in at the end of the presentation. It can be the very same content you give away in other formats like special reports or videos, but in this slide show format, it seems to connect with a different audience!

Start with a great title that grabs the attention of your would-be audience.

Add a compelling photo a cover shot that screams look at me

Make sure you write a solid description of the content and use lots of targeted keywords in the tags section, so you connect with the right traffic.

Make sure the content is solid, you will be dealing with a professional audience and they are not looking for a sales pitch.

Then of course at the end of your presentation give them a reason to opt-in to get even more of your great information. Last but not least encourage them to share your presentation with others.

16. Use LinkedIn Connections to Grow Your Lists

LinkedIn obviously offers a quick way to build various professional lists, but it's also a great way to add to your credibility.

- ✔ Invite your friends and colleges

- ✔ Upload any email lists you have into LinkedIn

- ✔ Ask them to recommend you to others

- ✔ Contact a small number of people directly each day if you do just a few they are unlikely to flag you. Technically you should only invite people you know but very few people pay any attention to that rule. Just do it gradually and you won't get locked out!

- ✔ When people invite you always send back a semi-custom response inviting them at once to get some of your high-value content for free.

- ✔ Do something similar every time a new contact accepts your invite

Thanks for Hooking up With Me on LinkedIn

This is not another boring auto reply... In fact, it's a custom designed welcome package, just for YOU to get us off to a great start...

First a Couple of Free Books for You

Followed by a Handful of Killer Golf Resources!

I think books give you a great insight into the way a person thinks. As a way of saying thanks for connecting and giving you a little more insight on how my marketing strategies may be of help to your business in the future, please find complimentary audio copies of two of my best-selling books:

Cunningly Clever Marketing – Packed full of great marketing tips

And Desperately Seeking Members – Short, fun read with lots of real world advice

If you prefer a hard copy of either book you can get that Free as well if you just take care of the shipping, it's the same link as above.

If you like to read as much as I do you can check out some of my other books that may be of interest here http://andrewwoodinc.com/book-tag/all-books/

If I can be of help in some other way, please let me know

All the Best

Andrew Wood

Marketing Legend

www.AndrewWoodInc.com

www.LegendaryMarketing.com

Direct 352 266 2099

PS. Great resource for golf social media content www.golfoperatorassociation.org

PPS: A few Facebook pages you might like

https://www.facebook.com/worldsbestgolfdestinations/

https://www.facebook.com/GolfOperatorMagazine/

https://www.facebook.com/CunninglyClever/

I send different reports to different people depending on their industry and position.

17. Use LinkedIn Groups to Grow Your List

Join all relevant groups to your target market you can join up to 50. As you can see I am in a lot of golf and business groups.

Join in the discussion and post meaningful content rich answers. Never just post links to your stuff without offing good advice first. Once you have offered a rich content answer, then you may offer links to your free solutions, reports and videos as additional answers to some of the questions that are posted.

For example posted question is:

Does anyone have any ideas on how to improve my club's golf outing business?

Joes here's ten quick things I recommend to all my clients:

1. Call everyone who booked last year.

2. Keep direct mailing everyone who is not yet signed up.

3. Keep direct mailing everyone who is not yet signed up.

4. Direct mail new prospects every month until they book.

5. Offer a value-added bonus for signing a contract early in the season.

6. Train your outing staff how to sells outings.

7. As soon as the contract is signed offer an upsell.

8. If it's a charity offer to promote the event to your e-list as a bonus.

9. Always ask for referrals.

10. Encourage events to sign multi-year contracts

If you would like some in-depth information on this subject, I have written a manual, which may be of interest. http://golfoutingsmarketing.com or just download my FREE Golf Outing Blue Print.

Always provide value before trying to get anything even just an opt-in?

You can use this strategy with any type of group or forum not just LinkedIn. Every industry has them seek them out in yours!

Post your own questions, especially questions that might lead to a discussion where your product or opt-in is the answer.

I am writing a report on how to boost self-confidence what are your best tips?

Once people post, you can circle back and offer them your report with thanks for contributing an idea.

Start your own group for people in your field. Let's say you have products on soccer coaching. Start a soccer coaching group, then invite people to join the group. As the group leader, you will be able to steer the conversations towards your solutions.

18. Use LinkedIn Pulse Feature to Grow Your List

Post articles on LinkedIn's Pulse, which is basically their blog platform. Make the article content rich with an opt-in suggestion somewhere late in the text. Then share the articles with all the groups you belong to. Once again I find that even if the same article is on my blog putting it on Pulse reaches a different market.

19. Your Other Social Media

Obviously, there are hundreds of options for social media beyond the obvious but at the same time life is short and you can't do them all well. Depending on your audience you might consider Instagram, Pinterest, Periscope and many others. But don't just do them to say you have an account you can only do so many well focus on the ones that give you the biggest bang for your time and effort!

20. Use Rented e-Lists

I own an ad agency and buy lots of e-lists for my clients, usually at their insistence, after I try to talk them out of it.

Why? Because 95% of them are garbage!

They are over-rented, overused and sent hundreds of campaign's a year that are of no relevance to the end user. Because they send so many campaigns, their emails are often blocked from many of the major IP's and never see the light of day!

Yes I know is sounds good that they have 55,000 people just like the ones you are looking for…

I know it sounds like a quick fix…

I know is seems like a great short cut…

All I can tell you is that unless you are ok with a very high acquisition cost maybe 50-100 sign ups out of say 50,000 names, then this is not for you. By all means, try it but test a small portion of the list first say 5,000. If they are not willing to do a small paid for test, then there is a good chance they know the list won't work.

Email lists from a legitimate magazine have a far better chance of success but I'd still be wary.

21. Buy Email Lists with Extreme Caution!

The fastest way to get a large email list is to buy one. There are thousands of people with cheap email lists to sell you, and it's easy to get seduced by the large number they throw around at very attractive prices!

Don't do it!

Even more caution should be used when of buying e-lists than when renting lists, in fact, it's even worse because when you buy a list those names are going to be sent from YOUR server and YOU are the one who is going to get BANNED!

Unless you know the person personally or have a good history of where the list came from DON"T DO IT!

It's a virtual guarantee to get banned by your email host and kicked off your ISP as well. I know of hundreds of sorry tales…

Here Is What You Can Buy!

On the other hand, I have had great success buying lists of struggling companies or companies that had already gone under. Many of my clients's in the golf industry will give me heads up when things are not going well. It may well not be the owner who gives you the head up but someone lower down who works there.

In one case, at my suggestion, I took a list of 50,000 good names in payment for a debt that was never going to be paid. I sold the list for $10,000 to other non-competing client and kept it for my own use as well. All of which was disclosed to the second client who bought the list and the seller.

I have also had success in soliciting lists from website owners who seem to have given up on their sites or blogs. You know the ones I mean where the last post was three years ago!

Subject: I'd like to buy your list

Dear Blog Master Dave:

I have a new website I like to promote that I think would be of interest to your blog's readers. Do you have an email list I can rent or buy that I might be able to offer them a Free Special Report on Making This Year Their Best Year Ever!

When a business or website closes down for good someone leaves with the list. Find who has it and approach them with an offer. (Look in Google archives to find a contact person) When a business is struggling, especially a small one, the thought of a quick $500 or $1,000 for nothing more than their email list can be very appealing!

Obviously what you pay depends on how big their list is, how recently they mailed to it and how good it is. While there is no hard and fast rule, these days a list that's a year old will have at least 30% deterioration. Any older and it may not be worth the hassle of cleaning it!

To do this ethically depends on the website/companies privacy policy but while most Fortune 500 companies have pages detailing theirs most small companies make no such guarantees. In fact they usually have none!

22. The All Important Ethical Bribe

Without an ethical bribe to help things along building lists is hard. Sure some people will sign up to be first in line or for your newsletter, blog or discount club but to really turbocharge things you need a bribe. The bigger and better the bribe the faster you will build your list.

In the last two months, on my main, golf marketing site I have opted in over 3,000 people using two special reports and a slide show. In addition to their name and email I also got them to answer three qualifying questions about their business!

It's important to remember that different types of people respond to different types of bribes so using only one type may severely limit your success. Some like to read others prefer to listen or watch. Some like contests and sweepstakes others might prefer discounts or VIP status! Some like free software, apps and technology.

The best list builders realize that people respond to different types of offer and incorporate all in their strategic plans.

23. Hand Craft Your List Using Free Special Reports

Over the years, this has been my absolute cheapest and best source of leads. Call it a special report, a white paper, insider's secrets, an ebook or a guide, it doesn't matter, free information is by far the quickest, most cost effective and quality way of generating leads in ANY BUSINESS that I can give you.

Who downloads a Free Wedding Guide? People who are thinking of having a wedding, right?

Who downloads a Free Internet Marketing Guide? People thinking about doing Internet marketing, right?

Who downloads a Free Golf School Guide? People looking for a golf school and so on.

The booklets can be 10-30 pages and should include lots of point specific information.

✔ Design an attractive cover

✔ Add a benefit laden headline

✔ Add a bio page

✔ 5-7 bullet points on why the reader MUST download this guide now.

✔ Make sure the content is point specific and of high quality for your target market. Use is to showcase your expertise not to sell. I lot of people run ads throughout the content for their actual products while I am not against doing this I usually try to keep mine clean.

✔ Make the last page an ad for your products or services

✔ Upload it to your website in a prominent spot on your home page (and the page that corresponds with the topic), and you are just minutes away from qualified leads.

✔ Set up some auto responder emails to upsell anyone who opts-in.

24. Free Sample Chapters

Another simple option is to give away the first few chapters of your book that not only gets you an opt-in but increases the chance that you make a product sale at the same time.

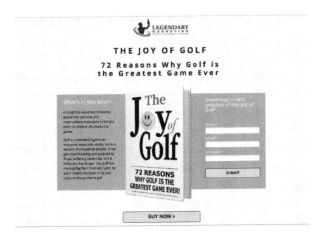

25. Use Free Audio to Hand Craft Your List

This is such a potent strategy, if "Free Reports" are the quickest and most effective way of generating leads, Free Audio Seminars about your products or services are by far the most potent. I have been using this technique since audiotapes, graduated to CD and now use podcasts or MP3 files.

While CD's are pretty retro, they still have value especially if your audience happens to be forty-five plus. The reason audios work in whatever format you use is that the prospect can listen to your content in the car, on their iPhone standing in line or while out jogging. So not only is it a great way to get data, it's a great way to sell!

Apart from the obvious convenience of downloading an audio remember from as sales perspective, there are three types of people:

- o   Some people like to read

- o   Some people like to watch

- o   Other like to listen

The more different ways you offer your opt-in information, the more people you will reach.

26. Build Your List With Informative Video

Seminars

We live in a visual world, and video is fast becoming every bit as important as copy. In my research people seem to be split 50/50 between preferring to watching a video or read copy, so I often do both!

Obviously, you can load your video's on YouTube, but the chances of them signing up for your channel are minuscule compared with the absolute certainty of a ClickFunnels-like squeeze page.

This informative series pictured above included a short intro full of amazing benefits and three, 30-minute seminars dripped over a 10-day period. The opt-in video generated over 1,800 opt-ins, in just two months.

I shoot my videos in a studio because I have one, but it's not necessary, a decent laptop video capture will do just fine. It's the message that's important not your Hollywood production quality!

The Key Factor on Great Opt-in Video is to Tell a Great Story!

In this case, a golf pro who had been teaching the same way for 20 years doubled his income. This when I shared a different way to sell his services in long term packages rather than one lesson at a time which amazingly is what 95% of the golf industry does.

Here's the perfect video opt-in formula:

Define the prospects problem:

Joe's a hard working golf pro, but he's not making enough money for his experience and expertise.

Show empathy for the problem:

I was once like Joe struggling to make ends meet

Show a budding hero just like them:

Then I met Mark Smith; he was a pro making two to three times what I was making and working fewer hours. I had to find out why!

Propose a solution:

His secret was Andrew Wood's the six-figure teaching pro program

Report the results:

I thought this was worth a shot and boy am I glad I took it. Within just days using the techniques in the program, I had re-vamped my programs and had an instant 30% increase in revenue with plenty more on the way!

Promise similar results:

Joe is not alone, in fact, over the last ten years thousands of teaching pros just like you have seen rapid income growth from using this program.

Tell them what to do:

Just leave me your email right here (point to the box) and I'll share three amazing videos with you absolutely free that details how a six-figure teaching income can be yours! Leave your email now and I'll see you on the other side!

Two minutes is ideal for the opt-in, but the actual video can be as long as you like as long as the story is engaging and entertaining.

27. Use YouTube to Build Your List

If you have not done so already start your own channel on YouTube. While not as good as a closed option like above as you can't make people subscribe to your channel or your list YouTube will reach more people and so is a complementary strategy.

Use informative segments to display your unique expertise. Always ask your viewer to opt-in for more info at the end and display a footer on screen at various points as well in case they don't make it all the way to the end.

Remember to ask them not only to opt into your channel which is good, but you don't get their data, but also to opt into your email list for your free info!

You can do this yourself with no technical skill by clicking on the enhancement button, which is the little wand icon next to the pencil. In addition to messages asking views to subscribe to your channel or opt-in to your list you can also place hyperlinks directly into your videos.

This simple tip will significantly increase response to your videos as you drive people to your landing pages.

28. Use Contests, Vacations and Sweepstakes

The quickest and easiest way to build a prospect list is to run a free contest, sweepstakes or prize giveaway. While you may think that people looking for free are not ideal prospects, studies show that people rarely enter FREE contests for prizes in which they have no interest in. Therefore, if the prize revolves around your product or service you can assume with reasonable certainty that the person entering is, in fact, a prospect.

You can qualify the entries further by asking two or three additional questions that remove all doubt such as their income, buying habits or time frame.

At several of our resort clients, we have had no problem in getting people to answer 20 questions or more in return for a free off season round or room! In most cases, we generate between 2,000-3,000 leads in a single month.

Here are the stats from the first promotion and this was one of three landing pages we used. The total sign ups were over 16,000!

29. Use Free Apps or Software to Handcraft Your Lists

Free apps or software can often be developed for very little cost and go viral fast especially with the mobile market, which is fast becoming everybody.

What kind of app could you develop for your market? The key to apps is to make sure you have an upgrade that makes the consumer register to get more features, without that all you get is a download, not an email address.

30. Use a Free, e-Newsletter as a Way to Build Your

List

Opt-in newsletters are one of the very best ways to build your list. But don't just put a subscription form on your website sell potential subscribers on why signing up is a good idea.

- ✔ Tell them what's in your newsletter.

- ✔ Tell them how they will benefit directly from its content

- ✔ Tell them how many subscribers you have already

DO NOT MAKE THE FATAL MISTAKE OF ASKING ONLY FOR e-MAIL!

You should try and get their snail mail as well. I know right now you may think you will never mail them... But you never know, plus even if you don't ever use them it's another asset you have to trade, sell or just add to the value of your business should you ever sell it!

To be effective, your free e-newsletter must be content rich with the type of information that will be of prime interest to your prospects.

My Golf Marketing Strategies e-Newsletter picture left, has grown to 56,000 subscribers, since its inception in 2000.

Remember, always be sure to ask a few qualifying questions on your subscription forms specific to your needs, not just their name and address!

31. Use Discount or VIP Club to Handcraft Your Lists

Other variations of this concept included asking prospects to sign up for special discount clubs, VIP clubs, e-special clubs or whatever you want to call your subscriber list.

Invite visitors to sign up for your discount or e-club. Be sure to let them know only e-club members get the best deals and watch your e-list grow!!!!!

Provide discounts, tee time privileges, and other special offers only to those who register. Registering on the site and the benefits of doing so should be mentioned at various points throughout the copy on your site. Always be promoting the idea of registering for additional benefits. People are more and more cautious about giving out their emails and being bombarded by junk they don't care to read. Make sure you offer compelling reasons to register on your site because your competition for that email address is worldwide. (Also tell people how you will use their name. For instance, that you won't sell their name and will use it only for your e-zine and special offers from the club.)

Make your registration instructions clear. Ask the visitor to type his email HERE. Re-explain the benefits the visitor will get by registering.

After they register, MAKE SURE your site sends an automatic letter thanking them for signing up. Take this opportunity to mention once more the benefits they will receive from doing so. Suggest they might want to refer the site to a friend so that they too might benefit from the same information. By making registration on your site rewarding and easy you can quickly build your email list and slash your marketing costs.

32. Use Online Surveys to Hand Craft Your Prospect List

Surveys are another simple and inexpensive way to generate a large number of qualified prospects in a short period of time. It doesn't matter whether you do the survey online, in an e-mail blast, at the counter, a trade show, or in a shopping mall. Simply put your survey in front of people wherever and whenever you can find them and you will with the right questions quickly generate enough qualified leads to do a Thunderbolt campaign.

33. Trade Old Lists With Others

Now, this is other than harvesting email yourself the best strategy of all but I have left it until later in the program simply because until you have a decent list yourself, you have nothing to trade!

One company's old leads can be a gold mine for another.

For example:

One of our clients generated over 4,000 real estate leads for their new development on Florida's East coast. Once these leads had be taken through the seven sales process to their logical conclusion, it was reasonable to assume that those people who had not bought were no longer interested in that particular development. That of course, did not mean that they might not buy somewhere else in Florida. So we swapped the names with a development in an identical price range on the other coast of Florida.

Think about that! 4,000 qualified names, of people with the money and desire to move to Florida!

Beg, borrow or trade with others to build your prospect list.

Once you do have decent list, people will line up at your door to get their hands on it!

34. Use Your email Signature to Handcraft Your List

Create a signature file at the bottom of your outgoing emails with your e-zine ad or contest included. You should have your email software set to include a signature file on every e-mail message you send out. This goes right after your name at the end of every email you send. Your signature file should include an ad for your opt-in list along with your free bonus for subscribers. Once they are on your list, you build a relationship with them and sell them.

Andrew Wood :: Founder
Legendary Marketing
"Increasing Your Business is Our Business."
Download my Free Special Report 12 Traits of Legendary Leaders

3729 S. Lecanto Hwy Lecanto, FL 34461
Direct: 1-352-266-2099
Office: 1-800-827-1663
Fax: 1-877-817-0650

35. Use Email Inquiries to Hand Craft Your List

Strangely enough, many great leads that come into companies in the form of questions, suggestions and comments via e-mail, NEVER make it into the company's prospect file!

Make a habit of including such requests in future target lists.

You should also look at your auto replies and bounced e-mails.

Very often these automatic messages contain a wealth of additional information that can be used to your advantage. This includes titles, phone numbers and addresses. The names and titles of other people in the organization and the messages that tell you Joe is gone and the new owner is Frank!

36. Use Print Ads to Build Your Lists

Yes, print ads are costly and are dying a death but they are not dead just yet. If the publication you are targeting is read by a vertical enough market, a small ad for the specific purpose of opting people into your list can pay dividends by reaching people you might not have otherwise reached. This is especially true of trade journals, association publications and B 2 B publications,

Most people run ads hoping they end up in direct sales. Because they want their ad to end in a direct sale, they waste space and copy trying to make a sale. The vast majority of print ads would be FAR better aimed at producing an initial contact rather than a sale.

This two-step approach is remarkably more effective in generating long- term results.

Direct your copy, graphics and call to action toward making an initial contact and you will produce far superior results. Use your print ads to advertise FREE Reports, Consulting, Contests, FREEBIES and other incentives that get prospects to identify themselves, preferably by filling in a contact point on your website. Once they are in your system, now you can contact them multiple times and make a sale.

If you can accept this simple but potent paradigm shift and Use your marketing dollars to build a qualified prospect list instead of trying to make a sale. Then you are well on your way to astonishingly better results!

37. Go to Conventions and Seminars With The Express Purpose of Building Your List

Although time-consuming and potentially expensive compared to other options, this is one of the surest and fastest ways to build a great prospect list of proven spenders!

Pick up The Show Directory

Many shows like the PGA show I attend every year in Orlando, has a very good directory with all the exhibitors listed. Many of the listings include titles and contact information!

Rent a Booth

Many of my clients go to trade shows for the sole purpose of generating a mailing list. Rent a booth, grab some i-pads, offer a contest and perhaps even hire some talent. I have clients who grab 3,000 emails in a single show.

Network

I sent an employee to a big info-marketing seminar as an attendee and he got the business card of 85% of the other attendees. Primo list of high spending people ☺

Very often the best place to network is at the bar at the event's official hotel right after the event and the last thing at night when everyone is back from dinner. Make it your goal to introduce yourself and swap cards not just chat! You'd be amazed at how many great leads you can get as you build your list.

Look For Opportunity!

I bought Marketing Guru Dan Kennedy a Heineken and chatted with him for 20 minutes. Gave *Chicken Soup for the Soul* author, Mark Victor Hansen a ride back to his hotel when the shuttle was taking too long and my car had just arrived from valet. Did the same for Harvey McKay of *Swim With The Sharks* fame and ended up playing golf with him.

38. Use Snail Mail Postcards

Wait you say; you want me to rent a mailing list of prospects and then print and mail postcards to it so that I can build an email list of the same people to mail to again?

Precisely Dear Watson!

Using the same offers, reports and FREEBIES you offered on your website and through e-blasts, rent a snail mail list of any target group "golfers, weight loss product buyers, dog owners" who might be in your target market and send out a postcard screaming that they respond. Postcards are relatively cheap, easy to produce and the most inexpensive thing you can mail.

This is an important strategy for two reasons:

One:

The availability of highly targeted and storable mailing lists is still far greater than e-mail lists. So if you need to reach golfing, Corvette owners who read *Forbes Magazine* and whose wife loves dogs, you can actually do it!

Two:

No worries about spam complaints, no worries about spam filters. In fact, very little worry at all that the great majority of your prospects will not, at least glance at your message. You will reach not only more people with a postcard than with e-mail but you will also reach different people.

39. Use Snail Mail Letters to Build Your Lists

I have had some amazing success with snail mail and I think that as fewer and fewer people send postal mail the response rates will only go up!

The beauty of a sales letter over a postcard is simply more space to tell your story and with a high price or more sophisticated audience that's important.

Yes, snail mail can be expensive if you do it wrong but you can test very cost effectively and check your conversion rates before you ramp up. This is only going to be cost effective if you have a relatively high-ticket product but you should not ignore it!

40. Use Tele-Research to Hand Craft Your List

I have saved telemarketing (tele-research) for near the end because it is relatively costly and time consuming to do. Of all the suggestions, it is one of the best methods to qualify prospects and build an excellent list.

If you outsource the job, it's painless and can usually be accomplished in four weeks or less! In the golf business, we have used telemarketing in three ways great success:

1) To build a targeted list of outing prospects for our clients

Since no such list was available for sales, telemarketing was the only way to accomplish this task. We started using online directories to identify those organizations most likely to hold a golf outing. These included charities, hospitals, fraternal organizations, schools, churches, car dealers, radio and TV stations, firehouses, police stations and large employers. To give you some idea of the task you face approximately 4,000 calls will produce a list of 400 good names; that is to say, the name and address of the person in charge of booking the event.

WE also ask when the event is held, where it was last held and how many players typically attend. Based on this information, we may vet the list at the source if it looks like their typical venue is too far down or up the food chain to apply to our client, although in most cases, we will mail everyone. There is always the chance they will move up or down in cost.

2) To build a list of membership prospects for our clients

Our membership program takes a similar track, although the target market is different. In the case of membership, we focus on calling high-income professionals such as doctors, lawyers, investment brokers and entrepreneurs.

3) To build a list of prospects for our ad agency

This is perhaps the most typical use of telemarketing in building a list that is suitable for Thunderbolt Marketing. Take a mailing list, yellow pages, Chamber directory, industry magazine, trade guide or internet listing and call with specific questions to narrow down your market to a list of people who are qualified and likely to be REAL prospects for you.

4) To re-qualify old data and out-of-date mailing lists

Many of our clients have large files of people who have done business with them in the past, sometimes the very distant past. Most of them also have decent numbers of people who have inquired but never bought. Then there are the various Excel spreadsheets handed down from previous employees, the origin and make-up of which are long since lost. Add to that file draws full of handwritten notes, business cards from long lost trade shows and a Rolodex no one ever bothered to digitize. You'll have a perfect source of great leads, just as soon as you call them all and re-qualify these multiple sources into a single Thunderbolt mailing list.

This is obviously a painful task; were it not, someone would already have done it for you!

Let me stress again most STRONGLY- Spending a few thousand dollars to get this end of your house in order will be worth 100 times the money you waste on mailing greater quantities or poorer quality names than the target list you will eventually contact seven times or more.

145

41. Hand Out Flyers at Your Speaking Events and Include Opt-in Offers in Your Slide Show

Sometimes the most obvious things we should do we just don't do. Whenever you are speaking at an event at the very least hand out flyers with a free gift for anyone who goes to your landing page and registers. I have a client who does seminars all over the world who simply never thought to do this, so busy were they setting up their various demonstrations. In one night they picked up over 1500 names!

It's shocking to me how many events I go to where they make no effort to get my name. Sure the organizer has it but the speaker often doesn't and often never gets it as they quote various "privacy" concerns.

Every time I speak, in addition to flyers, I will add several slides promoting my free gift for all participants good for 48 hours only and suggest they immediately write down the info. I have never had an organization be anything but delighted by the knowledge that I am going to give their audience a value added free gift. In fact, many include it in their promotion for the event. This always gets me over 50% of the audience and often far more depending on how many of the group are from the same family or organization.

42. Use Scratch Cards to Handcraft Your List

Not everyone will want to take your free flyer and a large percentage of those that do will ditch it long before they get in front a of a computer to sign up. Enter the scratch card. People love scratch cards and will eagerly accept them. The key is to have a large grand prize - perhaps a day of you consulting, or speaking or coaching time and a number of little prizes. Then have the cards set up, so everyone wins something like your special money saving report or lowering your golf score, weight loss or self-defense tips.

43. Point of Sale – Make Email Acquisition Part of the Checkout Process

For retail stores, or seminar sales asking customers for their email addresses at the point of sale (POS) is a proven technique that is quickly gaining momentum. In-person and in-store events were ranked second in acquisition quality and quantity, according to a recent research study.

To put this practice into action, it's important that your associates:

o   Ask customers for their email addresses

o   Explain the benefits of your email program

o   Let customers know exactly what to expect in terms of email frequency and content

o   Read back the email addresses to verify correct spelling and reduce the risk of error

44. Add Share Buttons at The Bottom of All your Emails and Content

Encourage your current email subscribers to share and forward your emails by including social sharing buttons and an "email to a friend" button in your marketing emails. That way, you'll gain access to fresh networks, friends, and colleagues who might sign up for your list. At the bottom of your emails, include a "Subscribe" CTA as a simple text-based link so that those receiving the forwarded emails can easily opt-in, too.

Add a share suggestion on all your PDFs and videos. Add it to everything!

SUMMARY

Whatever you do to acquire e-mail subscribers, treat them like the gold they are. Having the power to distribute your message to a large number of people with the touch of a button is marketing power you can't afford to miss. Remember he with the biggest database wins!

Before you can expect to make any money from your online marketing, **You MUST START by COMMITTING the time and resources to HANDCRAFT your PROSPECT LIST.** Success in this Endeavour is measured in quality NOT quantity but both is even better!

First, decide what your specific written criteria will be for inclusion in your mailing list. The tougher the criteria, the better!

Once you have determined your exact criteria, you will use a variety of methods to qualify prospects into your final thunderbolt list until you reach your desired number of prospects for the campaign.

Start by combing your computer, desk, files and pockets for all existing data, that even though not current can at least be re-qualified by mail or phone quickly.

Look at your local media every day it is swimming with leads. Make your website the focus of all your prospecting efforts. Use ads, direct mail, radio, TV and e-blasts to drive people to a contact point on your website. Entice prospects to register for contests, offers, e-mails, free stuff, DVD's, Audios, Green Fees, room nights, newsletters, special reports and e-clubs.

Don't forget the obvious, existing clients, x clients, referrals, trade show leads and existing vendors. Look for Alliances with none competing clubs to quickly enhance your prospect list by sharing data.

Use telemarketing to qualify new prospects in your area, re-qualify old lists, and to add an additional layer of quality to new lists.

Finally look for people of influence who can plug you into their network as well as the occasional dream contact, just for fun. The one contact, whom, if you got them to buy would bring with them an avalanche of other business.

CHAPTER NINE

Building the Perfect Web Site for Your Club

WHY YOU <u>MUST</u> HAVE A WORLD-CLASS WEB SITE AND BUILD ALL OF YOUR MARKETING AROUND IT!

I t's still tough to get some people to realize that your web site is the absolute foundation of all your marketing activities. It's better than print, radio, TV, billboards, and Yellow Pages. In fact, about the only marketing that gives your website a run for its money is landing pages.

Think about your club's website:

✔ It is the only employee you have who never calls in sick. It books tee times and answers questions 24 hours a day. (If your site doesn't do this and more, talk to us.)

✔ It's the only marketing you have that can send an instant and personalized response to prospective players or members at 3 AM on a Sunday morning by using pre-programmed autoresponders and follow-up letters.

✔ It's the only marketing you have that can collect detailed information on outing, banquet, or wedding prospects while you sleep by using dynamic request forms.

✔ It's the only marketing you can do that incrementally lowers your future marketing costs with almost every visit to your website.

There is no more important marketing tool at your club than your website, yet most clubs are content to trade out to amateur designers, members, or the owner's son-in-law rather than make the commitment to a world-class website. Even where clubs have made substantial investments with ad agencies or web design companies, they almost always miss the mark. While these vendors understand the technology and design aspects, they do NOT understand the marketing aspects of dynamic websites. Nor do most understand the golf market, and those who do come at it from only an online perspective rather than integrating online marketing into their overall marketing efforts.

Your website cannot just be pretty; it has to be a marketing machine to be an effective tool. Ninety-eight percent are not!

In this chapter, you will discover:

✔ How your current site measures up

✔ How to design an effective website

✔ What the most important features are

✔ Why you should use automation as much as possible

TYPES OF GOLF WEBSITES

There are basically three types of websites for golf businesses.

✔ **A site to service your existing members** and perhaps attract some new ones. This site would include a lot of interactive features, like your schedules, news, events, and perhaps have a password-protected section that helps make the members feel special.

- ✔ **A landing page** is mainly interested in getting local leads. There is nowhere to click, just a sales pitch to get you new business in the form of an e-mail address or phone call requesting information.

- ✔ **A retail site** would include daily fee courses, resorts, real estate developments, and golf schools, and all those looking to attract and retain ongoing play. These sites will often have an e-commerce feature so you can sell merchandise, tee times, or other items by credit card.

THE TWELVE MOST IMPORTANT FACTORS IN BUILDING THE PERFECT WEBSITE FOR YOUR CLUB

1. Your website must be a data collection machine.

The number one function of your website is to collect information. Only when you have good information from your clients can you meet their needs correctly. This is every bit as true for a private club as a daily-fee club, resort, or real estate development. You must know your customers' wants, needs, and trends before you can fulfill them.

For this reason, you need multiple data collection points incorporated into your site's design. If you just offer a single e-newsletter sign-up on your site, you are only collecting about 20 percent of your potential e-mail addresses. If you doubt me for a moment, look at your traffic and look at your sign-ups!

Some people are contest people; they respond to a chance to win! Some people are coupon people; they respond to discounts. Give *me* a chance to download information though (like 20 ways to hit it 20 yards further), and I will gladly give you my name, address, e-mail, and mother's maiden name! Everyone has a different motivation, so the only way to get maximum response from your site is to build multiple data collection points into your site. (Our latest websites have no fewer than five different ways to gather data. If your site doesn't, you are really missing the boat!)

With the importance of data collection in mind, the key goal of your home page should be to collect data, either through surveys, contests, downloads, request forms, or online bookings. Other pages should also make a strong effort to collect data such as outing pages, weddings, banquets, meetings, and so forth. Feedback pages and member surveys work well at private clubs, as do monthly giveaways of dinner.

2. Detailed information must compel the visitor to ACTION!

The second most important key to web success is to provide lots of information. One of the biggest complaints of web surfers is finding a site and then not finding the information they were looking for once they get there! Put as much information on your site as you can and let the visitors decide what's important to them. The more you make your website the center of communication at your club, the more you will gain from it. Post news, schedules, specials, reminders, photos of members and guests, and so on. When visitors know that the site is regularly updated with the latest information, they will use it. When they show up several times and nothing has changed, they won't be back anytime soon.

Merely providing detailed information, content, and news— which few clubs do—is NOT enough. On your site's key pages— membership, outings, banquets, lessons, real estate, golf, and so on—the copy MUST SELL. Ninety-nine percent of all golf websites ignore this vital truth. It's the *copy* that sells. Let me repeat—*it's the copy that sells!*

I was shocked recently to hear a so-called golf marketing expert speak to a seminar audience at the Golf Club Owners Convention and tell everyone that nobody reads, so it doesn't really matter how good the copy is! I couldn't believe my ears. The number one reason people use the web is for information. If you present that information using Marketing 101 features and benefits you will get a thousand times more response than if you stick to a "just the facts ma'am" approach!

Each page should be a sales pitch for something

Each page must be a mini sales pitch to move the prospect to do something. Book a tee time, make a dinner reservation, take a lesson, or whatever eventual action you want them to take. It should be a complete sales pitch with a beginning, a middle, and an end; features, benefits, testimonials, and a call to action. Only if each page contains all these elements can it be deemed a great web page—and that's not just one page, it's every page you have that ultimately pushes for a sale. There is no such thing as too much good information, only too little information or information that is not relevant to making a decision.

3. The site must be easy to navigate and easy to read!

A visitor to your site should be able to easily move from any page to any other page. Many golf sites I have looked at [thousands] break this rule. Use navigation menus that have a consistent look and location on every page at the top or left-hand side—don't put any obstacles in your visitors' way.

Menu design 101

- ✔ Menus on the right don't work well. People naturally look left or up.

- ✔ Menus at the bottom of your site are often below eye level on many computers, meaning there is no menu at all as far as those users are concerned.

- ✔ Don't have more than about eight or nine choices in the main menu. You should use sub-menus from that point. Sites with twenty or more items in the menu are not user-friendly. If you have that many, always used a left side menu

- ✔ Make the type style of your menus large enough to read.

- ✔ White text on a black background is 33 percent harder for the human eye to read. Why make it harder?

An easy-to-read, easy-to-navigate site.

Mobile or Responsive websites

You must have a mobile version of your website. Better yet, make your site responsive. With how many people use the web on smartphones, you cannot afford to have a website that does not change based on the device it is being viewed with. If you think size 12 font is tough to read on a desktop, try reading it on your phone. Impossible!

Not only does your site need to be responsive to mobile or tablets, your online booking engine and online stores need to as well. Visit your website on your phone right now to see if your tee time booking link is responsive. If not, get on the phone immediately and demand that it be done. If they say they can't, find a new online tee time provider. It's that important.

Google **heavily penalizes** any website that does not have a mobile or responsive version. This means that your search engine rankings will drop (or already have) and you will not stand a chance of ranking higher than your competitors if Google detects that you do not have one.

4. Your site must allow the visitor to complete a transaction.

There are few things as frustrating as investing time visiting a website only to find once you have made a decision to act that your next step is to call between 9–5 to actually book a tee time or make an appointment. The web is open 24/7, 365 days a year, and a great majority of web surfing is done after normal business hours. You must have online reservations, a shopping cart, and the ability to request dates for outings and banquets without having to wait until the next day. If you do not, you will lose business. Web surfers will rarely, if ever, take the trouble to print out a form, fill it in, then mail or fax it to you. If you don't offer online booking for tee times, your web visitors are likely to go to one of your competitors who do, rather than wait to call you in the morning.

5. The site must have marketing automation.

Perhaps the most radical difference between the Legendary Marketing systematic approach and other ad agencies and consultants is our commitment to relentless follow-up. Nowhere is that better demonstrated than in the automatic tools we build into our websites. These are the same tools you MUST build into your site if you are to get maximum results from your online investment.

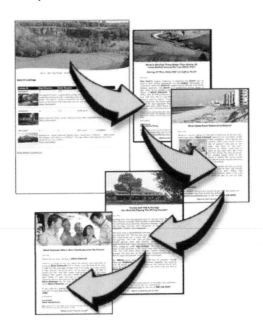

There are three distinct levels to marketing automation

1. Basic auto responder or series of auto-responders pre-programmed to fire when a prospect signs up for something

An autoresponder lets you pre-program sales letters and follow-up messages that respond immediately to any request generated from your site. For instance, when someone registers on your website, you can immediately send them a message thanking them and providing your latest offers. For outing or membership leads, three or four follow-ups can be programmed in. New clubs or real estate developments may follow up twenty times or more over the next year. Immediate, consistent follow-up increases sales, branding and income! Best of all, it's automatic and does not rely on anyone at the club remembering to do it!

For example, let's say you ask whether the player has any interest in Summer Junior Golf Camps. The person answers yes, but it's only January. Not to worry. Your marketing automation will AUTOMATICALLY follow up with an e-mail on May 15th letting ONLY the players who answered YES know the dates and details of the summer camps. It will follow up again June 1st with more information and a link so that they can go ahead and register their kids online! You do nothing! It doesn't matter whether you happen to be in your office or vacationing in St. Andrews!

Marketing Automation is designed to bolster every money-making aspect of your operation. Think about your extra income potential if just four more people signed up for every single event at your club. That's four to the power of 100 different events, that's 400 people who, even at only $30 an event, represent an extra $12,000 in revenue. If it drove eight people, it would be $24,000. If the eight people paid $40 a head, it would be an extra $32,000. And remember, this is all automatic.

WARNING: DO NOT make your auto responses passionless John Doe follow-ups that generate the excitement of the automatic train voice at the Atlanta airport!

Write them like great ads, with compelling headlines, benefits, testimonials, and calls to action. "Thank you for contacting us," doesn't cut it!

2) Visitor Tripped Automation Based on What Pages They Visit

Perhaps the most innovative and powerful feature you can use on your website for marketing is marketing automation.

For instance, our marketing automation features can be preprogrammed with an almost unlimited number of promotional custom e-mail campaigns, follow-ups and more. You can decide to send a series of e-mail messages to each player, inquiry, local association and so on. You can have a series of e-mails developed to contact people based on their answers to any question you choose to ask on your website.

You can automatically send emails to people who visit certain pages, click on certain links, stay on a page for a pre-defined amount of time, visited a specific sequence of pages and so on. The possibilities are nearly endless, and everything is set up to be automatic. This is true one-to-one marketing, automatically sending people offers on only the things that interest them the most.

3) Dynamic email Follow UP

Dynamic email content is a powerful way to update your emails to provide tailored, timely and useful information to each of your leads. It saves the time and effort of creating dozens of similar emails to tailor your messaging, by instead using one email and custom content merge variables to insert the most relevant information for your lead.

Here are just some of the possibilities available when using Dynamic Email Content:

- o Shopping cart abandonment to show everything left in the cart

- o For multi-location businesses, changing headers for different offices

- o Different service offerings based on lead demographics

- o Offer different coupons based on previous behavior

- o Informational content based on different topics of interest

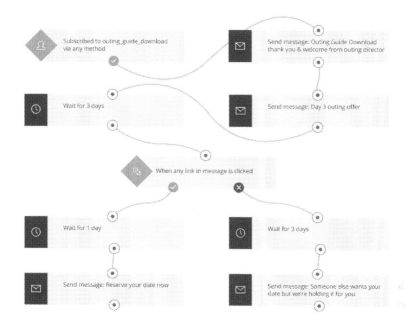

Marketing automation allows you to automatically send follow-up based on any action or combination of actions imaginable.

6. If your site is expected to create business, you must take the search engine rules into account.

Search engine rules and tactics change weekly so writing a definitive piece that lasts is difficult. But whatever the rules are when you build your site, you had better know them. Currently they include having 200 - 400 words of text on your home page, (which many clubs don't) and having lots of other sites linked to yours. It's also a good idea to have a domain name with your key word in it and name your title tags and pictures with keywords.

We keep up on the every-changing search engine rules and the new rules are constantly being programmed on our customers' web sites.

7. You must have excellent e-marketing tools that integrate with your website.

This is where the gold lies in e-marketing. E-marketing is even more effective if you can segment your target markets and make specific offers to those most interested. Based on the contact points you choose in your Legendary Marketing website, you can sort and send e-mail to specific target markets with the touch of a button. For example, you can e-mail only people who have entered outing requests, only women, or only players who live more than 50 miles away.

In fact, you can sort by any category you choose with the touch of a button. This allows you to promote "shrimp night" to the people most interested in dining, tournaments to those most interested in competition, and junior events only to people with teens. Because you target people's real interests, people receive what they are interested in and there are no spam problems. In other words, customers don't unsubscribe when you are sending them the information of most interest to them!

Is that how you do your current e-mail marketing?

8. Your site must have excellent reporting tools.

Your site's reporting tools are the mechanism that you will use to evaluate your site's performance and tweak your online offerings. There are four important areas you are going to want to generate reports from:

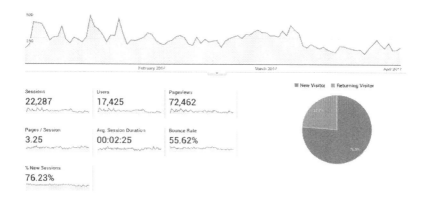

A. Web site traffic

Your site should be connected to Google Analytics to record the following key traffic information and review it monthly - if not weekly.

- ✔ How many visitors did you get?

- ✔ How many pages did the visitor view?

- ✔ What specific pages did they view?

- ✔ How did they find your site?

B. E-mail results

When you want to track the success of your e-marketing, you need powerful reporting tools on your site for the elements that matter most to making good decisions about your future marketing. You can quickly and easily find out the statistics you need including:

- ✔ How many e-mails did you send?

- ✔ How many bounced?

- ✔ How many were opened?

- ✔ How many people clicked through to your site?

- ✔ Which links did they click?

- ✔ How many opened on mobile vs desktop?

- ✔ How many people forwarded the e-mail?

- ✔ How many unsubscribed?

In other words, you can tell the results of your e-mails on almost any dimension, in any time frame after you send them. These reports should also be presented in various graphic formats for quick inspection.

C. Web form reports

Since there are an unlimited number of questions you can ask in surveys or contact points, there are an unlimited number of reports you can run depending on what data are important to your operation. Common reports might include:

- ✔ Player frequency

- ✔ Player price points

- ✔ What other courses they frequent

Month	Year	Orders	Payment Amount	Payment Authorized	Payment Received	Sales Tax 1
12 - Dec	2016	37	$3,432.25	$3,432.25	$3,432.25	$107.25
11 - Nov	2016	10	$1,587.15	$1,587.15	$1,587.15	$62.15
10 - Oct	2016	13	$1,528.75	$1,528.75	$1,528.75	$79.75
9 - Sep	2016	35	$4,169.66	$4,169.66	$4,169.66	$193.66
8 - Aug	2016	14	$2,344.00	$2,344.00	$2,344.00	$0.00

D. Transaction reports

If you are running a shopping cart, your backend will log all the transactions and provide numerous reports on customer spending habits.

9. Your site must be easy to manage and update!

This is a big deal because no one wants yesterday's news on the web; that's what newspapers are for! This is critical to your overall success because if your site is not easy to manage and update, your staff will never do it! Let me repeat that: *If your site is not easy to manage your staff won't do it!* Add to that a revolving door at most clubs for the position of *web site updater* and you have just washed your entire online investment down the drain.

Ah, you say, but our web company updates our site for us. Do they do it on weekends? Do they do it in the evenings? Do they do it within 24 hours after receiving your request? In my experience probably not!

This is a feature we build into all of our web sites, so that even clients with very limited web experience can make simple additions to their sites *without* having to call us or *pay* someone else for changes. In fact, it's because of its ease of use that we called our first product a Smartsite - the theory being that it is so easy and powerful to use that it makes everyone who uses it look smart!

All a person has to do, in effect, is log into the dashboard of your website, select the page they want to update, paste whatever he wants to update onto the page, then save and publish the page. It's instantly live. The editor is your standard WISYWIG, no code to learn, just a simple familiar interface! Legendary Marketing will of course update your site for you and, yes, we do work seven days a week. But even that does not deliver the personal satisfaction of waking up at 2 a.m. on a Sunday morning with an *ah-ha!* moment and being able to jump online and instantly add a special to your site or send an e-blast to your customers!

In less than five minutes we can train anyone at a club - and I mean anyone above the age of seven - how to update any time of the day or night. And, yes, I mean in FIVE minutes.

Make sure you have a feature like this built into your site, so that you are not held hostage to anyone and can quickly get news and information posted on your site to keep it fresh.

10. The site must look good.

Notice how far down the list this rule came. On many people's lists, design comes first. The truth of the matter is that while look, feel, and design elements are important, they are a lot less important than the copy or what your site does on the back end. As long as you follow key guidelines about menus, make your type large enough to read, and have plenty of copy, there are almost an unlimited number of good designs you can come up with.

Here are a few key considerations:

✔ Be sure not to confuse the eye; people read from top to bottom and from left to right. Don't mess too much with that pattern.

✔ Highlight your four most important products at the very top of your site. For example Outings, Membership, Book a Tee Time, and Enter to Win!

✔ Avoid reverse type (white on black) it's 33 percent harder for the human eye to read.

✔ Make sure background colors or shading contrast enough that the text can be read. Can it be read if they print it out?

✔ Pictures work best at the top of the site with a headline underneath or over the top of them.

✔ Pictures in the body copy should always face in so the reader's eye moves towards the copy.

✔ The pictures should be big enough to actually see!

✔ Avoid overuse of bolded, capitalized, and colored letters. Use modern fonts and understand that italicized words will slow down your reader (so don't use an abundance). Have you ever

168

come across a web site where the text stretches across the screen - and sometimes beyond? That is not the sign of a professional site. Generate a professional image by keeping your text in a narrow column - it makes for much easier reading.

✔ Make sure your site loads fast. Have you ever waited more than 10 seconds for a page to load? Probably not. And neither will your visitors. Compress all of your graphics for faster load times. Assume your web site is going to be viewed by the oldest browser on the slowest internet speed. You don't have complete control over this attribute, but what you can control, you should.

✔ Maintain a consistent look and feel. Be conscious of the rest of your course's printed material when you create your web pages. Be consistent in your graphics; use the same logo that appears on your letterhead and the same kind of color and style that's found on your other business material.

11. The site must have a sophisticated CRM

All of your data must be easy to find in one place, easily sortable and should aid you greatly in following up leads for membership, outings and events through a logical sales process. The CRM Legendary Marketing provides shows an entire customer history on one screen.

You can see:

✔ Which emails he has opened

✔ Which forms he has filled in

✔ Which web pages he has browsed and for how long

✔ Which videos he has watched

✔ Track your sales opportunities from creation to close.

✔ Move opportunities across deal stages with a simple drag-and-drop interface.

✔ View the entire funnel in one easy-to-manage view.

✔ Create custom deal stages, fields, filters and more to manage your unique sales process.

✔ Lead Scoring identifies hot prospects so you can zone in on those most likely to buy. His engagement with your site even produces a score which alerts you each day to the most active users. This can be very useful in the sale of certain products and it gives you invaluable feedback on which emails are resonating with which individual players.

Here are some of the other cool tools you might like to have that are built into our CRM system.

Behavioral-based tracking to truly understand what motivates each click. Receive a list of the day's hottest leads right to your inbox and act at the just the right time to convert to sales.

Identify Anonymous Web Visitors

Think about this: 98% of web visitors remain anonymous because they don't fill out forms. VisitorID uses reverse IP lookup to identify the companies visiting your site, and provides you contact info, including names, emails and phone numbers - effectively doubling or tripling the number of leads that can be harvested from your existing web traffic.

Track your Known Leads

Is your website just a glorified brochure? Turn it into a two-way communication tool. Track and notify sales by email as soon as a lead that is currently in your sales funnel comes back to your site to check out your pricing, or a specific page like golf outings or wedding. Arm your sales people with the knowledge they need to close the sale in real time!

Daily VisitorID Email Allows You Focus Your Efforts Only on Those Most Likely to Buy!

Put anonymous web visitors, leads, opportunities, and customers that have visited your site each day directly in your inbox. Quickly scan through contact information, Lead Score and other fields without even logging into the app!

Page Visits, Referral URLs and Search Terms

Visitor ID times page visits, recognizes when someone views an important page, checks out where they came from and identifies which search terms led to your site.

12. Be reliable; be protected.

Last, and by no means least, your site should be reliable. 24/7 is the colloquialism for expressing the expectation that the web, including your site, should be available twenty-four hours a day, seven days a week. If you are running your own server, it's advisable to have some degree of redundancy built into your system to meet this expectation. The day will come when your server will crash or you'll need to perform maintenance on it. You'd be surprised at the number of large companies that operate their sites with no back-up in place. Most that do regret it at some point in time. If your hosting service is operating without some sort of backup, find a new provider (We back up every one of our sites in two places).

OTHER WEB-SITE FACTORS YOU SHOULD CONSIDER IN DESIGNING YOUR SITE

Think globally - the world can be your market

There's no shortage of consumers online. On the web your prospects are the entire world. In fact, nothing gives me a greater kick than signing up a new client in Sweden, or selling a set of clubs to a man in Pakistan! You'll experience the same euphoria when you start selling green fees, memberships or products in places you don't even know how to find on a map.

Since most of your competitors will be focusing on their home markets, you can get the jump on the long-distance market. Visitors to your area often do web searches before they travel to look for attractions. For example, if you run a golf course in Orlando, why wait until golfers arrive from the UK or Canada and pick up a hotel guide. Help them find your web site ahead of time and offer an "out of towners" special. You can also run Facebook ads and other online ads in other markets to get them to your web site before they even set foot on a plane. That's the type of marketing that makes millions (or even an extra round now and then!).

Add a media section to save time and money

Does your site offer a media section where the media can download high resolution pictures, logos and fact sheets when they want instant information on your facility? This is a simple example of using your web site to save time. By having a media section, you increase your chances of getting your course free PR. You also don't have to spend time and money shipping out high resolution pictures or logos to people who want to design brochures and flyers for their outings or want to write articles on your club. Simply direct them to click on the picture of their choice and it instantly downloads a high-resolution image to their computer! Now that's instant gratification. Like most additions to our product, we came up with this idea when I realized how much time and money we were wasting hunting around for clients' pictures or logos and overnighting them to various magazines or graphic designers.

Private club sites

Private clubs need specialized options to serve their members. Consider adding options to your site if you are a private club to increase members' communication and participation in your activities. There are many member-only options you can offer through password-protected gateways. These might include:

- ✔ **Photo gallery.** Special section to allow you to post club photos that members can view, download, and e-mail to friends or family.

- ✔ **Member directory.** Real-time updates of member information to keep your directory current. Members will always have contact information available to schedule golf and social activities. Directories can also be printed out in hard-copy format.

- ✔ **Reservations.** Offer convenient reservations to enable members (or others) to sign-up online for tournaments, dining, court times, and other events.

✔ **Calendar.** Post images and calendar messages to remind members of your tournaments, social events, and important dates. The calendar can be printed out for easy use with most day planners.

✔ **Online statements.** Allow members to access their monthly statements.

✔ **Menus.** Design and enter menus for your snack bar and dining facilities, and update special menu items daily, in seconds.

An excellent example of a daily fee course that incorporates all of the key elements into their web site.

✔ **Meeting minutes, rules, and regulations.** Better distribution of business information that is for members' eyes only.

✔ **Custom member "dashboards."** Each member has a custom, personal area where they can keep a calendar of your events (and their entire personal schedules), fully password protected, of course.

✔ **Specialized member info.**

✔ Fitness info

✔ Tennis info

✔ Dining info

✔ Activities info

✔ **Specialized information.** Other info pages should also be customized to your membership's exact needs—for example, bridge info, ladies info, kids info.

✔ **Real-estate opportunities.** If you are selling homes or land, a real estate engine to display available property is also a good idea.

As you can see, these are many factors that make up a great web site. Some publicize you to the outside world, others help you better serve your members or players. Your web site should be more than just a pretty brochure online. It should be the heart of your marketing.

SUMMARY

My discussion above of how to use the web comes from our experience doing thousands of golf sites over the last few years. Legendary Marketing has built our website product from the ground up and enhanced it with feedback from several thousand clients. We have designed our sites as more than just web sites, but as command and control centers for all a club's marketing efforts. Regardless of whether you choose to use our technology or go it alone, the items discussed above are the key elements you must build into your club's site if you are to use the web most effectively.

CHAPTER TEN

Landing Pages

L anding pages are one of the most important elements of lead generation for your teaching business. According to Marketing Sherpa, landing pages are effective for 94% of B2B and B2C companies and according to a recent marketing benchmarks report by HubSpot, companies see a 55% increase in leads by increasing landing pages from 10 to 15.

In this chapter, you will discover:

✔ What exactly a landing page is

✔ Why landing pages are so important

✔ Why you need to be using them

✔ The six principles of high-converting landing pages

✔ The various types of landing pages

It's not rocket science, more content, offers, and landing pages = more opportunities to generate more leads!

The use of landing pages enables you to send prospects to targeted pages and capture leads and convert at a much higher rate than through other means. Visitors are on a landing page for one and only purpose based on the type of landing page you're using: to complete the lead capture form or to purchase your product or service.

Landing pages are essentially the heart and soul of any effective marketing strategy. These pages are the destinations for your numerous prospects to find out more information on your offer, product or service. Whether you're looking to generate leads, sell products, or simply to collect data for future sales, your landing pages are where it all happens.

Well-optimized landing pages allow you to take the prospects that you have attracted and convert them into leads. Unless you have a massive stroke of luck and something causes your business to go viral and it launches into the stratosphere, landing pages are your primary means for generating leads for your business and it is absolutely critical that they are *well designed, highly optimized, and relevant* to the wants and needs of your potential prospects.

What is a landing page?

A landing page is the webpage a potential customer arrives at after expressing interest in one of a multitude of forms of advertising.

For example:

- o A search engine result
- o Social media advertising (Facebook, Instagram, Twitter, Pinterest, etc.)
- o Banner ad
- o Google AdWords or AdSense
- o A link in an email
- o Print advertising
- o TV or radio commercials

The purpose of a landing page is to convince the visitor to convert taking a specific action. This conversion can be anything from collecting an email address to the sale of a product or service.

What do I need landing pages for?

If you sell products, generate leads, get online bookings, give away free trial lessons or use sales funnels, you need landing pages.

Ideally, you should have a landing page for *every* different source of targeted traffic you wish to produce, such as:

- Each of your free ebooks or special reports Like *How to Hit it Further*

- PPC (pay-per-click) Campaigns

- Promoting new products, books or sales

- Advertising in offline media such as TV, radio & newspapers

- Contest landing pages

- Building your email list

- Targeting a particular type of client women, kids, elite players, summer camps

At this point, you may be thinking, "I have a great homepage, why would I need to use landing pages?" Too many people send their advertising, email, or social media traffic to their homepage.

Simply put, there is no point in spending money on advertising if you are not driving traffic to a page created specifically for the people you are targeting. The following are six landing page principles that will help you convert at higher rates generate more leads than ever before.

Six Principles of High-Converting Landing Pages

1. Message Match — Your ad and landing page must be consistent!

Message match is a measure of how well the headline on your landing page matches the call-to-action on your ad. This consistency is especially true for PPC (pay per click) marketing. A strong match = more conversions as people know they've landed in the right place.

The great thing about message match is that there are really just two main things you need accomplish: matching the headline to the CTA (call to action) and matching the design to the ad (if the ad has a visual component).

For example: If you are targeting a women's golf school use pictures and colors that are female friendly. Not pictures of men and headlines in screaming red!

2. Headline and Offer

A few months ago I read an article in the NY Times called the "Eight-Second Attention Span" that discussed a survey of Canadian media consumption by Microsoft which concluded that the average attention span had fallen to eight seconds, down from 12 in the year 2000. We now have a shorter attention span than goldfish!

This is why your headline is so important!

The headline is the first thing people see on your landing page. It should clearly convey your USP (unique selling proposition) while matching the copy in the ad that was clicked.

Great landing page headlines cut right to the chase, are relevant only to the offer at hand, provide the benefits of what you're offering right away or hold the actual offer itself in them. It's best to keep the headline simple and utilize a headline/sub-headline combination.

You can add a *sense of urgency* to your headlines to boost conversions:

- o   Limited supply of FREE rounds of golf!

- o   Act Now!

- o   Offer expires in 7 days!

- o   First 10 new students ONLY!

3. Main Image, Video or Graphic

The purpose of the main image or video is to show how your service actually works so your prospects can picture themselves using it or experiencing it.

People are visual, so it's no coincidence that landing pages with better images are higher converting than those without. You want your visitor's to read the headline, see your image and understand what they're looking at within those first eight seconds that we discussed in #2.

Getting the main image, video or graphic right is another very simple step that a lot of landing pages somehow screw up - if your product is an e-book, you should include an image of the e-book cover. If you are giving away a swing evaluation show a swing evaluation or a launch monitor.

4. Benefits

Now that you've got your visitor hooked, it's time to show them your benefits and answer the all-important question – "what's in it for me?" Not to be confused with features – they only describe your offer - benefits show the value people get from your product or service.

- o   Hit it 20 yards further

- o   Never slice again!

- o   Break 80 fast!

A large number of people, over 75%, are going to scan your landing page rather than read word-for-word (at least until they find what they want). To solve for this, show your benefits as bullet lists in addition to short paragraphs.

5. CTA (call-to-action)

The call-to-action is the one and only thing you want people to click on your page. It's the big button you're trying to steer attention toward, it's what *every* campaign is built around.

Call now, click here, download it now, share this, join now for FREE are examples of typical call to actions found on a landing page. You want to use phrases that make the visitor feel like they *need* to take the next step to download your e-book, purchase your product, take your free trial, etc.

Taking action is the ultimate goal of the landing page. It is what you want your visitors to do in response to your offer. Like the headline, your call to action should be clear, benefit oriented and action centric. It should be asking to get clicked. Since it is the goal of the landing page, it should be easily discoverable – use bright colors to make it stand out and try not to just use the word "submit!"

6. Endorsements or Testimonials

The last principle of a high-converting landing page is endorsements or testimonials, which can be verbal, written or video.

Powerful testimonials are one of the best ways of building social proof on a landing page. The best testimonials tend to describe the resolution of a specific pain, describing how your offering solved it for them.

These testimonials should be short and to the point, and should ideally include a photo of the person giving the testimonial if you can get one to make it more authentic. Even better are video testimonials, which are proven to increase conversion rates more than any other type of testimonial. When using testimonials you must be careful, people pick right up on testimonials that appear to be fake (even if they're real) and will immediately discredit your product or service.

Types of Landing Pages

There are essentially five main types of landing pages: sales, click-through, lead generation, viral and squeeze.

Not all landing pages are created equal. Each type follows a different approach, but each has the same goal – generating sales or high-quality leads at high conversion rates.

Sales Landing Pages

A sales page is used to sell a product or service. The purpose of a sales page is to give all the information needed to make a purchase. There are a number of different types of sales pages, but they are generally either short or long form.

Short form sales pages are used when the value of your product or service is easy to communicate or when the investment is not large.

Long form sales pages are used when your product or service requires a more in-depth explanation or is a larger investment.

The more you need to explain why your product or service is worth the price or the commitment, the longer the landing page needs to be. Think about every possible objection your potential customer may have and answer it on the page.

For a personal growth program we recently launched, we opted for a long form sales page as the investment was quite large and the program itself required more explaining than could be accomplished in a short form page.

How do I know when to use short form or long form sales pages?

You should use short form when:

- o Potential customers are highly aware of your product or service
- o Your product or service is straightforward
- o Your product or service is low-cost, low-risk or low-commitment

You should use long form when:

- o Your product or service carries a big price tag like a membership or week-long stay and play package
- o Your product or service is complicated
- o Potential customers have low awareness of your product or service

o Your product or service is high-commitment – i.e. a year-long membership

Ocean City, Maryland
Spectacular Stay Where You Play Savings!

"Everyone enjoyed the trip. River Run continues to do an outstanding job. And that steak dinner is really hard to beat. Looking forward to next year already!" – Al W., Hanover, PA

ABOUT
River Run Golf Club

The Golf Villas at River Run offer the perfect golf vacation with options to fit any budget. Play multiple rounds on their Gary Player Designed masterpiece or add in a round or two and other nearby championship courses designed by masters of the game. Whether you are looking for a spring getaway, a summer golf vacation with a round or golf or two or a longer stay where you can play every day, The Golf Villas at River Run have what you need.

WHY
Choose River Run?

Gary Player created a course that is very enjoyable to play. The golf course is sometimes called a "tale of two nines" with itsriver1.jpg open front nine and tighter back side that winds through the timber. The course is fair for the beginner, but is certainly no walk in the park for the scratch player. The greens are medium sized and not especially difficult, the fairways are generous from the tee and modestly bunkered. There are a few lakes to avoid and some marshy areas which common when you're only seven miles from the ocean.

River Run is an active golf club where guests have fun in a relaxed atmosphere on a Gary Player Signature Course.

Click-Through Landing Pages

A click-through page is a landing page without a form. A click-through page is most often used to quickly inform your visitor about what you're offering to get them to click through to your product or service. The goal of click-through landing pages is that when the potential customer clicks through via the CTA, they land on your site ready to buy or take your desired action.

Lead Generation Landing Pages

The main goal of lead generation pages is to gather information about your visitor that you can use later on to market to your prospect.

The contact forms must be the center of attention, so design your lead gen pages around them. Copy on lead capture pages need to be able to explain the product or service thoroughly, in a brief period of time, so that the visitor becomes emotionally invested in the page and clicks the CTA button.

A lead generation page could be for a:

- o Contest or sweepstakes
- o Free e-book
- o Webinar registration
- o How-to guide
- o Newsletter sign-up

Squeeze Pages

A squeeze page is specifically designed for visitors to submit their email address in order to proceed further into the site or your marketing funnel.

The copy of your squeeze page can either consist of a list of all the benefits that your service can provide to your prospect in order to grab instant attention or it can just be a teaser designed to quickly get the prospect's email address.

Unlike a lead capture page, the lead capture form on the squeeze page needs to be short. An email address field is sufficient for you to collect your visitors into your funnel.

Viral Landing Pages

Viral landing pages are usually fun flash games or funny videos with just a subtle reference to the company in the form of a logo or a reference in the video.

The goal of these pages is to have them spread around to as many people as possible via social media, email and word-of-mouth.

Viral landing pages utilize two key elements:

Great Content: Your content has to be cool or funny enough to be shared by the masses.

Sharing Enablers: Make sure you have a URL that is easily shareable vocally. You don't technically need social share buttons, but it helps.

SUMMARY

Used correctly, landing pages should be the heart and soul of your marketing campaigns. The use of landing pages allows you to send highly targeted traffic to pages designed specifically for that traffic. They are designed to not feature any distractions and have one goal – to get a conversion. In order be effective you must not ignore the Six Principles of High-Converting Landing Pages, then start up your ad campaign and sit back and watch the leads roll in.

CHAPTER ELEVEN

Legendary Promotions

OVER 50 PROVEN STRATEGIES TO GENERATE LEADS AND DRIVE MORE BUSINESS FOR YOU

Promotions are special offers or activities designed to bring people to your course, lessons, or other services. The important thing to remember about promotions is that different people respond to different offers. Some people use coupons whenever they can; others wouldn't use a coupon if you paid them. Some like free information, golf books, or tips; others couldn't care less. Some will enter every contest; others wouldn't take the time if you guaranteed a prize. Some will jump at a sleeve of balls; others won't respond unless the balls are a certain brand. Only by trying and testing different types of promotions in your market can you get a true idea of what your response will be.

Offering a free $20 golf cap may only motivate 30 people to show up and pay full green fees. But it will very likely be 30 different people than will show up for $20 off your green fee. It's the difference between a discount mentality and a value-added mentality.

In the same way, the player who enters your contest to win a Free Year of Golf will often not be the same person who signs up for a free download of your best selling golf book *Shanking for Distance*!

With this in mind, you need to take a varied and segmented approach to promotions. As your database grows, you will increasingly segment your market so that you are only sending offers to the players most likely to respond.

There are two types of promotions that we are interested in: those that generate leads and those that generate immediate income. Lead generation promotions are primarily used to help you collect data and identify prospects, but they very often result in extra business as well.

In this chapter, you will discover:

- ✔ More than 50 tried-and-tested promotions
- ✔ Web-site lead-generating promotions
- ✔ E-mail promotions
- ✔ Creative value-added promotions
- ✔ Community promotions
- ✔ Pro-shop promotions

WEBSITE PROMOTIONS

Free coupons

Coupons can be offered effectively online. Upload a number of coupons with offers from each segment of your business. For example:

- ✔ Cart
- ✔ Dining
- ✔ Pro shop
- ✔ Range

Send an e-mail blast offering $50 of money-saving coupons at XYZ Golf Club. Once they register for the coupons, the website automatically e-mails them to the player.

Win a golf outing for you and 50 friends

A headline offering the chance at a golf outing for 51 people is a great way to generate daily fee and outing leads. The contest can be announced on the front page of your website or as an ad in local golf magazines.

You can further target the response by offering the deal only to charities or fundraisers. You will quickly build a list of outing prospects.

Make a big deal of the event (which you can hold during off- peak time) with the local newspaper. Send them a press release announcing the offer and the winning organization. This will help generate more response and interest next year!

E-MAIL & DIRECT MAIL PROMOS

Free golf when you participate in our survey

The results of this promotion have been astonishing in both the amount of data gathered and the additional income generated at traditionally slow times.

Online surveys are a great way to gain feedback and insight into your market. They can mine amazing amounts of data if the incentive is attractive. Quite frankly, there is nothing more attractive than free golf to motivate players to respond.

At one club, 1,250 golfers completed the survey in less than 48 hours and over FIVE HUNDRED (yes 500) tee times were booked for the week—that's just Monday through Thursday!

When players showed up at the club, they were also invited to participate in a one-day spring sale with 20 percent off almost everything. The income and traffic were very welcome after a horrible winter, but the real gold, as always, was in the information that was collected about players.

Additional revenues are generated by cart fees, food and beverage, pro shop sales and bounce back offers. Remember, these promotions should only be used in the shoulder season when the weather makes normal play marginal.

That way you gain data, gain income, and do nothing that will negatively affect your P&L bottom line!

Enter our tournament & win free golf!

A promotion to win free golf through "tournament" participation drove lots of midweek play for a client.

If you had a choice of 20 comparable courses, but one of them offered you a chance to win free membership just for turning in your card, where would you play?

Here's how Twisted Dune Golf Course did it:

> Every time you tee it up at Twisted Dune between now and June 15, Monday–Thursday, you will be playing for more than just the lunch tab. Our FREE tournament gives every player a shot at FREE golf for the rest of the season!

Simply book your tee time at Twisted Dune and tee off before 3 PM, Monday thru Thursday at our regular rates. Play from the designated tees, hole everything out and have your card signed by your playing partners. Then hand it in at the pro shop upon completion of your round.

Gross and net winners in each flight win free golf for 2004 (Flights: 0–7, 8–14, 15–22, 23–30, and 31–40). Plus we will have an open division for all golfers who don't have a legitimate USGA handicap.

Winners in each flight will receive free golf at Twisted Dune from June 15th to December 31st, cart fees not included.

The more you play, the more chances you have to win! Enter as often as you like Monday thru Thursday. The more you play, the more chances you have to win!

Buy X number of rounds in advance and get X bonus rounds!

Prepaid sales are a great way to raise cash up front (and many rounds are not even used). You can restrict rounds from Monday to Thursday if you wish. Always put an expiration date on these rounds.

Suggest in your e-mail that customers:

✔ Split the cost and share the rounds with friends

✔ Use them for business incentives or employee rewards

✔ Just take advantage of this amazing deal themselves

The grand-opening special

"Grand Opening Special" - these words alone will attract attention. But here is one that will appeal to the male ego: When opening a new course, whoever finishes the course first will (by default) be the course record holder! Who doesn't want to tell his buddies about that! Run a contest for the privilege of being the first to play and frame the card in the locker room.

VALUE-ADDED PROMOTIONS

While occasionally it does pay to use discounting, I always favor testing value-added promotions first. A cautionary word on discounts: Discounts do work, but—and it's a big BUT—if you keep discounting, players will wait for a bigger and better discount rather than play your course on a regular basis. For this reason, you should mix up your offers with value propositions, not just discounts. Here are some examples:

- ✔ Pay for three and the fourth player is free. Actually, you are cutting the green fees by 25 percent.

- ✔ A free box of balls. Sounds like a $30 deal, but it really only costs you $12 and can be used instead of slashing your green fee.

- ✔ A free cap is an $18 value but costs you just $8. Plus it gets others to serve as walking billboards for your course!

The more you mix up and test your offers, the less likely you are to build a discount mentality in your players and the more likely you are to hit the right combination of offers. Timing is also an important factor. If an offer works one Labor Day, chances are it will work next Labor Day as well. So be sure to make a note not only of what offers work but when they worked.

Double your e-mail response

Here is a quick and simple tip to seriously increase the reach of any of your e-promos. Simply instruct the reader to forward the offer to a friend at the bottom of each of your promotions. You'll be amazed at the additional response you can generate by adding this one simple line of text.

Play this week and get a FREE $XX gift!

There are many ways to use this value-added promotion. Test what works best for you, including:

- ✔ Golf book
- ✔ Club cap
- ✔ Club towel
- ✔ Golf glove
- ✔ Sleeve of balls
- ✔ Golf shirt

Free lesson before you play!

Everyone wants to play better, but only 13 percent of golfers in any given year ever take a lesson. Here's a painless way to add value, help a customer, and get more people interested in your lesson programs.

- ✔ Free video lesson
- ✔ Free putting lesson
- ✔ Free chipping lesson
- ✔ Free bunker lesson

U.S. open-style championship

Pick three players, add their Sunday score to your net score and win valuable prizes. This tournament-based promotion works well with avid players. The value of the prizes will also dictate participation.

Free car wash with green fee this weekend only!

Out-market your competitors by offering players a time saving and value-added service like a car wash. This can help you attract more players even though your green fee might be higher than the course down the street.

This works especially well in busy urban areas. Simply hire some kids on your own or call a local detail shop.

Demo day - hit the very latest equipment!

Players of all abilities love to try out the latest equipment. You should organize several demo days throughout the year with your equipment reps.

Demo day - every weekend all summer long only at XYZ Golf Club

Since demo days work, why not continue the concept all summer long? You would quickly establish yourself as the club with the latest equipment! We're talking extra play, extra range revenue, and plenty of club sales.

Putter-only demo day—over 100 different putters to try!

A different twist on a popular concept. Everyone likes trying new putters. They don't even have to be new—just clean out your garage!

Who said there's no such thing as a free lunch?

There is at XYZ Club when you play Monday through Thursday. Throw in a free burger and fries and you're sure to satisfy some appetites.

DISCOUNT PROMOTIONS

You play free when you bring three other players

Phrasing the promotion this way is simple and works to varying degrees depending on the day and time you make the offer. By carefully tracking the results you will see when it truly helps you increase business.

Two for one

A standard discount promotion that can bring in extra play midweek. Use judiciously.

Play now...get a free round later!

This has worked well for many of our clubs in the Northeast to drive mid-week business in the summer by offering a free round in the shoulder season when the weather and business are marginal.

Play free on your birthday!

Most people don't play alone on their birthdays, so you gain by getting three paying players. This program can be run all year. Once you have the player's birthday, you can automatically e-mail him the birthday offer every year two weeks ahead of his birthday. It will also send him an e-birthday card on his birthday—a nice touch, indeed!

Register yourself and your friends for free!

Register yourself and your friends for our free birthday gift package. Package includes:

- ✔ A free round
- ✔ Free golf e-book
- ✔ Personalized e-greeting

Kids play free with a paid adult

This is a simple but effective way to drive play at off-peak times and lay the foundation for future revenue. It can also be used in conjunction with your range!

Father-son or mother-daughter day

Do this on your own or in conjunction with one of the national events sponsored by the PGA, NGCOA, or others.

Become an XYZ staff player

How about creating a special bond between your club and your customers? Put together a staff package: tour bag, golf shirts, cap, and several rounds of golf. Offer it at a very attractive price and get 20 to 30 players on your staff. Work out some additional perks for them throughout the year. (See Chapter 19 on Loyalty Programs for more details on Opinion Leader Programs.)

Team colors

At Legendary Marketing, we are far more interested in results than image. But that doesn't mean image and branding should be ignored. Here is a promotion to get you some real branding in the community. Pick a team color—say, purple—then order 1,000 low- cost purple shirts with oversized logos on the breast or arm. This is now your team identity, like silver and black is for the Oakland Raiders. Your goal is to get at least 5,000 players all over town wearing your colors.

Display the shirts in your shop with a $39.95 price tag, but offer them to everyone who plays that day for just another $10 on top of their green fee (assuming you can buy your shirts for $10).

"Sir would you like one of our XYZ Club staff shirts for just an extra $10, that's a savings of $30?"

SEEKING OUT NEW PROSPECTS

Car wash booth

Nobody coming to your club? Then go to them! This may seem like a strange promotion for a golf club, but you'd be amazed at how successful it can be.

I came up with the idea partly by accident. I walked into one of my karate schools in California on a sunny Saturday morning to find it totally dead. I asked the manager what was going on and he joked "Everyone's at the car wash."

His words hit me right away! I had just passed the car wash on my way in and it was jammed. There were people with expensive cars and SUVs, people with absolutely nothing to do for at least 20 minutes while they waited for their cars.

I immediately went down there and asked for the manager. I offered him free lessons for himself or his kids in return for us putting a table outside his office where I could promote my school.

On a good weekend, 1,500 people a day went through that car wash. We never spent a day there where we did not sign up a new student, and karate only appeals to 0.5 percent of the population. At 10 percent for golf, that means 150 of them would have been golfers with nothing to do for 20 minutes!

How many of these bored golfers could you get interested in your club in a single day? How about every one of them! Depending on how upscale the area is, you can do everything from collect data to generate leads for lessons and membership.

Mall booth

This next idea is an upscale version of the previous one and can be used at Christmas. Ninety percent of all retail shopping is done between Thanksgiving and Christmas. That's great if you are located in a mall, not so great if you are a golf course far away from a mall. But here's a solution. Rent one of those little handcarts in the middle of the mall walkway. That way you get all the traffic at a fraction of the price and with no long-term commitment.

Load up the handcart with brochures, information kits, booklets, flyers, gift certificates, and promo items. Play your course video on TV. Hand out surveys, take names, have drawings. Sell rounds, lessons, memberships, and generate leads with contests and giveaways. Give away water bottles, pens, T-shirts, key rings, or whatever makes sense for your club. Have a special "Christmas present package" that includes a gift-wrapped product or ornate gift certificate.

TARGET MARKET PROMOTIONS

The more targeted and exclusive your offer is, the greater your response will be! Seniors don't want ads for kids' camps and avid players don't want to receive promotions for the nine-hole ladies group.

- ✔ Headlines should qualify the group.

- ✔ Offers and copy should speak to that group's unique needs and motivation.

✔ The offer should be of interest to that specific group.

Locals-only day!

Locals-only days work well in areas with high tourist traffic. Give locals or state residents a special rate during specified days or months.

Beginner's day!

Stress a no-pressure, quiet day at the club. Provide free tips on the range. Let them know that beginners are welcome at your club.

Ladies day!

Simple things like changing colors can have an effect on generating additional response. Think pink, or at least more pastel colors when marketing to women. Offering a free rose on ladies day might well work better than a sleeve of Pro V1s!

Seniors day!

Since seniors are far more flexible as to when they can play, you can designate a Seniors Day that fills a hole in your schedule. Seniors typically respond well to value. That often means discounts but it could just as easily mean including the cost of a hamburger in their green fee! Also, consider providing a weekly prize from the pro shop. Like anyone else, seniors respond to personal attention.

Feeling lucky?

Try a simple promotion that randomly lets one out of 10 players play free on any given day. This only amounts to a 10 percent discount and generates more extra business than that. Require them to register on the website to qualify.

ON-SITE PROMOTIONS

Monster day!

A Halloween promotion can be used to drive play to a midweek day near October 31st. The course could be set up super-tough and prizes given for the best scores, closest to the hole, and so forth. Add a few decorations and some eerie noises and you're in business.

Sell gift certificates that double in value if they hit the green

Have the ranger or cart girl stationed by a par three. Offer the players a chance to double their money in pro shop script if they hit the green. Let them decide how much to "wager," from $5 to $20.

GET LOCAL BUSINESSES TO ATTRACT NEW CUSTOMERS FOR YOU

Have stores give out (free) gift certificates from you to their customers. Your certificates are a free bonus for the stores' customers. The first step is to seek out compatible stores for your particular club. Golf courses typically target local golf shops, dry cleaners, video stores, and so forth. How many gift certificates you give the store is entirely up to you, because the purpose is to get your gift certificates in the hands of prospective customers who meet your demographic profile. The gift certificates should look valuable, not like some second-rate photocopied coupon. (These businesses in turn can give you prizes for your tournaments or promotions.)

How to solicit the help of other businesses

Ask the person in charge of your target business, "How would you like to provide your best clients with an extra bonus of X amount of dollars for every purchase they make, say over $100?" Either wait for his response or let the person know at once that you're not trying to sell him anything, just offering him a win-win deal. Once he agrees to the concept, you can offer him as many gift certificates as you wish.

Make sure that the merchant understands this is a no-strings- attached offer for him and his clients and you will more often than not meet with success.

How about going to all the dry cleaning stores within 10 miles of your club and giving each of them 50 free $10 gift certificates that they can give to any client spending over $50? How many new faces will that bring to your club? Plenty! Then it's up to you to treat them right and turn them into full-fledged customers.

The key is to remember that this is not merely a discount coupon, but an actual gift certificate that is being added to the store's sale in recognition of a substantial purchase or customer loyalty. This creates a huge difference in whether or not the certificate is redeemed and avoids a discount look. (Of course, you can make the gift certificate good for only green fees or only carts or only lessons or whatever you choose.)

What about the cost?

If the thought of giving away your product bothers you, look at it this way. If you run a full-page ad in your local newspaper, it's going to cost you $600 or $700 (or even more), and you still can't guarantee any new business. If you give away sixty $10 gift certificates to your dry cleaner, you are virtually assured of getting some new business. Second, it only costs you $10 for the certificates that actually come back. And third, it's not real money that you're spending, just a discount on extra business you might not get!

Let's say that half the certificates are redeemed by people who are already customers and half are new customers. That means it costs you $20 per new customer, which is not bad over the lifetime of a typical customer. Think of this type of program as an alternative to advertising with far better results since you only pay for the leads you actually get!

FRIENDS AND FAMILY

Another way to distribute gift certificates is to get your existing clients to distribute them to their friends and family. Every Christmas, I used to send all of my karate school students two free $80 gift certificates, the price of a month's lessons. Along with the cards was a letter letting them know that the gift certificates could be passed along to friends as a gift and would be treated as such when their friends arrived at the school. The letter also pointed out that the certificates were only redeemable for lessons and that they could not be used by existing students. Sometimes the students asked if the certificates could be used by another person in their family, which of course was allowed because after a month they became regular paying clients.

SELLING LESSON PROGRAMS

Take a look at this sample letter:

This Holiday Season Give Gifts That Last A Lifetime!

There's no better feeling than finding a perfect gift for that special person on your list. Not just another gift that will be forgotten in a couple of days, but something that will be remembered and appreciated for years to come.

However, it isn't easy to find something special and different, something that can really make the recipients feel great about themselves and you.

This year, Beech Creek Golf Club offers golf gifts that last a lifetime: Confidence, Satisfaction, Enjoyment, and the wonderful feeling that comes from knowing you are in control of your golf swing. All these gifts can be developed through our unique teaching program.

The game of golf is more than just a way to pass the time. It gives you the ability to look inwards and know yourself. Playing well improves your self-image and your whole outlook on life, and it brings you a new circle of friends and business acquaintances. Much more than a tie or gift certificate to a restaurant, the instruction we offer at Beech Creek develops mental and physical vitality and can be life changing. Surely you know of others who would benefit from a gift like this.

For more information on the benefits and lessons programs available, call us at (803)499-GOLF and be sure to take advantage of our Holiday Special!

A happy and healthy holiday season to you from all of us at Beech Creek Golf Club

CHARITY REQUESTS

Most golf clubs are regularly solicited by charities and organizations to donate a free foursome. The smart clubs let it be known that they can always be counted on to respond to such requests with the following understanding:

"We will be happy to donate X to your program with the understanding that next year you give us a shot to hold any golf event at our club."

At the very least you pick up the name and address of the event and event planner. At best you book the event next year!

MORE IDEAS

Golf swap meet

This is probably best suited for a daily fee club, but it can work anywhere. Set up a golf swap meet in your parking lot once a month or even once a week on your slowest day. Charge a small fee for each table. You will make money on table rental and players sticking around before and after to play golf. As an alternative, you could offer a free table with the purchase of a green fee.

You could have your staff run it. Players show up and drop off the clubs they want to sell at a table. Your staff tags and prices everything. The player goes off to play and your staff makes the sales, keeping 15 percent of the sales price for your efforts.

18 members will have a hole named for them

Here is a neat way to get your first few members to pony up that initiation fee! Name a hole after them!

Daily fees: Have a hole at XYZ Club named in your honor!

Even at a daily fee you can use this concept to drive extra play. This could be done yearly.

Double your income and double your players' fun by playing golf at night!

Why limit your club's profit and your players' fun by playing only in daylight? It's relatively easy to set up your course to play at night. One company, NiteLite, has specialized in helping clubs run evening tournaments. With over 200,000 successful tournaments worldwide, they've shown it can be fun for your members or guests. And it's largely extra profit for your club. NiteLite is a commercial service that you can work with, but you can also arrange your own evening events with lighted balls and other available material. How about flashlights with your logo for every player? Or a bonus for players who use regular balls?

An evening golf tournament can:

✔ Increase your green fee revenue

✔ Drive cart-fee revenue while other fleets are parked!

Evening golf tournaments are also ideal for fundraising. They have raised millions of dollars for charities of all kinds, including hospitals, medical groups, churches, schools, Rotary Clubs, Fraternal organizations, foundations, fire departments, police departments, sports teams, and more!

For details, you can contact NiteLite Golf at: 800-282-1533, ext 21 or visit their website at http://www.nitelitegolf.com.

Tie-in promotions

Create excitement on and off the course by tying in with the hottest shows and movies. Use a theme and decorations for a special event or weekend. For example, Sponge Bob is great for junior events. When every big new movie comes out, local golfers will think of your course.

On-hold phone marketing

In today's world of cost-cutting and shrinking staffs, being put on hold is simply a reality of business life. A simple, effective, and low-cost way to market your upcoming events or ongoing specials is to have an on-hold message that continually repeats. On-hold machines can be picked up very inexpensively at Radio Shack. You simply insert a regular cassette tape, which should be changed on a weekly or even daily basis depending on the message. This is an excellent way to give customers the special message you want and to increase response to your events. If you add a little humor, it's also a way to keep them entertained and less irritated while on hold.

Promoting social events and club tournaments—automatic marketing

Your website can be programmed to automatically send out promotions all year long. It can also send out customized promotional material based on visitors' answers to questions on your site. For instance, our Legendary Marketing Campaign Manager can preprogram an entire year's worth of golf and social programs. E-mail promotions can be triggered by date or by the player checking a specific box in a survey. This way, members get the right promotion for their unique interests at the right time.

High school golf day

Talk to the local high school golf teams. Have a fundraiser for them. Let them sell tickets for a special tournament and gift certificates for other times. You can add lots of touches:

✔ Ask your members to bring in equipment to donate to the team

✔ Have your ground crew collect balls for them.

MEMBERSHIP PROMOTIONS

Member for a day

Bring prospective members to your club for a day and make them feel special. If they come alone put them in a friendly foursome with some existing members.

VIP executive outing

This is a great way to identify membership prospects and give them a little taste of what to expect at your club. We can provide more complete consulting on this program but here are the basics:

First, using the power of the Internet, build a database of leading professionals within a certain socioeconomic bracket (depending on your club's unique needs). Typically you would target attorneys, doctors, executives, business owners, and entrepreneurs located within a 30-mile radius of your club.

Make ten calls for every lead you want to generate. So you need 4,000 calls to generate at least 400 prospective members. During the initial call, invite the prospective members to come to the club for a special VIP Executive Golf Outing. This will include breakfast, a 15-minute presentation on the benefits of memberships, 18 holes of golf, and a short awards ceremony.

SUMMARY

There are many special promotions you can use for your course. As you experiment with them, you'll find the ones that work for you and they can be repeated every year (or more frequently). As you develop a routine, events will get easier to run; you just have to get started.

CHAPTER TWELVE

Legendary Print Advertising

HOW TO DESIGN A GOLF AD THAT WORKS

Frankly, most golf print advertising is a giant waste of time, money, and trees. That is not to say that print publications are not worthy of your ad dollars or that they're not an integral part of your overall marketing plan. The problems lie largely in how the ads are done.

For starters, most ads fail by not grabbing the readers' attention in the headline. Research shows that 90 percent of readers never get beyond the headline. The text of the ad frequently fails by not expanding on the headline and by not turning features into real benefits. People buy for emotional reasons backed up by logic. The ad fails if it doesn't spell out benefits clearly.

Misuse of graphics is also common. Many ads feature pictures or graphics that are indistinguishable from their 50 closest competitors. Poor layout of the ad components often draws the reader's eye away from your sales message instead of towards it.

Failure to ask for specific action can turn an otherwise good ad into a waste of money. The whole purpose is to lead the reader to action, yet many ads do not spell out the action.

WHAT MAKES A GOOD AD?

An advertisement is not necessarily good just because it is funny, clever, or even easily remembered. A good ad effectively motivates people to ACTION—to sign-up for your offer, visit your website, book a tee time, inquire about membership, or buy a shirt. In other words, a good ad gets response!

In this chapter, you will discover:

- ✔ Why most golf ads fail

- ✔ How to capture your readers' attention

- ✔ How to write response-driven copy

- ✔ Which "gimmicks" can help you garner additional response

- ✔ How to prove your value

- ✔ How to create compelling offers

- ✔ How to test your ads for effectiveness before they run With these ideas in mind, let's look at ten factors that will determine the success of your print advertising.

TEN KEY FACTORS TO PRINT ADVERTISING SUCCESS

First, let's look at what printed material can and cannot do for your club. Print ads can educate, qualify, generate leads, and even handle some objections. In some cases, ads can sell your product or service. Ads cannot interest a 69-year-old woman in buying a golf membership to your Pete Dye golf club. Nor can they realistically attract a member of an exclusive country club to play an $18 municipal course!

Ads can only attract and heighten the interest of someone who wants to buy your product. You do not design printed pieces to be everything to everybody. You design them to attract either people who are already buying your product or people who may be thinking about your product.

In the golf business, you can figure that about 10 percent of the readers of any given newspaper have some interest in golf. It matters not whether your ad is brilliant, the number of people who glance at it stays roughly the same.

The key is to increase the number of people who actually read your ad

Recent studies have shown that of the thousands of ads people are exposed to each day, only 4 percent gain more than two or three seconds of attention.

While each different print vehicle obviously has its own nuances, these factors will hold up for all vehicles: Yellow Pages, direct mail, magazines, newspaper ads, and brochures. Ignore one of these ten key factors, and you instantly decrease the power of your marketing message!

1. Respect every inch of printed space. The biggest reason that most printed material is a waste of trees is that most people treat printed matter as a challenge to fill up space. Logos are too big, pictures don't relate to headlines, and worthless copy explains the club's history rather than your sales message, benefits, and call to action!

To increase the effectiveness of each piece you print, you must treat each inch of each ad, flyer, letter, and brochure with the respect it deserves. That innocent piece of white paper is going to cost you lots of green paper, so make it work for you for all it's worth. Never make a casual decision about even an inch of space. Make your paper into the best salesperson your club has by committing to maximize its full potential. That means doing your ads well in advance of any deadline!

The simplest way to maximize your ad is to remind yourself constantly that people buy for their reasons, not yours! This is Sales 101, but for some reason when people try to sell someone on the idea of visiting their club or inquiring about a vacation, logic goes out the window. They suddenly spew a host of mind-numbing statements like "committed to excellence," "in business for twenty years," and "we're the biggest resort in town." The reader doesn't care. Use space to sell, not to build your ego!

2. You must capture the reader's attention in three seconds. Your headlines have just three seconds to capture a reader's interest. If they don't, you're doomed to failure. This is just as true for a two-cent flyer as for a $10,000 brochure. There are several methods you can use to accomplish this, but by far the most predictable way is to make sure your headline states a clear benefit to the reader. What can your course offer him? How will it benefit his life or his work?

Here are some examples:

✔ Play in Less than 4 Hours Guaranteed!

✔ Play the Number One Course in Maryland!

✔ Never 3-Putt Again!

✔ Play a Great Scottish Links without Leaving New Jersey! Spend What You Save on Airfare at the Bar!

Each of these headlines would grab the attention of anyone looking to play quickly, notch up another #1 course, or stop three putting! The benefits of reading further are obvious from the headlines.

Another way to create a good headline is to pose an intriguing or thought-provoking question like:

Why Is the Back Nine at XYZ the Best Nine Holes of Golf in Virginia?

Another way is to make a bold and provocative statement that grabs attention, similar to what you see in the supermarket tabloids, "Martians Land in London!" While the last two approaches are both acceptable ways to use a headline, they are harder to test than simply offering real benefits. Start with benefits before you test "fancier" approaches.

3. You must capture your reader's attention with the picture you use. Pictures should capture your readers' attention and show your course in effortless, happy, exciting, and wonderful use! With a few exceptions such as fashion merchandising, pictures do not sell your product or service; rather, they attract readership and complement the copy. By all means, use a photo of your best hole. But be warned: if it is not something spectacular—think 18th at Pebble Beach—it's just another golf hole.

You will do far better in attracting readership, especially in a golf magazine, if you add an element to stop the reader dead in his tracks. For example, a man or woman in a swimsuit playing golf on your signature hole would get people to STOP and look at the ad, read the headline, and then decide if they want to read the copy. We're not saying to do something like this just for shock value; the picture MUST relate to the copy and the offer. In this case, perhaps the theme might be how relaxing your resort is or how close the course is to the ocean. The point is that by adding an extra element, you can greatly increase how well your ad stands out.

Use graphics to point out features and benefits of your product or service. People believe what they see. Show how fun your course is to play. Show how much enjoyment it brings; show how your readers' lives will be enhanced if only they buy!

For the most part, headlines work better if they are placed below a picture, not above it or next to it.

Very often readers will scan captions to determine whether they want to go back and read the copy. Never waste caption space by describing what's in the picture—the readers can see that. Instead, use that space to remind them of key benefits, or restate your offer in different words.

4. Learn the difference between benefits and features. People tend to list lots of meaningless features rather than opting for a handful of potent benefits. A feature tells you about a product, a benefit explains how the prospect can benefit from it.

Most ads contain short bulleted phrases like "convenient location." By using more words, you can take that simple feature and turn it into thought-provoking benefits that connect with readers:

> Our convenient location next to I-95 makes our club
> easy to get to when you feel like a fast nine or just want
> to hit some balls on your way home from work!

Now the reader can't help but think for a moment about the proposition you have put before him.

You may think that if you list lots of features, the prospect will put two and two together and figure out how that feature will benefit him. He won't. Instead, he will scan the feature and move on to the rest of your copy without ever having made the connection. Had he scanned copy with real benefits, he may well have stopped, re-read a key point, and been enticed to buy.

Other than poor headlines, the greatest waste of money in printed matter is generated by volumes of text that say absolutely nothing about what your club will do for the reader. Most people are so afraid of filling their ads up with words; they opt instead for meaningless features or bulleted highlights that don't tell the reader much of anything.

Words sell! They sell your reader on the concept of picking up the phone or driving down to your club. They sell the reader on the need he has for what you offer, on the pain he will feel if he doesn't see you, and on the joy she will feel upon joining your club!

Do not be afraid to fill your ads with copy. There is no such thing as copy that is too long, only copy that is too boring! The biggest myth in advertising is that people don't read. Book and magazine sales are at an all-time high despite 300 channels on TV and the lure of the Internet. *People do read things that are of interest to them.* The most successful print material of all time is full of long, interesting, benefit-filled copy. Write as much as you can about your product or service. Write two or three times more than you need, then go back and pick the very strongest statements that make your offer sound exciting, reliable, the best in town.

5. Back up all your claims with proof. People are very skeptical of advertising. That's why it pays to back up all your claims. Use quotes from magazines, statistics, charts, study findings, and testimonials. Show people that you are giving it to them straight by bringing in third-person endorsements for your club. Quote satisfied members, outing customers, and wedding planners, and use their real names and titles. Use well-known people in your community to heighten awareness and build your credibility.

Don't be afraid of lots of copy—just make sure it's interesting to your TARGET reader.

6. Do not assault the reader's eye or make your ad hard to read. Do not confuse the reader with off-the-wall type styles, fancy designs, and strange layouts. Some graphic designers understand the principles of effective advertising as do some advertising sales reps. About as many understand the principles of nuclear physics! Please remember that neither graphic design or advertising sales have anything in common with designing printed material that increases your business!

People read from top to bottom and from left to right. If you make their eyes jump around too much, they will give up. If you make the type too small, they will pass. If you print your flyer on bright red paper, they will give it a miss. By all means be creative, but never at the cost of making your piece difficult to read.

Using colored paper is good unless it prevents or handicaps you from reading the material, as many colors do! Also, if you ever need to fax any of your printed material to customers, keep that in mind when choosing background colors. Red, for example, reproduces as black, making it impossible to read if faxed or photocopied.

To get views this spectacular you could take a balloon ride
Or you can just Tee it Up at Treetops!

Rick Smith

Come and enjoy 81 holes of spectacular championship golf with five distinctly different courses including a Fazio, a Jones Sr and two Rick Smith signatures. We have also hosted the world's top players on the world's best par 3 course. Choose from **238 cozy guest rooms in our hotel or 2 and 3-bedroom condominiums.** Nearly every room takes advantage of our majestic setting and offers sweeping vistas of ski hills, golf courses, pristine woods or wetlands. After golf, relax with a massage in our spa, hit the hot tub and **party like a Tour star in our Legends bar** and lounge. There you can relive the birdies of the day with your favorite beverage and fine food close at hand!

Call now to book your spectacular vacation!

Treetops RESORT

Michigan's Most Spectacular Resort
Golf • Ski • Spa

www.Treetops.com

1-888-TREETOPS

Notice how a strong photograph draws your eye to the headline.
The copy highlights benefits. The call to action is at the bottom.

7. Use all known gimmicks to increase customer response. There are a great many little tricks you can use in a printed piece to greatly increase its effectiveness. On their own, each may seem insignificant, but put them all together, and you can increase the effectiveness of your ad ten-fold or more!

- ✔ End the headline where you want the reader to start reading, not on the far side of the page.

- ✔ Always use a caption under a picture. It's the second place everyone looks.

- ✔ Make sure the caption sums up your key benefit or offer—you may not get another chance!

- ✔ Make sure all photographs with people have the people oriented looking towards the text, so the reader's eye follows the picture and begins to read. Photographs of people who appear to be looking off the page take the reader's eye to the next ad.

- ✔ Use a graphic of a phone next to the phone number; it can increase response by up to 25 percent.

- ✔ If you want readers to clip a coupon, show scissors— you'll get up to 35 percent more responses.

8. Always ask the reader to do something. Not asking the reader to take action is the biggest sin of all. Surprisingly, it is often committed by people who up to this point have passed most of the key tests. They have grabbed their readers' attention, expanded on benefits, used the right pictures, and have their readers salivating like Pavlov's dogs. Then, their copy ends. Readers are left lost, empty, and wondering what to do next. Should they file this information for future use? Should they throw it away, or should they pick up the phone and call right now? Better still, why not ask them to get into their vehicle and drive right on down, because you are ready and waiting to see them?

Use strong calls to action, such as:

- ✔ Go to our website right now and claim your coupon.

- ✔ Pick up the phone right now and call!

✔ Don't wait another minute to get the rewards you deserve. Clip out this coupon and mail it today!

Never end a printed piece without direct and specific instructions for what you want the reader to do next. Don't blow it by arousing their interest in what you have, and then letting them go to a competitor first.

9. The more compelling the offer, the greater the response. Much retail advertising in golf is price-based. Yes, some people are drawn to this, but if you want to build a real reputation in your community, make a statement about who you are and why people should do business with you.

*M*ake Your Special Day
One You Will Always Cherish
Celebrate It With Us At Pine Needles & Mid Pines!

Whether you are looking to host your reception, rehearsal dinner, bridal shower, or bachelor party, our all-inclusive resorts can accommodate any aspects of your wedding. At Pine Needles and Mid Pines we'll create the perfect ambience for your wedding day, complete with delectable cuisine and superb service from our staff.

Our outdoor romantic ceremonies with blooming flowers and breathtaking lawns set the tone for an elegant wedding.

Your reception can be held in one of our exquisite banquet areas, which accommodates 25 to 400 guests. Whether you choose a casual intimate dinner or a grand formal affair, we feature a variety of dining options from cocktail receptions to sit down dinners.

To make an appointment to meet with Sarah Losee at Pine Needles or Patsy Smith at Mid Pines, please call 1-866-375-5894 to request further information.

 PINE NEEDLES   Visit www.PineNeedles-MidPinesWedding.com   MID PINES

Use your copy to make statements about your experience, your service, your selection and your reputation. Then tie each statement into a clear and specific benefit to the customer.

10. Put all printed matter to the test before allowing it to leave your office. All printed material should be put to the test before it ever gets to print. By all means, use family, friends, other business owners, graphic designers, and ad reps to gain feedback. But be warned. If you have followed any of our advice until now, they may tell you that you have too much copy (you don't). They may tell you to use fancier type styles or, worse yet, put your headline in reverse type (which makes it 35 percent harder to read). They may encourage you to use a picture of yourself or to make your logo bigger. Resist the temptation. Instead, do the Legendary Print-Ad Test below.

LEGENDARY PRINT-AD TEST

Use the following tests to evaluate the design readiness of every print ad:

Headline test

Does the headline promise a clear benefit to the prospective customer, such as:

Be the First to Play XYZ Club!

Alternatively, does the headline make a provocative statement or pose a very interesting question? If your headline does not pass the above criteria, it stands a 99.5 percent chance of failing.

Picture test

Look at each picture in your ad. Will it capture your prospects attention?

Does it CLEARLY differentiate itself and stand out from the host of other ads it is competing against?

Does it show people just like your target reader having fun?

Copy test

Is the copy written specifically for your most probable prospects? Does each line state what's in it for the client with clear, compelling benefits?

The classic test we have developed is this: Read two sentences of any printed piece, then ask, "So what?" If one of the previous two sentences did not answer that question go back and rewrite them. Of course, the answer to "so what?" must relate to the customer's point of view, not yours.

Gimmick test

Have you used all the gimmicks you can to incrementally increase your response?

Have you used the captions underneath each picture, to sum up your offer, rather than merely telling the reader what he can already see in the picture?

Are coupons flanked by a graphic of scissors?

Is there a picture of a phone next to the phone number?

Does your ad avoid hard-to-read type styles, colored paper, all capitals, and reverse type?

Is your ad designed so that the eye follows a natural path from the top left to bottom right?

Call to action and offer test

Have you asked for action? What do you want the customer to do? Be specific!

Tracking test

Have you used a unique web address and a unique phone number to track all response to this ad?

Media test

Is this the right media to run your ad? Sure, they may have lots of readers, but how many of them fit into your "Perfect Customer" category?

MATCH THE MESSAGE TO THE MEDIUM AND DON'T BE SEDUCED BY NUMBERS

Even taking all of the above ten key ad-design factors into account, an ad can still fail. Many club owners are unwittingly seduced by the lure of large numbers. They think, "Well if 100,000 people see my ad in the newspaper I am going to get X number of calls. Or if I mail out a flyer to 10,000 people, I ought to get X response." Ad reps love to seduce you with the power of large numbers, but a smaller number of the right target group will always beat a larger number of just anybody. Choose your media with care. Don't waste money on people who are not your prospects.

Ninety thousand people who see your ad but don't play golf won't make you a dime! Nor will people who read your ad and play golf, but only make $55,000 a year, join your $100,000 golf club.

SUMMARY

The sole purpose of your print ads is to get people to take action— for example, to drive them to your website to register for an offer. Once you have their information you do not need to run ads to reach those people again—they are yours! Let your competitors squander their money building their images! Design your ads to elicit response.

Most print advertising by golf courses and clubs is poorly done. Use the rules and guidelines from this chapter to design effective ads. When you are preparing ads, run them through the Legendary Print-Ad Test and make sure they pass muster before proceeding with them.

CHAPTER THIRTEEN

How to Design a Direct Mail Campaign that Works

O ther than the Internet, direct mail is by far the best form of advertising for golf clubs, resorts, real estate, and golf schools. Yet many clubs have tried and failed with direct mail. There are usually two reasons for this: poor lists and the absence of a sales-oriented message. Instead, they hope pretty pictures and a few *"impotent"* features will sell. They will not!

Direct mail is the most scientific form of advertising. The majority of factors, such as lists, timing, offers, copy, and space, are all in your hands. Each variation can be precisely tested for effectiveness. There are proven techniques that boost response. Unfortunately, many people ignore proven techniques and try to be "creative!" Instead, you should be testing each incremental improvement in the copy, layout, and design that can have a far-reaching effect on the success of your campaign.

No other type of advertising lets you target market so specifically with income ranges, demographics, gender, even occupation. Email and Facebook are rapidly catching up in this area, but they are still not there yet. Direct marketing is not cheap. But if systemized, the results can be quite astonishing.

In this chapter, you will discover:

✔ Why most direct mail campaigns fail

✔ What makes an effective direct mail campaign

✔ The most effective lists to generate response

✔ The importance of the offer

✔ The keys to copy and design success

✔ How to test properly

LEGENDARY DIRECT MAIL

Why most direct mail campaigns fail

First, let's explain what I mean by a mail campaign. At Legendary Marketing, we frequently talk to course owners who've just run a direct mail campaign with terrible results. Upon questioning, we learn that their idea of a mail campaign is a 2 × 3 coupon included with 50 other coupons in a shotgun mailing to anybody with a mailbox. That is not what we mean by a direct mail campaign!

We also talk to many course owners who eagerly rent a mailing list of everyone who just moved to town. They print a one-sided flyer with no letter, no offer, no headline, no sweetener, and then send it to four thousand people. They are shocked when the phone doesn't ring. That is not a direct mail campaign, either.

Sending a one-page John Doe invite letter to a list of golf magazine subscribers doesn't cut it either!

Creating your campaign

There are no hard rules about what a mail package should contain. It could be as simple as a one-sided sales letter or be as complex as a 14-page letter complete with a color brochure. However, if you take a look at the type of mail you receive, you'll find 70–80 percent will contain the following:

- ✔ An envelope with teaser copy that entices you to open it and find out what is inside

- ✔ A 3- or 4-fold brochure

- ✔ A 2–4-page letter

- ✔ A clear, compelling offer

- ✔ A reply card or other response device

Mailing lists—the first key to success

The best direct mail package can fail miserably if you don't send it to the right people. If you're not careful, your letters will end up in the hands of old people, dead people, and people who can't afford your services. Lists can be ordered and sorted in almost unimaginable combinations. You can rent lists of people categorized by race, income, zip code, property value, business, or a thousand other identifying factors.

Even with golfers, there is a huge difference between the performance of good lists and poor lists. For example, if your club is high end, you will need a clear income qualifier.

First, figure out what your ideal prospects look like. (See Chapter 4, Defining Your Market).

What characteristics do they have?

- ✔ Do most of your customers live in the same zip code or same part of town?

- ✔ Do they have a certain level of income?

- ✔ Do they have children, drive a Corvette, or root for the Redskins?

Once you've pinpointed the characteristics of your ideal prospects, check to see what lists are available with those exact criteria.

Lists are usually available in minimums of 5,000 names and can be rented for one-time or multiple uses. I suggest a one-time use and asking for a credit if you want to reuse it within 60 days. By then you'll know what the response rate was. Make sure you use a reputable list broker or call us; there are plenty of sharks!

THE MOST EFFECTIVE LISTS TO GENERATE RESPONSE

While good lists can be found from third parties, the most effective lists you will ever use are the lists you build yourself. All the data you collect from your website and at the counter will pay off big time with direct mail. These are people who already have had contact with your club, and that will translate into far greater response rates than any cold list you buy or rent. (That's providing their experience with your club was positive.)

The first trick is to get your mail opened

When a prospect gets a letter from you in the mail, the VERY FIRST CHALLENGE is to get your letter in the interesting pile! Fail to do that, and I don't care what you spent or what you sent, your campaign is DOOMED!

Have you ever watched someone open their mail? It's a very interesting study in human nature; take me for example, I'm a sorter.

First I look through the stack for checks and bills. That's the accounting pile—pile A. Pile B is anything for my wife. Pile C is the "later pile"—catalogs that might be of potential interest (golf, car stuff, and, at Christmas at least, possible gifts for my wife) and periodicals. They get put on my magazine rack for later reading at night or for my next plane trip. Pile D is my favorite. That is the interesting stuff—a handwritten letter from a friend, books or tapes I ordered, brochures for interesting vacations, and direct mail offers for things that interest me (books, tapes, cars, golf, and so forth). Catalogs and mailing pieces of no interest to me (credit card offers, insurance solicitations, stock pick newsletters, car dealerships of brands I don't care about) get instantly trashed.

Which brings me to pile E. Pile E is direct mail offers which might be of interest to me—only pile E almost never exists because very few pieces make it through the sort and trash process.

For sure there are other methods of sorting your mail, but they all have one thing in common, some stuff gets thrown out without a glance, some gets saved for later reading, and some actually gets OPENED and READ!!!

So how can you massively increase your chances of getting our letter opened and read?

How about an envelope with a handwritten address and a Bobby Jones golf stamp affixed, and a tee, pencil ball marker, or some other lumpy trinket inside the letter to create some interest? I have used everything from ball markers to tea bags and seed packets to divots! They are not going to trash that letter like the rest of the "Junk Mail"!

They are going to first put it on the interesting pile.

Grab readers' attention with your headline

When they open it to see what the lump is, a giant headline is going to grab their ATTENTION at ONCE! If you don't grab them by the throat with your headline, 95 percent won't make it past the first paragraph. (Which means no matter how long or short your letter is it won't work!)

Just as in print advertising, writing good headlines is critical to the success of your direct mail campaign. Without good headlines everything that follows is a waste of time and money for it will most likely never be read.

With direct mail, you have more space than a print ad and traditionally see much longer headlines. Longer headlines give you a better chance to hook the reader.

Some of the more effective ways to write good headlines are:

✔ An expose-type headline that gets people to look!

Amazing True Story: How a Mentally Tortured Woman Found Peace and Happiness through a Golf Outing at GlenEagles

✔ "How-to" headlines also work well.

How You Can Be the Hero of Your Next Golf Event with This Incredible Limited-Time Offer!

How I Talked My Wife into Buying Property at My Favorite Golf Resort

✔ Put the key benefits of your product in the headline or, better still, put the key benefits *and* the offer in your headline.

Designed by Golf Professionals for Golf Professionals— Starters Hut, The World's Most Powerful, Easy to Use Electronic Tee Sheet...

And It's Yours FREE for Six Months to Put It to the Ultimate Test...in Your Pro Shop!

✔ Put your guarantee in the headline

You Will Cut Your Handicap by at Least 20% or Your Money Back!

✔ Offer secrets

The Inside Secrets to BOOKING 10 Extra Outings This Month

Whichever method you choose, you must work and re-work you headlines until the promise created in them motivates your reader to dig into the copy that follows.

Make sure the person writing your copy is a DIRECT RESPONSE MARKETER, not a typical agency copywriter. Based on my search for copywriters, such a person can be found in about one in 200 people who call themselves copywriters!

Go back and READ the letter in Chapter Two that starts on page 18 for an excellent example of GREAT COPY!

Long, relevant, interesting letters sell

Once you have your prospect's attention, the letter needs to tell an INTERESTING story AND make a COMPLETE SALES PITCH as to why the reader should act NOW!

Which brings me to my favorite topic, long copy. Almost all successful direct response packages have a lot of copy. Most letters are 2–4 pages or more. Now, you might think that is too much to read. This is the biggest fallacy people have about direct marketing.

For those who are truly interested in golf and your club, the more information, the better.

Long copy always outsells short copy! Yet ask anyone and they won't believe it! In fact, they will flat out tell you that nobody reads anymore BUT...

If people don't read anymore, why were there more books printed last year than in any year in the history of the world?

If people don't read anymore, why are there more magazine titles on the newsstand than at any time in history?

If people don't read anymore, why has the size of a local bookstore grown from 1,500 square feet to 20,000 square feet (and that doesn't count the cappuccino bar!)?

If people don't read anymore, why is the number one complaint of web surfers that they didn't find enough information when they got to a site?

I'll tell you why—because despite what the amateurs tell you, people do read but they ONLY read things that are of strong interest to them!

At the very first marketing seminar I ever conducted, I asked 40 small business owners whether they thought people would read letters that were 4, 8, or even 12 pages long. They all said no. I then asked how they learned about the seminar they were attending and they all said they received an 11-page letter with a four-page brochure and a personal note, a total of 15 pages of text. I asked them how many had read the entire letter before committing $600 for the seminar along with airfare, rental car, lodging, and meals. All but one said that they had read the entire letter before making the commitment. Some even admitted to reading it twice, including a husband and wife who had driven 2,000 miles from Houston!

Has time changed anything? No, last year I repeated the experiment, this time attracting 93 people to my Golf Marketing Boot Camp at $1595 a head with an 11-page letter! When the group was asked if anyone would read an 11-page letter every single one said NO!!! But when I pointed out it was the only way the seminar was marketed most agreed to having read every page, with some admitting to reading the entire package three times before making their decision to buy! What people say they do and what they *actually* do is often different!

Don't be generic

Make your copy of great interest to your readers. Get them emotionally involved in what you have to offer! Do not settle for generic descriptions of what you have at the club.

- ✔ Make it LIVE, make it breathe, make it real!

- ✔ CONNECT with the reader in a personal way!

- ✔ PAINT a picture with your words, with them in it!

- ✔ What will it feel like to hit the ball 20 yards further?

- ✔ What will it feel like to play golf with your son every evening when you buy a golf course home?

- ✔ How will your wife feel after a day at the resort's spa?

Ninety-nine percent of all copy in the golf business is impersonal corporate-speak with no passion, no connection with the reader, and no reason to act now. Therefore it FAILS! (In fact, half the text in the golf business is obviously written by people who don't play golf. I saw one recently that compared a course in New Jersey to the great ones in Scotland like Ballybunion!!!!! I saw another at a very high-end real estate development that gave the approximate length of the fairways in feet! I mean what do they want to do land a plane on it?)

To sell golf, speak like a golfer, think like a golfer, act like a golfer, relate like a golfer, quote golfers, and tell golf stories! All of which should happen as part of the natural sales presentation you are making in your letter.

People need reasons...they need benefits...they need proof...they need motivation—and it takes more than a few lines of puff to connect on a meaningful level. Don't be afraid of writing letters long enough to prove your case. There is no such thing as a letter that's too long, only one that is too boring! If people are interested in any given subject they want more information, not less.

✔ Why is your course or resort better?

✔ What are the other members like?

✔ Why is your teaching philosophy different and more effective?

Remember, when developing a direct mail campaign, design the letter, brochure, and everything else NOT for the people who will regard it as junk mail and just throw it away, but for the ones whose attention it will catch and whose interest it will pique. Inspire them by providing more benefits and reasons to pick up the phone and take advantage of the unique offer you have made.

Have a conversation with your reader

The letter copy should be written as you would write a letter to a friend. It should be conversational and use simple, explicit language, free of technical jargon. It should excite the reader to want to learn more about your club, resort, real estate, or teaching program. It should be laced with benefits, testimonials, and true life stories that will categorically back up your position.

Tell your reader a story about someone who's benefited from a particular service, someone who saved their sanity, made a business deal, or beat the odds and vastly improved their lives...thanks to you. Back up your story with lots of testimonials...fill them up with benefits, benefits, benefits. Add that real-world touch to your letter. Make it down home and folksy, like you've helped the person next door and can help them.

Grab readers' attention, then tell them a story

Here is part of a letter to event planner that goes with one of the dramatic headlines mentioned earlier.

Amazing True Story

How a Mentally Tortured Woman Found Peace and Happiness Through a Golf Outing at GlenEagles

Dear Event Planner:

Glenda (not her real name) worked for a demanding doctor. This particular doctor was a big philanthropist in the community and head of a well-known local charity. Anyway, one day right out of the blue he had a great idea, "Let's hold a golf event to raise some money!" he said to Glenda.

That's where the problems started for Glenda. You see, Glenda did not play golf, so she didn't have a clue about how to run a golf event.

How To Survive Your First Outing

What she did know was that the doctor, all his friends, and the charity's major donors did golf, and all eyes would be on her performance! She was petrified.

The first night she tossed and turned in bed waking up in a cold sweat as one horrendous golf outing disaster after another (all starring Christopher Lee) filled her mind with images.

On day two she started looking on the Internet for a venue, biting her nails to the bone as she surfed the web.

Wow! She had no idea there were this many courses. They couldn't all be good ones, could they? They all seemed to offer outings but none had very much information.

It was the third day now, and poor Glenda was no closer to booking her event. She was paralyzed with fear.

GlenEagles Makes It Easy

Fortunately for her, a caring friend intervened before it was too late and suggested she simply call GlenEagles. Glenda thought this was particular- ly odd since while surfing the Internet, she had found the club was located in Scotland and did not want to add booking 144 plane tickets to her already full plate. Her friend filled her in...

(Continued)

240

As the letter on the opposite page shows, run your text to the next page so that the reader will have to go there to finish the sentence. Underline, circle, or highlight key words and phrases. Indent key paragraphs and double space your text to make it easy on the eyes. Use lots of bold headlines to break up the text and to allow your reader to scan your letter just by reading the headlines. Sometimes that's exactly what people do first to decide if they will read your letter. Once their attention has been gained and points scored with benefits and testimonials, the real object of the direct mail letter must be revealed.

The following page contains another example of a direct marketing letter. Again note the headline, breaking the text mid- sentence at the bottom of the page, and the various devices used to highlight keywords and phrases.

YOU NEED A GREAT OFFER

I want to expose the truth to you, one that no one else in the advertising industry dares to tell you—99 percent of all your marketing is doomed to FAIL because of one KEY missing ingredient: The lack of an irresistible offer!

The truth of the matter is you can take an average list and average writing ability and still make a success of it if you have an irresistible offer! However, most do not.

This is where it gets tricky. You see, most people in the golf business have a totally distorted view of what it takes both physically and financially to get a new client.

This makes them very reluctant to devise an IRRESISTIBLE OFFER since they think that ANY offer is giving away or cheapening their product!

**An Invitation to Experience
the GOLF CLUB OF YOUR DREAMS!**

Dear Golfer:

This invitation to join Pine Barrens Golf Club is not for everyone.

It is reserved for a select few who appreciate magnificent golf and pristine, awe-inspiring surroundings. It's for those who wish to play, entertain, and relax in the friendly ambiance of other successful professionals just like you.

At the same time, it's for people who yearn to belong to a world-class golf facility without the huge up-front fees, assessments, and politics so often associated with stuffier clubs.

If I am correct, you are one of those people. If so, I'd like to share with you more about Pine Barrens and give you a glimpse of the privileges that await you as a member.

Solitude and Tranquility Are Closer Than You Think

Carved from sandy soil and dotted with pines, Pine Barrens sits in scenic Jackson, New Jersey--just 90 minutes from New York City, 55 minutes from Atlantic City and 75 minutes from Philadelphia. It has the virtue of easy access plus a mild maritime climate that makes year-round golf possible.

"The staff here treats you like family and the course and membership just keep getting better every year!"

- Mike Jensen, Member, Since 1999, Brielle, NJ

From the moment you arrive at our gorgeous, Adirondack-style clubhouse, you'll know you're in for something special. First, you'll notice there are no

(continued)

What is a player, member or home buyer worth to you?

If you get a new player to show up at your club for a $50 green fee, you make $50. But if you get that player back ten times this year, that player is worth $500; get him back 20 times and he's worth $1,000! And that does not include pro shop or F&B revenue, referrals, and so forth! That player's true value as a client might well be $2,000 for which you should gladly pay $100 or more to get him in the door.

Now, let's say you spend $12,000 on a direct mail campaign to 10,000 golfers in your area. What will the response be?

I could tell you the typical response to a good list, with good copy is 0.5 percent, but even that would be a stretch.

What's a great offer?

The truth of the matter is that all things being equal, the number of people who respond will be based on the quality of your offer!

You can get 1 percent, 3 percent, or even 5 percent response rates and higher BUT ONLY TO IRRESISTIBLE OFFERS:

- ✔ Offer a $5 discount on your green fee and the response will be lukewarm at best!

- ✔ Offer a dozen Pro V1s and you'll do way better than 0.5 percent!

- ✔ Offer a FREE lunch and response drops back to alarmingly average.

- ✔ Offer a FREE green fee and watch response SOAR!!!

- ✔ Tell people to come see your golf homes in Florida because they are exclusive... yawn.

- ✔ Offer two nights in the Ritz, a round of golf, and a property tour at a very attractive discounted rate and, BOOM, they are already on SouthWest.com booking their flight!

To determine your optimum offer you have to track your leads, conversions, and up-sells. It may well be okay to give away $600 worth of gifts per person to attract 30 new members as we did recently at a club in California.

Sure it's a loss leader, but it's one that pays off VERY QUICKLY in the form of monthly dues!!!

What works?

We had an amazing response to an $80 tee package in closing over $150,000 of outing business in just 30 days at one of our resort clients.

We have had excellent response to books, DVDs, and Audio CDs as premiums.

Property discovery packages, free room nights, and replay rounds all work in the right situation.

Like most effective marketing, the key to finding effective offers is to test, test, test.

Spell out the action you want from the reader

What do you want the reader to do? What is the offer they should act upon at once? The more compelling your offer, the greater your response will be. Whatever you decide to offer, be sure to emphasize the value. For example, if you're offering a free room night, be sure you let your people know that it is a $200 value. The higher the perceived value, the more response you will generate. In addition to the actual offer, direct mail campaigns often include some kind of sweetener or bonus if you act now. You might want to offer a T-shirt or free golf glove, a free book, or some other kind of inducement to get people to respond immediately.

Your letter has to create a sense of urgency, a sense of loss if they don't pick up the phone and act right now. Here's a letter for the club where I live:

"Where to Live If You Live For Golf"

Dear Golfer:

There are obviously lots of great places you can choose to make your home in Florida if you like to play golf.

But...if you truly love golf, there is simply no better choice than **BLACK DIAMOND**. Our facility features 45 holes of spectacular, uncrowded, Fazio golf. Great weather all year round, luxurious, yet affordable homes and a diverse and active membership that is always ready to invite some new blood into their games. No matter what your scorecard looks like you'll find a group to match your game. Unlike many top clubs, you don't have to bring your game with you at **BLACK DIAMOND**. In fact, you'll find year-round play with a group that's a perfect match for your game!

Of course, once you are a member of our "**Top 100 Club**" that boasts (according to noted sports writer **Dan Jenkins**) *"The best five consecutive holes in the world,"* you might find plenty of friends flying in to see you as well!

You'll find our clubhouse facilities an excellent place to conduct business and entertain friends. While our world class fitness center, tennis and swimming facilities will help keep you in great shape.

For a very limited time, we are offering the opportunity for you and your spouse to experience the spectacular beauty of Black Diamond, our world class golf courses, cuisine and accommodations for the nominal fee of just $495 per couple.

Here's how it works: Fly to Tampa, Florida where you will be met and welcomed by the Black Diamond limousine. Then just sit back and relax as you enjoy the tranquil beauty of Florida's Nature Coast on your journey to **Black Diamond**.

Once on property, you will be shown to your spacious cottage accommodations. Next, it's time to take a tour of the property before you experience the beautiful rolling terrain of our **Ranch Course**. In the evening enjoy a sumptuous dinner in our clubhouse and meet some of our friendly members. Tour the area once more in the morning before an early afternoon round on our famed **Quarry Course.**

To take advantage of this spectacular offer go at once to www.GolfBlackDiamond.com and register now. This offer is for a very limited time so even if you plan to visit us later in the year, please register now to avoid disappointment. If you have any questions, please feel free to contact me directly at **888-328-8099.**

Yours sincerely,

Ken Breland

Director of Sales

P.S. Will Rogers once said he loved investing in real estate because *"It was the only thing they weren't making any more of."* Nowhere is that statement truer than in the pristine beauty of Black Diamond. We are in the final phase of development and soon it will all be gone! Don't wait too long to come and see us and take advantage of our special offer today at www.BlackDiamond.com.

The importance of your P.S.

Many people read the headline of the letter and then go straight to the end to see who signed it and read the P.S. For this reason it is extremely important that you use both your headline and your P.S. to state your case as succinctly and powerfully as possible. Excite the reader and promise him specific and tangible rewards for taking his valuable time to read through the body of your text.

THE BROCHURE

Your brochure should be a graphical representation of your club and should expand on the major points of your letter. The majority of direct mail campaigns use either a 4-page format (an 11 x 17 page folded in half) or a 3- or 4-fold format that is 8.5 x 11 or 11 x 17, printed on both sides.

Use the front cover for a good clean photograph or graphic that demonstrates the end result of your service. If you sell a vacation experience, show relaxed people smiling. If you improve players' golf games, show their scorecards. The better you can visually demonstrate the end result of your services in your lead photograph; the more effective your brochure will be. And don't forget to promise a clear benefit in the headline.

The inside of your brochure is where you repeat your story. Use a less personal approach that is full of facts and benefits. Make every line read from the golfer's perspective. If your benefits are unclear, remove that copy at once. To break up your text, use descriptive headlines, graphics, pictures, and charts. Always use captions under pictures or graphics to sell yourself or your service, never to describe what is in the picture. (Many brochures stupidly don't use captions or headlines with their photos!) Use facts, figures, statistics, surveys, comparisons, awards, and anything else to prove that you will do exactly what you say you will. Use the back panel or back page for summarizing all your benefits point-by-point, a brief biography dripping with benefits, or a new set of testimonials elevating your reputation. Also, include a strong call to action.

The envelope

There are two different strategies when it comes to the envelope. One is to leave the impression that this is important and personal. That means using no copy, a first class stamp, and at least a laser- printed address. (Handwritten is always better!)

The other strategy is to make it clear that the envelope contains a solicitation, and make it so appealing that people open it anyway! Use a graphic and teaser that gets people excited and eager to open it up. Promise a clear benefit like lower scores, a better deal, or a VIP invitation.

Testing

Finally, test, test, and test. Mail some to one list, some to another list and see which letters and lists pull the best. You'll find that you can use your best lists and letters again and again with excellent results. Some say the typical response rate for a direct mail campaign is 2 percent. Don't count on it! Figure closer to 0.5 percent until you've proven differently. Until you have a willing list of clients and followers, always figure on the low end. But follow-up telemarketing can boost your response rate much higher.

Pitfalls of marketing golf by mail

There is a lot of information that most people in the marketing business not only won't tell you but often deny!

Let's say you decide to do a direct mail campaign to boost your membership. You write and design a wonderful package with a strong offer, print up 10,000 pieces and trust them to the good old US Postal Service. Then you sit back and wait for your 2 percent response because that's the number you have always heard thrown around!

Two hundred people rushing to the phones!

Sadly, this is fantasy because there is NO AVERAGE RESPONSE RATE. Response is driven by a multitude of factors and if you are going to guess what yours will be before it happens, start at 0.5 percent and you won't be too disappointed.

So you take my word for it and re-adjust your sights on getting 50 responses, but, sadly, my friend, you are still mistaken. You see, you are counting on a .5 percent response from the 10,000 pieces you think you mailed when the truth of the matter is you'll be lucky if 9,000 of them ever make to the right mailbox!

NO! You say, how can this be?

First, no list is perfect, most claim only 96 percent delivery which means do not be surprised if you get back a whopping 400 envelopes for every 10,000 pieces you send out!

And be prepared, no matter who you rent your list from: Some lady WILL call up and tell you her husband's been dead for seven years!!!

Some do a better job of updating their lists than others but even the real clean lists don't necessarily generate a better response, you just feel better that less mail came back.

So of the 10,000 you thought you mailed, you are already down to 9,600.

I actually got ahead of myself because the "10,000 pieces mailed" assumes that your printer delivered all 10,000 pieces to the mailing house. Most printers work on a plus or minus 5 percent tolerance and all it takes is the press to jam for a few seconds and you're down another 300 or 400 pieces. (Ever spend a day in a print shop? I have!)

Then, of course, there is the mailing house itself, a massive, poorly lit warehouse, staffed mainly by illegal aliens with hundreds and hundreds of mail sacks just sitting on the floor. It is surprisingly common for mail to be sent to the entirely wrong list! (It's already happened to me once this year! After finally admitting their mistake six weeks later, the mailing house reprinted the mailing piece and mailed it at their expense.)

Then there are mailing houses that mail, say 10 percent less mail than they say they did. Just one sack, you understand, nothing that will be missed...but that sack of unstuffed, un-mailed letters creates a tidy profit when you add the mythical postage!

And, as for that official looking U.S. Postal Service receipt, that's about as reliable as those blank ones you get from cab drivers. The mailing house brings in the forms saying that 10,000 pieces are being mailed and the USPS clerk signs a receipt for it. The postal clerks don't count the pieces. At some point, postal employees will estimate the size of the mailing by weight. For example, if one of your pieces weighs .8 ounces and the form that was presented at to the post office says you're mailing 10,000 pieces, then the total weight of your mail should be 500 pounds. If the mailing house only brought in 9,000 pieces, the weight will be less than 500 pounds, but you'll never hear about it as the postal service doesn't mind getting paid for more pieces than are actually getting mailed. The only time you'll hear about an error is if you've mailed more pieces than you've paid for.

With all those direct mail sacks and tubs lying around, one of your sacks could easily be missed by accident. But even the potential incompetence or larceny of your printer and mailing house pales in comparison to that of the U.S. Postal System.

Don't get me wrong. It's amazing that you can send a letter 3000 miles in a couple of days for less than 50 cents and, yes, there are lots of wonderful people who work in the postal service BUT...and it's a big BUT...I could fill a book with personal examples of incompetent morons as well. And I can vouch that several of them work at my local post office!

When you send bulk mail, it does not get treated like first class mail; it gets treated like NO class mail. If you're like me, you've received mailings sent via bulk mail whose offers are long expired. Bulk mail sometimes sits for days or even weeks until the people sorting it deem that they have the time to process it after getting all the regular mail on it's merry way. The longer it sits, the more chance it has of getting lost or dumped. (Whenever you do a bulk mailing, always make sure your name is on the list, so you have some idea about when the pieces are delivered.)

Yes, dumping mail is a crime, but you can read about it every month in your local newspaper! It happens. Joe, the postman, is having a bad day, his wife is mad at him, the dog tore up the rug, his '88 Camaro needs a valve job, and his back is aching. He's got a whole tray of JUNK MAIL to deliver, and who needs this stuff anyway? Why not just leave it in the van and do it tomorrow when he feels better; it's not like anyone is going to miss it. But tomorrow for this particular mail never comes and Joe eventually just disposes of it! Yep, that's right, he throws it away it and it often happens, far more often than you would believe! (People do not become government employees because of their incredible entrepreneurial zeal!)

Admittedly I get a lot of mail, but never does a week go by without me getting a piece addressed to someone else. I bet this happens to you too!

To say that 90 percent of the mail you thought you printed and mailed gets delivered to the right person is pushing it! Some people estimate as little as 70 percent of bulk mail gets through!

So with all these factors going against you, is it actually worth doing direct mail?

Absolutely! Done right, it is still the best, most responsive form of marketing money can buy! I just want you to be aware of the pitfalls, so you'll work harder on the key factors that can make your mailings successful.

SUMMARY

Direct mail is the purest form of advertising and can pay the greatest rewards, but only if you do it right. A great offer with dramatic headlines sent to a good list is a start. Then test and refine until your mailings pull predictable, repeatable responses.

CHAPTER FOURTEEN

Legendary Email Marketing

Done right, e-mail marketing is low cost, generates high returns, and provides instant gratification. Done wrong, you'll spend weeks trying to clean up the mess you leave behind, with irate customers who may never return. You have gone to great length to build a large email list. Now it's time to monetize it properly which, is not quite as simple as it seems!

Many clubs get luck luster results from their campaigns rarely seeing any significant spikes in business. Many more murder their lists with offer after offer quickly destroying its' marketing power in a storm of unsubscribes.

On the flip-side at legendary marketing have been able to help clients sell two and a half weeks of tee times from a single e-mail. In another case, we were able, to increase revenues by $1500 per weekend with a simple, last-minute e-mail to sell prime tee times that had been cancelled. A Florida resort we work with sent a blast to Canadian golfers just as a winter storm hit. This perfect timing (we waited for bad weather) generated $28,000 in room nights plus the same again in golf for an investment of just $1500.

In another case we had a blast ready for when the airlines started a price war in the Northeast. It hit e-mail in-boxes within an hour of

Delta's announcement of $99 flights from all New York airports to all, of its' Florida destinations. A good e-mail marketing strategy is power at your finger-tips.

In this chapter, you will discover:

✔ Ten ways to connect with your customers using e-mail

✔ The power of creating your own e-zine

✔ How to segment your lists for greater response

✔ Ten ways to make your e-marketing more effectively

✔ How to personalize your messages for greater response

✔ How often to mail your list

✔ 12 ways to avoid spam filters

Connecting with your customers using email

Email is a wonderful way to market your course locally, nationally, and even internationally but there are many reasons to use email not considered by most clubs.

Ten Ways Your Club Should Be Using e-mail Marketing to Increase Your Business – But Isn't!

1. **Sales** – This is obvious but is often the last of the seven things you should be doing not the first and only thing which is what most clubs do! Even when you do sell it's often better to wrap your message in a content sandwich rather than an all-out sales pitch!

2. **Data collection and enhancement**– This should be first on your list of email strategies. Emails change often and you must be constantly asking your people to update their data. You should also be using your emails to enhance your customer pro-files. Trading something of value for additional insight in to their

playing habits like how often they play golf and how many of those rounds they play at your club!

You should also request they forward your emails to their friends so they too can enter your contest or download your coupon and continue to expand your database.

3. **Entertainment and additional value** – Again this is something few clubs really consider but your emails should be an extension of your club's experience. In other words your emails should provide additional entertainment to your players, members or guests so the good feelings they get at your club extend into their daily lives.

4. **Customer retention** – Few clubs think of email as a customer retention tool but again high quality emails expounding on the benefits of golf for health, fitness or business remind people of the value of your club.

5. **Nurturing** them towards a large purchase like a membership, outing, wedding, vacation or home. This is a big one and once again one many club's ignore this in the scramble for fast dollars. People need to feel comfortable with large purchases email someone over time a series of educational message and you will enhance the trust needed to make a larger sale.

6. **Brand awareness** – Constantly emailing constantly high quality information will build a positive brand for your club. Constantly sending out discount offers or cheesy low end graphics like the emails you get daily from the 3rd party tee time vendors whose only purpose in life is a book fee or reseal of your trade time will and often does accomplish the reverse.

7. **To follow up** and thank your customers for their business. Once again although the technology is built into many POS systems and websites few clubs do this. Those that do often opt for nothing more than the basic default message that has long since failed to impress anyone. Chance the message often, using dif-

ferent graphics and offering frequent value added to the message will make an impact.

8. **To connect and engage** with your customers by soliciting feedback in the form or comments, surveys and various forms of consumer rankings such as Trip Advisor, Yelp or Facebook.

9. **To drive customers** to specific event landing pages.

World Masters Golf Championship
Hua Hin, Thailand

11-17 JUNE, 2017 IN HUA HIN, THAILAND

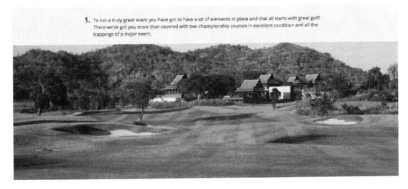

Thailand's Must Play Amateur Golf Event

The fourth annual **Centara World Masters Golf Championship** hosted in the royal city of Hua Hin, Thailand has quickly earned the reputation of Asia's best week of golf. Golfers from 23 countries across all continents were in high praise of the previous events with the golf courses, caddies, event organization and tournament functions all rated five star. So long as you are over 35 you can tee it up at the Masters and there are 15 tournament divisions based on age and handicap. Playing with golfers your own age and standard is one of the event's great traditions while at the heart of the event's success is the camaraderie and friendship among participants.

Here are ten reasons you need to make this event an annual tradition...

1. To run a truly great event you have got to have a lot of elements in place and that all starts with great golf. There we've got you more than covered with two championship courses in excellent condition and all the trappings of a major event.

10. **To keep them informed** on the happenings at the clubs with a monthly or weekly newsletter. To included upcoming events, pictures of past events and winners. New members, holes in one, members success or charity involvement beyond the club.

9:36 AM	10:32 AM	11:44 AM
ert Dunes - Robert Trent Jones Jr.	Desert Dunes - Robert Trent Jones Jr.	Desert Dunes - Robert Trent Jones .
$49.00 /player	$49.00 /player	$49.00 /player
2 to 4 players	2 to 4 players	1 to 4 players
You Save 51%	You Save 51%	You Save 51%

1:39 PM	2:33 PM	3:36 PM
ert Dunes - Robert Trent Jones Jr.	Desert Dunes - Robert Trent Jones Jr.	Desert Dunes - 9 Hole Times
$49.00 /player	$39.00 /player	$25.00 /player
1 or 2 players	1 to 4 players	1 to 4 players
You Save 51%	You Save 28%	You Save 58%

nesday, April 17, 2013

6:08 AM	7:04 AM	8:00 AM
ert Dunes - Robert Trent Jones Jr.	Desert Dunes - Robert Trent Jones Jr.	Desert Dunes - Robert Trent Jones .
$49.00 /player	$49.00 /player	$49.00 /player
		2 to 4 players

How to destroy your email list

If all you do is send discount tee time offers after discount tee offers and offer nothing else of value to your readers, you will appeal to a very small percentage of your list! You will rapidly increase your unsubscribes or people will simply just ignore your emails altogether. That's assuming they get them at all as many of the 3rd Party emails are instantly sent to the junk folder. Why because THEY send out discount tee time offer after discount tee time offer for multiple clubs every day and are labeled SPAM by a large majority of the internet providers thus ensuring less of your legitimate emails get through to your customers when using their servers!

Most damaging of all in the long term is you will brand your course as being at the very bottom of the food chain. A place that's very difficult to come back from.

As a private club it's important to segment your members into special interest groups don't keep sending ladies 9 hole information to a 30 something single male and vice versa.

Another good way to destroy your club's good name is to send out cheesy templates

Lots of the low-end website companies like Course Tends, Golf Now and Cyber Golf and the like offer these and they make your course look amateurish and destroy your brand! I see several of these a day in my inbox people so lazy they paste a header on top of a header.

Ten Keys to Effective e-mail Marketing

1. Clean lists

Before we get into the nuances of good email design let's start with something far more important… your email lists:

✔ How good are they targeted, opt in segmented?

✔ How clean are they?

✔ Poor lists maintenance results in poor delivery rates!

The low-end web providers and tee time traders DO NOT clean your lists no matter what they say it takes real time and effort to keep a list clean every time you mail and if you think they are really managing your list for a few hundred bucks a month or a tee time you are sadly mistaken.

Manage Your Bounces

This is probably the most mismanaged process in the golf industry. If your provider isn't doing this correctly they are flushing your email database down the drain.

There are two types of bounces that occur:

Hard Bounces – These are bounces that occur because the email address just isn't active anymore. These should be immediately removed from your database once confirmed as bad!

Soft Bounces – There are many of reasons a soft bounce can occur. The most common are reasons like "Mailbox Full", "Email Account Unavailable", or "System not Accepting Message".

Hard bounces should not be immediately removed from your email database because the receiving server isn't telling you it's a bad email address. Your system should try resending to them and monitor the bounce that is received.

- If it continues to receive the same bounce message after a few tries then it is acceptable for the email address to be removed, however if it receives different messages, it shows that the receiving server is having issues. This is EXTREMELY common with a lot of the major mail providers such as AOL.com, Yahoo.com and Hotmail.com

- Resend to Your Soft Bounces: Soft bounces are usually errors that are occurring on the receiving end. Usually these issues are solved within a few hours and the email addresses start functioning again.

2. Target list demographics with your message

The more ways you sort your lists by interest, gender, preference and geography the greater your open rates and the less unsubscribes. This is important data you can gain from the questions on your landing pages and over time build an insightful profile of your players.

Sort your lists into logical groups:

- o Members
- o Non-members
- o Ladies
- o Men
- o Seniors
- o Juniors
- o Locals
- o Out of town more than 25 miles
- o Discount club
- o Korean, French, Spanish language
- o The more targeted the message to the list the better the open rates and response.
- o Frequent players
- o Occasional players
- o Plays in tournaments
- o Does not play in tournaments
- o Likes theme events wine tasting, cigars, Italian night, etc
- o Play tennis

260

- o Swims

- o Has kids

And 101 other questions you can ask to create small responsive groups, after all it makes no sense to invite a non-drinker to wine tasting or to pound the men's group with info on the ladies nine hole events!

Targeted messages and offers can be designed for each group so that you can maximize your success. As with everything, the more targeted your groups and the more specific your offer is to meeting that group's needs, the more effective your marketing efforts will be. While it may sound like a lot of work, it's really just a couple of hours spent on programming. The computer will take care of the rest if you have the right software.

3. Great subject lines

The difference between an e-mail blast that gets open and therefore potentially acted upon, usually hangs in the balance of less than six words. Just like an ad your emails will live and die on your subject lines. The difference in open rates between an A and B subject line can easily be 500% or more!

The subject line is your ad for your email, make it count! The best email subject lines are short, descriptive and provide the reader with a reason to explore your message further. Trying to stand out in the inbox, by using splashy or cheesy phrases, will invariably result in your email being ignored. Promise the reader a benefit for opening your email.

Great headlines

- o Funniest Golf Video Ever?

- o Hit it 20 yards Further!

- o Complimentary golf cart!

- o Golf -Two for One!

- o Seniors Golf Only!

o   Play a round on us!

o   Shocking golf news!

o   Best ever golf joke!

o   I hate Andrew Wood! (entertaining)

You will notice that I often try to get the word GOLF into the headline so it's clear to the reader that golf is involved. I get hundreds of emails a week where it's not clear to me in the subject what I will read about in the email and while that can work in some cases you will do better in the long run sticking to the basics.

Best Value when you BOOK ONLINE! AT WWW.PROVIDENCE-GOLF.COM

TUESDAY NIGHT GOLF LEAGUE STARTS APRIL 4TH AT 5PM....GUYS AND GALS WELCOMED... CALL TO SIGN UP .... 863-424-7926 EXT. 1

BOOK ONLINE AND SAVE

Don't miss out on exclusive daily deals when you book on our online booking site.
www.providence-golf.com

- Secure
- Easy to Use
- NO BOOKING FEE AT WWW.PROVIDENCE-GOLF.COM
- EXCLUSIVE DEALS

Click here to BOOK ONLINE Today

Available Online ONLY at PROVIDENCE GOLF CLUB!

Please call 863-424-7916 with any questions.

Typical of thw weak efforts I see daily!

4. Attractive design

Attractive is often in the eye of the beholder judging by the deluge of pitiful emails in my inbox from "golf marketing people" at clubs. Large pink type, purple block capitals, neon greens and red do not actually make the email stand out at least not for the right reasons.

The email should first and foremost be easy to read. That means no 9- point type, little to no reverse type, no block capitals and no type over pictures unless it's very, very contrasting. Designers love all of these elements but trust me you will make more money if it's readable not pretty.

Consider using a larger typestyle, 55% of Americans over 40 can't read 12-point type without glasses. Have on key focal point and don't forget your social media buttons on the footer!

5. *Emails should add value to your readers' lives*

Think of your emails as an extension of your club's service, or an additional way to entertain your members and guests. With this key point in mind, you MUST add value to your emails, don't make them ALL about sales!

Make your reader pleased he opened your email even if he is not of the mind to book a tee time, vacation or lesson today!

- Make your emails a careful mixture of engagement, entertainment and education
- Build value into your emails not just offers
- Make the golfer glad they opened it even if they are not ready to book a tee time or join your club!
- Videos
- Contests
- Cool pictures
- Cartoons
- Stories
- Jokes
- Quotes
- News
- Events
- And of course offers!

Example

Subject: The Funniest Golf Video Ever

Funniest golf video EVER?

This may be the funniest golf video I have ever seen. It's a candid camera style clip taken at a local driving range.

The look on the players faces when the local redneck shows up and starts shooting, at the golf balls in flight are priceless!

Click here to see for yourself

I hope it you enjoy it and share it with your friends.

From Your Friends at XYZ GOLF club

PS. Don't forget to check out this weeks news and special offers on our website – **click here.**

Check out our blog
Click here to visit us online

How did it do?

o   Great subject line!

o   64% open rate

o   106% pass around rate

o   And we sill had links to special offers, tee times and the
    website

o   LEGENDARY!

Going viral

The second reason that the open rates where high is because the content
was entertaining. The e-mail got opened more than once and got passed
around to thousands of additional people as readers shared it with their
friends. <u>You simply don't get that type of response from the typical
canned, generic looking golf offers, most web companies provide.</u>

Entertaining, engaging content like we include in programs will get
passed around at astonishingly higher rates! More pass around means
more traffic and it comes with the healthy endorsement of a friend, who
thinks this is worth reading!

Join us for some
Presidential Golf

Presidents love to golf and so should you! Beginning with William Howard Taft,
almost all modern-day presidents have counted golf as one of their favorite
pastimes.

Join us at Legendary Golf Club as we celebrate President's Day Weekend and
take advantage of our Presidential Special - just $39.95 for golf and lunch
after you're through with your round.

6. Engaging graphics

Most clubs are happy with a single header image for their club and at least that's consistent but custom graphics add to the reader's engagement and entertainment so should be used frequently. The more creative you are the better!

If it makes you smile it will most likely make them smile and that my friends is entertainment!

You're probably wondering... so, what's the catch?

Well, the fact is there is no catch! We're just welcoming the golf season in the best way we know how, by offering all of our VIP (very important players) a free 18 hole green fee. A promotional cart is required for only $15 per person.

Our offer is valid Monday – Friday any time and after 12 on weekends. Simply fill out a short form by **clicking here** to receive your certificate by email that needs to be printed and brought on the day of play along with photo ID.

Please only one certificate per person and will be tracked. Not valid with other discounts, specials, leagues, outings, or tournaments.

Be sure to forward this to your friends so they can join you.

<u>Click here</u> **to get your FREE green fee!**

Only 3 Saturday Outing Dates left in 2017!

We know it's early in the year but time is running out if you want the best dates for your golf outing, especially if your date is a Saturday.

We know you want the golf outing but if you are looking for the perfect date you'd better act now!

Here at Legendary Golf Club, we have several outings ever year. We take seriously how important your golf outing is to you. So, when it comes to your outing, we don't get a "Mulligan" - we treat your outing as if it were the most important thing we have going - because it is!

Our professional staff is committed to the success of your tournament. From the planning and implementation to final wrap-up, we're here to make sure every aspect of your event is run in a manner in which you can be proud.

Click here to contact your personal outing coordinator today and receive a FREE copy of our golf outing planning guide to help you along the way.

7. Call to action

I see very few emails with specific calls to action, but the more time sensitive, the more limited and the more explicit your demand for action is, the more response you will get. You must try and create some urgency to ACT in your emails.

> o   Limited to the first twenty callers

- o   Only 4 spots left in the event

- o   Only 3 Sundays left this summer for wedding dates

- o   Only two Monday outings available this fall

- o   Deadline approaching for summer kids camp

8. Timeliness and Creativity

Getting Creative - How to Make Your Emails More Interesting, Engaging and Effective

There are lots of simple ways you can make your e-mails stand our from the crowd of boring corporate speak and mindless discount offers! Make your emails memorable, timely and effective.

Who says Friday the 13th is Unlucky?

Consider this Friday the 13th your LUCKY day when you play golf at Legendary Golf Club.

Play before 11am on Friday and pay less than $30!

… and if you can't make it out during the week, play this weekend before 11am for less than $60!

There are an extremely limited number of tee times available at these low rates and they are going fast.

These and other great rates are only available when you book through our website by clicking below.

BOOK A TEE TIME
CLICK HERE

Memorable Dates

The more timely your email subject matter, the better it will be received by your audience.

The calendar is your friend:

o   Holidays

o   Tour events

- o Birthdays

- o Current events

- o Use custom graphics

- o Interesting copy

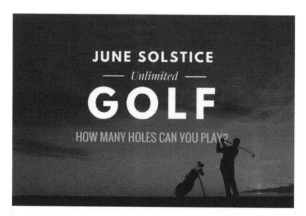

How many can you play on the longest day?

The summer solstice is June 21st and is the longest day of the year with just over **12 hours** of daylight. Come out and play ALL day for just $39.95 with our **Unlimited Golf Solstice Special.**

Enjoy unlimited golf for the price of one tee time and see how many you can play.

To give you something to shoot at...

According to *Guinness World Records,* the record for most holes of golf played in 24 hours with the use of a cart is 851 set by Canadian Robb James.

The longest day of the year is approaching, click here to book your tee time. Even if you only get in 36, it's still a great deal!

What makes this good?

- o Price point offer

- o Custom picture that matches the subject

- o Offer tied into the actual day

- o Fun fact included to spur them to action

o   Easy to read

o   Facebook icon

Birthdays

Famous golfers' birthdays, present and past, make great emails as name recognition is a sure way to make them open your email:

Remembering the King

September 10th would have been Arnold Palmer's 88th birthday, join us as we take a look back at some of the greatest golf moments in the King's career:

Come out to Legendary Golf Club and have an Arnold Palmer in memory of the King and take advantage of our $39.95 golf and lunch special this week only.

Click here to book a tee time or call us at 123-456-7890.

Tie into major events

The "unofficial" start to the golf season is here!

To get you in the mood for the first major of the season, check out the best shots in Augusta history:

Then grab a few friends and head on out to Legendary Golf Club and play a round of golf. **We'll even throw in a free bucket of range balls so you can shake off some of that winter rust - you're gonna need it!**

Click here to book a tee time or call us at 123-456-7890.

PEOPLE LOVE CONTESTS AND SWEEPSTAKES

Enter for a chance to win the Ping Putter Sweepstakes!

We are giving away a 50th Anniversary Limited Edition Putter of the 1966 Anser Tooling Putter. $1,500.00 Value!

Click here to enter to win now!

*Only ONE entry per person is allowed. Multiple entries over the course of several days or weeks will not be counted. The winner will be selected by Premier Irish Golf Tours on 5/2/17 and the winner will be contacted by phone. All decisions made by Premier Irish Golf Tours and World's Best Golf Destinations are final.

Try to do at least one contest every couple of months:

- o   It creates excitement

- o   It provides additional value

- o   It refreshes your database with updated info

- o   It often goes viral with people sharing emails

- o   It mixes up your content and keeps it fresh

- o   Vacations are great because of the high perceived value

This is something we also do every month for our clients that generally gets great engagement:

Best Golf Quotes EVER!

With its long and distinguished history and host of colorful characters, it's no wonder golf has so many amazing anecdotes and memorable one-liners.

Here are a few of our favorites:

1. "The more I practice, the luckier I get." - Gary Player

2. "99 per cent of all putts you leave short don't go in." - Hubert Green

3. "Golf is a game where the aim is to hit a very small ball into an even smaller hole, with weapons singularly ill-designed for the purpose." Winston Churchill

4. "Golf is a good walk spoiled." Mark Twain

5. "Competitive golf is played mainly on a five-and-a-half-inch course, the space between your ears." - Bobby Jones.

Here's the best quote of all, 18 holes and a cart for just $39.95 before 11am! Click here to book your tee time today!

- o   Entertainment value

- o   There will be some viral action

- o   Tee time link clearly visible

- o   Offer tied into the email content

- o   Facebook link

- o   Easy to read layout

- And of course it would have a club header and footer for positive association with your brand

9. Personalize your subject lines or the intro of your email

Most good list servers allow the addition of fields such as a player's name so the offers you send are more personalized. One- to-one personalization is a proven key to building long-term customer value and higher response rates. We use our Campaign Manager to implement a true one-to-one marketing solution. Personalize your mailings to the people who have already indicated their interest in specific offers. It's all automatic!

10. Solid branding

Every email you send should have a solid header at the top with the clubs branding which on longer emails you may choose to repeat at the bottom.

12 ways legitimate emailers can avoid spam filters

Recently several subscribers informed me that their spam filters were not letting their copy of **Golf Club Operator Magazine** through. I decided to check and, sure enough, several factors were causing my own e-zine to get rejected. It's a sad fact that because of the massive amount of spam perhaps as much as 20%–30% of legitimate e-mail does not get through to its intended recipient. Various spam filters such as Spam Assassin block some legitimate e-mails in addition to spam. That's bad news for golf clubs looking to use their lists to attract players. The good news is that by paying attention to some key factors, you can still get most of your messages through!

Spam filters these days are much more sophisticated than the typical e-mail filters of the past. The new ones can be made to delete an e-mail message that contains a number of "bad" words. Filters such as Spam Assassin look for patterns and add or delete points for certain factors. If your total score reaches a predetermined level, the message is flagged as spam. By looking at what adds points (bad) and subtracts points (good), you can learn to construct e-mails that will do better with the filters, if not escape them entirely.

Make Sure You Get Delivered to the Inbox!

1. **You MUST authenticate your emails** – If you're not authenticating the emails you send from your mail platform, receiving servers automatically assume your email is more likely to be SPAM.

   Ways to Authenticate Your Email

   o **Sender Policy Framework (SPF)** - This record is a type of Domain Name System (DNS) record that can help to prevent email address forgery. This method adds IP Addresses of the servers that are allowed to send email from your domain name. SPF is the oldest authentication method that is still accepted by mail servers.

   o **DomainKeys Identified Mail (DKIM)** – This is another type of entry that is made to a Domain Name System (DNS) record. DomainKeys Identified Mail (DKIM) allows sending servers to associate a domain name with an email message, which will show it is authentic. This is done by "signing" the email with a digital signature, a field that is added to the message's header when it is sent from the server. The receiving server can then validate the digital signature using the DNS records and allow delivery. DKIM is currently the most popular authentication method.

○ **Domain-based Message Authentication, Reporting and Conformance (DMARC)** – DMARC is the final type of authentication method, although it has not gained the popularity of SPF or DKIM. DMARC works with both DKIM and SPF and builds off the success each technology has created. It uses both SPF and DKIM record to validate email, by testing the Domain Name System records. If either record fails, the email immediately is flagged and can be handled by the receiving server to either be flagged as SPAM or rejected completely. DMARC is expected to grow in popularity over the next few years given the success it is having.

2. **Offer a Simple Unsubscribe Option** - Having an easy unsubscribe link is important to avoid being classified as spam. The link to the unsubscribe page must be functional, instantaneous and easy to find in the email, meaning put it at the top or bottom.

    Do not send users a follow-up email to confirm their unsubscribe. The majority of them will flag you as spam, blocking your sender address.

3. **IP Reputation** – Monitoring your IP Reputation is very important. If your email provider uses the same IP Addresses to send email for hundreds of different golf courses, all it would take is for one golf course to import a bad list and cause SPAM complaints to hurt **YOUR** deliverability.

Legendary Marketing has many dedicated IP addresses meaning that you don't have to share the reputation of your IP Address with 100 other users on your mailing platform. Systems are in place to monitor them regularly to avoid any problems that might occur. We also give partners and clients the option to upgrade to their own private IP Address virtually eliminating any deliverability problems.

4. **Use a Domain Name That is Linked to Your Website** – You always want to use an email address that is linked to your domain name.

   Example: Andrew@LegendaryMarketing.com

   If you use any other type of email address, even if you have all the proper SPF/DKIM/DMARC records created, your email delivery will fall dramatically.

5. **Make Sure Your Email Provider Can Use Throttled Delivery -** Throttling is the practice of adjusting your sending rate based of the rules ISPs(Internet service providers) and ESPs(Email service providers) have set. Yes, it is shocking to believe, but Gmail, Hotmail, Comcast and many other providers do not want you sending 10,000 emails to them in under one minute.

   Your technology must be able to throttle based off of:

   o   The number of emails sent per minute or hour

   o   The number of connections per minute or hour

   o   The number emails sent per connection

6. **You Must Monitor Spam Complaints and Use Feedback Loops** – Many ISPs and ESPs allow you to receive an alert when your email is flagged as spam, also known as a "feedback loop." When your email platform receives one of these alerts, it is best practice to immediately unsubscribe the email address that

reported you as spam. If you do not, and you continue to deliver to the address that reported you as spam, your deliverability will be hurt.

7. **Manage Your Email Bounces Properly** - This is probably the most mismanaged process in the golf industry. If your provider isn't doing this correctly, they are flushing your email database down the drain.

There are two types of bounces that occur:

Hard Bounces – These are bounces that occur because the email address just isn't active anymore. These should be immediately removed from your database.

Soft Bounces – There are many of reasons a soft bounce can occur. The most common are reasons like "Mailbox Full," "Email Account Unavailable," or "System not Accepting Message."

These should not be immediately removed from your email database because the receiving server isn't telling you it's a bad email address. Your system should try resending to them and monitor the bounce that is received. If it continues to receive the same bounce message after a few tries then it is acceptable for the email address to be removed, however, if it receives different messages, it shows that the receiving server is having issues. This is EXTREMELY common with a lot of the major mail providers such as AOL.com, Yahoo.com, and Hotmail.com.

You should instead be monitoring your bounces to see if any problems are occurring. Your provider should be showing you the reasons for what types of bounces are occurring, if they aren't, they probably don't want you to see something.

8. **Send Emails Out Regularly** – If you do not send emails out on a regular basis, your subscribers will forget they subscribed. They

then will most likely report you as spam, hurting your deliverability.

9. **Remove Inactive Email Addresses** – This one will be painful, but it's something everyone should do that no one does. If someone hasn't opened an email from you in the last 12 months, remove their email.

   Yes, I know, you've spent so many years building your club's email list to the size that it currently is but, the greater the number of inactive contacts, the more your IP reputation rate suffers which will impact your deliverability.

10. Avoid suspect spam phrases. There are hundreds to avoid if you want your e-mails read, but here are a few key ones.

    ✔ Free

    ✔ You won

    ✔ Amazing

    ✔ Special offer

    ✔ Promotion

11. Be careful with your subject lines. Spam Assassin is particularly interested in subject lines. Here are a few subject line no-no's to learn from:

    ✔ Contains "FREE" in all caps

    ✔ Starts with "Free"

    ✔ GUARANTEED

    ✔ Starts with dollar amount

    ✔ Subject is all in capitals

    ✔ Subject talks about savings

12. **Mobile Responsive Email Design -** Over 50% of all emails were opened on a mobile device in 2016. If your emails do not look correct on a mobile device, it hurts your deliverability and causes unsubscribes!

How often should you mail?

This is one of the most asked questions at my live speaking events. Everyone one has an opinion on this topic, but like most untested opinions about marketing, they are usually wrong. Most people email too little, yes too little. It's a simple fact the more you mail, the more you make. As long as the email is interesting, fun, entertaining, valuable to the reader!

General guidelines:

o   Newsletter once a month

o   Updates twice a week even three in season but segment and target different groups

o   Make your emails add value to your customers' lives!

o   Make your emails add entertainment to their lives!

o   Make your email marketing a positive extension of your club's overall experience!

o   The key to email marketing success is consistency and creativity.

o   Send emails at least once and preferably twice per week

o   Stay on a schedule find the best days and best times for your club

o   Use a creative mix of offers and content

o   Variety is the spice of life, YET the typical club sends the same type of emails week after week, which quickly turns people off. You have to keep readers on their toes by mixing it up, so they open your e-mail just to see what you are doing this week!

Give your emails a personality

One of the biggest mistakes I see being made by course owners is not inserting their own personalities into their e-mail. Part of the advantage of having a small business is that you are a real person. Readers can contact you, agree, disagree, and so forth. All of your articles could be from other people. The key is to add some of yourself to your content. What you need to do is add in a few paragraphs you wrote yourself at the top of the e-zine. Do an editorial section, just like in magazines to talk about what's going on at your club. Tell your readers how you feel about your course, how it was built, what the design philosophy was, its history, and so on. Talk about current events, politics, or what you love about golf. Be personal. You may be so afraid of making mistakes in this area that you don't do anything. So make some mistakes; we all do. It's part of being human.

What you say may offend some people, and they may unsubscribe from your e-zine. So what? They weren't planning on buying from you anyway. I'm not telling you to purposely offend anyone, just letting you know it's going to happen. Use spell checkers and have someone edit your writing for you. But guess what? There are still going to be mistakes people will let you know about.

People always ask me how I have gotten my name published all over the web. Here's the secret...

Be a real person.

It's not what you were expecting, is it? It's not exciting or highly technical. It's just the truth. People online are looking for people who are real, who have opinions, and who make mistakes. One of my most popular articles being published around the web mentions my dog, Winston. Some people won't like you mentioning "daily- life" items such as this. Let them unsubscribe. The ones who stay on your list will buy more once they know you. Personality is one of the most underused tools in the marketing arsenal.

Open 24 hours with an e-mail auto responder follow-ups

By installing autoresponder software on your website, you can, in effect, be in business 24 hours a day. This option lets you preload a series of letters, answers to questions, tips, or any other printed material, and then e-mail the specific information about your business back to the customer on demand. It's like the old fax-on- demand but quicker, faster, and in clear print.

Use Marketing Automation to take follow-ups to the next level

It's now possible to have custom emails triggered just by people spending time on specific pages, or watching 30 seconds of your video (see *Chapter 12 – Building the Perfect Website for your Club* for more on this exciting topic.)

Check your e-mail often

Speed is king on the Internet. Customers don't expect to wait until tomorrow for an answer. Check your e-mail and respond throughout the day, not just at the end of the day. Many courses we talked with don't even do it every day.

Using these strategies will allow you to connect more often, provide better service, and acquire and keep more happy customers.

SUMMARY

Email is a powerful tool for golf marketing. With its speed, low cost, and ease of customization, it should be your favorite tool. Always keep in mind however that your email is an extension of your club's experience.

CHAPTER FIFTEEN

Legendary Sales

GETTING READY TO MAXIMIZE SALES

R ecently I had a call from a major resort asking what one idea I could give them to instantly improve revenue. The answer was easy and would have been the same had the caller wanted to sell more memberships, more banquets, more real estate, or even more tee times.

Train your people how to sell!

Nowhere in this entire book will you get faster results in terms of pure income than in this and the following chapter on how to sell.

Few people in the golf club business genuinely love selling. Fewer still are good at it! (Read the bonus chapter for some horror stories.) In many ways, it's not surprising that most people don't like to sell. Selling not only has a bad image in many people's minds, *it often deserves it!* Telemarketing calls at dinner time, pushy salespeople who won't take no for an answer, and products and services that don't live up to the sales claims. These have all contributed to the bad image that sales has today.

In defense of sales, almost everyone sells in their everyday lives. Teachers need to sell students on the benefits of paying attention. Spouses sell their ideas to each other. Children sell their parents on staying up for that special TV show, and so on. Practice will bring comfort if you have the right attitude.

Increasing your sales skills by even a few increments can dramatically increase your club's income. Imagine if you closed two out of ten leads instead of one—you have just doubled sales at NO cost! Even small improvements in how you answer the phone, handle objections, and close can have a massive impact on your club's bottom line. Few, if any, clubs engage in meaningful sales training.

Before you can sell, there are several things you will need to understand in more detail. First, you must understand the fears that hold most people back from maximizing their sales potential. Next, you must learn about bonding with prospects and developing rapport. Finally, you will discover secrets for quickly qualifying your prospects, so you focus more of your time on those people most likely to buy.

In this chapter, you will discover:

✔ How to overcome typical sales fear

✔ How to develop instant rapport

✔ How to separate suspects from prospects

✔ How to qualify prospects

GETTING MENTALLY READY TO SELL

> *It is not the mountain we conquer, but ourselves.*
> —Sir Edmund Hillary, first man to stand atop Mt.
> Everest

Sincerity sells

If you believe in what you are selling, your sincere attitude will communicate itself to your prospective customers. But you must have a positive attitude about the sales situation as well. If you feel uncomfortable selling, your prospect will feel uncomfortable buying from you. I'll use membership sales as my major example here, but the concepts apply to selling lessons, real estate, or clothing in the pro shop!

CONQUERING THE THREE GREAT FEARS

Before you can set off in pursuit of your quest for sales excellence, you must overcome the three great fears that hold back mere ordinary mortals. These fears exist in almost everyone, even great salespeople to a degree. They are:

- ✔ Fear of money
- ✔ Fear of responsibility
- ✔ Fear of failure

Until you have confronted these fears and put them behind you forever, you will not achieve your true sales potential.

FEAR OF MONEY

Believe it or not, many salespeople are afraid to ask for money. I was giving a seminar in South Carolina when I realized that the membership directors I was dealing with were victims of this dreaded affliction. I devised a simple little exercise where they paired off, and each of them said to the other, "Our memberships are $50,000."

I had trouble deciding if the results were tragic or hilarious! The first few times we did it, three of the membership directors actually couldn't get the words out of their mouths. We practiced for half an hour, going up and down in various increments until they could say "$100,000" just as easily as "ten bucks." By the membership directors participating in this exercise, and then my explaining the reasons for their reluctance to ask for large sums of money, they were able to conquer this long-held fear.

Why should membership salespeople be afraid to ask for money?

Salespeople may be afraid to ask for large sums of money because they don't have enough money to buy the memberships they are selling. The fact that they are selling a club they cannot afford may lead them to believe, at least subconsciously, that other people can't afford it either. Membership directors too often place a mental barrier on themselves and, in doing so, thwart their own efforts to obtain the success they deserve.

In my work with the PGA I have found that despite the fact that golf professionals are working with some of the most affluent individuals in the country, many of them are desperately afraid of asking for money. In this case, it's not because they don't make decent money themselves but because they don't want to be thought of as salespeople. What they don't seem to appreciate is that 90 percent of the people they deal with are businessmen or former businessmen who aren't offended by being asked for money. They expect it!

Overcoming your fear of money

It's okay to make money selling memberships or anything else! The more people you help to enjoy the benefits of what you offer, the more money you deserve to make. Whether or not *you* can afford to join your club does not mean that others can't. Whether or not you think it's expensive doesn't matter at all. Put your personal thoughts and prejudices away. Let your prospects decide whether or not they will spend their money. It's your job to give them the opportunity.

FEAR OF RESPONSIBILITY

The "demented mole" syndrome: Time management

A key factor in accepting responsibility is how you manage your time. Since every salesperson in the world starts the day with the same amount of time, it's the way you use that time that ultimately determines your success.

Treat your work time like gold so you can enjoy maximum results in a shorter period of time (a strategy that will provide you with greater free time). Follow a carefully scheduled plan of appointments and follow ups, and never fall victim to the dreaded demented mole syndrome that has struck down so many potential salespeople in their primes.

I first witnessed the effects of the demented mole syndrome at my local golf club when I was a teenager. I was helping a friend who had secured the contract to rebuild the 16th green. At one point during the afternoon, we were waiting for the arrival of some gravel trucks. I watched a workman fill up a wheelbarrow with soil, then move it to the other side of the green and dump it. This was a distance of approximately thirty-five yards. After wandering around for a few minutes doing nothing, he filled up the wheelbarrow again and moved the soil back to its original position!

There were, of course, a million and one other more productive things he could have been doing, but this worker chose instead to focus on waiting for the gravel. In his mind, there was absolutely nothing else of importance except looking busy and waiting for the gravel trucks.

99% of failures come from people who have a habit of making excuses.
—George Washington Carver

There are always papers to be shuffled, mail to be read, reports to write, and desks to clear. There are always things that can take your attention and time—the economy, the weather, the time of day. The trained eye can easily spot the afflicted. They plan extensively. Despite always looking busy, they never actually accomplish anything! I'll bet if you look around your club, you'll find someone already displaying advanced symptoms.

Get a day planner, a laptop computer, a contact program, and a cellular phone. You don't need anything else. *You are now armed and dangerous!*

Take responsibility for your own actions, time management, and results.

FEAR OF FAILURE OR REJECTION

One of the reasons mature people stop learning is they become less and less willing to risk failure.
—John Gardner

Sometimes the problem that holds salespeople back is fear of failure or rejection. If membership directors had real faith in their clubs, they wouldn't feel rejected when prospects say no but would sympathize with the prospects for not having the wisdom or money to take advantage of the opportunity they are being offered.

A young up-and-coming executive with IBM approached the company president, Thomas Watson, Sr., and asked him the key to success. The older man turned to the younger and announced, "Fail twice as fast." The young man, perplexed, asked the question again. "But, Mr. Watson, I really, really want badly to make it. Please tell me what should I do?" "In that case," replied Watson, "fail three times as fast."

Sound advice, indeed, from one of the smartest salespeople who ever lived. Watson had learned that rather than fear failure, you must embrace it in order to become a Legendary Salesperson.

What the younger man failed to understand is that the quicker you get the inevitable failures behind you, the sooner you will reach success. If you double the number of phone calls you make in a day, it will probably double your failure rate. But it will almost certainly double your sales at the same time.

What's the worst that can happen?

When you make a phone call, greet an appointment, or welcome a "walk-in," what is the worst thing that can occur? I mean, after you have introduced yourself, made a presentation, and asked them to join, what's the absolute worst thing that can happen to you?

The prospect can hang up, walk out, call your mother names, or say no. That's it! Those are the worst things that can possibly happen. Compared to the millions of people who are dying every day, rejection is pretty minor! Great! Now let's move on.

There is one small problem we didn't mention—**EGO!** Our fragile human egos are such that when a person rejects our proposition, we take it as a personal affront. We feel humiliated, embarrassed, or even belittled. Rejection attacks our self-confidence and self-esteem.

Yet if we can let it go for what it is—a rejection of a sales proposition—we will have jumped a hurdle that many never cross.

Sales is a numbers game

You know that when people don't buy a membership, they are *not* rejecting you! You know that when people can't afford a membership, they're *not* rejecting you. You know that when people are looking for a free round of golf, they're *not* rejecting you. How could it be personal when they don't even know *you*?

Yes, it can *feel* like rejection; but come on, it's not!

Membership sales is a numbers game. Depending on the quality of your leads, only 1 in 20 or 1 in 30 of the people you see has any interest in buying a membership. So when most people say no, they're *not* rejecting you.

Yes, many people will say no to you if you're doing your job. But every no gets you closer to the person who wants to join. And even the people who say no can give you referrals to friends who are more serious about membership.

So even if you *feel* like you're being rejected, you're NOT. You can't get over your feelings immediately, but you can begin. Take control of your feelings and move on to successful membership sales.

Our greatest glory is not in never falling, but in rising every time we fall.
—Confucius

The power of persistence: The five reasons you must persist

Persistence is a virtue that many salespeople overlook. There are five key reasons why you must be persistent if you are to join the ranks of Legendary Salespeople. Knowing them will benefit both you and your members.

1 The customer doesn't always know what's in his best interest at first. You may have new information for him. You have to persist and educate him.

2 Prospects are almost always reluctant to change. You must persist and help them realize what the cost will be if they don't change.

3 Your prospects often have difficulty comparing different products and services and become confused. Confused people are afraid of making a mistake so instead of buying they procrastinate on making a decision. You must persist in your attempts to minimize the confusion and provide them with a clear path to enjoying the benefits of your club membership!

4 Prospects have many different priorities. You must persist and help them arrange their priorities in such a way that your club moves up the list and helps them achieve their goals.

5 Some prospects are just not ready to buy right now. They might, however, buy next month or next year. You must persist to make sure you are still in the forefronts of their minds when they eventually do!

BUILDING RAPPORT

Rapport is the ability to bond with another person as you would with a friend, and, for a Legendary Salesperson, it is the most sought after of all conditions. Good rapport puts other people at their ease. They treat you as a *person* they are comfortable with, *not a sales*person.

You start most sales relationships with one strike against you. People assume that you have *your* interests at heart rather than theirs. Thus, they naturally don't trust you until you can demonstrate that you are interested in them and can be helpful to them. Because of this negative conditioning, it is essential that you go the extra mile to be courteous, friendly, and professional as you start building rapport.

Calming your prospects' fears

When people walk into your club to explore membership options, it is very probable that they do so with some degree of trepidation. They are unsure of what to expect. Maybe you'll put a lot of pressure on them, and it will be unpleasant. Maybe they won't be able to justify the purchase to their wives. Maybe they won't feel that they fit in.

One way to make most people more comfortable is to immediately tell them what will happen. For instance, you could say something like:

> Here's what I was planning to do in our time together: Ask you a few questions about your golfing interests, tell you about our club, show you around, and answer your questions. Does that sound reasonable? Is there anything you want to know before we get started?

Your foremost task in the initial sales contact is to make your prospect feel comfortable with you. Until this happens, it will be impossible for the prospect to make a buying decision. Use the first few minutes to remove the prospect's fear and help him or her to relax.

If you don't sell yourself first, you won't sell anything

Men in general judge far more from appearances than from reality.
All men have eyes, but few have the gift of penetration.
—Niccolo Machiavelli

If prospects don't like you, they will not buy from you! That's pretty simple, isn't it? Consider for a moment. Do you buy products and services from people you don't like? No? Neither do most other people. Above all else, selling requires *selling yourself* to the prospect. If you don't do that, no sales technique in the world is going to save you.

The first few seconds of your contact with a prospect can determine your success in any sales interview. First impressions are lasting impressions and are usually the right impressions, at least as far as your prospect is concerned.

Your appearance

The way you dress is very important in selling. Always be careful to strike a happy medium between *over*dressing and *under*dressing. Smartly attired people have an air of success about them. Without overpowering the audience you will be selling to, make an effort to improve your image by improving the quality of your clothing and tailoring. In the words of Henry Ward Beecher, "Clothes and manner do not make the man; but, when he is made, they greatly improve his appearance."

Is your office destroying rapport?

If you are selling from your own office or sales area, take heed. The way your office looks and feels can cost you sales. Be sure to avoid displaying anything that could create a negative response in a prospect or customer. The power of one negative image is almost ten times stronger than the power of one positive image. Your ultimate sales skill is to create in your prospect a powerful mental image of enjoying the benefits you offer.

Making your office sales friendly

Make your office the image of what you want to accomplish. If you want to sell memberships, decorate your office to inspire the prospect to want to join your club. Try hanging beautiful pictures of your best holes. Add pictures of celebrities playing at your club, big social events, and so on. Impress them with the quality of your club. Testimonial letters from current members are never out of place!

The best sales organizations in the world set up their offices in a very carefully thought-out way to inspire trust and positive feelings. They remove clutter and distraction so that the prospect's focus remains on the sales process.

Develop winning personal traits

When asked what great secret he had found to influence people to his way of thinking, Abraham Lincoln replied, "If you would win a man over to your cause, first convince him that you are his sincere friend." To a great extent, the way people react to you depends on the little things—like smiling. When you are introduced to someone, always respond with a warm and friendly smile. Shake hands firmly because there are few things that turn people off quicker than a limp handshake. Stand up straight with your shoulders back and chest forward. Make good eye contact and generally let the other person know by your body language that you are a successful, professional, friendly, and confident individual who is genuinely glad to meet them.

How do you sound?

Next, to your appearance, the tone of your voice and the way you deliver your words are the most important parts of making a good impression on the prospect. Make your conversation enthusiastic, friendly, and professional. If the prospect talks in a loud voice, raise yours slightly above its normal level. If the prospect speaks quietly, lower your voice a couple of decibels. Mirror your prospect's speech patterns by speaking a little slower or a little faster as appropriate. Remember, people establish the highest levels of rapport with others who are just like them! Your voice can indicate to prospects that you are indeed like them.

Body language

The value of matching your prospect is equally true of basic body language. If the person you are dealing with has a military bearing and stands straight and tall, rather than lounging or slumping, it will definitely pay you to do the same. In your office, if the prospect leans forward, so should you. In short, mirroring your prospect's largely unconscious physical demeanor is one of the most effective ways to rapidly establish rapport. Be sure to use this technique in conjunction with the others mentioned in this chapter.

Compliments

Giving genuine compliments about your prospect or his possessions will almost certainly bring a favorable response. However, use caution in this area. Prospects easily detect insincerity. If you are insincere, you will lose their confidence, never to regain it. There are ways to make sure this never happens to you. Never make a compliment you do not mean, and add a qualifying statement to all your compliments for added weight.

Qualifiers prove your sincerity. Your compliment is made more meaningful and personal if you add a brief remark to prove you mean what you say. For example, you might say to a woman who walks into your place of business, "That's a beautiful sweater." Then immediately add a qualifier. "I gave one just like that to my wife, last Christmas." You have demonstrated your sincerity. Why would you buy a sweater for your wife if you didn't find it attractive?

What's in a name?

One of the surest ways to develop rapport is to remember a person's name. In his classic book, *How to Win Friends and Influence People*, Dale Carnegie stated, "The sound of a person's name said correctly is one of the nicest sounds in the world, at least to them." Using someone's name is indeed one of the sincerest compliments you can pay a person. It builds self-esteem and lets him know you think he is important.

How to open a rapport-building conversation

In order to build rapport beyond the superficial stages, you have to get the prospect to talk to you. The best way to accomplish this is to ask open-ended questions. Open-ended questions are questions that can't be answered with a simple yes or no. They demand a more detailed response. Not only does this method build rapport, since you allow the customer to respond without interruption or contradiction, but it also provides you with valuable data for use in the sales presentation. After you exchange names, it's time to start questioning as discussed in the next chapter. This time, however, we will be using the responses not just for data, but also to develop future questions.

> Where are you from, Jack? [In states with rapidly expanding populations, like California, Florida, Arizona and Nevada, this is a good question, since the majority of people were born elsewhere.]

> What line of work are you in?

Move smoothly from basic questions to more specific lines of inquiry.

> How long have you lived here?

> That's an interesting occupation. How did you get into it?

The more others talk about themselves, the more rapport you will be building, especially if you use active listening techniques.

Developing active listening techniques to increase rapport

Active listening means showing the prospect that you are not only listening to what he has to say, but you are interested in what he is saying. Here are some of the ways you can do this:

   ✔ By holding eye contact and not looking around at anything else

✔ By nodding your head at appropriate points

✔ By raising an eyebrow (like Mr. Spock in Star Trek!) to express surprise

✔ By laughing, smiling, and making occasional comments like, "Yes," "Uh-huh," or "I see" to show you are an active participant in the conversation, even though you aren't doing the talking

You will find that such active listening will draw people out and they will consider you an interesting person.

How people process information affects rapport

After all, when you come right down to it, how many people speak the same language, even when they speak the same language?
—Russell Hoban

Essentially, people process information in one of three main ways—visually, aurally, and kinesthetically. Knowing which of these applies to a particular person can give you a much better chance of getting your point across.

If a prospect asks to *see* the course or comments on the view, he is almost certainly visual (and the majority of people fall into this category.) If he wants to *try* it for himself or comments on the *smell* of the trees, he is probably kinesthetic. If he asks you to *tell* him about your course or *explain* membership benefits, then he is probably auditory. In cases where someone displays a combination of two or even all three of these forms, you can use multiple approaches, but one of them will usually be dominant. Understanding this human characteristic can be invaluable to your presentation by helping you to communicate better and faster with your prospect.

Asking a kinesthetic prospect to look at something is not nearly as valuable as having him do it himself. If you prevent a kinesthetic person from "feeling" things, you risk losing the sale. In the same way, if you simply talk to a visually oriented person you will soon lose his interest.

If you can't tell which method your prospect uses to process his information, try to use all three in your speech patterns. (It takes a little practice!) You will either find out what you need to know or at least will be sure that you have covered all the bases.

QUALIFYING YOUR PROSPECTS

Once rapport has been achieved, the next step in the sales process is to qualify your prospects.

One of the biggest complaints by salespeople is that they are receiving "unqualified leads." The corresponding complaint from managers is that their salespeople can't close sales from the "great leads" they are given. To have success in any sales, you need to set up a system and then measure the results to demonstrate its effectiveness. You need to produce qualified leads, train your salespeople well, and measure performance.

What is a qualified prospect?

Traditionally, a qualified prospect is someone who has a need for your product or service and the means to pay for it. If you are a golf course selling daily rounds, any regular golfer in your area— or even visiting— would be technically qualified. With golf, you're usually talking about a "want" rather than an actual "need."

If you are a club selling memberships or a golf realty development, you will want further qualifications, such as high income. And you will need further information about their "means."

You need to help them justify the purchase. You need to find out how they would pay for it and if financing will be involved. And you need to find out how they will measure the value they receive for their investment.

Some prospects are more equal than others!

If you look at your prospects as a whole, you will get a very wide range of people—from those chomping at the bit to sign up to those with no intention of ever buying. Think of them as A, B, C, and D prospects.

The success of membership programs is based on generating the total number of leads needed to reach your goals. Successful programs recognize that leads come in various qualities even with qualifiers in place:

- ✔ "A" leads include referrals, golfers moving to the area, members of other clubs unhappy with their current clubs, and social climbers.

- ✔ "B" leads include daily fee players with no permanent home who can afford what you offer if they are shown the service and value they expect.

- ✔ "C" leads might be prospects or might not. They could be a source of future members and should be kept on a tickler program.

- ✔ "D" leads are simply not real prospects.

Referrals and people new to your area are often the best prospects. Direct mail leads offer the next best prospects since they can be prequalified by income, zip code, and other demographics. Telemarketing produces a wide range of leads, but most tend to do better than average simply based on the professions that are targeted such as doctors, lawyers, and so forth.

Web inquiries and telephone inquiries from newspaper or magazine ads tend to be far less qualified unless the ad was specifically written to discourage people from calling, which is an art in itself. (For instance, an ad might mention the financial qualifications needed to buy.)

The bottom line is that all leads should be counted and standards created for the conversion of each kind. Referrals might sell at the rate of 1 in 2 or 3, while web leads might sell 1 in 20 or 30. You should measure an average return from each source.

Questions to ask

You need to develop a series of questions that not only qualifies people but goes further to expand their thinking about their needs and your offer. For instance, confirming that prospects play golf and fit your income category isn't enough. You need to cover frequency of play, specific reasons they don't play more often, social influences, and so on. Prospects need to see you as helping them satisfy their needs, not selling to them to meet yours! Your questions need to be interesting to them. They need to enjoy the conversation.

The key qualifying questions you ask will depend on the nature of your club, your offer, and your location.

Here are some examples:

✔ How often do you play?

✔ What's your handicap?

✔ Where do you play now? [If you know your market well, you should know if the answer is public or private, high- end or low-end, is the prospect looking to move up or down?]

✔ What three things do you enjoy most about playing?

✔ Does your spouse play?

✔ Do you have children? Do they play?

✔ What type of other activities does your family enjoy besides golf? (swimming, tennis, etc.)

✔ What type of work do you do?

✔ How often will you be visiting the area? (second memberships)

✔ Do you entertain clients on the course?

✔ What are the most important aspects of club membership for you? (get a game, great layout, convenient, etc.)

Casually work the three or four most important questions you need into your initial conversation.

Qualified is not motivated!

The key flaw in most sales systems is that they don't acknowledge that *most technically qualified prospects are not motivated to act now*. For outings, weddings, and banquets, motivation is usually not a problem. That is, those prospects need to contract with a facility in a specific time frame, so they are motivated.

For lessons, golf real estate, and club memberships, motivation can become a problem. Prospects may have an interest in making a purchase, but they have no urgency. The decision can be put off forever. Selling daily rounds falls in between. A regular golfer doesn't have to play at any particular time, but they are likely to want to play fairly soon.

Another reason people will delay acting is because they don't feel a connection to you. There is no relationship. They have no reason to trust you. They have no desire to please you. This is where long-term qualifying can come into play. If you approach prospects realizing that many will take a year to commit to action or make up their minds, you will design a sales system that allows you to keep in touch and build the relationship in addition to finding the short- term sales.

Qualifying prospects out?

There are cases when finding prospects is very expensive for you, but they are also worth a lot, for instance, when you are selling golf real estate or memberships in an expensive club. In these cases, you have to decide how much a prospect is worth to you and how "hard" you want to qualify them.

Each case is different depending on your prospecting and closing systems. To decide what is right for you, you'll need to test.

Let's take a typical case we've worked with in selling memberships for various clubs. Say the membership is $100,000, excluding any special offers, rebates, and so on. And let's say that most of the club is built or is a conversion. We call wealthy people in the area of the club and invite them to a free round of golf, and a presentation on club membership that usually includes breakfast. We might organize these events for groups of 20 prospects.

It could take a month or two to produce 400 membership prospects. All prospects are qualified in the sense that they say they play golf, are interested in playing the course, can afford the membership fee, and know that they will be subject to a sales presentation. Here is where further qualifying and screening begins. Some people don't show up for the presentations. During the tour and golf, salespeople talk to the prospects. Perhaps only three have any serious interest in membership. After the presentation, these are the ones you focus on, as well as any other prospects who put themselves forward.

This level of qualifying means that most of your money is spent on people who aren't good prospects. With a well-designed sales approach, this still pays off handsomely in sales. However, you could take a harder line. By requiring people to take an action step, you are qualifying them further. For instance, you can require them to send you something, to meet with you, or to give you further information.

A simple way to screen out people who are only interested in a free round of golf but don't care enough to work for it is to require prospects to sign up for your presentation at your club's website. You direct them to the proper page, and they have to answer some qualifying questions there. In our experience, this cuts out about half of your "prospects."

You have to track your results to decide what screening and qualifying approach is best for you. Is it better to have 20 prospects of whom three are serious or ten of whom one to two are serious?

The answer is not simple. Some people end up buying when they didn't plan to. This can be the case with memberships or real estate. People may come for the free golf and become more interested when they see your offer.

As we said earlier, the only way you can see how your sales skills match up best with your prospect pool is to test different approaches and see which one is most cost effective for you. We generally like to get more prospects there, even if they are weaker. People can't judge your club until they've seen it. And more people seeing it creates more word-of-mouth and referral possibilities.

Why qualified prospects don't raise their hands

One complication in qualifying people is that sometimes your best prospects won't say that they want what you have to offer and can afford it. Why do people deny being good prospects?

They do it for many reasons that vary from wanting to stay in control of the situation to wanting to make you jump through a few hoops. Some reasons can work for you; others create problems.

Perhaps the most common reason that the wealthy "hide" themselves is that they don't want to be bothered. Many of the well-to-do are approached every day with a new offer. Many companies go to great lengths to identify the wealthiest one percent of the country who can buy almost anything. (The same goes for the top 5–10 percent as well.)

Another reason for sales resistance is the desire to see how good you are—how persistent and how skilled. These people are sophisticated in business. They are familiar with most sales approaches. If they have time, they may entertain themselves watching how you sell to them. They may also use resistance as a way to test your sincerity. They throw up obstacles but expect you to overcome them. They reason that if you're willing to put a lot of effort into signing them up, you may be more likely to put effort into making them happy once they buy.

False prospects

On the other hand, there are people who will lie about their interest. These people may be retired and miss the action of business. Or they may simply like whatever freebies you offer. Some prospects are even fantasizing. By pretending that they will buy, they get some fantasy pleasure at little cost.

Interestingly enough, there are situations where people who have no intention of buying end up doing so. Timeshare vacation rentals are a prime example. Almost no one who goes to a presentation intends to buy, but enough do to keep the hard-sell sales practices going. So you'll have to make your best guess on how hard to qualify prospects and then test to develop a better profile of actual buyers.

If you're selling something like memberships where you're willing to spend some money on prospects, you can use credit checks as one way to screen out false leads. You will also find that people who are referred to you are much more serious than people who respond to ads. And the more freebies you offer, the more "Looky Lous" you'll get.

SUMMARY

To maximize your sales potential you must understand and overcome the common fears that hold back most people in sales— fear of money, fear of responsibility, and fear of rejection. In sales, success is up to you. Manage your time well and realize that the more no's you get, the more sales you will make.

Learn how to quickly build rapport with your prospects by asking open-ended questions, demonstrating active listing techniques, and being aware of your body language. Once rapport is established, probe to qualify the prospect. There is no point in spending time selling to people who don't want to buy. By setting up a qualifying system, you will improve your results, make prospects happier, and have more fun selling. Design your system for both short- and long-term sales. While you harvest the "low hanging fruit," you will be building relationships for long-term sales. Even prospects who never buy may become sources of referrals and positive word of mouth when they are treated professionally and respectfully.

CHAPTER SIXTEEN

Legendary Sales Part 2

PRESENTATIONS, OBJECTIONS, AND CLOSING

Once a prospect has been greeted, bonded with, and qualified, it's time to get to the meat of the presentation, handle objections, and close the sale. All presentations should be scripted and orchestrated for optimum results. If you do not approach presentations in a scripted systematic manner, your approach and results will differ from day to day and person to person—but you won't know what is causing the variation!

To get the most from your sales, you must follow a system and be prepared with perfect answers to any question. Since you can double your profits by doubling your sales results, it will pay you to keep track of what you're doing and what works!

Objections are a natural part of the membership sales process. While you might prefer that people come in with their checks in hand, already all made out to your club, it's natural for people to have questions or concerns just as *you* would in any major purchasing decision. These concerns are generally expressed as objections. An objection is nothing more than a question in the mind of the buyer that has to be defined and answered. It gives you the chance to clarify or improve your presentation. A prospect who does not raise objections is not engaged in thinking about your presentation.

Most sales are lost simply by not asking for the sale! Close early and close often. Find the closing techniques that best suit your style and audience and use them!

In this chapter, you will discover:

✔ How to build a perfect presentation

✔ How to uncover and isolate objections

✔ The five-step process to deal with objections

✔ The *feel, felt, found* way to deal with objections

✔ Exactly what to say to specific objections

✔ How to spot closing signals

✔ How to close

> *I never learn anything just by talking. I only learn things when I ask questions.*
> **—Lou Holtz**

MAKING AN EFFECTIVE PRESENTATION

Because each presentation is different, this book can only give you pieces to use and an approach to put "standard" pieces together with your own custom material. (On a consulting basis, Legendary Marketing can develop custom presentations for you, as well as train your staff.)

As you design your presentation, start by assuming that everyone who has qualified as a prospect wants to buy and buy *now*. This may eventually prove to be incorrect but assume it anyway. Many people who are on the "edge" will make the decision to buy without your having to make a great deal of extra effort simply because you are so confident they want what you have to offer and today is the day they should buy.

Getting the audience involved in the action

The more senses you can bring into play during the presentation, the better your chances of making a sale! Clearly, with golf, you have many senses involved: the visual, the feel of the club, the smell of the cut grass, the sounds of players, and so on.

Using questions for involvement

Questions can be an important part of your presentation by getting the prospects *involved* with your points. Prospects can't just sit back and pretend to listen when you ask them questions. And often, even if they wanted to remain detached, good questions will "hook" them into considering your club more seriously. Open-ended questions—questions that can't be answered yes or no—are best. Ask questions that get them talking about things that relate to features or benefits of your club, such as how they find business contacts now or what their wife likes to do.

The points you need to cover

Many people think that giving a great presentation requires a gift of gab or a certain type of personality. Not so! There are many ways to give a winning presentation, the best of which is to write a script and practice it until you can deliver a legendary performance.

A good presentation script will read a lot like a good direct mail letter. It will be full of features and benefits. While features are more objective, your emphasis should be on the benefits. There are usually more benefits than you think, and many of them are several levels deep. For instance, playing golf may be relaxing. That's a benefit for your prospect. Being relaxed may mean your prospect is more cheerful with his wife. That's a benefit for her. And when spouses treat each other better, it improves their relationship. The kids are less stressed by their parents fighting. That's a benefit. (And more kids may be on the way, which we won't talk about!)

You see the point. You can spend a long time listing multiple benefits, which may be subtle but more important than the obvious benefits. Another example: Most people like more money, yet your club costs money. But they'll make contacts that can lead to better jobs, more business, and so on. And when you have more money, you can afford to relax more, like at a club! So you'll be able to relax *and* make more money to pay for your membership. Instead of having to wait to relax, you can relax while you're investing in your future. Not simple, but workable.

List the features of your club that you want to cover in your presentation. They should include features such as:

- ✔ History
- ✔ Regional points of interest (for recent movers)
- ✔ Types of members
- ✔ Social activities
- ✔ The club house
- ✔ The course(s)
- ✔ Tournaments
- ✔ Other facilities
- ✔ Membership costs and financing programs

Now list the benefits that come from your features. (You may skip many features and go straight to benefits in your presentation.)

- ✔ Family recreation and togetherness
- ✔ Safe place for the kids
- ✔ Relaxation
- ✔ New friends
- ✔ More social life
- ✔ Exercise

✔ Business contacts

✔ Status

✔ Meeting the "right" type of people

✔ A place to take customers

✔ Money saved on vacations and entertainment

When you simply spell out each benefit you want to convey, you have your basic presentation. Add a few member testimonials, and you're well on your way.

Quitting while you're ahead

One thing that epitomizes Legendary Selling is knowing exactly when to stop presenting and start closing. The key to selling golf is getting the prospect excited about your offer. Once that has been accomplished, you must provide him with logical reasons why he must buy *today*. Then you must close. Continuing to talk after the prospect is ready to buy is overkill and often leads to lost sales rather than successful closing.

Anticipating objections

When Abraham Lincoln was a lawyer, he always summed up his opponent's arguments before he gave his side. That way the jury saw him as a fair man, and he got to "frame" his opponents points the way he wanted to. If you *know* that certain concerns will be in the prospect's mind during your presentation, you are usually better off dealing with them as part of the presentation. Otherwise, prospects will tend to not listen to *your* points as they think about the problems on their own. For instance, price is often a concern, so acknowledge it and show how the value your club delivers outweighs the cost. Another example is competitive clubs. You need to know how they compare to your club on all important dimensions. When people are looking at other clubs, you need to deal with them briefly in your presentation. Never "bad-mouth" other clubs. Say something like you hear they are very nice, then cover your relative advantages.

How to present to a couple

As a general rule of thumb, sell to the person of the same sex. If you are a man, direct your main attention to the man, and vice versa. However, you'll need to use eye contact and body language to make sure the second person is not excluded. Most wives are used to the husband receiving more sales attention for golf-related activities. They won't be offended if you direct things to their spouses. Just make sure that you keep in visual touch with them to let them know nonverbally that they are not being excluded. Husbands are often a little more sensitive about *not* being the center of attention.

Too many choices

Complexity is your enemy. It only confuses prospects. Design your presentation to offer no more than three options. If you have to present more than three options, do it in stages. For example, if you have nine options, offer three groups of three. Help your prospect to reach a decision on which group of options appears to be most suitable, then concentrate on those three options in detail. When you give people too many choices, they become confused. When they are confused, they become scared, and when they are scared, they rarely make a buying decision.

Reduce risk, build trust

Another thing you can do is use guarantees to reduce people's perceived risk. Make their choosing you a safe choice so that they can reap your benefits for themselves and their families. Written testimonials can produce some trust effect, especially if the testimonials are from people similar to them.

The to-the-point sales presentation

The entire sale process should, in most cases, take no longer than fifteen minutes from contact to close, unless you play a round with them! If you take too much time, your prospect will probably become bored or confused as the presentation drags on, and you will be frustrated as a result. Tighten up your presentation. Be fast, fluid, and professional. Act as if completing the sale is second nature to you, and you do it every hour of the day, week in and week out. After all, selling *should* become second nature to you!

Use emotion backed up by logic

You want to use emotion: the excitement the prospect experiences as a result of his perception of the benefits your club will bring him. Your prospect should feel that this pleasurable sensation is real and waiting for him and him alone.

Once prospects have decided to buy, they use logic to come up with good reasons to justify their decisions. Back up their reasons with your own supporting evidence. Indicate features and benefits that they may not have considered, and you will make the sale. Help them to see that their emotional reasons are also logical ones. Reinforce the buying decision by complimenting them on their choice and assuring them, sincerely, that you know they will get satisfaction and pleasure from their membership.

What's in it for me?

A basic motivating force that drives nearly everybody is "What's in it for me?" Some membership directors are so busy selling that they can't see the forest for the trees. Few, if any, potential members will be initially interested in the *quality* of the service you offer them.

That may come later. Initially, they will be much more concerned about what the club, and *you*, will do to make them better people — to improve their lives. You must understand that their decisions are often exercises in positive selfishness.

While your prospect *is* concerned about himself, there are multiple ways you can approach this. For instance, even if he is motivated by playing golf with "the boys," he may respond to looking good with his family by providing them with swimming or other activities. So you could show how he can justify the purchase to his wife (and himself) with family benefits. For instance, kids who play golf can get college golf scholarships. The kids will make better lifelong social contacts at the club. The family will save money on vacations, and so on. The more wants you can satisfy, the more problems you can solve, the more needs you can meet, the more that's in it for them, the more likely your sale. And the more personalized and reliable your service is, the more successful you will be!

Write it down

You should address all the above points and type up a script for selling memberships, outings, banquets, and anything else you sell. This should include diagrams of the very best places to stand as you deliver your lines and point at something of interest! It takes time, but once you have done it you will reap big dividends, and the script will always be there for training as staff comes and goes. (Legendary Marketing also offers custom sales manuals and follow- up training for everything from real estate sales to membership sales for those not wishing to tackle the project themselves.)

OVERCOMING OBJECTIONS

Objections are a necessary part of the membership sales process. Learn to deal with them, and you will close a much higher percentage of the prospects you meet. Unfortunately, many salespeople take objections personally, and their ability to complete the sale is adversely influenced by this negativity.

It's not personal. They are turning down buying, not turning down you!

Think of objections not as rejections but as steps toward your final goal. Rather than fearing objections, you need to ask good questions to bring them out. An objection is not the *end* of the sales process; it is the beginning! Many objections mask a real or perceived problem. For instance, if the prospect doesn't know anyone at your club, they will hesitate to join but may not bring up their "shyness" as a reason. You should anticipate this issue and others such as cost, and deal with them early by asking them if they have friends at your club, assuring them that there are other people like them, and so on.

Hidden objections are often associated with money. They will not want to admit that they are not qualified or don't have decision authority.

Overcoming objections is usually taught in a one-step sales approach, and it *is* one step for smaller items such as one lesson. But for memberships or real estate, you can't expect everyone to make a fast decision. As long as you have permission to keep in touch with the prospect, you are in the game. Keep in touch for the short term when they're in the decision-making mode. And if necessary, keep in touch for the long term if they either don't decide or join another club. Some objections will dissipate over time—"I'm happy with the course I play now." Either their course will make a "mistake," or you will use the repeated sales contacts to better build value. When you keep in touch with them, you build your credibility and sincerity. Put them on your e-mail newsletter list, and they will see all the activities they are missing!

That gives you something to build on to resell them on membership.

Sometimes, you have to break out of the sales–sales-resistance cycle that can be created between you and a prospect. You have to step back and say "George, I've talked to you several times about membership here and we don't seem to be making any progress. I don't want to keep bothering you—should I just leave you alone?" This will often turn the situation around—they'll start to sell you on why you should keep in touch! And they'll often tell you their true objection. The key is for them to talk to you person to person, *not* prospect to salesperson!

Some objections arise as the result of nothing more serious than a lack of understanding. Your presentation didn't come across. In these cases, it is necessary to further define and explain the benefits of your membership in clear and simple language. Use your membership kit as the excellent business tool it should be. Put it in front of the prospect and check off the listed benefits, giving a short explanation of each benefit as you go. When features and benefits are there in black and white, any misunderstandings should soon vanish.

Anticipate the objection

As mentioned earlier, many objections can be dealt with in the sales presentation by bringing them up before the prospect does and taking away the objection before it is even voiced. Those that can't be dealt with during the presentation should have already been anticipated, and a perfect answer scripted out as the response.

In a system, there can only be one perfect answer to any objection.

The answer to each objection should be carefully crafted to be the best answer possible, then should be learned and used by everyone on staff exactly as scripted. This is the type of approach used by Disney, Ritz Carlton, and other world-renowned companies for a simple reason—it works!

This may sound very rigid, but, if you think about it, it's true at least 95 percent of the time that a scripted answer works best. Sure, intuition and experience can come into play 5 percent of the time, but 95 percent of the time a well-orchestrated response will produce better results. That's why movies have scripts. That's why comedians have scripts and practice them, so they don't sound like scripts. Remember, 95 percent of the jokes you ever heard from Jim Carrey were scripted, rehearsed, practiced, and timed to be delivered as if they were natural and spontaneous. Let me give you an example.

Suppose the prospect asks: "How long does it typically take to play a round?"

Now let's look at how three different people could choose to answer that simple but *deadly* question.

That question could be answered in several ways:

✔ It takes about 4 hours and 45 minutes.

✔ It depends on what day you play; sometimes it's fast, sometimes it's slow.

✔ We are committed to a pace-of-play policy that ensures maximum enjoyment for all of our members.

Now all of these are possible answers to the question, but only one is the very best answer. I am sure you know it is the last one. The best answer will produce better results for you than an off-the-cuff answer every time. And not just for you, for everyone on the property.

There are five important things to remember when you are dealing with objections:

1 Listen carefully to the objection. Resist the temptation to jump in before you have heard the full objection. Sometimes the prospect will talk himself out of it before you say a word.

2 The first thing you should do after an objection is thank them! This changes the tone of your interaction from adversarial to cooperative.

It shows that you're not defensive or trying to avoid the objection. For instance, after you listen to an objection you could say, "I'm glad you brought that up." Or "Thanks for asking that question. It gives me the chance to explain…"

3 Never argue with a prospect. Remain calm and pleasant. They may just want you to listen to them.

4 If the objection is unclear, as in, "Well, I have to think about it," then ask more questions to isolate the real objection.

5 When you have the information you need, you can deal with the root of the objection.

Convert objections to benefits

Remember, objections are not a surprise for you. And they should not lure you into an argumentative situation. After some study of this chapter, and consideration of your club's situation, you will know the issues that people will raise. Each concern they bring up gives you a chance to clarify a point and build further rapport.

OTHER WAYS TO DEAL WITH OBJECTIONS

"Fast forward" your prospects to help them understand the benefits

In order to overcome an objection, it's very helpful to involve your prospect emotionally in how his future will improve from the moment he agrees to join your club. This is particularly true when dealing with money issues. By "fast forwarding" your prospect into the future, you can help him see how different his life will be if he joins your club.

I understand your hesitation about the investment Mr. Miller. Lots of our new members felt the same way. Even when they could easily afford it, they didn't want to make a mistake. For instance, George had his doubts but found that he actually made a *profit* on his membership because of the new business he did. Plus, he and his wife made many new friends and are enjoying life much more. And, by the way, the value of his membership has gone up as well.

The biggest problem in the world could have been solved when it was small.
—Witter Bynner

Feel, felt, found

In the fast-forward process above, we used a *feel, felt, found* method that can be adapted to handle many types of objections. When the prospect raises an objection, you sound agreeable by using three steps:

13. I understand how you *feel*. [This avoids being argumentative and takes their objection seriously.]

14. Many of our members *felt* that way before they joined. For instance, Mr. Miller is in your business/church/age group, and so forth. He worried about that but...

15. He *found* that [answer] plus his family enjoyed the club facilities, the contacts were valuable to his business, and so on.

The Feel-Felt-Found approach has been proven for over 50 years as a good way to respond to an objection and create a little story about someone with whom the prospect can identify. You can adapt it to almost any objection you encounter.

Testimonials

Just as examples about another member are important in dealing with objections, written testimonials can be invaluable. Gather a portfolio of letters from your satisfied members. Together they should address all the objections that your prospects will have.

The easiest way to obtain a range of testimonials covering different issues is to ask satisfied members to address particular issues. Your portfolio of testimonials will be impressive by itself. It can even be given to prospects while they wait. By organizing it according to type of objection, you can also use it when specific objections are raised. For instance, after you answer a couple of objections, as a change of pace, you might say "Instead of me answering that question, why don't I let one of our members do it for you," and bring out the relevant testimonial.

Isolating objections

There are two times when you need to isolate objections. When people make vague objections like "I need to think it over," "I'm not sure," or "I need to talk it over with," you don't have much to work with. In the specific objections dealt with later, we show you how to ask for the real objection. These approaches acknowledge prospects' need to think it over and then ask them what they need to think over.

The second time you need to isolate an objection is to find out if this is THE KEY objection. When there are several objections on the table, many times most of them are minor. Don't be distracted with secondary objections. Focus on finding the major wants and the major objection. For instance, if there is an objection that you know you can answer, don't just say yes. Say something like "If I can arrange flexible payments for you, are you ready to join today."

By isolating the objections that really matter to the prospect, you can answer them and move to close the sale.

What will others think?

A key decision blocker that is often overlooked is how others' feelings and views may affect the buying decision of your prospect. Where most membership purchases are concerned, the question is, "What will my wife think about the buying decision?" (This is even more important if you sell family memberships.) Sometimes, but by no means always, this question is verbalized as an objection. However, a man's ego may not allow him to tell you that he must consult with his wife before making a buying decision.

Any time a third person is brought into the sales decision, your presentation must take them into account. You need to give your prospect the ammunition they need to "sell" the spouse.

Business to business

If you sell corporate memberships, the other significant party to the deal tends to be the boss or department head. You must make sure your benefits work at the corporate level.

"I'm not sure head office is going to like it" is often heard from a corporate buyer. Try this solution. "That's why I suggest we get everyone involved in the decision. In my experience, when your executive officers participate, they'll have complete confidence in your decision." If you don't have all the decision makers present for your membership presentation, you may not have qualified the prospect properly.

Answering objections is NOT solving every concern

While I can give you a *lot* of ammunition here to answer objections, some can't be eliminated. For instance, your club doesn't have a tennis court, a pool, or whatever. You can't change that. You can only suggest that it is not crucial. (You may also be able to create a reciprocal arrangement with a non-golf club for the use of their facilities.)

You'll add to your rapport and credibility by being frank about things you can't change. At the end of answering objections, you or the prospect might agree that there are a couple of points that are not perfect. But that can still compare very favorably to other clubs, or them not joining anywhere. Nothing is perfect. Help your prospects make a decision anyway.

COMMON CONCERNS, OBJECTIONS, AND STALLS

In our 40-hour, five-day sales training course, we cover over 60 objections in detail. Here are eight examples of scripted responses to common questions and concerns.

I would prefer a course that does not have houses all around it—something a little further out of town.

I can certainly understand what you mean. Other members have said the same thing before they joined. The upside is that because the course is so close to the major highways and the places people live and work, they get a lot more use and value from their membership.

There are rumors the club is in serious financial straits.

I'm glad you brought that up since we want you to have every confidence about that issue. We have the certified financial statements of the club available. The owners have deep pockets and have committed $XYZ to demonstrate their commitment.

- or -

Interestingly, those rumors are being spread by a few unprofessional salespeople who are selling for competitive clubs and find that they can't match our benefits.

The price is too high!

I understand. Prices today are certainly higher than they used to be in the past and will no doubt keep rising. This, of course, may work to your advantage for your investment.

- or -

Too high compared to what Mr. Miller? After all, this is the only Top-100 golf course community in Chicago, and it's certainly the only 45-hole Fazio community in the area. What other community would you say was comparable to the Legendary

Country Club?

I can't play enough rounds to justify joining.

The value of joining a club is a lot more than just multiplying your golf games by a green fee! Looking at it the other way around, many people in businesses like yours say that the business contacts pay for their membership and the golf is free! For example, there are great networking opportunities for businessmen like yourself that some members would consider priceless. And of course, that's exactly the value of the many new friends you will meet at the club as you socialize with other members and their families.

I don't see anyone my age [like me] around. [Or why are there so many kids, seniors, and so on?]

We have lots of members like you and part of my job as membership director is to make introductions. Not only can I think of X people right now who are in your occupation, but we have tons of people with handicaps like yours. And we can line up games for you with just a little notice. We also have a number of members who would probably like to hear more about your business since they buy services like your regularly. [Name sample names here and get back to them with more.]

I hear not all the members are happy.

As Lincoln so aptly said, "You can please some of the people all the time and all of the people some of the time." I suppose there will always be people who are unhappy about something, sometime. Our member surveys show satisfaction levels as high or higher than any other club around here, and we're always trying to further improve our service.

Do members have a voice in how Legendary Country Club is managed?

For Legendary to be successful, the members must be involved.

A   Because we are a member-owned club, you have a direct say in everything through your board of directors.

B.   Our professional management is always open to input from the membership. We conduct membership satisfaction surveys on a regular basis. A Membership Advisory Committee advises management and acts as a liaison between the membership and management. If you'd like to volunteer to serve on the Committee, I'll pass your name along to them.

I want to think it over. [This is your classic objection. Expect it often. You must pin them down to a more specific objection to deal with the true objection.]

I agree that a decision such as this should be thought about carefully. May I ask, is it the location or the price that you are thinking about the most? [Probe and close on the issue that is causing the procrastination.]

LEGENDARY CLOSING

Well done is better than well said.
—Benjamin Franklin

Closing a sale is the key step in the sales process and the first step to starting a series of lessons, welcoming people to membership in your club, or handing them the keys to a new home. You've spent time and money to generate leads, given free rounds and tours, and answered questions. Now you need to communicate your enthusiasm for your club to the prospect and sign him up. Just as in a golf game, a great drive and approach shot become almost meaningless if you take five putts to get the ball in the hole!

All the money, time, sweat, and skill you've put into your sales effort mean nothing if you can't get the prospect to buy. Many membership directors get so caught up in their sales pitches that they fail to observe that the prospect is radiating all kinds of buying signals. The prospect is ready to buy, but the salesperson doesn't know when to be quiet and go for the close.

In fact, studies show that an astonishing 63 percent of all sales presentations are given without the salesperson actually asking the prospect to buy!

Close early and often

As you probably know by now, "closing" a sale means that your prospect has agreed to purchase. To be even more specific, they need to have signed the contract and given you a check (that clears the bank!).

Closing is *the purpose* of the sales process. Many people are uncomfortable actually asking for the sale. As mentioned in the last chapter, most of us have a bad image of sales and don't want to seem "pushy." That's one reason people don't close enough. Another is that they think closing should come only *after* all the other steps in the sales process. In fact, sometimes the prospect is ready to be closed early. You won't know this unless you try.

The prospect may be ready to buy when he walks in the door. You will make more sales if you ask for the sale early and often. Another benefit of trying to close early in the presentation is that it will get you over your discomfort about asking for the sale in general.

Early attempts to close the sale are called "trial closes." You don't necessarily expect them to work, but they sometimes do.

Here are a few examples:

When Mr. Miller walks in your office for your appointment, you might say:

> Welcome to Legendary Country Club Mr. Miller. Are
> you ready to join today or do you have some questions?

A similar but more extreme approach can be used with people who are in professional sales, such as car dealers or realtors—and also with people who act impatient. With the salespeople you could say:

> Welcome to Legendary Country Club. You're in professional sales yourself, so you can probably help me do my job for you by telling me what I could cover that would let you make a decision to join today.

While immediately asking for the sale is an unusual approach, you'd be surprised how often it can work. And you can see how it gives you more information, flatters the prospect, and focuses the interaction on the sale.

In response to the first question, Mr. Miller might say yes, no, or maybe. Exactly what he says, and *how* he says it will give you information to better direct your sales presentation. For instance, if he says "I might be interested if you can show me XYZ benefit," then you know what you need to start with.

Another point where you might try a trial close is when the person looks bored or distracted. You might say:

> You look as bored as my husband does when I'm telling him what he needs to do around the house. Is there something else you'd like me to cover, or are you ready to join now?

If you don't feel comfortable using a humorous approach, you could say:

> It looks like you may not need more information on this point. Is there something else you'd like me to cover, or are you ready to join now?

The exact words you say for these trial closes can vary. You need to adapt your script to your circumstances and personality. By asking early, you'll get more information about the prospect and his interests. You'll have a chance to better focus your presentation on what he wants to hear.

Asking early and often makes closing a natural part of your presentation—not something you put off until the end when it may be too late to make adjustments. So ask—you never know when you'll get a pleasant yes.

SPOTTING CLOSING SIGNALS

Let's look at some common closing signals that will alert you to when your prospect is ready to buy.

Verbal closing signals

Often you can tell that a prospect's level of interest has risen by the type of questions he starts to ask. These questions suggest that the prospect is now thinking like a Member.

- ✔ Do you have other doctors who are members?

- ✔ Can I pay my initiation fee in three payments?

- ✔ Will my wife and children be able to play on my membership?

- ✔ How often may I bring guests?

- ✔ Can you prorate my dues for the rest of the season?

- ✔ What month is__[a specific event]?

Stay focused on closing

When the prospect asks questions like the ones just mentioned, try another trial close. Answer each question quickly and professionally in accordance with the answers in your presentation and objections scripts and then go directly for the close. Ask for the sale.

Note: Do not allow yourself to become distracted from selling by answering a series of questions that do not lead to the close. Always draw your prospect's attention back to closing (or your presentation if necessary). If the prospect persists in a series of distracting questions, excuse yourself and leave the room for a moment. This will help you regain control of the conversation. When you return, sit down and get right back into your closing sequence or structured presentation. Lead and remain in charge, but never be "pushy."

Just because someone asks a question doesn't mean you have to answer it immediately, or even at all. For instance, you could say, "I'll be getting to that point a bit later." You are in charge of the situation. It's up to you to dictate the pace and control the interaction. When a prospect asks if he can pay his initiation fee in three parts, don't say yes. Instead, say, "Are you ready to join if I can arrange a three-part payment?" The answer will tell you if it was an idle question (or one trying to distract you), or if the prospect is ready to go.

Sometimes questions that indicate a readiness to buy aren't as clear as the previous example.

"What month is the member-guest championship?" This question is a subtle indication that a prospect is identifying with members. If you give a quick answer with the month, you will miss a closing opportunity. Instead say something like, "Do you have a guest you'd want to bring to this event?" If they say yes, try closing them immediately. While they may bring up other questions—like the financing one—they may also be ready to buy.

Nonverbal closing signals

You must not only listen to what your prospect *says*, but watch his body language as well. The majority of communication is *not* based on *what* your prospect says. Below are some of the clues you may observe that will help you pick the right moment to close.

- ✔ Nodding in agreement
- ✔ Making more frequent eye contact
- ✔ Leaning towards you

✔ Picking up your sales literature and intently studying it

Be alert for such signals. When you observe any of them, bring your presentation to a pause point and try a trial close. You will find your sales volume increases significantly when you raise your level of alertness to nonverbal signals.

GETTING TO THE CLOSE

In order to ask for the sale smoothly, you need to set it up in advance. The way to do this is with your trial closes. As just mentioned, usually you'll attempt a trial close after the prospect has shown buying signals. If the close works, great! If not, follow the procedures in the objections section to isolate and answer any concerns and then float another trial close.

SAMPLE CLOSES

The professional salesperson knows that every prospect has a close that fits him or her—one that appeals to him on a most personal level. The secret is to find out which one will resonate most deeply with your prospect, so you can obtain a favorable response and make the sale.

There are several closes below that have been successful for decades in selling golf. Although you might know them by other names, anyone who has been in sales for even a short period of time will recognize many of them. Others may be new to you. Some of them you might like; others you might hate. It's important to be completely comfortable with the closes that work best for your style and personality. As you go through the following closes, adapt them to match your style and selling situation. Whichever closes you choose to adopt, practice them, role play them, and perfect them. The more you practice, the more they will flow naturally. The one thing that is certain is that if you don't ask prospects to buy, they won't!

The straightforward close

Mr. Miller, based on what you have seen, do you think that Legendary Country Club is the type of club in which you would like to become a member?

The assumptive close

Always assume that the prospect is going to buy. The assumptive close handles the sales interaction as if you were certain that the prospect would buy.

> Mr. Miller, based on our conversation it seems like Legendary Country Club meets most of your criteria. Would you like to start your membership at once before the initiation increase?

The alternative close

The alternative close is perhaps the best known of all closing techniques and has many variations, depending on the exact circumstances. Another common name for it is the "either-or" close. This close gives the prospect the choice between buying and buying, between yes and yes.

> Are you interested in a corporate membership or single membership?

> **- or -**

> Would you prefer the $500 pro shop credit or twenty free green fees for your friends as your welcome gift?

When your prospect is on the verge of making a buying decision, the most direct way of closing the sale is to ask how he intends to pay for it. This approach can best be used when a prospect has made the decision to buy but is asking unrelated questions—the kind that prevent him from giving you the order! At this point, "Will you be using a credit card or check?" is the best way to take control of the sale and complete it. Each one of the previous alternative closes offers the prospect a choice. No matter which one they choose, they will feel committed to buying once they have made the choice.

The action close

In the action close you ask the prospect to *do* something to accelerate the process and help them make a positive decision.

> Mr. Miller, would you like to go to the locker room now and pick out your locker?

> - or -

> Mr. Miller, I've gone ahead and filled out most of the membership application for you. If you would like to go ahead and approve it, I can get your application processed at once.

Hand the prospect a pen and casually slide the membership agreement across the desk.

Or, end your presentation in the pro shop:

> Mr. Miller, every new member gets a welcome gift of a new logo shirt. Would you like to pick yours out right now?

Once the prospect accepts whatever action you have asked him to take, he has already mentally signed up for membership.

The Ben Franklin Close

The Ben Franklin Close is ideal for prospects who are considering additional clubs or who are very detail oriented. It is so named because it was the method employed by the legendary statesman to help him and others make a decision. It is an excellent way to summarize your benefits and the positive response you have received from the prospect during the sale presentation about various features the club has to offer. When written down in black and white, the impact of the words is greater than the spoken word.

Start with a blank sheet of paper and draw a large "T" on the page. At the top, write on either side of the line Pro/Con. Look at the prospect and say:

> Mr. Miller, when Ben Franklin had an important decision to make, he'd make a list of the pros and cons and make a decision based on them. I always think it helps in any important decision to write things down on paper. Would you like to give it a try?

Now give them the paper and pencil and ask them to start with the "pros."

> Why don't you start with the things you liked that we offer here at Legendary Country Club?

One of the keys to this close is that your prospect states the pros and cons and that you give him lots of help with the pros.

> You agreed that this is one of the finest courses in the area, right?

> You liked the fact that, unlike most clubs, we have no food minimum and offer exceptional dining. And as a member, you enjoy a 20 percent discount on pro shop items.

> You liked the fact that there are no assessments ever, so you know exactly what your investment in membership will be.

> You mentioned that you enjoy working on your game and you saw we have excellent range and short game practice areas.

> You mentioned that our location is convenient to your office so you will be able to enjoy the range at lunch time or fit a quick nine in after work.

Prompt the prospect to contribute additional positive benefits to his list.

Then tell your prospect to write down the negatives. Because he's done the positives first, his mind will have a harder time changing gears to come up with negatives. And you don't help! This is one reason it's important to have the prospect do the writing (unlike some ways this close is taught). You might even say, "Now that you've got the hang of it, list all the negatives you can think of and I'll be right back."

When the prospect is done, he will typically have ten or more items in the positive column and no more than three items in the negative column. This alone gives you a psychological advantage in closing. You may be able to say "It looks like the positives far outweigh the negatives. I guess that's it," and go into final closing mode. For instance:

> Mr. Miller, it certainly looks like the benefits of membership at The Legendary Country Club are in favor of you joining our club. What do you say we go ahead and complete the paperwork?

If there any important negatives, you now have the chance to deal with the objection and close. It's the hidden objections that create problems. [See the Objections section for more details.]

The making-a-life close

> John, one of our new members, said the other day, "I spend so much time making a living that I ignore making a life." It seems to me that many people are in the same position today, wouldn't you agree?
>
> One of the reasons people join Legendary Country Club is because it helps them to get their priorities in better order by putting their money into something that will be a positive lifestyle investment. Lots of people say they want to spend more time on the golf course or with their friends, but they never get around to it. Life is

short. What good does it do a person to work hard and not spend money to enjoy life?

Can you see how becoming a member at Legendary Country Club would give you a great deal of personal enjoyment?

The minutes or cents close

If you have a prospect who is stuck on price, the way to handle it is to break it down to ridiculous proportions. This is how life insurance has been sold for decades, but this type of close works just as well selling memberships, especially to value-oriented prospects. When you show people how little your club will cost them on a daily basis, it makes it much easier for them to justify, or rationalize the purchase.

> Mr. Miller when you think about it, membership at Legendary Country Club works out to be less than $15 a day. Wouldn't you agree that's an amazing value for a world-class club?

When all else fails, there are three more closes you can try to get a positive outcome.

The reverse close

Occasionally, someone will come in and announce up front that he is not going to sign up for membership right now or that he is just looking around at the clubs in the area. This is a classic "shield" or defensive technique designed to give the prospect a clean way out if he doesn't hear exactly what he wants to hear. Now is the time for reverse psychology.

Thank him for coming in and offer to put his name on a waiting list for membership tours. Explain to him that you have so many people who are interested in joining right now that you can't possibly spend time with someone who is not ready to make a decision. Be polite but be firm; ask the prospect to pick a date for his tour a month from now. For example:

I'm sorry, Mr. Miller, but I have so many people scheduled for membership tours this month who are ready to decide that I will have to make an appointment for you next month. Tell me what's a good date for you and I'll be happy to add you to the list.

This never fails to change the prospect's mind. The moment he hears he *can't* take a tour, you have dissolved his shield. Suddenly he wants the membership. An interesting turn of events occurs at this point. Now the prospect is actually trying to sell you on letting him buy! A side effect of this close is that it automatically builds value and credibility into your club. What kind of restaurants have waiting lists? Good ones!

The Columbo close

Over the last thirty years, there have been hundreds of cop shows on television. Few TV detectives have been less glamorous in appearance than the seemingly bumbling Columbo. After interviewing a suspect, when he reached the door he would always turn back and ask if the suspect could just help him go over the details one more time so he could understand.

> **Membership:** Mr. Miller, I understand that you're not joining the Club but wonder if you would do me a favor?
>
> **Prospect:** Sure! [At this point they will drop their sales defenses because you have acknowledged that they said no. They are now more willing to help you to cushion the blow of them turning you down.]
>
> **Membership:** You see, I truly believe that Legendary Country Club has the most incredible membership program that I have ever seen...I feel so great about what I do that I just don't understand why I fail to get others as excited about membership as I am. I would really appreciate it if you would tell me why I didn't

337

> communicate that same feeling to you, so it will help me
> in the future. Can you tell me where I went wrong?

At this point, Mr. Miller will do one of two things. He will either tell you exactly why you didn't convince him, or he will reveal his hidden reason for inaction. In either case, this gives you an opportunity to provide him with additional information and ask him for a response to the new and improved proposition. In the process, it doesn't hurt that you have stroked Mr. Miller's ego and self-esteem by asking for his advice.

The puppy dog close

This close is often used when a prospect is hesitant to purchase because of price. The "giveaway" close, or puppy dog close as it is often called, allows the prospect to enjoy membership (or a set of clubs) without a final commitment for a period of time before making a final decision on whether to buy. Once the prospect has experienced membership in a risk-free way, made new friends, and been treated well by your staff, he will almost always buy! He'd almost be embarrassed not to.

> Let me do this, Mr. Miller. I am so sure you will enjoy membership at Legendary Country Club that I am prepared to offer you a very special deal. Give me a credit card on which to bill your monthly dues and member charges and try us out as a member for 90 days.

> Meet the other members, play in some events, and experience exactly what it's like to belong to our club. At the end of 90 days, you can make your decision on whether or not this is the right club for you. How does that sound?

If your prospect doesn't respond to this offer, you probably haven't uncovered his real objections, or he is not financially qualified.

SUMMARY

Your sales presentation should be carefully scripted. However, you don't need any special gift of gab to be a Legendary Salesperson. You just need to involve your prospect and explain your benefits in a credible way.

Overcoming objections to your presentations is one of the most challenging parts of the sales process. Yet, if you believe in your value, you will be helping people to see the benefits more clearly. As you learn to deal better with objections, you will also improve your qualifying and presenting. The sales system works together to make you more effective. Just remember, your benefits can overcome any objections for the right prospects. Look for them, find them, and help them see how your offer meets their needs.

There are almost an unlimited number of ways to close a sale and I've covered the most successful ones here. Try them out, say them out loud, and roleplay them with your staff. Find the ones that seem most natural for you and put them into action at once!

Additional Resource:

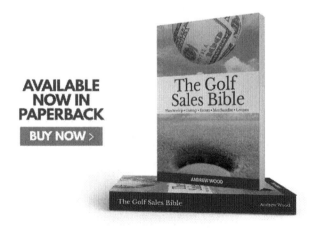

CHAPTER SEVENTEEN

Building a Referral Machine for Your Club

A sk any good golf club how they generate most of their membership or real estate sales and they will instantly and enthusiastically tell you they do it through referrals. However, if you ask them to explain their referral system to you, you are very likely to get a blank stare or a shrug.

I recently asked the vice president of a major golf real estate development and the president of a high-end country club what type of referral systems they had in place. Both had the same answer; they didn't; referrals just happened. So does death, but it doesn't mean you should wait around for it!

Referrals are the best way to bring in new customers for three simple reasons. First, other people are doing the marketing for you, usually at no cost to you. Second, when other people promote you, they are seen as more objective and credible. Third, referrals are generally made in order to help prospects improve their quality of life. A prospect who comes to you referred by his family, friends, or neighbors is already leaning towards a purchase decision.

Referrals are the lifeblood of any good golf club or golf real estate development. There is simply no quicker and less expensive way to build your customer base and increase your income than to double or triple your referral rate. It doesn't matter what type of business you are in; referral business makes you more money than any other type of new business (not surprising as referrals cost little or nothing to get).

While some referrals will happen by accident, you cannot build a reliable marketing system on accidental events. You have to plan, measure, and implement a referral system that ensures two or three referrals from every single person with whom you come into contact.

In this chapter, you will discover:

✔ The difference between word of mouth and referrals

✔ How to measure referral success

✔ The psychology of referrals

✔ The best time to ask

✔ How to ask

✔ Who to ask

✔ Seven ways to get referrals

✔ Setting up an ambassador program

YOU ALWAYS GET WORD OF MOUTH, BUT IS IT GOOD OR BAD?

Perhaps you hadn't thought about it, but you are always getting word of mouth, whether you ask for it or not. While the terms "word of mouth" and "referrals" are frequently used interchangeably, there is a difference. Referrals are specific attempts to help someone— either the person you refer to a business, or the business you refer

to an individual, or both. Word of mouth can include a referral, but it can also include general comments. For instance, someone might say "I would have made par my last time out, but the green was all torn up." Or "I hear that they've made some improvements on that course." Or "I hear that the scenery is great there."

You get the point. People talking is word of mouth. Sometimes it helps you, and sometimes it doesn't. By combining a strong USP, a program to communicate to all your staff and players, and a system for driving referrals, you can generate more and better word of mouth *and* more referrals.

REFERRAL GOALS

The age-old business adage that what gets measured gets done is just as true for referrals as for any other part of your business. Referrals are far too important a part of your marketing strategy to leave them to mere chance as most clubs do. They must instead be sought from every customer, every client, every contact, and every supplier that does business with your club. Furthermore, they must be sought out from all your personal relationships from your accountant to your dry cleaner!

The only way you can see whether your referral program is working is to set goals in each category and measure your progress against them monthly!

Depending on your facility, you should set monthly goals for referrals in the appropriate following areas:

✔ Family memberships

✔ Corporate memberships

✔ Social memberships

✔ Sports memberships (tennis, swim, and so forth)

✔ Outings

✔ Banquets

✔ Weddings

✔ Lessons

✔ Special events (tournaments or theme nights, for instance)

✔ Real estate

✔ Room nights

THE PSYCHOLOGY OF REFERRALS

Start building your referral machine by first understanding the psychology of referrals. Giving referrals involves two contrary impulses. First, people like to give referrals because it allows them to help others at a low cost to themselves. It makes them feel good about themselves and be a "hero" to others. Second, people worry about giving referrals because if something goes wrong, they get the blame. If things go right, the thanks they get is usually small. Because of this ambivalence, it's easy to get some people to give referrals and hard to get others to. The same people may change their attitudes over time, or be more comfortable giving referrals to some types of people than others.

Clearly, your job is to encourage referrals and also make it *safe* to give referrals to your course. One way to tilt the odds in your favor is to provide a reward for referrals.

People like to give referrals for three important reasons

1 Ego. When someone buys a new home, membership, car, or investment, he wants his friends and neighbors to be impressed. He wants them to know what a great deal he got. When was the last time someone who bought a new car told you what a schmuck he was for buying it? It simply doesn't happen, at least not in the first few weeks!

2 Most people like to feel important; they like to be the center of attention or information. When the opportunity to take center stage arises by giving a referral, they are more than ready to step up to the plate.

3 Birds of a feather flock together. People like their friends and neighbors to share and experience the same things they do! There are two parts of this equation. The first is that people want their friends to share in the joy of the same experience. The second and less talked about motivation is that people want their friends to share the risk. A person who has spent big money to join the Country Club wants a friend to join as well so if it turns out not to have been such a great idea at least they are in it together. Few people talk about this side, but it exists nonetheless—the "I'll do it if you do it" syndrome!

There are many other reasons for giving referrals, from trying to help people, to hoping for referrals in return.

WHEN IS THE BEST TIME TO ASK FOR A REFERRAL?

The short answer is anytime; ask often. Early in the relationship can be the best time. Asking for a referral is a good habit to get into when you talk with people. The second best time to ask for a referral is as soon as you have developed a rapport with the prospect. He may not buy, and you may never see him again so you should never let the prospect leave without asking for a referral. After someone has told you no is also a good time. Often, a person who has just turned you down feels bad about having done so and will give you a referral to compensate.

The very best time to ask for a referral is right after you have completed a sale with a new customer. People who have just purchased from you are very open to helping you. Over 80 percent of all referrals happen within six to eight weeks of selling a prospect. This is the time when excitement and anticipation are always at the highest level. After that period, people tend to fall into their regular routines, they join cliques and tend to be more reluctant to bring others into their new world.

A similar scenario happened at the country club I used to belong to in California. When it first opened, we all promoted the club at every opportunity because we wanted new people to play golf with. A few years later, the club was fully established, and we long-time members remembered the days when we could play whenever we wanted and didn't even need to book a tee time. When I resigned my membership, there were 900 members, and you could hardly get on the course at all. None of the golfers in my group wanted more members. On the contrary— they wanted fewer. Consequently, they didn't refer anyone. New members, on the other hand, who didn't know what a paradise it had been ten years prior, put up with abysmally slow play and encouraged their friends to join.

HOW TO ASK FOR REFERRALS

Many people are bashful or just downright scared of asking for a referral. They don't want to seem pushy, desperate, or—heaven forbid—both. While I assure you that most people do like giving referrals, you can make the process even more painless by reframing the way you ask for a referral. Plan your referral requests in advance, so they flow smoothly and effortlessly from your mouth.

As mentioned earlier, *how* you ask for referrals can make a big difference. The most important point is that you have to develop a method that works for you, remembering that it takes a little practice before you'll feel completely comfortable asking for referrals.

There are many ways to ask for referrals. The way you ask will depend on your club's specific offer, positioning, and your personality. Some people just **come right out and ask,** business person to business person like this:

> Joe, just as you probably do in your business, we find we get most of our new members from referrals by other satisfied members. Who else do you know who plays golf regularly?

Notice that we asked "who else," assuming that they know people who play golf rather than "Do you know anyone?" This subtle difference creates very different results!

Or you might ask Joe if his customers, rather than his peers, could benefit:

> Joe, which of your clients want to get their games in shape this year and who might enjoy some golf lessons?

If the answer is affirmative, get a name and phone number. If the prospect doesn't know, or is reluctant to give you this information, try to recruit him to your team. Ask if he would convey one of your brochures, or at least a business card, to any potential prospect. If you have established any degree of rapport during the sales process, your customer should at least be willing to do that.

Another type of appeal is a **personal appeal:**

> George, it would really help me if you could suggest two or three other people I could talk to about the wonderful membership programs we offer here at Legendary Country Club.

Notice that we set an expectation by asking for two or three other people.

You can use a **personal favor** approach:

> George, I wonder if you could do me a favor. I'm looking for a few new students, and I'd appreciate it if you could suggest some people who might be appropriate for me to approach.

If they give you names, ask if you can use their name as the referral source when approaching the new people.

You can offer **rewards:**

> You may not know that we have a program here that provides a $50 gift certificate for every qualified referral you provide the club who makes an appointment for a membership tour. And should they join, we give both you and the person a $200 certificate.

Notice that we reward both the tour and the sale. It costs money to get leads - usually far more than $50 a lead - so why not spend some of your ad budget in the place most likely to pay off by rewarding your members for leads? Notice that you're asking for *qualified* leads? You set the qualifications.

You can provide tools to **make it easy** to give referrals:

> George, here are five bag tags (etc.) to give out to your friends. There is an offer on them to play the course.

Here are some other examples of ways to ask for referrals. You should pick or develop ways that fit your own style and your club's position in the marketplace.

> George, we're trying to build up our outings business here at the course on Mondays. It would really help me if you could suggest a few groups you're a member of who might hold a golf event or a local company. Are you in Rotary or any other group that might hold a tournament for charity?

If the first answer is "No." try a few probes with specific examples. For instance:

- ✔ Are you a member of the local Chamber of Commerce?

- ✔ Do you have any kids in schools that have fund raisers?

- ✔ Do you work with any charities that raise money?

If this doesn't work, try for the names of other people who are better leads.

- ✔ Can you suggest someone else I can ask about group events?

- ✔ Who do you know that is a member of a local association?

- ✔ Who do you know who knows the most people? Who do you ask for a referral when you need a new contact?

If you were looking for members, your questions would be similar:

✔ We're always looking for good new members. Who do you know that you'd like to have in the club?

✔ As a new member, we want you to be comfortable here right away. Here are three free guest passes if you want to fill out your own foursome. Whose names should we put on them?

✔ Who do you know who plays golf the most often?

✔ Who do you know who might be dissatisfied with conditions at their current club?

WHOM TO ASK FOR REFERRALS

The short answer is, ask everyone you know or do business with for referrals.

Did you ask the UPS truck driver to buy today? I did. When I say everyone, I mean everyone. I include the mailman, the fire inspector, and the plumber. Hey, you won't know if you don't ask and everyone has friends who can afford to buy or is affiliated with a group that holds a golf outing!

SEVEN GREAT WAYS TO GET REFERRALS

There are seven key groups from whom you can gain referrals

1 Ask new clients to buy again. The reason we get referrals is so that we can sell more, right? Well, the first thing to consider before we ever work on the referrals to others is self-referrals: Can we sell anything else to the new golfer in front of us right now? Can they upgrade their membership to a multi-year membership? Can they buy a corporate membership and get their employees and partners involved at the club? Can they book an outing or give us the name of a cause they support that raises money through a golf event? Can they book a wedding or a birthday party at the club? Can you develop new things to sell them?

2 Ask new clients who else might benefit. Even if your most recent customer doesn't want to buy something else from you, it's almost certain that he knows someone in his line of work or situation who has similar needs. Everyone is an opinion leader—at least to a few people. A special few are opinion leaders to hundreds, or perhaps even thousands, of people. (See Chapter 19 on Customer Loyalty.)

3 Ask non-customers for referrals. Even when a sales presentation has not been successful, there is absolutely no reason why you should not ask the prospect for the name of a person who might benefit from what you have to offer.

The landscaper who did my yard dropped by recently to see if I could refer him to any potential new customers. He told me that he had contracted to do two new jobs in my area in the last month.

Each was worth almost $50,000, and both had come as a result of asking for a referral from homeowners who had turned his bids down because of the cost.

Simply say to the prospect:

> I'm sorry I don't seem to be able to meet your needs today. Who else do you know who might be interested in looking at Legendary Country Club?

4 Ask ex-customers. Just because a golfer is an ex-customer doesn't mean he or she can't or won't refer your business, especially if you parted on good terms. Make it a point to stay in contact with ex-members at least a couple of times a year and let them know you are still in business. I frequently get referrals from ex-customers who have since moved on to other things but still have friends or contacts in golf. And as a bonus, often ex-customers come back because you bothered to keep in touch.

5 Ask business suppliers for referrals. Remember, you and your club make purchases. You buy goods and services from others. You are a good customer to someone. That *someone* should be glad to give you referrals as a reward for the business you give him. At the least, suppliers should keep you up on industry happenings, but they also know people who golf. They may belong to groups that have outings or charity events. In sales, just as in other areas of your life, you won't receive if you don't ask, so be sure to remind your suppliers that you are always in the market for new leads.

Don't forget personal suppliers

You bought a car locally, a home locally, and have relationships with dry cleaners, gardeners, and a host of other personal service companies. They have *your* business; have you asked them to help your business?

Get everyone on staff involved

Make it a clear policy at your club that SALES is *everyone's* job! Remind employees that "Nothing happens until a sale is made" and that the club's success and their PAYCHECKS depend on a constant stream of new business! You can also reward them for each referral or sale.

What about your club manager, golf professional, super intendent, and chef? Have they leveraged their personal relation- ships by asking for referrals?

How about bartenders and wait staff? They come into contact with hundreds of people a week and often have jobs at more than one place. They can be a huge source of referral business. The more people on your staff you get involved at a grass-roots level, the quicker your referrals will grow exponentially.

6 Catch bees with honey: Get referrals from your competitors. Most business owners would be surprised to learn that your competitors can often be a good source of referrals. Before you think that I'm a couple clubs short of a full set, think about it! Sometimes you get a request for an outing on a date you're full. Or you and the prospect simply don't hit it off! She's from Venus, you're from Mars, he wants a club closer to home, or whatever. In these cases, instead of letting the prospect bounce around to three or four more people, take the proactive approach and refer them to someone who can help them at once. Then call that person in advance to let him know what you can about the prospect. When you give referrals, others should return them out of courtesy.

You can also set up a formal alliance whereby it's agreed in advance that all extra business gets referred. In one case, two of our clients in Orlando have this arrangement and give each other a 30 percent commission for the referral. THINK ABOUT that; a day when your course is full, and you generate more than 100 percent of revenue!

7 Give referrals to your members. Getting referrals is your goal, but you have to *give* referrals to get them. That's often the best way to generate referrals—and if they don't reciprocate, find someone else to refer to! (Good referrals also reward your members, thus making their memberships more valuable, and thus more likely to be renewed.)

It may be hard for a golf course to give referrals to some people. In that case, there are at least two things you can do. First, you can talk up your contacts. For instance, you can plug the local Chamber, banker, or housing development. Second, you can facilitate business among your members. When you learn that a new member is in a business that might be of use to one of your other members, immediately ask for that person's business card. Ask for several cards, so that you can pass them on to your clients. It will make your member feel good, and it will build your list of resources.

There are many ways you can facilitate contacts among members. Maybe you can plug new members in your newsletter, host networking events, or provide a bulletin board for business cards. You should make yourself a central source of information in the networking among members. Then they'll keep you in mind.

For instance, one club makes their meeting room available to nonprofit groups for free. Since meeting rooms are scarce in town, many opinion leaders appreciate the facility. And, of course, it's easy for members to arrange the room for their favorite groups. That makes them look good with their groups, exposes new people to the club, and gains the club publicity in the group newsletters and the local newspaper's event calendar.

BUILDING YOUR REFERRAL MACHINE

With all your tools in hand, it's time to commit to the development of a referral habit that will pay untold dividends over the course of your business career. (Even if you're not in sales or marketing, the ability to generate business—to be a rainmaker—makes you more valuable in any position.)

The first thing you must do to build a referral machine is to make a serious commitment to gathering referrals and following them up. You can often double or triple your referrals by simply asking for them. Not sometimes, not when you feel like it, not when you are having a good day, not if you feel the prospect likes you, but every single time in as many different ways as you can until you get what you need. In the book *Marketing Your Services: For People Who Hate to Sell*, the author (Rick Crandall) says that most people have a "prayer" referral system—they simply *hope* that someone will give them a referral! They say it takes 28 days of constant repetition to develop a habit, so give yourself more than a prayer of a chance for referrals—get started today!

Be specific when asking for referrals

Once you are given a referral, make every effort possible to get a little background on the person you will be dealing with. When I was selling my consulting services for golf courses a few years ago, I asked each client to provide me with three referrals. One client in Mississippi faxed me right back with the names of three people.

The first was mildly interested.

The second told me that if this client was using me, then he certainly wouldn't.

The third started shouting at me on the phone at the mere

mention of the client, and went on to tell me what he would do with the "son of a #@!#@" if he ever got hold of him.

I was completely confused and called the client back to ask him what was going on. He said he had simply referred people to me whom he knew needed my services. He didn't know they had to like him!

Whenever you get a referral, try to find the connection between the person referring and the referral. Ask how Joe knows Harry. Ask how long Sally has been friends with Chelsea. Ask what line of work the prospect is in. The more information you have about the referral, and the clearer you are about the referee's relationship with the referrer, the better are your chances of a successful outcome.

CULTIVATE REFERRAL SOURCES

Some people don't give referrals no matter what you do. Some people like to give referrals. It might be a manager of a sporting goods shop, a realtor, or the Chamber of Commerce that is a good referral source. When you find one, look for more that are similar. Most important, when you find a person who gives referrals, build the relationship. Keep in touch. Give them referrals back. Put them on your newsletter list. Find out what they like. Treat them or their family and friends as special people.

Show your gratitude

Once you have received a referral, whether it works out to your advantage or not, make sure that you thank people. When a customer gives you a referral that results in a sale, make a big production out of the event. At the very least, you should send him a "thank you" note. If the amount of money involved in closing the sale is substantial, consider sending the customer who gave you the referral a suitable gift for his assistance. A book on a subject that interests him or a bottle of his favorite wine will go a long way towards ensuring that this particular person will continue to refer good prospects to you.

Reward with money?

Many clubs offer a financial inducement to encourage referrals, but they do not always work. Studies show that a large percentage of people feel uneasy about being paid for referring their friends unless their friends benefit equally in the process. For instance, they get a $500 credit and so does the new member. They get a staff bag and so does the new member. They get a cruise and so does the new member. You get the idea. Coming up with a reward whereby both parties benefit is by far the most effective way to say thank you for a referral and encourage more.

Ask again for referrals

Every time you thank a customer for a referral, you have the opportunity to repeat the cycle by asking for another referral. Always end each thank-you communication, whether it's a letter or a phone call, by asking if the customer knows of anyone similar who might benefit from what you have to offer. Remember, the best time to get a referral is right after a sale. Strike while the iron is hot and ask for more names at once.

Make it easy to give referrals

The easier you make it for other people to promote you and your club, the more they will do it. Provide free postcards or discount passes for visitors at the pro shop, restaurant, or front gate. At a seminar with over two hundred people in Las Vegas, I distributed 200 postcards and asked the audience members to write down the three most important things they had learned and sent the postcard to a friend who could then remind them to take action on these items. At the next break I announced that if everyone would drop the postcards up front, my secretary had a bunch of postcard stamps and would take care of mailing them. Ninety percent of the people dropped them off for mailing! 180 referrals in the mail at very little cost! Now, to me, a program like that makes a lot of sense.

The law of large numbers

The more people you know, the more referrals you get! Now that's a pretty simple concept, but far too many people fail to take advantage of this simple fact! Join the club or association in your town that will bring you into contact with the largest number of prospective contacts!

Okay, so there are already ten people in your field involved in the Chamber who are more established than you are, so now what? Well, before you take the next step, consider this: More than half of them never go to a meeting anyway. Of the half that go, they only go once a year or spend their time in aimless socializing rather than building relationships. As Woody Allen said, "Ninety percent of success is just showing up." If you still feel there is too much competition in the local chapters of whatever organizations you have considered, try a jump to left field and change the game. Join a related organization rather than the most obvious. Join the Chamber in the next town over, or instead of the realtors' association join the builders' association or the mortgage association.

Word of mouth is the lifeblood of any golf course. And you receive good words a whole lot more predictably and effectively when you develop and follow a system so that good leads don't just slip through the cracks.

LOOK FOR OPINION LEADERS; THEY ARE EVERYWHERE

In Joe Girard's remarkable book, *How to Sell Anything to Anyone*, he talks about the "250 rule." Basically, this states that everyone knows at least 250 people, and each of them knows another 250. Get the idea?

I know many more than 250 people, and I conduct seminars and give lectures to thousands across the country. What if the person to whom you are selling something is in the same position as I am, coming into contact with thousands of new people every year? What appears to be an individual, isolated sale could turn into hundreds of sales. Ask questions after each sale to find out what you can about your customer's sphere of influence. (Also see Chapter 19 for more information on Building Customer Loyalty.)

SALES CYCLE LEADS

Certain products have sales cycles. On average, people buy a new home every seven years. When golfers in the Northern states hit their late forties or early fifties, they start looking for a home in the SUN! Being aware of your product's life cycle gives you the edge in knowing when a previous customer will be ready for another purchase. Keep an active file in your computer's database that lets you know a couple of months in advance when these previous customers will be at their hottest to replace the golf course membership or house. But let me give you an even simpler example. Everyone has a birthday. Do you approach a member's spouse a month in advance and suggest a party at the club? Perhaps even a surprise party? If you're not sure of the timing, follow the first rule of referrals, ask early and often!

SETTING UP AN AMBASSADOR PROGRAM

Why take care of all referrals yourself when you can enlist the help of others? Develop your own Ambassador program.

In short, your goal is to have a group of your members dedicated to reaching out to the community on your behalf to find new members. Look for people who want to have an official role in your success. Maybe they are retired and have time. Maybe they are in fields like insurance where they want a reason to meet more people. They are likely to be naturally outgoing.

These will be the people who will play with, introduce and bond with prospective members. Having a friendly person show a prospective member around the club and introduce them to the various groups is a very strong way to create a positive impression. We often forget that a great part of the golf experience is social interaction, not just the quality of the course. Members can be assigned by age, geographic background, and skill so that similar people get to play together.

A formal rewards program should be set up to thank ambassadors based on their success in attracting new members.

SUMMARY

There is no quicker or less expensive way to increase your business than to build a referral system rather than leave it to chance as most clubs do. Your system must be structured and measured. Then your staff must be trained and rewarded for following it. No less important is the recognition and rewarding of those who are doing the referring.

CHAPTER EIGHTEEN

Developing Legendary Service and a Customer Friendly Culture

O ne of the most overlooked parts of marketing at any club is service! While a reputation can be built, enhanced, and even achieved with marketing, at some point your reputation is going to be put to the test. You may be the fastest gun in the West on all the wanted posters, but when the other guy staring you down draws, reputation doesn't count for much unless you really are fast! When you can back up your reputation with legendary service, you immediately vault yourself to the top echelon in your field. Great service drives repeat business, referrals, and long-term relationships with members and guests.

There is a lot of talk about providing great service in the golf business, about making your members and guests feel special. We all want it yet so few places deliver it! In fact, when you ask the managers at most clubs what good service is, you won't get a very straight answer. Instead, you will get a bunch of vague platitudes about being friendly and "taking care of our customers' needs." All very nice, but how often can you truthfully say that your service is not just good, but exceptional? Not just exceptional, but outrageously great?

In this chapter, you will discover:

✔ How to define great service

358

✔ How to determine what a customer is worth to you

✔ Why customers leave

✔ The ten commandments of customer service

✔ Whether or not your club's policies are customer friendly

WHAT IS YOUR REPUTATION?

How are reputations for service, good or bad, formed in the minds of the public? How much of any person's or club's reputation is true and how much is hype? In the minds of your customers and prospects, perception is reality. Your reputation is based on word of mouth and observations. It may be accurate, or it may not be.

If we see someone stepping out of a limousine in front of a ritzy hotel, we automatically assume that the person is rich, successful, and perhaps even powerful or famous. If we see that a company's stock is rising, we assume the company must be doing well; if it's falling, we assume the company must be doing poorly. If other people tell us a particular restaurant is good or bad, we are inclined to believe them. The fact that our taste may be totally different from theirs doesn't enter into it; a good reputation is good and a bad reputation is bad. Most people won't take the time or effort to confirm either way; Instead, they will just accept what they hear or read as the truth right up until something happens to change their minds.

WHAT MAKES YOU THINK YOUR SERVICE IS GREAT?

The hype, the posturing, the positioning, marketing, the promotions, and the advertising must take a back seat to good old-fashioned service. As yourself these questions:

✔ Can you deliver the goods?

✔ Can you back up the position you've claimed?

✔ Are you who we think you are?

Everyone *says* they give good service. And everyone probably *means* to offer customers a great experience. But most have no system in place with standards, measurement, and rewards.

Great service is partly intangibles. It's people who treat you like a real person, not as an indistinguishable unit passing through their facility. It's a friendly tone of voice. It's a personal connection, not a "professionally friendly" employee. It's personal recognition.

Unfortunately, it's all too easy to come up with examples of bad service even when dealing with "quality" businesses. Here are three examples where, as a customer, I expected a big service response. Instead, I received, well...

New home

When I bought my current home, it generated a very large commission for the real estate agent who was both the listing and the selling agent. She spent a grand total of one day with my wife and me before we bought. When we moved into our new home, did we have fruit waiting in the kitchen, a bottle of Dom Perignon, or a thank-you card? Or perhaps something more creative like a refrigerator stocked with food, a certificate for a babysitter so we could go out, or a little party to introduce us to local contacts. NO! In fact, we got nothing—way to build your reputation for service, lady!

The sad thing is that while I felt the business I brought her was unappreciated, if this realtor had made a small gesture of acknowledgment, she would have received positive word of mouth and several referrals from me that would have earned her tens of thousands of dollars.

Golf club championship

Two decades ago I won the club championship at my golf club in California. Did I get my picture in the club's newsletter? No! In fact, I didn't even get my name mentioned in the club's newsletter, let alone my picture! I was the most excited I had been since I was fifteen years old, but not being acknowledged was a huge letdown! Way to make your members feel special, guys! (The fact that I'm still talking about this incident years later illustrates how important it is to acknowledge and appreciate your customers.)

Foggy service

On a recent trip to Ireland, I paid nearly $300 for a round of golf on a very memorable course. There were, however, a couple of incidents that dampened my overall experience. First, I never received a response to my initial e-mail request for a tee time. Then, faced with a fog delay at 10 AM, my friend and I decided to have breakfast at the club. There were five items on the breakfast menu. I ordered a Danish and coffee, my friend a cocoa. No Danish. No problem. I ordered a scone. No scones. No problem—what do you have? The waitress left, then returned and suggested a croissant (not one of the five menu items). I gladly ordered it and was duly served a fresh croissant accompanied by one of those little individual strawberry jam pots. As I opened the jam pot, my friend and I both burst out laughing! The jam was half-eaten. By this time, soured on the service, I just dug in and didn't even bother to mention it!

After a two-hour fog delay, all of the tee times were reshuffled (fair enough). I told the starter that we were both scratch players and would like, if possible, to play with a couple of better players. He responded two minutes later by asking that we go off next, with two 68-year-old ladies from Boca Raton. To their credit, they played admirably well, but with us playing all the way back, it did not enhance our day and I doubt it did theirs! Still, all was well again when we found the bar 5 hours and 45 minutes later! (Anything longer than a three-and-a-half-hour round is generally a negative experience for me.)

We all have stories similar to these, about people and businesses from whom we thought we would get superior service, but didn't. Fortunately, there is the other end of the service spectrum.

OUTRAGEOUSLY GOOD SERVICE

Several Times I had the pleasure of playing golf at the Robert Trent Jones Golf Club in Gainesville, Virginia. This story is about the third time I have played in a tournament there, which only goes to prove that the exceptional experiences I have had there were not a fluke but, in fact, a tradition of outrageously great service!

I find it hard to quantify just why my experiences at RTJ are so great. Like many, I am quicker to tell you when service is not good. I am also far slower to appreciate exceptional service, so I thought I would try to quantify just why the experience there is so great in the hope that it may help you in setting standards you can measure at your club (see Benchmarking in Chapter 3). How many of these can you claim for your club? What extras do you offer during your customers' golf experiences?

16. **An immaculate course.** From the greens that run 13 on the stimpmeter to the tees that look like greens.

17. **Gorgeous setting.** The setting and design along the shores of Lake Manassas with the dogwoods and azaleas in bloom is truly exceptional.

18. **Comfortable clubhouse.** The clubhouse was immaculate and tasteful.

19. **A welcoming pro.** The pro, Cary, greeted me by name although he had not seen me in 363 days. He also greeted the rest of the group by name and no doubt the majority of the 21 other four-man teams!

20. **Personal attention from wait staff.** The wait staff knew my drink of choice and offered it at once on the second day. (It was like being on a cruise.)

21. **Great caddies.** The caddie I had, Dennis, was as knowledgeable and professional as anyone on the PGA Tour. Plus, he read the greens really well.

22. **Locker-room attention to detail.** When we walked into the locker room they already had our names on lockers.

23. **Practice-round pin sheets.** We were given pin sheets even for the practice round.

24. **Locker-room service.** When I left my golf shoes in my locker with a missing spike, the following day my shoes had a NEW SET of spikes!

25. **Outstanding food.** The food was as good as that served at any of the best restaurants I have ever eaten in, anywhere in the world.

26. **Outstanding rooms.** The accommodations in the clubhouse were on par with the finest hotels in the world.

27. **Memorable tee gift.** The tee gift was memorable and something I will keep and use—unlike the dozen Titleist low-end golf balls I got for paying $1,000 to enter another club's member-guest tournament. (I was also told I could not swap the Titleists for the Pro V! balls I actually play since they said "member guest" on them. Like anybody really cares!)

28. **Well-run tournament.** The tournament was run professionally with a full printout of standings delivered to each table at lunch and dinner.

29. **Social aspects.** Camaraderie was promoted and encouraged as much as the competition itself.

30. **I played well.** Last, and by no means least, I played well. Maybe the service helped my game, but even if I hadn't played well, it would still have been an awesome experience!

While it's easy to dismiss this as a high-end club with the money to do things right, that fact is only a small part of the equation. Plus, there are lots of high-end clubs that don't do it right! Not everyone can have a world-class club in perfect condition, but the commitment to world-class service can be made even at a nine-hole public course in a bad location. It's all about vision, desire, attitude, and—most important—trying to quantify, measure, and develop a service program that elevates any course, regardless of its physical plant.

YOU NEED TO KNOW WHAT A CUSTOMER IS WORTH TO YOU!

One of the most important marketing facts to discover in running your club is: What exactly is a customer worth to you? Knowing this information not only helps determine how much money you should spend on advertising and marketing to get a customer but also how much time, money, and effort you should spend on trying to *keep* a customer. If your customers spend only a few dollars a year, then you certainly can't send them a hamper full of goodies at Christmas time. If however, your customers spend thousands of dollars with you, then it might well be worth the extra goodwill!

I remember, back in the mid-Eighties, reading Carl Sewell's book *Customers for Life*. At that time he found that the average Cadillac buyer at his dealership would spend over $375,000 with him as long as he kept them happy! In my karate school, I figured out that an average student would, over the course of his training, spend about $1000. In my marketing business, my average client is worth far more than that!

✔ Take a look at the best 20 percent of your clients—what did they spend with you last year?

✔ Take a look at your bottom 20 percent—what did they spend with you?

✔ After throwing out the bottom 5 percent and top 5 percent that might throw off the scales, what is your average client worth to your business?

You might be surprised by how much your best clients spend with you in a year. (And you probably haven't counted the referral business they bring in.) Now, project that number over five years, ten years, or perhaps even longer.

For example, I use a local limo service at least once a month to go to the airport and back at a cost of $100 plus tip per trip. This means that if I continue to use them, I will be worth well over $12,000 in business to them in the next five years and close to $30,000 over the next ten years when you take inflation into account.

As a good customer, I ought to rate the occasional upgrade from a town car to their stretch limo. I should make their Christmas card list and maybe get a small token gift once in a while. Going the extra mile and spending $25 to $50 a year on me is going to be well worth the cost and will be far cheaper than finding a new client to replace me!

The value of clients cannot, and should not, be measured only in terms of dollars spent. There are other intangible measures of a client's worth that are equally important in terms of building your business. For example, I have several clients who don't do a great deal of business with me but account for a large portion of my referrals. They are always telling others how my business has helped them. Their worth in terms of referral business adds up to far more than the dollars they spend.

Other clients are worth far more than the books show because of their marquee value or brand name. I just picked up the marketing account for a large and prestigious resort. Although the dollars involved are small, having their name on my list of clients will undoubtedly produce more business for me. Your club will encounter the same sorts of situations. Certain people or companies with whom you do business will add to other people's positive perceptions of your club. That makes those customers special!

Going through this process and figuring out just what your customers are worth, both tangibly and intangibly, on an annual basis, can go a long way to helping you focus your efforts on the customers who most deserve your attention.

CUSTOMER SERVICE IS EVERYONE'S JOB

A fact that often goes unnoticed by executives is that, despite the best advertising, media relations, and all the good intentions in the world, reputations are won and lost on the front lines. An airline is not judged by the quality of its captain or management, but by its flight attendants and its ticketing agents. I do not use a certain major airline because their ticket lady called me an idiot when I asked her to sign me up for their frequent flyer program and she found that my travel agent had already done it. Then she told me to make sure I had the second number removed when I got off the plane in Dallas. Despite my better judgment, I asked her to do it for me. She refused, saying she only had thirty minutes before the flight took off and had to deal with other passengers.

Now, you might be thinking that maybe this ticket agent was just having a really bad day, but the following week when my Delta flight was canceled due to an equipment problem, I found myself once again standing in line with this same agent at the counter. This time, it was the person in front of me who suffered her wrath. I just smiled and never flew Delta again! A car dealership is not judged by the models it sells, but by its salespeople and customer service staff in the shop.

The point is that your staff has your success in their hands. Do you pay them minimum wage, give them no training, and yet expect great results? Or do you put your staff first so they, in turn, will put your customers first?

WHY CUSTOMERS LEAVE

It is easy to forget that the people we serve can leave at any time. If they leave with an unsolved problem, they are liable to tell a whole bunch of people about that problem. According to the best studies, here is a breakdown of why people stop doing business with any particular person or company. The greatest percentage of loss can be avoided if you train your staff well.

- ✔ 1% get injured, ill, or die.

- ✔ 2% just disappear or get lost in the shuffle.

- ✔ 4% move away from the area.

- ✔ 6% change activities because of friends.

- ✔ 9% leave because of cost.

- ✔ 10% of people just love to change.

- ✔ 68% of customers leave because of indifference to them or their child.

Let's take a moment to look at that last statistic. Almost two-thirds of all lost customers leave because of perceived indifference.

THE TEN COMMANDMENTS OF CUSTOMER SERVICE

Customers these days have plenty of options and plenty of others vying for their time and money. Make the most of your opportunities by following the ten commandments of customer service!

1. Stay close to the wants and needs of your customers. Ask them for honest and critical opinions on your operation. Do not argue or try to defend your position, just shut up and listen. Use surveys, telephone interviews, and idea boxes to solicit and generate ways to improve your service. Almost every innovation we have added to our consulting services over the years has been born out of a client's suggestion for improvement.

Ask your customers questions like:

✔ How do you think we could improve the appearance of the clubhouse?

✔ How could we have a better merchandise display in the pro shop? Is there merchandise you'd like that we don't offer?

✔ Do our hours of operation suit your lifestyle?

✔ What specific improvements or additions could we make to serve you better?

Just the fact that you ask their opinions will make your customers feel more special. If you implement a customer's idea, that customer could be yours for life!

Get a consultant to help you make amazing discoveries

In addition to direct customer feedback, another invaluable tool is to get a different pair of eyes examining your business, even if from a totally unrelated sector. You are never the best person to judge your own operation. Quite simply, you can't see the forest for the trees. You need to have an outside person come in and point out obvious things that you can't see.

Solicit opinions from friends, colleagues, and peers and, if all else fails, a consultant. Invite them to ask dumb questions about your membership procedure, sales pitch, your follow up, and your service. By encouraging them to do so, you will often discover areas that could be improved. You will make amazing discoveries such as that your office smells funny, that what you think is a clean bathroom doesn't cut it when you ask a woman. You might discover that you confuse your clients with too many choices during the sign- up conference. You might find you are charging too little for your service, as is often the case when I consult with a business. Not all of this feedback will be useful, of course, but it really does pay huge dividends to have outside people look at your operation and open your eyes to what is going on around you.

2. Existing customers are more important than ones you don't have yet. Don't treat new customers or prospects better than old customers. It is very easy to fall into this trap and it's a surefire recipe for the destruction of your reputation and your business. For example, it's not unusual for a business, in an attempt to gain more clients, to cut prices for new customers to attract business while charging established accounts more money. All the explanations in the world, even if they are heard or read, are not going to change the perception of the older customer that he is getting a raw deal.

A great way to make sure you are doing your best is always to act like your client has just told you he is considering another club. What would you do differently to try and keep that client from leaving? Well, first of all, you would likely try to find out what was wrong But let's suppose there is nothing in particular, or at least nothing the client is willing to share with you—then what?

You should develop a system to aid in getting clients back on track. Here are some possible steps you could take:

- ✔ Ask everyone on staff what they know about the golfer. (They may have shared some problem with the bartender, but not the club pro.)

- ✔ Give him personal attention. Invite him to join a foursome of people he'd like to meet. Take time to chat about his interests (which you should have in your database).

- ✔ Get him involved in an event that is in the future— preferably, one that will occur after his membership expires.

- ✔ Invite him and his wife to dinner at the club with another couple.

✔ Ask him to chair a committee, become an ambassador, or otherwise be part of the "inner circle."

✔ Come up with your own list of other things you can do, such as giving him coupons he can give to friends for free rounds.

In short, you need to go out of your way to do anything in your power to see that he doesn't quit!

Of course, you know as well as I do that most members or golfers do not give a warning before riding off into the sunset never to be seen again. There is a solution, though: Treat each and every client as though they were going to quit each and every month, and you will soon see a dramatic improvement in your customer service and retention.

3. Follow up on all the things you say you will do or don't say anything. One of the simplest ways to ensure good service is to schedule a follow-up call at the very same time you resolve to fix a problem or respond to a request. Murphy's Law pretty much guarantees that if you have a problem with the client that you resolve to fix, something will also go wrong with the planned fix, adding insult to injury. The best way to ensure that such events don't permanently damage your reputation is to outline the proposed action, then immediately schedule a follow-up call to ensure that such action has taken place. When fixing problems or responding to requests, you must always have a fail-safe system to ensure that the actual requests, however simple, were carried out. In fact, nothing damages a reputation more than a few simple requests not carried to their successful conclusion. People then start to wonder: If he can't take care of such a little thing, how can he take care of the bigger problems I entrust him with?

4. Remember and use customers' names. Remembering someone's name is one of the sincerest compliments you can pay a person.

It builds their self-esteem; it lets them know you think they are important and they have made an impression on you. The sound of a person's name, pronounced correctly, is one of the nicest sounds in the world, at least to that person.

Staff should be trained to remember and use people's names. Some people are just better at this than others. Don't put the inept ones in customer contact positions.

If you doubt the value of using names for even for a moment, think how you feel when someone sends you a letter with your name horribly misspelled. Does that start you off feeling good about the person and his abilities? Not likely. Instead, it will tend to make you shake your head, roll your eyes, and mutter under your breath. The same is true when a person continues to verbally butcher your name.

It is vital when you engage in a conversation or are introduced to someone, to remember their name. The fastest way to lose any rapport that you are building is to forget the name and have to ask it again. It has been shown that calling someone by their name, first or last, dramatically increases the bonding and communication. Other people feel as though they know you if you call them by their names.

Some people are good with names. Almost everyone at the pinnacle of success is excellent. People like former President Harry Truman could call literally thousands of people, from senators to scullery maids, by their first names. Can you imagine the feeling of joy and satisfaction you would get by having the President of the United States call you by your first name? Can you imagine the lengths a simple attendant might go to please when the President took the trouble to remember his name? The answer is clear. If you really try to improve your retention of people's names, you will soon discover the astonishing power of this simple act.

The simple effort of correctly pronouncing a person's name is a hundred times more powerful when the name has its origins in a foreign country. Learn how to correctly say a particularly difficult Greek name, or Japanese name, and you may be the only person they have ever met who has made the effort. That makes for a powerful bonding in your relationship that will have very deep roots. The person can't help but like and respect you when you alone have gone to the trouble of learning to pronounce his or her name correctly.

Unfortunately, not everyone has the natural ability to instantly put a name to a face. To remember names or other data the first time you hear them, you must pay attention. Be really mentally alert when you are introduced to a new person. Listen to their name closely and repeat it several times in your head. Ask them to repeat it if you are unsure you heard them correctly. Ask them to pronounce it for you if it is unusual. Echo the name back to them in a way that encourages correction if necessary. "Nice to meet you, Darin..." Or you can echo the name to simply acknowledge and confirm that you have understood. Use their name as often as you can in the first few minutes you talk to them. This will help reinforce the name in your memory.

Some memory techniques suggest that you look at the face and link a facial feature with the sound of the name. This could be something like, "Roberta, for her rosy cheeks," or "Stan, for a strong jaw." The idea is to be looking at a facial feature and linking their name with that feature. This technique greatly improves your ability to retain a name.

Another technique is to link this new person to a person you know well. For example, if I meet a "Ron," I link it to my good friend Ron. I find something that is similar between the new Ron and the familiar friend Ron. In this way, your mind links the two names and individuals together, making it easier to remember the name. These types of techniques will greatly assist you in recalling and remembering the names and faces of new people. This will also help you in bonding to these people quickly, which will make meeting new people fun and rewarding.

5. Give personal attention. Many business relationships today come down to just that—relationships. The deeper you understand your clients' wants, needs, prejudices, and personal interests, above and beyond the actual business, the greater the chance you have of serving them for the long haul. Simple touches like birthday cards, Christmas cards, and anniversary cards go a lot further than the dollar you spend. Keep credit card numbers and sizes on file, so you don't have to continually ask for them. Make mental or written notes of their favorite beverages, cigars, and foods. In fact, developing a customer profile in a database is a must for legendary service.

The profile I use has over 50 questions about my clients that over time, through various conversations, I fill in. It contains information like where they were born, where they went to school, what their parents did, what sports they like, what teams they support, which cars they drive, what religion they are, how many children they have, and so forth. Some of these things I ask point blank; others my clients tell me over time in the natural flow of conversation. All of this information is deeply valuable in building a relationship and turning conversations toward their areas of interest rather than mine.

Having taught karate for many years, one of the most interesting observations I can give you about the hundreds of hours I spent teaching private lessons is that the most important skill in teaching is, in fact, listening. (This is just as true for most golf professionals.) Over half the time I spent giving lessons was actually spent listening to my clients vent frustration, share excitement, and use me as a sounding board for their hopes, plans, and dreams. Rarely did they actually talk about karate! Find out what your golfers want to talk about. The more you know about them, the longer your relationships will last!

Remember, everyone in the world has this great big badge on their chest which reads "MAKE ME FEEL IMPORTANT." Succeed in that endeavor and you will succeed in everything. No matter what else is going on, at least smile, nod, or wave whenever someone meets your eye.

6. Make employees—all employees—service oriented. The best way to get all employees in a service mode is simply to tell every new employee that their number one job, regardless of position or job description, is customer service. Let them know that if they cannot answer a question or help a customer, they are to help that customer locate someone else who can, or to take that customer's name and have the appropriate person call them back later that day! Employees, like everyone else, will rise to the level of your expectations only if they are given those expectations. If you hire a graphics designer for your office and tell him that his job is graphics, on the occasions when he may be the only one in the office to answer the phone, he is not going to be very helpful. However, if he is told in no uncertain terms that he is a customer service graphics designer, he will be much more in tune to making an effort on this front. Set yourself up for service success by making customer service everyone's job!

7. Be accessible. When clients want to reach you, they want to do it now! Few things are more irritating than calling a service provider and being shuffled to voicemail automatically, with little or no indication that the person you are looking for is in the office or traveling through Kenya on safari. If nothing else, tell your receptionist when you will be returning calls, so that the person waiting for the call can continue with his daily life. Nothing irritates me (and most other people) more than being told I will be called right back only to be hanging by the phone for two hours or more waiting for the call.

Provide real people to your web site's visitors

You are going to think I am making this up, but I assure you I am not. Recently I had a general manager call me and yell at me because I put his contact information on his website. He told me in no uncertain terms that he did not want his members e-mailing him at all hours of the day. In fact, he didn't want them to e-mail him at all.

Don't play hide-and-seek with your customers and potential customers. Include your name, phone number, e-mail address, and street address, to show that you are a real person and a real business with real products and services to sell. A mark of the company with poor service is that it doesn't have any contact information displayed on its site, or hides it so no one can find it. (Another sign is that they don't answer their e-mail!) Show your visitors that you care by including your contact number and the times you wish to be called. Offer a feedback e-mail section to get players' opinions on your course and service. It's better they tell you there's a problem than all of their friends!

8. Never tell your customers about your problems or the club's; they don't care. Often, especially in situations where you spend a lot of time with a particular member, there is the temptation to cross the boundary and share personal problems with a client. In the norms of conversation, they may even ask questions or probe about your personal life. In reality, they are not interested in your problems. Do not be conned into sharing them. Find out everything you can about your customers, while saying little or nothing about yourself. As the Chinese say "keep the tiger behind the bamboo!" This will only add to your sense of power and help build your reputation faster.

9. Be consistent in all your actions. Simple, consistent actions build reputations. It is through your simple actions that you can build your customer service. And if you combine several simple actions together you can take giant leaps over your competition as you build your reputation. After each visit to the dentist, my dentist called my house that evening to make sure I felt all right. Not only that, but when he referred me to surgery with another physician, he found out when the surgery was scheduled and called me that night to see how it had gone, even though he was not personally involved. When my child was born, he sent me a bottle of wine with his label on it. Now, this is someone whom I only saw every six months, yet he acted as if he was almost part of the family. The result was simple:

Even when I moved my business over fifty miles away, I still drove to his office. He had backed up his reputation with service!

Showing up is 90% of the job

As an employee of various restaurants in my youth, I built my reputation not on knowledge of fine wines or excellent service, but on the one thing that mattered most to the owners and managers— I showed up. Not once in a while, not when I felt like it, and not just when it was raining outside. I showed up and showed up on time, every single day I was scheduled to work, without fail. In the restaurant business that simply does not happen! In getting jobs every season, my ace in the hole was the restaurant's knowledge that I would show up, and so time and time again I cut the season's job search down to just one or two calls. At nineteen I had a reputation for nothing in the world except showing up, but at nineteen, that was enough. As Woody Allen once said, "Showing up is 90 percent of success."

10. Always smile! One of the surest ways of giving good service is to project the type of attitude you expect to get back.

Pay careful attention to your body language, posture, and facial expressions. Always look as if you are having the time of your life, no matter what is going on around you! Unless you are running a mortuary, smile at all times; if nothing else, people will wonder what you are smiling about.

ARE YOU DOING YOUR BEST?

A question I often ask in my seminars is, "Are you good at what you do?" To which—surprise, surprise—most people answer with the most resounding YES of the day. Then I ask them if, in fact, they are settling for being good when they could be GREAT! Usually, it gets a little quiet around that time. In today's competitive climate, good is the standard—if you aren't good, you won't be around for very long. But how much more could you accomplish in building your reputation for service (and your income) if, instead of just being good, you actually were GREAT!

You must build your reputation first with your employees, then with your customers, then with your prospects.

CUSTOMER SERVICE GOALS FOR THE SUPERIOR BUSINESS

I devised the following customer service goals that, with a little amendment, you might find useful in applying to your particular club.

Collect information about customer preferences and habits, and use this information to personalize relationships and services.

Keep our present clients.

Keep our clients delighted, not just satisfied, with our services.

Help our clients improve their lives with our service so that we, in turn, can enjoy ours more from their compensation.

Ensure that our clients always speak well of our business and employees.

Help our present clients help us attract new customers and keep them happy as well.

Maintain excellent communication with our clients at all times and greet clients by name. Treat our employees well, so they'll treat our customers the same way.

Realize that all client complaints give us a chance to improve. Act quickly and fairly to resolve all complaints.

Make every single employee responsive to customer service.

Be known as a business that has superior customer service and retention.

QUANTIFYING SUPERIOR SERVICE

Goals like the ones above are a great place to start when it comes to improving service, but what exactly is great service? Ask that question of most people and their answers will be, "I can't quite describe it, but I know it when I get it!" Great service is like good taste; it varies with the eye of the beholder. Despite this, you must specify what great service is.

A major reason that poor service happens is that in most business and organizations, great service is not *quantified*. It may be talked about, talked about, and talked about again, but rarely is it taken to the next step and measured in a host of different ways. As you no doubt already know from other areas of your business, what gets measured is what gets done.

With that thought in mind, I suggest that you sit down with your staff and identify as many areas as you can in which service is given. For example:

- ✔ Answering the phone: How many rings is acceptable?

- ✔ How often will you send follow-up cards, thank you cards, or reminders?

- ✔ How quickly will you resolve any billing problems?

- ✔ How and when will you thank people for their referrals?

- ✔ What level do you want to keep your number of monthly complaints below?

- ✔ How clean will the clubhouse be?

- ✔ How well-stocked will the pro shop be?

- ✔ What will you give players if their scheduled start time is delayed?

By specifically quantifying how you intend to measure performance, you will take a quantum jump in your ability to achieve higher levels of service performance.

Policy must back up your position

A key factor many forget is that once a reputation enhancement plan is in place, policies must allow your employees to carry out their mission without conflict. You can't tell golfers your greens are the best and then not give your employees enough budget for seed, fertilizer, and labor. You cannot build a reputation for honesty and then tell an employee to lie about you not being in the office when you don't want to take a certain phone call. If your employees don't believe your commitment to great service, you can be sure no one else will! You can't create a friendly atmosphere if signage all over the property tells you WHAT YOU CAN'T DO!

ARE YOUR CLUB RULES & POLICIES USER-FRIENDLY?

One of the biggest responses I ever had to my e-newsletter that reaches over 69,000 owners and managers weekly was the one titled "Are Club Rules & Policies Killing Golf?" While about 70 percent were in agreement with my position, a solid 30 percent were quite vocal in their dissent! Nonetheless, I feel that archaic rules and policies at many clubs are a detriment to good customer service! Now let me preface this by saying I am not against policies and rules that have a basis in logic, nor do I want guys playing without a shirt, clubs in one hand and a six-pack of Bud in the other! (Although in some places a policy like that would improve a club's income, I just don't want to play there!)

Here's a novel idea. Slay some sacred cows and let your members and guests actually enjoy themselves!

16. Relax or Eliminate the Dress Code, Cell Phone Policy & Other Stupid Rules

They say attitude is everything and your club's attitude to everyday decisions, that many people feel are "personal" makes a huge statement to the golfing public at large.

Are they welcome? Or are they likely too embarrassed by failure to adhere to some long lost rule or club policy held sacrosanct like the holy grail by the club's "old guard"?

A Golf Development Wales (GDW) poll of nearly 2,000 people revealed how important a 'welcoming' golf club is to membership recruitment, while another poll of over 1,000 golfers found that 71 percent believe that dress codes do deter people from taking up the game.

In many ways, I'm a traditionalist. I play blades, would prefer the balls stop going any further and love the older classic courses. But I've never been much for club rules, and in fact, **I think club rules hurt golf in a bigger way than anyone realizes or cares to admit.**

For example, at club in Scotland on a damp and foggy morning, I was asked to remove my $100 navy blue, water resistant, sleeveless sweater with an RTJ logo on it as according to the steward, it constituted rain gear which was not allowed in the clubhouse. I protested that:

A.   It was my only sweater, and

B.   It was cold.

To which came the reply, "You'll warm up in a wee minute as soon as ye get yer coffee in yea! (Which loosely translated means "I don't give a damn… take it off if you want to come in!") I did, but was cold for 15 minutes while I waited for my coffee to arrive and thus warm me up! To what end?

(I understand since I first told that story on my blog they have radically changed their policy. If so good for them.)

At another famous course in Scotland a monster of a course at almost 6200 yards, with the fairways hard as rock after weeks of high temperatures and no rain, (unusual I know) thus ensuring that even a miss hit went 300 yards, we were forbidden to play the back tees. (Very typical in England and Scotland, as they consider it a privilege for the members and even then only in tournaments.) And so we played this course as we did at Royal course in Scotland at 5800 yards or less with a driver and a Sand Wedge. If I had wanted to play pitch and putt, I could have done that on the free course at the village green! I likely not go back, to that golf club. The pub on the village green was excellent!

My previous club in the USA (as most clubs do) banned jeans, which in my club's case, cost them about $3,000 in my business because I can't be bothered to change to go to the club for lunch. Besides I look better in a pair of $150 Armani jeans than Bob Lynch looks in his 1978, brown Polyester Sears slacks! In some club's they allow black denim but no blue jeans?

In France where golf is actually growing, you see a lot of 30 something couples playing the game, a large percentage, 50% or more of them in jeans. Yes, blue jeans!

How about this set of rules from a club I played recently:

Club Dress Code

Management has been directed by the Board of Directors to enforce the following dress code. These guidelines pertain to all members and their families. Members are responsible for ensuring all guests follow these guidelines. Please do not embarrass the management, your guests or yourself by not following the rules currently in force.

31. All male members, guests and children must wear collared shirts throughout the Club except at the Pool. Turtleneck and mock turtleneck shirts may be worn on the Golf Course only if they have sleeves long enough to cover the elbow. Anywhere in the Clubhouse (except the Locker Room and the Men's Grill) a jacket or a collared shirt must be worn over turtlenecks. All shirts must be tucked inside pants or shorts.

32. All female members, guests and children must wear either collared shirts with or without sleeves or collarless shirts with sleeves. All shirts which are manufactured to be worn out must be 3 inches below the waist all the way around and must be bonded or finished. All shorts, shorts or skirts worn must be no more than 4 inches above the knee.

33. No member or guest, male or female, may wear any type of denim (shorts, pants, dresses or jackets) anywhere on the Club property including the Pool area. This rule pertains to children of all ages.

34. Rally caps are forbidden anywhere on the property.

35. Bathing attire, including cover-ups and flip-flops, may only be worn in the Pool Area.

36. Shoes or women's dress sandals must be worn in the Living Room and Main Dining Room. Sneakers are acceptable in other areas.

37. Bermuda length and golf shorts are the only acceptable shorts to be worn on the Golf Course. Cargo shorts or cargo pants are not allowed anywhere in the Club.

38. All members and guests must wear proper tennis attire on the Tennis Courts. Tops must be predominately white in color.

39. Proper tennis attire may be worn in the Terrace for lunch. Tennis attire is not acceptable for dinner, except in the 19th Hole (seasonal).

40. Clothing that appears irregular or extraordinary in size or fashion is not acceptable anywhere in the Club.

41. If you are coming from the Pool, Tennis Courts or Golf Course to have dinner in the Terrace, you should not enter the Dining Room at any time if you are not dressed in proper Dining Room attire.

42. Cell phones and other electronic devices (including Laptops, IPads, Blackberry's, PDA's and "Texting") are NOT PERMITTED in most Club areas, INCLUDING the Dining and Public Areas, Outside Patio and the Tennis Court area.

Cell phones/electronic devices ARE PERMITTED only in the Locker Rooms & Parking Lots. They are also PERMITTED Poolside and on the Golf Course, but with discretion.

Please put on vibrate in all areas, and do not answer them or make calls in prohibited areas.

Please use good judgment and respect your fellow members and guests.

Management, including the Starter and Service Staff, have been given the authority to enforce the dress code and cell phone policy. Their decisions are final and the Board will not tolerate any abuse of the Hempstead Staff by a member or guest.

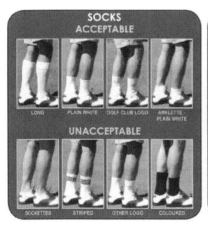 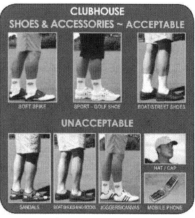

How about the no hat rule in the bar?

What if you are bald? What if you use your hat like some people surely do as a sort of sportsman's toupee? I know that after walking 18 holes in the Florida sun, my hair looks a lot neater if I keep my visor on!

I was asked to leave one club in the UK for wearing sneakers, actually $300 Ferrari driving shoes, it even had stamped on the back "Driving shoes for seriously fast drivers only." I took one off and showed him to prove they were driving shoes and not sneakers to no avail.

My friend a doctor, and a member at Pine Valley was asked to leave for wear Crocks! Clubs seem to forget that when you travel, you may only have two pairs of shoes!

Okay, here's a good one… for years almost every course on the planet, including mine, had a no collar no play rule! Well… that was until Tiger started wearing T-shirts to play in. Oh, but that's Okay they tell me because it has a mock collar? A mock collar? What the hell is a mock collar? Is that like a fake collar? It's also what the most famous CEO of the Century, Steve Jobs, wore every day of his life!

Now does anyone enjoy the game less because now you can play in a T-shirt and before you couldn't?

At most clubs, I have to wear shorts to my knees which makes it hard to walk especially when it's dripping hot! What is wrong with tailored tennis shorts to play golf in? I've seen "Jack" play in them several times and if it's good enough for "Jack" it ought to be good enough for everyone else!

Besides, the people who make these stupid rules are not the ones walking in 90-degree heat and carrying their bags anyway.

Troon Takes a Lead in the Relaxation of Golf

A senior vice president of Troon's International Operation said Troon's recent relaxation of dress code rules had produced a positive effect on the clubs' bottom lines.

"Based on our consumer feedback, we found that clubs 'stuffiness' and overbearing rules were barriers to some visiting," he said.

"Having strict rules on attire meant families and friends were going elsewhere for lunches, drinks and dinner, which was therefore negatively affecting a critical revenue stream for our owners. Our new dress code has allowed a family to come and enjoy the facilities without having to worry so much about what they wear."

Clothing Optional

While I was gone one summer my previous office manager adopted an 18-point dress code policy; I changed it to a one-point policy. "Clothing is optional" except on days when clients visit where you will wear staff uniforms of orange and black.

Think about this: in the 20's and 30's all golfers played in a jacket and tie. In the 60's no salesman was ever without a hat. In the 70's every CEO wore a suit. When was the last time you ever saw Richard Branson or Mark Zuckerberg in a suit? Things change, get used to it!

Do I still tell my kid to tuck his shirt in? Yes, but I have no idea why, just conditioning I guess!

Tee Policy

Let's take the tenth tee policy at most clubs. They treat teeing off there like some privilege reserved for high-ranking members of the Senate. If there is no one on the back nine and no one on the 9th tee, why the heck can't you play the back first?

Or take the tee time policy, which at most clubs is seven days. What if you have a guest coming from out of town and you want to make sure you can get a tee time that coincides with his flights in and out four weeks from now?

At a private club, why would that be a big deal? Isn't it member-centric to take care of situations like this for the enjoyment of the member and guest? Try doing it most places, and you'll get the old "My hands are tied" story.

Access Numbers Are NOT Customer Friendly!

A look at the UK for a couple more points ... **Every club has code pad access** to the clubhouse, so to get in you must first visit the pro shop, who usually although not always can provide it, (when they are open). The other option, banging on the door until someone lets you in, is often quicker and no one ever asks who you are anyway!

And my favorite UK "Screw you all" (and I seem to remember this at Merion too?) **Visitors are NOT allowed** in the members' changing rooms at many clubs. Guests have their own TINY locker rooms creating a two-tier system long since banished in most educated countries. (It's not even like the members changing room are nicer, most would be put to shame by a high school locker room!)

Many clubs have ridiculous rules as to when singles or four balls can play. Meanwhile, the course is half empty while you wait for 2 hours on the putting green for your allotted time!

At a private club, why does the range close at 5 or 6 pm, except the day the range is being cut? What the hell difference does it make if I want to hit balls until dark? I really don't need any supervision.

Cell Phones

I don't like cell phones on a golf course, but I absolutely see how allowing them will increase, NOT decrease play. Guys who sneak away from the office want to stay in touch, simple as that. Others, like doctors on call, have to stay in touch. By all means, limit their use in the dining room, but that's about it! Keyword vibrate.

Two recent reports underline how important this could be to golf clubs in 2014 – *England Golf* surveyed 55 golf clubs that were performing well and concluded that one of the key reasons was a relaxing of bans on mobile phones. And a poll by Syngenta of thousands of people found that not having WiFi capabilities on the course was the fourth biggest reason why people aged 15 to 25 are not playing golf.

Anyway, by now I am sure you get my drift, and you may have many of your own pet peeves to contribute.

I say get rid of one and all of your clubs stupid rules and mindless policies if they don't contribute to helping players enjoy the game. Go ahead slay some sacred cows and make your club 100% people friendly! The old guard will complain about lack of standards for a few weeks and life will go on. A life set up to attract rather than repel people from your club's doors!

Take Down ALL the Negative Signage!

The only thing that's more productive at turning people off the game than stupid rules are stupid signs that serve to reinforce the old-fashioned, stuffy attitudes and regimes that have gone before.

These are not perhaps as damaging overall as poor policies, but signs do make up part of the player's initial impression about a place and almost all signs I see at golf courses around the world are negative!

✔ No Mulligans

✔ No practice swings

✔ No coolers

✔ Don't steal range balls

✔ No starting on the 10th

✔ Members only car park,

✔ Members only lockers

✔ Members only patio

✔ Members only table

✔ No chipping

✔ No Putting

✔ No pull carts

✔ No cell phones

✔ No five balls

✔ No climbing up the face

✔ No changing in the parking lot

First of all these sign are an eyesore.

Secondly they are annoying and...

Thirdly no one pays any attention to them anyway!

If a guy cold tops his first shot he's going to re-tee no matter what the sign says. And he can always say he didn't see it and declare it a provisional to flaunt his superior knowledge of the Rules of Golf anyway!

Let's start a national campaign to ban useless signs on golf courses!

And another campaign to eliminate the word NO from the club experience!

Four star resort!

Hand the players a RULES sheet before they start IF YOU MUST, but take all those tacky signs off the golf course.

Gee REALLY... and I was thirsty too!

Am I advocating anarchy?

No, just some common sense. If we are to grow golf we must appeal to a wider audience than we do now. We must be user friendly. The Rules of golf are complicated enough without adding all kinds of meaningless signage, rules and restrictions.

Take all that money and effort and put it towards making sure members and guests have a great time at your club!

If you have to have signage at least use a more entertaining option!

Improve Your Customer Service and Be Friendly!

I don't think golf has ever been viewed as a friendly or accommodating sport, which is a shame as it's one of the few sports anyone regardless of size or age can enjoy! The interaction customers have with staff is often how a club or for that matter any business is judged, "Do they want my business?"

Ask any club how good their service is and 95% will tell you it's great! Even those that don't will tell you they are "friendly." But poor service and aloof attitudes drive many away from the game and stop many more from ever starting. How do you even know if your customer service is good… do you measure it? Most clubs do not but all you have to do is take a quick look on line at the hundreds of review sites to see the real state of customer service in the golf industry.

Phone rings without being answered or the phone is picked up to book someone a tee time while you stand at the counter trying to do the same thing and finishing second! The club secretary raises a disapproving eyebrow at your choice of shirt and the starter goes through a list of 99 things you should not do on the course before wishing you a nice day☹ Then you tee off and the real problems start.

Let's just take a quick peek:

amcritic

Senior Reviewer

⭐ 7 reviews

🌐 Reviews in 6 cities

🏅 4 helpful votes

"Terrible course with an annoying nazi course ranger."

◉○○○○ Reviewed 23 January 2012 📱 via mobile

I was playing with a group of well-played golfers, including one ex-pro only to have the course ranger follow us onto 3 of our 9 holes and had the audacity to tell us we were behind play, he had time to come tell us while we were waiting on the tee for the group in front.

I think he was a little bored and took his job a little too seriously. The kind of person that would make the perfect parking inspector.

Didn't end playing the 18 holes we were planning. Such a shame. Great location but felt like the hungry jacks of the golf world.

Was this review helpful? Yes   Problem with this review?

Ask amcritic about Victoria Park Golf Complex

This review is the subjective opinion of a TripAdvisor member and not of TripAdvisor LLC

Bryant M.
Irvine, CA

👥 2
📷 4

◼◻◻◻◻ 2/21/2012

WOW!! Are you kidding me Customer Service???? All I can say is WOW!! I came here on my birthday, and as you may or may not know, if you sign up online, they will send a free day of golf to be redeemed on your birthday, so I was like cool, awesome, I can play for free at this really nice course, and I can get my friend on for like $65 (which we split so we each paid $33ish).

So we haven't golfed in a while, not going to play great. We tee off on number one, we both hit pretty crappy shots, and the first few holes take a while, the marshall is up on our A%$, no problem, I can understand that.

Ok, so after the 4th hole, we pick up the pace, we are warmed up, now there is no one on our tail, no one we need to hurry up for, so we just cruise through the rest of the front nine.

So we finish the 9th Hole and the marshall comes up to us and says this.." Not to bust your chops or anything, but you guys really need to pick it up, that nine took you 2 hours and 9 minutes." So I said, there was no one behind us, and I thought we played in a pretty timely manner, is that bad?" He said, "yes," in a very rude tone. "You need to be on pace for 4 hours, even if you aren't holding anyone up, or bothering anyone"!

Guy was a total Jerk, and then another guys said the same thing to us!!

What a bunch of A&^ Holes who work here, never coming back, even it is for FREE!!

Worst customer service ever!!!

1 review from our community

Write a Review

mwalno
Chicago, IL

Top Contributor

⭐ 174 reviews

20 attraction reviews

Reviews in 62 cities

69 helpful votes

"BUGS, bad rangers, but Great Golf"

⊙⊙⊙◯◯ Reviewed June 24, 2013

The one thing that REALLY BOTHERED me was the PACE OF PLAY....we flew through the first 5 holes and then ran into a foursome....we were right on them and they never let play through. I had enough at the turn when we reached the tee after they were in the 1/2 way house and they still would NOT let us through (even after I axed). So we walked in to get a beer and I went into the the pro shop to let them know...the young kid said he would send the ranger out. So we hit our tee shots, and the ranger approached when we were on the green, he asked if we were the ones who "complained" and said he would talk to the group in front....he did and came back to say they were playing just fine.....EXCEPT there were two holes open in front of them......I have never had a ranger who was like that.....

So, great course (great value), shi**y rangers, and lots of bugs....I would try somewhere else next time.

Total - 2 green fees (walking) - $64.00

1 review from our community

Write a Review

mwalno
Chicago, IL

Top Contributor

⭐ 174 reviews

20 attraction reviews

Reviews in 62 cities

69 helpful votes

"BUGS, bad rangers, but Great Golf"

⊙⊙⊙◯◯ Reviewed June 24, 2013

The one thing that REALLY BOTHERED me was the PACE OF PLAY....we flew through the first 5 holes and then ran into a foursome....we were right on them and they never let play through. I had enough at the turn when we reached the tee after they were in the 1/2 way house and they still would NOT let us through (even after I axed). So we walked in to get a beer and I went into the the pro shop to let them know...the young kid said he would send the ranger out. So we hit our tee shots, and the ranger approached when we were on the green, he asked if we were the ones who "complained" and said he would talk to the group in front....he did and came back to say they were playing just fine.....EXCEPT there were two holes open in front of them......I have never had a ranger who was like that.....

So, great course (great value), shi**y rangers, and lots of bugs....I would try somewhere else next time.

Total - 2 green fees (walking) - $64.00

82% of All Your Bad Press Is Generated by a Single Person...the Club's Ranger!

This makes sense as once a player tees off the ranger is the person they are most likely to see while out on the course for 4 or 5 hours. Unless they actually do want to see him, in which case he is usually AWOL looking for golf balls!

Your ranger can have a huge effect on the public's impressions of your course and judging by the hundreds of comments I reviewed, that impression is generally negative, very negative!

He might be a nice old guy in the coffee shop, but on the course, he morphs into a regular Napoleon. So …. **It's 11:27 am do you know where your ranger is?**

At almost every course I have ever been to the answer is NO and that's a problem! Not only is it a customer service problem but it's also an income problem!

The rangers at most courses are retired guys who often don't get paid and get free golf in return. (Not technically legal but common enough anyway.) Since they don't get paid, they are not really employees, which is good because they usually don't really work either!

Instead, they cruise around the course like General MacArthur in his Jeep looking for golf balls and avoiding contact with players that might result in them having to actually do something! LIKE SPEED THE GROUP IN FRONT UP! (As discussed earlier, I'm not the only player in the world who enjoys playing in 3 1/2 hours or less? And yes I do mean for 18.)

The problem is that rangers are one of your club's most important employees and usually the only person your players have interaction with once they are out on the golf course. While most courses talk about *"service"* or *"creating a great golfing experience"* few do actually anything about creating it, and that includes many private clubs!

Public or Private, Many Rangers Suffer from Napoleon Syndrome

Just the other day at my exclusive private club the ranger ran over to the tenth tee in his cart and yelled even though he was just 20 feet away from my foursome "HEY! You guys are supposed to be starting on the

1st of the other nine!" It was cold, windy and raining (sure reasons not to play when you live in Florida, and consequently there was hardly anyone at the club).

We trudged over to the first tee and found a foursome of women who were as daft as we were and duly went back to the tenth where ranger Bob appeared again. "YOU GUYS are supposed to be on the 1st!" he yells exasperated at his dim-witted members.

"Call the shop," we said, "and see if they care!" He did, and they didn't! We completed nine holes in 1.15 without seeing another player on the course.

The point though is not the rights and wrongs of the incident itself, but rather the way in which our group was addressed and how the problem, or in this case non-problem, was handled. None of us were addressed by name although he knows us all. At not one point did he offer to check with the shop to solve the problem without creating one. In fact, he seemed more intent on showing us who was boss instead of helping facilitate our golfing experience!

This is just a small personal example of the problems I hear about every week from players at the various clubs I work with. *"I'll never pay XXX club again because your rangers are rude."* This is a very common e-mail that comes back to me when I send out various promotions for my clients.

Few courses seem to realize just what damage a ranger can do to their business. If you doubt me even for a moment just look at Trip Advisor, Yelp, Golf.com or anywhere else people can leave comments about a course. An alarming number are about the ranger, and they are not the positive type!

And of course, it's not just the rangers; it can be anyone at the club:

My friend and I were playing an early morning practice round at St Million, a high-end resort in the UK for a scratch event the following day. We specifically asked to play the back tees as this is where we would

397

be playing from in the tournament. As mentioned earlier, in England for some reason known only to the gods this is a huge issue. However, we were granted permission. There was no starter at the tee, so we teed off. We were about 50 yards up the fairway when the ranger came running after us:

"Hey guys you can't play the back tees!" he yells."

"We can," I said, "We just asked."

What did he say next …"Okay, no problem, have a nice day?"

No, he said, and I quote, "WE will see about that!" and got on his radio to the pro shop who then confirmed what I had told him.

On the second tee, a member of the ground staff asked us if we knew we were playing the back tees. We said we did. He, of course, asked if we had permission and even took us at our word when we said we did. On the 5th the greens keeper himself drove up to us and asked again.

I stood in a pro shop in Orlando at a well-known daily fee as the assistant pro recounted his previous days round in a pro-am, hole by hole on the phone while I stood in front of him. About the 13th he got embarrassed and turned his back to me!

I watched a caddie master lambaste a guest at an exclusive private club for taking a cart to the range because, although it looked identical to all the others, in fact, belonged to the club president. I mean he yelled at the guest for several minutes. In any other setting, the guy who was about six foot five would have probably knocked him out. Instead, he took it like a five year being scolded by his mother front of 15 to 20 people!

You Are Not Worthy!

I played in the Florida State team championship at an exclusive club in Naples, Fl. There were about 50 four-man teams, and it was the practice day. Our team, from an exclusive club, went into the clubhouse at around noon to get something to eat before we teed off at 1 pm. There was a huge buffet set out and about three people, (members I assumed) eating. We greeted them, grabbed a plate and headed for the food only to be told not only could we not eat, but we were not allowed in the clubhouse.

You run a statewide event and ban the players from your clubhouse?

Yep, you can't make this stuff up! We were told there was a girl on the course with sandwiches whom we eventually saw, about 3.15!

A Royal Welcome!

A few years ago I walked into the secretary's office at Royal St. Georges at 8 am on a Tuesday (I one of only three cars in the parking lot) to inquire about a practice round for the English Amateur Championship a few days hence. He looked at me incredulously and without even the thought of a greeting said in a very unpleasant and arrogant tone

"Didn't you read your package?" as he brandied a large manila envelope.

"Well," said I, "Since the English Golf Union did not see fit to e-mail any details, and I left home four weeks ago that package might well be in my mail box 3,000 miles away but I haven't seen it personally."

"HUMPH!" he says and proceeds to make a big show of photo copying two pages, which he hands me. "Practice rounds were last week," he says emphatically.

"Fine then can I pay to play?" I inquire humbly -- well at least politely.

He said I could for 150 pounds, but I couldn't play until 2 pm. 6 hours from then!

Fine I say and head to the range to beat several buckets of balls. By 11.30am I am worn out and walking back towards the clubhouse for a cup of tea. As I pass the cart shed the caddie master is sending home two boys as there are no players! I said I'd be glad to take a caddie. The caddie master is very grateful as he doesn't want to send them home empty-handed.

"Only problem is I can't play until 2 pm according to his highness in the secretary's office." I venture.

Forget that he says, you can go now, and I'll sign you in at the guest of a member rate. (Nice, 110 pounds saved)

There is no one on the entire course except the two members in front of me. They hold me up for 18 holes although I am playing 4 or 5 balls a hole to kill time.

When I am done, it's now after 4 pm, and I walk in the clubhouse to get a cup of tea. Suddenly the secretary rushes out to tell me I can't come in the clubhouse after 4 pm without a jacket. I apologize profusely for my ignorance but tell him I had only ventured into the clubhouse to THANK HIM for his hospitality ☺

He mumbled something and scuttled back into his office!

I took tea outside on the patio; it was a lovely day!

I could go on and on about the hilarious lack of service and attitude in the golf business; only it's never very funny at the time.

✔ Clubs must train staff to be MORE people friendly and accommodating. The customer is not always right, but he's not always wrong either!

✔ Body language and tonality are just as important as what you actually say, sometimes more so!

✔ Staff should be trained to recall the names of members or frequent guests.

✔ Clubs should provide employees with simple scripts to deal with common situations like they do at Disney or Ritz Carlton, or any other top-notch organizations.

✔ Special care must be given to women, children and newcomers, as Club Corp founder, Robert Deadman used to say "Warm welcomes and fond goodbyes!"

✔ Both tangible and intangible customer service points should be measured and reviewed monthly.

✔ Rangers, starters and people answering the phone should be properly trained!

✔ Buy copies of *How to Win Friends and Influence People* for all staff!

SUMMARY

Backing up your reputation with the real McCoy is essential for the long-term establishment of your legendary reputation. When it comes to service, it is the frontline people and the little things that can make or break your reputation.

Understand why customers leave and what their most common complaints are, then take action to address them. Stay close to your customers and always solicit feedback on how you are doing and how you might improve. Remember that existing customers are always more valuable than customers you don't have yet.

Follow up on everything you say you will do, and check that it's been done. Make an extra effort to remember all your customers' names and give them the special attention that everyone craves. Make sure your employees are trained and that they understand that, no matter what their positions, customer service is everyone's job.

Always be accessible, or give clear instructions on when and where you can be reached. Never discuss any of your problems with customers; they don't care.

Re-evaluate your rules, regulars and dress codes do you really need them all? Remove all negative signage! Train your rangers and first tee hosts!

Continually question whether you are doing your best to set customer service goals and, most important of all, quantify superior service. Once you decide what you will do to create great service, back up your goals and policies by giving those who work for you the power, authority, and moral guidance to provide superior service.

Last, but not least, always be consistent in your actions and don't forget to smile!

The words of Henry David Thoreau ring just as true today in the new millennium as they did when he first spoke them, "What you do speaks so loud I cannot hear what you are saying."

Additional Resources: Ranger Training Program

The *Ranger Systems Manual* I developed to solve this problem is 60 pages plus a video and includes detailed checklists, routing plans and times so that you can answer the question "Do you know where the ranger is at any given time?" by looking at a sheet of paper, not picking up the walkie-talkie. Using this manual as a guide, you also know exactly to the word what the rangers response will be to any of 19 key situations from slow play to trespassers on the golf course.

Like Disney, everything in the manual is scripted. Whether the group responds with a positive "No Problem" or negative "@#$%& you" there is another scripted response, and it's not "@#$% you too!" By training the rangers to respond in the correct way and having a real checklist of tasks, they must perform on their way around the course at specific times (like filling divots on the par threes) you eliminate a huge number of problems and increase their value to your operation by 1000%

While a ranger systems manual like this does not solve every problem, it solves many of them before they happen. This, in turn, makes their job easier, your job easier and the quality and consistency of your club's response to problems the same no matter whether ranger Bob, John or Sally happens to be dealing with the problem. This helps speed up play, increasing your potential for greater revenue and delivers the type of consistent experience that players associate with great service.

Whether you agree or disagree with any of my examples, at least consider reviewing your club's policies once a year and see if they still make sense to anyone under eighty!

CHAPTER NINETEEN

How to Develop a REAL Customer Loyalty Program

I have told you about the importance of generating leads and getting people to your club. I have stressed the importance of giving your customers good—outrageously good—service. Now, let's talk about keeping your customers loyal. Let's look at how to turn occasional golfers into loyal customers who sing your praises to others. Customer loyalty seems to be the buzzword of the moment in the increasingly competitive golf business—and it should be. Courses are rightly taking a look at their existing players and trying to figure out how to stop them from going elsewhere.

In this chapter, you will discover:

✔ How to identify your best customers

✔ How to show customers that they are special

✔ How to outsmart your competition, steal players, and make them loyal to your course

✔ How to turn your members and guests into evangelists for your club

✔ How to turn a few letters and cards into GOLD

LEGENDARY LOYALTY

The problem with most clubs' attempts to start loyalty programs is that they start by offering discounts to their frequent players. Think about that. They offer their very best customers discounts for showing up! The problem with this strategy should be clear. Let's use a restaurant analogy. My favorite restaurant is the Crystal River Wine & Cheese Company. I spend over $1,000 there every single month. If the restaurant decided to start a loyalty program and give me a 10 percent discount, I'm not going to show up any more frequently than I do now. The restaurant would simply lose $1,200 a year in revenue!

I'm a loyal customer because the food is good, the atmosphere friendly, and the owner greets me by name and makes a big deal every time I walk in the door. On top of that, I know I can always get a table no matter how busy it is. In other words, I am treated like a special customer and therefore am a loyal customer.

The point is simple:

You cannot buy loyalty with discounts.

Instead let's suppose I received an occasional bottle of wine as a gift or was invited to a special wine-and-cheese tasting. In the latter case, I would probably buy a case of wine just for the invitation. You can buy play with discounts but you cannot buy loyalty! You buy loyalty with special service, small gifts, and special attention.

Think of the airline frequent-flyer programs. They are about much more than getting free flights. They're about first-class upgrades, free access to club rooms, early boarding, and other intangibles that are the real benefits since free flights take so long to earn these days. Your best customers will pay a fair price if you treat them right. Use incentives to get golfers to try your course, then convert them to loyal players with your service and extras!

Grass-roots marketing will always pay big

dividends!

A best-selling marketing book explains how Hush Puppies, the famous shoe company, had all but made the decision to shut down operations in 1995 when sales of their once-popular shoes dipped below 30,000 pairs. Then a very strange thing happened. Some kids in the Village section of New York started wearing the shoes, probably because no one else was. No one knows for sure how many kids started doing this, but the book suggests fewer than 50. While their numbers were few, their influence was not! These kids were opinion leaders in the local dance-club scene of lower Manhattan. Their friends and followers started to buy Hush Puppies.

A famous New York designer noticed that the "cool kids" were wearing Hush Puppies. He featured the shoes in his fall collection. Another designer noticed the same trend and opened a Hush Puppies store in Manhattan. Suddenly a bunch of kids had done something that no amount of marketing dollars could have done— they made Hush Puppies cool again! The following years the company sold over a million pairs of shoes.

When I built a karate-school empire in the mid 1990s, I realized early on that the fractionalized world of martial arts was controlled by the opinions of fewer than 200 school owners. Each of these 200 people had an association or a network of other schools. By convincing one opinion leader to join my organization, three or four other schools would automatically follow suit. By targeting these 200 school owners (rather than the other 12,000), I was able to sign up 120 franchisees in less than 18 months.

By targeting influential opinion leaders, the masses will soon follow.

DEVELOPING AN EFFECTIVE LOYALTY & OPINION-LEADER MARKETING PROGRAM FOR YOUR CLUB

The power of the Pareto principle

Within every business exists the phenomenon of the Pareto Principle, or the 80/20 rule. It posits that 80 percent of your business comes from 20 percent of your customers. While most understand the concept, few courses actually try to identify their opinion leaders!

Let's go back to the restaurant example. In any restaurant there are X number of customers who come in frequently and often bring friends. If the restaurant could get these "super customers" to go to the restaurant twice a month instead of once a month, it might be worth an extra $5,000 a year per super-customer to them.

The same is true of daily-fee golf clubs and of private clubs interested in member retention. A golfer might play a particular course and bring three business guests once a month. Chances are the guy is an avid player and plays six to eight times a month. If you could get him to bring guests to your course twice a month instead of once, it would be worth an extra few thousand dollars a year. That doesn't even count the potential for him to bring other "A" type players to the facility. These "A" players would in turn bring all of their guests!

While quality (whether of a restaurant's food or a golf course's greens) does play a part in customers' decisions, it plays only a minor role. Far more important is the connection customers feel to the particular business. Ask yourself:

- ✔ Does your bartender or starter remember players by name?

- ✔ Is the player acknowledged as a good customer and given an occasional free drink or golf cart?

- ✔ Does the player get a thank-you card or a Christmas card?

Scott Wyckoff, the pro at World Woods, always sends me a thank you card for taking a lesson, even though he won't take my money! In a shameless pitch for Scott (he is much too modest to have anything to do with this), if we ever opened a golf club this is the guy we would hire, and

PAY HIM TWICE WHAT HE ASKS FOR.

He is worth three times what he asks for! (You too, Rudy!)

✔ How about an occasional free gift for your best customers? A sleeve of balls, a golf book, or something that doesn't cost much but makes the player feel special?

The first club in your area to offer players more than just a good golf course will slowly but surely get more of their business, and others like them! Customers' positive opinions lead other people. They do your marketing for you. Word of mouth from these opinion- leader players will do a better job than you ever can!

✔ Who are your opinion leaders?

✔ Are they tagged in your database?

✔ What have you done for them lately?

DEFINE YOUR PERFECT CUSTOMERS, YOUR OPINION LEADERS

Can you describe the qualities of a perfect customer to yourself? (See Chapter 4.) You probably immediately thought of someone at your club who's the perfect customer. That's good because the first step in finding more perfect customers is to truly understand what perfect customers should "look like."

What age are they? What kind of income do they have? What type of job do they have? Where do they live? What do they read? Where do they work? What exactly are the qualities of a perfect customer for you? (See examples on the next page.)

Do this exercise with your staff and try to come up with 25–50 people who seem to be the perfect clients. Take a look at the profiles of who the perfect client is because from now on they are the only clients you want to attract! Take the time to establish profiles of your key customers. Build the model customer, the type of customer you want to attract.

Once identified, these are the people we are going to put on our opinion leader program.

OPINION LEADER PROGRAM

Identify 25–50 opinion leaders from the people who play your course on a regular basis and are your very best clients.

These are the people who:

✔ Pay full green fees

✔ Bring guests

✔ Give you referrals

✔ Buy stuff in the pro shop

✔ Take lessons

✔ Attend special events

✔ Play in tournaments

✔ Spend money in the bar and restaurant

These are your very best customers, the type of people you need more of to maximize your club. These are your "A" clients, the top of the 20 percent from which you derive most of your income. More players like this and...well, you wouldn't need more players like this!

The idea of your opinion leader program is to design a system that makes these players feel special. By using a system, you can implement the program on a carefully planned basis and make sure that everything gets done. The players, of course, have no idea that it's a system—they just think you provide great service to them because they're special.

By making these opinion leaders feel more special and with some subtle hints, this program will turn your top 50 players into evangelists for your club.

Are you treating your clients like dogs?

Some years ago my dog, a Black lab named Winston, needed a vet. My wife took him to the nearest local animal hospital. They took care of his problem and sent him home with some tablets. A few weeks later, we moved to a new home some 30 miles away. Soon we began receiving truckloads of junk mail from realtors, insurance agents, landscape contractors, and charities. However, one piece of mail stood out—a letter addressed to Winston Wood. I thought someone must have really screwed up—imagine trying to make a cogent sales presentation to a dog! However, when I opened the envelope on Winston's behalf, I discovered that it was no mistake. The contents were indeed intended for Winston Wood. Inside was a birthday card from the animal hospital. Immediately, I felt a little guilty because I didn't even know it was his birthday. So I jumped in my car and rushed down to the store to get him a bone. My wife and I laughed and later told all our friends about the incident.

The 1040-DOG form that made me a customer for life.

Over the next few months Winston received several additional pieces of mail, all addressed to him personally. There were Christmas cards and get-well cards after shots. Believe it or not, Winston even received a 1040 DOG form at income tax time.

Though this animal hospital was over 30 miles away, we continued making the drive whenever Winston needed a vet. Why? Because this animal hospital took the time and effort to send cards and letters to my dog. The fact is, people don't care how much you know until they know how much you care. Show them you care!

For example, do you send your members or best customers Christmas cards, birthday cards, or simple thank-you cards? Do you reward them with an occasional small gift? What would it take from you to get golfers who play 15 times a year to play 16, 17, times or even 20 times? You'd be surprised how simple that is to do, and without discounting! And with incremental growth comes exponential profits!

Opinion leader program examples

✔ Thank-you card (costs about 83 cents mailed)

✔ E-mail a golf story ("I thought you'd enjoy this...")

✔ A book such as *Good Bounces Bad Lies* (retails for $24.95, but your cost is just $2—$4.50 mailed)

✔ A sleeve of balls ($3)

✔ A survey (40 cents)

✔ A copy of a great golf article or story with a note "I thought you'd enjoy this..." (40 cents mailed)

✔ E-mail another golf story

✔ A golf audio CD (retail 14.95, your cost is $1.99–$3.49 mailed)

✔ A video such as "Golf's Greatest Trick Shots (retail $24.95, your cost $2)

✔ A $5 gift certificate to golfbooks.com (your cost is zero by sending via e-mail)

✔ A birthday card on the player's birthday (costs 83 cents mailed)

✔ Three guest tickets for free play (your cost is zero)

✔ Golf print of a hole from your course (your cost $1 each)

✔ A Christmas card (mailed 83 cents)

All of this would cost around $14.98, but let's round it up to $20.

Multiply that by 50 people, and your total cost is just $1,000!

Why contact people 14 times a year? As mentioned in the Direct Mail chapter, because that number has been shown to create the optimum response. That's why catalog companies mail 14 times a year.

Now you might wish to spend a little more on your best clients or substitute some of the items for others depending on your situation.

You could also use the following as gifts:

✔ Hat

✔ Metal bag tag

✔ New-design glove

✔ Yardage book

✔ Gift certificate for a free lesson

✔ Gift certificate for free club fitting

✔ One box of the 700 dozen close-out balls you bought that are still in the bag room

✔ Lunch at the club with you

✔ A special dinner and focus group to gather input from "special customers"

SUMMARY

Not all customers are created equal. Identify your best customers using the good old 80/20 rule. Identify opinion leaders in your community as well. Target the right guys at a competing club and 20 more will follow them to yours. Find out who these people are and develop an opinion leaders program to reach them. Make your loyalty program based on gifts, service, and special touches so that your best clients don't even know it exists. They just think that you and your club are superior!

CHAPTER TWENTY

Creating a Legendary Entertainment Experience for Your Players

ENTERTAIN OR DIE!

P erhaps the most profound breakthrough I made in my former life in the karate business was the discovery that, unlike any of my competitors, I was not actually in the karate business. Nor was I in the self-defense business, health club business, or the more generic service business. I was in the personal development business helping people "Maximize their potential physically and mentally." That meant that our ads were different, our look and feel was different and, of course, our curriculum was different. While 21 other schools in the city of Irvine, California, battled it out for the karate business, I was the only school competing for the personal development business by using karate as the delivery method!

Too many people in the golf industry have lost sight of the business they are actually in, which for most clubs is the entertainment business. That's right, the entertainment business— NOT the service business, not the people business, and not the golf business. Golf is the vehicle by which you entertain your members or guests. Having a good course, good conditions, and a great staff are entry level items in this game. Merely adding the word "experience" to your sales literature doesn't mean much if there are no extraordinary experiences to back it up!

In this chapter, you will discover:

✔ Why we are living in the experience economy

✔ How to enhance your players' experiences

✔ How to adapt creative ideas from outside the golf industry

✔ How to change players' focus away from price

✔ How to create WOW moments

✔ The power of the One Strategy

WE ARE LIVING IN AN EXPERIENCE-DRIVEN ECONOMY

Can you imagine buying a product on a regular basis where the price you pay for the exact same product varies by as much as 800 percent on any given day?

Can you imagine charging your customers 300 percent more than you do right now and getting them not only to accept it but to recommend you to all of their friends?

Can you imagine being the most expensive club in town (in your market segment) and having people lining up at your door to get in?

I hope so, because in this highly combative, oversaturated golf market your club's future success—perhaps even your club's survival—depends what I am about to share with you.

If you buy a bottle of imported beer, for example, Heineken, at a wholesale store, it will cost you about a buck. If you buy the same beer at the local hole-in-the-wall bar, it will cost you about two dollars and fifty cents. If you buy the same beer at my country club, it will cost you four dollars. And, if you buy the exact same beer at the bar of the Hotel Splendido overlooking Portofino Bay in Italy, you will pay a whopping eight dollars for the very same drink. Since the beer didn't change, why am I or anyone else willing to pay such a wide range of rates—a difference of 800 percent—for the very same green bottle filled with 12 ounces of the identical liquid? The answer, of course, is that we are all conditioned to put a premium on *the experience* rather than on the actual product itself. This is true today more than ever; consumers want an "experience." They want a taste of the good life, their own 15 minutes of fame or fantasy, and they are willing to pay highly for it.

AutoWeek magazine now lists over 50 places where, for a couple of thousand bucks, you can learn to drive like a NASCAR or Formula One driver in real race cars. Talk about an experience for the average red-blooded male! For about the same price you can pilot a MIG fighter in mock combat or float across the Serengeti in a hot air balloon at sunset searching for wildebeests.

Back a little closer to home, you can take a very average business and double your income by improving the experience. A hairdressing salon I used to visit used this strategy to almost triple their prices. One day it was a regular unisex haircut place, the next, a posh salon. The difference? Fancy tile on the floor, a new paint job, better-looking fixtures, and a new name. But what really did it for me was the glass of champagne that magically appeared in my hand as soon as I walked in the door. I hardly noticed that the price of a haircut had tripled because I enjoyed the experience more than before!

It's Not All About The Golf Course

Far too much emphasis in the golf industry is put solely on the course, which for better or worse is usually about where it's going to be. On invisible "service" or in creating an "experience" which in most places exists only as a word in their outdated brochures!

I bet you have had some of your most memorable days ever at some sheep infested club in the Scottish Highlands, with awful weather, a colorful caddie and wee dram of local whisky afterwards as you warmed yourself around a fire in the pub! The total sum of club membership, a nice day out at your local daily fee course or a weekend away at a resort includes far more than just the quality of the golf course. Some of it is tangible some of it not but the "experience" they get, whichever one it happens to be, is what will bring them back or not!

PEOPLE WANT TO BE ENTERTAINED—THEY WANT AN EXPERIENCE!

Last week, to prove a point to a course owner, I called my neighbor from my office. I said, "Allen, remember that great tournament we played in at the Robert Trent Jones Golf Club in Gainesville, Virginia? Tell my client about it."

"Okay," he said. "It's hard to know where to start since everything was so fantastic. The food was great, the entertainment was great—and, man, that magician was good!"

"The entertainment?" I asked

"You remember," he said. "That magician at the event...he was unbelievable! The best I have ever seen!"

He went on to describe some of the magician's tricks in detail for another two or three minutes. Finally, I prompted him to talk about the course. "Best course I have ever played," he said casually, but it was the magician he kept talking about (in fact, we all did!).

The One Strategy

I coined a phrase to describe this strategy I call it the "One Strategy" your goal is to provide one thing at each touch point in your club that is memorable. Memorable enough to snap a picture and share it on social media!

How do you entertain your customers in the golf shop?

Do you have a putting carpet set up for guests to try out a new putter right at the counter? A TV in the corner playing the instruction videos you sell? Big pro shop, little pro shop, low end or high end it doesn't matter. What does matter is that your customer remembers ONE thing that you do better in your pro shop than anyone one else in your immediate area or golf club category!

For example:

- o   Best selection of putters new or used
- o   Best selection of wedges
- o   Best selection of shoes
- o   Sun glasses
- o   Custom club fitting center
- o   Largest selection of pre owned clubs
- o   Takes trade-in's
- o   Free coffee and cookies anytime
- o   Indoor putting green
- o   Indoor net or simulator
- o   Cheapest priced on used golf balls
- o $5 or $10 gift certificate with every purchase of X or more
- o   Free lessons with every new set of irons
- o   Free lesson with every club purchase (could be 15 minutes)

On the Range?

Most ranges are boring, a large field with a small hitting area and a few flags or signs at various distances. Obviously the higher end clubs have real looking greens and bunkers to add to the ambience, but it doesn't have to stop there and if you can't afford that there are other simpler things you can do.

My buddy Mike Warbeck, PGA, DRP* owns a Tin Cup range in Florida where the star attraction is an old VW van about 180 yards from the mats. It looks horrendous and I told him so. His response was simple, "If I took that out I'd go broke."

Sure enough as I took a club fitting, car after car pulled up and put money in the ball machine with the sole goal of hitting the van. "Hooting hollering and having a blast!"

In the UK I have a client that has stand up wooden cows on their range that fall down and moo when you hit them. It's really a family course so it goes down big time.

If all this is a little too slapstick for you there are more conservative and even temporary things you can try to prove just how more engaged people will be with more interesting targets.

- o A large bell
- o A gong
- o A net
- o Carpet bulls eye targets
- o Small pools filled with water
- o Western movie star cut outs mounted on plywood

As I write, we are looking at getting involved with a high-end club in Colorado, it's a very Western theme with a huge range. If the deal goes through I am going to buy life sized Buffalo statues and put them out as targets I know it will be the talk of the state! Do you have a selection of the latest swing aids in a barrel for players to try out? Swing aids are cheap and players love this!

How about having a demo day every Saturday or Sunday morning? If players know they can try out the latest equipment at your club perhaps that will be enough of a factor to spend their money with you?

Do you have video equipment and computer software for analyzing your students' swings?

In the winter, do you have a golf simulator where players can enjoy playing Pebble Beach while six feet of snow covers the ground outside?

How about playing music on your range? That would set it apart from others and perhaps attract a younger crowd.

Do you have clear yardage marked on the hitting area? Players really appreciate that.

Do you have a grass tee this is a huge factor especially in the UK. I would gladly pay extra to hit off grass!

Do your golf balls have dimples it's amazing how many balls in a bucket do not! A friend of mine in Scotland told me his range business went up big time after investing in new high quality range balls. People know the difference!

How about adding a short game with a bunker, green and some rough many clubs still don't have one.

I just spent a small fortune at club in Portugal for one simple reason, they had the best grass range and new range balls. I hit balls there and had lunch there several days in a row choosing them over 25 other options within 10 miles! (I also eat their fresh shrimp and avocado salad everyday!) Two ones made me a good customer!

DRP* Stands for Driving Range Pro, he wore the badge at the PGA Show after the President of the PGA started out his speech with the words, "From the lowest driving range pro to the director of golf at a top resort" …Oops!

Entertaining on the Course

If there was ever a clear endorsement of *The One Strategy* it's the TPC golf course in Ponte Verde, Florida. The TPC is one of the most famous courses in the world and while it's an excellent course all round its fame is based on a single hole. A hole which depending on where the tee is played between just 100 and 154 yards! Their entire pricing (very high) and fame is based on that hole alone!

There are two holes at your club you want to make special if you can, the first and the eighteenth. If you use two tees to start let's add the tenth and ninth. The first and last impressions of your course are most important so if you spend any money on the course on non-essential work spend it there first.

For example on the 1st tee:

- o   Raise the first tee to give a better view of the landing area

- o   Increase the size of the landing area (no one likes a bad start)

- o   Put a picket fence, hedge or boulders around the tee to frame it

- o   Add some flowerbeds around the tee

- o   On the tenth tee offer free bottled water, iced towels or complimentary apples displayed in a barrel!

- o   On 9 install a phone to call ahead to the snack bar or just post a sign suggesting they call in on their mobile for quick service

- o   Put in some makers to guide players

- o   Let the rough grow up 100 Yards off the tee with a path mown through the middle like the British links courses, provides a nice look and saves on maintenance.

Most courses are already what they are ever going to be, but if you can make one solid improvement a year people notice. Cleaning out a pond or a stream to make it more esthetically pleasing. Adding a new tee at a better angle. Putting new yardage markers on the fairways, better tee signs with hole maps or new unusual tee markers.

If you do have the money to redesign the course remember, all it takes is one hole to become famous, just one hole!

Entertaining with Your Golf Carts

Ok so golf carts come in three makes and about three colors. That would be white, beige and green. Very occasionally blue, maybe gray but that's about it.

Boring!

How about adding a couple of FUN carts to your fleet and charging a premium for them? Or offering them to good customers as an upgrade just like the rental car companies do, or say they do!

Golfers especially occasional golfers or golfers on trips, like to have fun, take pictures and splurge a little. One or two upgrades in the fleet will soon pay for themselves and add to your customers' enjoyment of their day!

Gentlemen start your engines!

Entertaining in the Restaurant

In my last twenty-five years of private club membership I can count on two hands the times I eat dinner at the club with the exception of the occasional special event. It's not that the food was bad my last two clubs where both high-end, both had nice dining rooms, but both were totally boring. Their fine dining was the usual steak, chicken, one catch and pasta. While their casual dining was uninspiring, so we'd drive twenty-five miles and get Sushi, Indian, Italian or Tapas!

What's the one item on your menu you have just got to eat?

That's all you need ; one killer item! It isn't the steak they can get that anywhere; it most likely isn't the burger either! All it has to be is one thing that WOW's them like the Tapas plate above from St. Mellion, in Cornwall, England. I took this picture two years ago long before I ever thought of writing a book and shared it on my social networks, it was that GOOD!

Likewise this six-pack of appetizers from a club in Florida was so good we went back several times and took friends just to get it!

If there is nothing on your menu they can't get anywhere else in town it's just not good enough! It does not have to be gourmet it does not have to be expensive, it does not have to be exotic it just has to be great!

Please don't tell me all your players' want is a bacon sandwich for breakfast and a hamburger for lunch. If that were really true hundreds specialty restaurants in your area would not exists!

For example:

A great foot long Italian sausage served with onions, peppers.

A giant barbeque turkey leg

An awesome cheese plate

Healthy Options:

A Turkey or Buffalo burger

California Pita: Turkey, avocado, sprouts and low calorie Italian dressing

It doesn't matter what end of the food chain your club is on from snack bar to fine dining you need ONE item that's awesome. One item every server jumps to recommend. The dish every guest is told by existing members to order. At Black Diamond when I first joined it was the Portobello mushroom sandwich. If you can do two or three so much the better but start with one! Challenge your cook or chef to come up with one, get servers buy in, get customers to buy in and go from there!

While most clubs struggle with F and B, there are many clubs around the world whose food is the major attraction. We all have to eat and if a player knows they are going to get something WAY better than average at your club it can be enough to tip their custom in your favor... Food is after all the way to a man's heart!

Entertain with Your Menu

Your club's menu is a very important element of your overall F and B success and one that you should pay careful attention to, to get right. The menu should not simply be treated as a list of the food you have for sale as it is at most clubs, but as a real sales and entertainment tool in the same vein as your club's brochure or website.

Many clubs simply treat the menu as an afterthought. It is not just a place to list the food items you have decided to serve in any old order with little to no description of the uniqueness of your recipe or preparation. Your menu is your selling tool and it needs to be treated with as much care and planning as anything else you do in your business. Any club can make their menu special regardless of the actual food offered!

Your menu should be an attractive and inviting presentation of the food you have decided to serve, laid out in a logical manner and highlighting the items you particularly want to sell either because they represent your best achievements or your highest margin items or preferably because they are both.

Where Do Customers Look First?

Research shows that most people look to the top right, corner of your menu first. This is a good place to feature one of your most popular menu items. From there, a customer's eyes generally drift down and to the middle of the menu page. This is a good place to feature your most expensive menu item. Even though many may pass on this particular dish because of the high price, you can put *other* popular (and fairly expensive) menu items *around* your most expensive item. The contrast in prices makes people more likely to buy the items you place around your most expensive offering.

Food is the only art form that engages each of the five senses. Explore each one in your menu description

Your menu description should make a guest's mouth water. Don't be afraid to explain what is in a dish and use ethnic names if they fit. They'll add a bit of authentic flair to the menu description.

For example:

Chicken Margarita sounds better than just Chicken topped with spicy tomatoes. You can explain what is in the dish (spicy tomatoes) in the description itself.

Incorporating geography or local history into a menu item name is also a way to make your restaurant menu unique.

For example:

Maine Lobster Roll sounds inviting, whether you eating it in Maine or somewhere else, as does *Texas Barbecued Ribs* and *Georgia Peach Pie*.

In the UK now it's very common in better restaurants and even some pubs to actually state which farm the produce is coming from and which butcher made the sausages! They did look at me funny when I asked which pond the duck came from but there you go.

Even if you are working out of a shack bar by the pool, "Joe's Famous Burgers with Grandma Mildred's secret sauce" sounds better than just burger!

The more of a story you can build into your food the more of it you will sell.

When only the best will do. Private Reserve Tenderloins are hand selected from the finest quality beef found anywhere, then naturally aged and carefully trimmed into mouth-watering perfection. These exquisite filets give you the melt-in-your-mouth tenderness and juiciness you crave. Private Reserve Filet Mignons are crafted to give you and your loved ones the ultimate Filet Mignon thrill. Tender, succulent and impressive beyond belief, they'll transport you and your lucky gift recipients to moments of sheer bliss.

Make sure your type is large enough for people over 40 to read, especially when the light is dim, and make sure your background designs don't make it harder to read. You shouldn't have to work to read the menu.

You want to intrigue the customer with your menu and your descriptions. If they have more questions, their server should be able to give further information about a dish or recommend a house favorite.

Entertaining with Your Crockery

Recently I was at a city-run golf club in Colorado with a clubhouse that looked like a German bunker. Frankly, I was not expecting much more than a hamburger or a hot dog when the manager offered me lunch.

Instead they served an awesome Mexican menu on oversize plates of different shapes and bright colors. That simple touch made me feel like I was in a fine restaurant rather than in relatively ordinary surroundings. It also made the food taste better!

They would have made the experience even better had they painted the metal chairs the same colors as the plates and put something on the walls other than a lone Bud Light sign!

Why do so many clubs and restaurant have white plates? White plates are

Boring! You can take an average menu and put the food out on colored plates and make it look way better than average!

Entertaining in Your Bar

This is the world famous Sombrero Margarita at "The Margarita Grill" it's their signature drink and people go there just to have that one drink! They often take snap shots like above and of course they share those snap shots on their social media, it's that memorable! If all you have is Miller Lite and Bud you are not creating much of a unique experience!

Any Bar Can Be Memorable

When I was in my early twenties, we used to go to a hole-in- the-wall bar in Delray Beach. It was twenty miles out of our way and had no ambience, no girls, and no music. In fact almost nothing whatsoever to attract business. What they did have, or at least claimed to have, was a bottle of every beer in the world. Since, at the time, we didn't have the money to travel the world, my friends and I decided to do the next best thing and drink our way around the world!

Every time we went in the barman would say, "What country will it be tonight?" We traveled from the Trappist monks' beer in Belgium to the Taj Mahal beer of India and back again.

The Signature Drink

Having one or two signature drinks will bring customers back with friends to share the experience. For that is what a signature drink aims for fun, unique experience in drinking that is not offered on the bar or menu down the street.

Infusions are one way to make something truly special to your bar. An infusion uses fresh herb or fruits soaked in vodka for three or more days allowing the flavors to "infuse" in the alcohol. These flavored vodkas can then be used to create unique mojitos, martinis, and other drinks that can easily become a signature cocktail. Infusions and micro distilled artisan liquors is the number nine on the top twenty trends in the NRA's chef survey.

Another top trend includes culinary cocktails, so another area to consider when planning your menu is what food to serve that goes well with your selected drinks. Small plates and tapas are very popular and offer many wonderful options for food that pairs nicely with wines, beer and mixed drinks.

What is your specialty drink, the one drink you MUST try if at your club's bar?

- o José's world famous Mojito?
- o A yard of English Ale?
- o A stein of German beer?
- o Local hard cider?
- o Local vineyard?

Entertaining in your club's fitness center?

Recently I spent the night in a hotel that had a small but world- class fitness center. In most respects it looked just like any other gym except that several of the machines were interactive. The rowing machine had a video screen that allowed me to row against another opponent. It led me on a mad quest to keep up with the Olympic rowing team, which I did for nearly five minutes before collapsing with exhaustion. After a short rest, it was on to the stationary bike, a piece of equipment that usually bores me to tears. Not so today as my video screen allowed me to race in the Tour de France. Would the novelty wear off? Perhaps. Nonetheless, if such an experience- enhancing option were available in my area, I would be willing to pay a premium price for it. While your club's gym won't compete with a 60,000 square-foot health center, you could add a few such machines to create a better experience.

In the restrooms?

In the restrooms—sure, why not? In fact, this is what started the whole Idea i=of the one strategy when I returned again and a again to a small pub and restaurant in England where the men's urinals where French Horns.

It could be as simple as pinning the sports pages from today's newspaper to the wall of the Men's Room, or a more sophisticated approach like different-shaped wash basins or toilets. It could be as simple as just having a restroom with a running waterscape on the wall or unusual faucets. It all counts when it comes to building the experience.

In large cities many department stores actually attract customers because people know they will get clean, safe comfortable restrooms if they go to a particular store, albeit on the tenth floor! The point here is to think out of the box—don't think like a golf course owner or manager— pretend you work for Disney and enhance every area of your club's experience!

CHANGING THE RULES

I have visited several courses lately in what can only be described as "very tough markets." Play is down, prices are slashed, and everyone is running bigger and better coupon offers! Everyone is competing for the same dollar in the same way—by cutting prices!

While everyone agrees this race to the bottom is not a great way to do business, no one seems to have any idea of how to stop the trend. But have no fear, faithful reader, I do have the solution. Change the rules!

For example's sake, let's say you are in a market with twenty other daily-fee clubs all charging half what they did two years ago. All twenty are decent courses with 18 holes. Each one has a similar product and each one charges about the same fees. They all are trying to do the same thing—get as many people on the course as possible! There are many ways to change the rules, but the key issue is to change your customers' focus from the price they are paying to something very different—the experience. Now, I agree that there is a large percentage of seniors and others to whom price is, and always will be, a major factor, but that doesn't stop Cadillac from selling $60,000 SUVs. In other words, there are plenty of other people out there who might respond to a different offer.

Change the focus

As a busy person, I hate, repeat HATE, playing golf if it takes more than three and a half hours. Yet at several courses I have been on this year, three and a half hours only gets me through about 13 holes!!!

Now, suppose that Wednesday is your slow day. Why not move the tee times back to 12-minute intervals. Add a second ranger and up the green fee ten-bucks-a-player and guarantee players will complete play in less than four hours or they get a free round of golf? Everyone will be instructed on the first tee that they will be given a clear hole start and that if a group catches them, they must wave them through at once (as is the custom in Britain). If you have lost your place, the guarantee does not apply! With this offering, you become the only course of the 20 to guarantee a round of golf in less than four hours. Now you are instantly in a different game than the rest of the courses. They are selling green fees; you are selling time!

Customers are willing to pay a premium for time. Earlier in this book I told you how I paid $10 more to ski at a resort that guaranteed lift-line waiting times to be ten minutes or less. Judging by the crowds there, their pricing strategy didn't hurt their business one bit (a lower-priced ski resort was essentially next door).

As mentioned earlier, Domino's Pizza made billions selling time (with their 30-minutes-or-less delivery guarantee), not great pizza, simply by changing the rules. Will offering shorter play time work in every market? No. Are there some bugs you might have to work out? Yes. Can it add thousands to your bottom line and differentiate you in a crowded market place? Yes, again!

Improve their games

Okay, your players don't care about playing fast? Then how about playing well? The standard of play I witnessed on my last daily fee outing was pitiful. Hardly anyone young or old alike kept the ball in the air for 100 yards or more and I drove all 18 holes. NGF statistics show that 84 percent of golfers surveyed said they would "Play more often, buy more equipment, eat more hot dogs, and drink more beer at the course" if just one thing happened—if THEY PLAYED BETTER! The same surveys also showed that only 13 percent of golfers took a lesson in the last 12 months! So what we have here is a GIANT market that obviously has not been satisfied.

Now, let's switch to Marketing 101. How many times have you been to McDonald's and been asked whether you want fries with that burger? Okay, every time. How many times have you been at the counter in a pro shop where the pro has invited you, suggested, or even vaguely hinted that you might want to take a lesson. I've been playing golf for 28 years now and it has never happened to me!

So back to our problem of changing the rules. How about selling a 20-lesson game-improvement package? You are guaranteed to hit the ball further and score better. Or a Wednesday and Saturday clinic package with a $1995 value for just $1595—and you get *free golf* while you are learning! (At $20 a round they would have to play 80 rounds in 10 weeks to make out on the deal! IF they play 40 rounds you made $40 a round, if they play 20 rounds, you made $80 a round! Sure the pro and the assistant have to get paid, but I am sure you can work out an equitable split. The other upside is that you end up with better players, fill a need, and build relationships! You could add free club fitting, a free video, a free book, or whatever else you can think of to add value to the package.

The whole point to this strategy is to change what people think about—from thinking about discounts to instead thinking about time, playing better, or anything else so that it is no longer an apples- to-apples comparison between your course and the one down the street.

REMODEL AND REVAMP

You don't have to redesign your holes for a PGA tournament to benefit from making changes at your club. Little upgrades in the bar, the restaurant, the clubhouse, or on the tees can increase your business and your free word-of-mouth advertising. After all, if you want people to talk about you, you have to give them something to talk about.

Some businesses like banks and insurance companies might thrive on longevity and consistency in the marketplace; however, most businesses don't. There are plenty of examples of once-solid business that no longer exist. In fact, in most businesses if you don't consistently reinvent yourself you are in big trouble.

Look outside the golf market for concepts that you could use

Take the nightclub business, for example. A "hot" club is a license to print money for two or three years. Then the bubble bursts and a new club across town suddenly becomes the "in" place. While inexperienced owners ride the tide to the very end, crashing in bankruptcy, astute club owners do just the opposite. They reap the rewards while the going is good, then close the club for several months as business starts to decline, but before it's lost completely. Then they remodel, rename, and reopen it all over again. Bars and restaurants can also benefit from this strategy, especially in a competitive market place.

Time for a new logo? A new name? A new attitude?

The interesting thing about remodeling, even if it's only a quick facelift with new carpet and a lick of paint, is that it almost always attracts new business and allows you to increase sales with existing clients. Change creates excitement, and excitement creates more sales.

Theme restaurants are now popular all over the world. My personal favorite is in West Palm Beach, Florida. It's the 391st Bomber Group restaurant located on the site of Palm Beach International Airport. As you approach the parking lot, you pass under a barrier with a sentry post and an old army jeep. The main building has been created to look like a bombed-out French farmhouse complete with shell holes in some of the walls. Out back, two huge World War II bombers sit on the tarmac at the edge of the airfield. The bathrooms are done from floor to ceiling in sandbags while they pipe in speeches from Churchill and others. The waitresses are dressed in Red Cross uniforms and the waiters are dressed as airmen. In the bar, there is a dance floor. Early in the evening, they play music from the 1940s; each hour, the music advances a decade until the current dance tunes hit around 11 PM. To top it all off, they provide headphones so you can listen to the pilots of incoming planes talk with the tower. Everything there creates the perfect illusion that you have, in fact, gone back in time. The food is great, too, but that is secondary to the actually experience of the place.

The Hard Rock Cafe, the All Star Cafe, Planet Hollywood, The Harley Cafe, The Race Rock Cafe, and hundreds of other theme restaurants all sell hamburgers for ten dollars—not because the food is special but because the places are special. The experience for the rock fan, race fan, or sports fan seeing the actual sunglasses Elvis, Jeff Gordon, or Andre Agassi wore is what counts; the food is secondary.

Let your customers experience being a king

The Five Feet Restaurant in Laguna Beach, California had some of the best food in the world before the owner died, but it also had a unique feature reserved for its' best customers. The restaurant itself had very high ceilings with that open industrial look. The walls are decorated with a huge mural of various individuals, each one a good customer of the restaurant. Now, if your face was immortalized on the wall of one of the best restaurants in town, where would you take your out-of- town guests for dinner? Not rocket science is it? Also what does that do for the self-esteem, ego, experience, and general dining pleasure of the customer?

Another simple example is the bartender who changes all the regular names of drinks and renames them with the initials of his favorite customers. So when Joe Peterson comes in and sits down at the bar the bartender asks, "You want a JP?" and serves him a gin and tonic with a twist of lime. When a stranger sits down at the bar and asks for a gin and tonic with lime, the bartender laughs and says "Oh, you mean a JP." You may think this is a dumb example but I've seen it done and it makes Joe's experiences that much greater. Speaking of Joe, in Sedona, Arizona, there is an Italian restaurant called Not Your Average Joe's. The walls are lined with pictures of famous athletes named "Joe" like Joe Montana, Joe Lewis, Joe Dimaggio, and so on. Once again a simple concept turned a fairly ordinary Italian restaurant into a place that I've talked about to hundreds of people, even though it was closed the day I was there!

So how are you doing in the entertainment game?

Having a good course, good conditions and a friendly staff are entry level in this game. Every course claims these things and remember it's not just courses you compete against it's every other form of recreational entertainment. If your customers are taking pictures and frequently sharing aspects of your club's experience on social media you have created a WOW factor! If not you'd better start doing something soon…..

What most clubs fail to understand is that the total entertainment package doesn't begin on the 1st and end on the 18th

Once you understand and accept that your job is to entertain your members and guests at every level, it creates a radically different mindset that attracts people to your doors!

If you are to be successful, your club must not only be more entertaining than any club in its market segment, but it must also be more satisfying than the bowling alley down the street. It must be more entertaining than the baseball game on ESPN, the Strawberry Festival, Chili Cook-off or whatever 101 other events are listed in your local papers activities section this week!

Take a look at your club as an entertainment business and brainstorm with your staff how you can increase the entertainment level at every touch point of your club from the parking lot to the restrooms and everywhere in between!

Specialize in creating WOW moments, if players are taking pictures with their cell phones of your amazing burger, cool restrooms, or awesome golf carts and sharing it on their social media with hundreds of their friends then you are on the right track!

SUMMARY

Remember, your golfers want an experience, not just to hit a little ball around a course. Maybe they want to get away from home. Maybe they want to be with friends or do business. Maybe they like being outside. It's up to you to understand what can make the golfing experience better and offer it. How can you enhance the experience you offer your customers? What can you add to offer more value? How can you use sight, sound, and smell to make your products and services more appealing? How can you increase the entertainment value of your products and services?

To succeed, your club must not only be more entertaining than any club in it's market segment, but it must also be more satisfying than the bowling alley down the street. It must be more entertaining than the baseball game on ESPN, the Strawberry Festival, Chili Cook- off, or any of the other 101 events listed in your local paper's activities section this week.

Additional Resources:

http://andrewwoodinc.com/book/making-your-business-the-one-they-choose/

CHAPTER TWENTY-ONE

How to Dominate the Outings Market

HE WITH THE BIGGEST DATABASE OF OUTINGS PROSPECTS AND THE BEST FOLLOW-UP SYSTEM WINS!

Outings can be very profitable for your club. A wise man once said that fishing for whales made more sense than fishing for minnows. For daily fee clubs, going after group business can be a lot more rewarding than looking for 288 new players every day. For private clubs, outings can provide a welcome source of additional income.

In this chapter, you will discover how to build your outings business in five ways through:

- ✔ Repeat business

- ✔ Referral business

- ✔ Your web site

- ✔ Targeted direct mail

- ✔ Telemarketing

You'll also book outings through walk-ins and other "accidental" means. These bookings are not predictable or controllable, but will increase when you implement the systematic programs discussed here.

ENCOURAGING REPEAT BUSINESS BY STAYING IN REGULAR CONTACT

The easiest and most obvious way to increase your outing business is to sell your existing clients again.

As simple as this idea is, of the hundreds of courses I have visited, only a handful do more than send last year's outing planner for a particular event the traditional John Doe thank-you letter (and perhaps an additional postcard) some time near the start of next season.

This, of course, is not enough! Not nearly enough. You need a systematic plan to keep your club in front of outing planners regularly. Treat past clients as valued friends and do what you can to help them. Some groups like variety for their events. Even if a particular group doesn't come every year, they will come back more often if you keep in regular touch.

Follow up with calls to each of your outing contacts at least three times a year after their event at intervals of:

✔ 90 days

✔ 180 days

✔ 250 days

But your phone calls are only part of your new contact program. Your existing outing database of past clients should be contacted on a continuing basis throughout the year with a series of letters, postcards, and calls—and small gifts, depending on the value of the business. You cannot afford for another course to gain their attention or business. Stay in touch monthly! That's right, 12 times a year.

If you follow this step, and this step alone you will guarantee yourself more business. Just make sure the letters you send are creative!

If you contact your past clients every month, you will generate more than your share of inbound outing calls. In fact, if your database is big enough (over 400), you might well generate enough inbound calls to meet your outing goals.

If you stay in touch with past outing clients each month, the resulting increase in business will astonish you!

BUILDING OUTING REFERRAL BUSINESS

Most of the methods discussed in the Referrals chapter work for outings, so I'll be brief here. The main point is that you should be cultivating—and regularly contacting—referral sources as well as direct prospects. This means that you ask people about groups that have outings. Cultivate possible referral sources. Ask for leads from:

- ✔ Your members or regular golfers ("Does your Rotary Club hold a golf outing, or could they use a new fund raising idea?")

- ✔ People who book outings with you now ("Who else do you know who holds outings?")

- ✔ Local high school and college golf coaches

- ✔ Influential people in town (bankers, board members, politicians)

- ✔ Your personal contact list

- ✔ Golf courses in other towns (their outing clients might like variety, and you can return the favor)

- ✔ Local sporting goods and golf businesses

- ✔ Everyone else you can think of

A web page promoting tournament events. Note that the first links to request information appear just to the right of the top photograph so prospects don't have to hunt for them.

BOOK MORE OUTINGS ON THE INTERNET

Make sure that the outing portion of your club's web page is presented in the form of a sales letter and feature the outing button prominently on your home page and elsewhere. This is much stronger than simply announcing to the world in bullet form that you are in the market to hold an event if one happens to be going! (Also see Chapter 12 on Building the Perfect Web Site.)

Having the proper sales pitch on your web site is important for several reasons:

1 People buy for their reasons, not yours. You need to provide them with clear benefits for booking their events with you. That means not simply listing what you offer, but providing REAL BENEFITS! Think of the outing page on your web site as an infomercial, an electronic salesperson representing your club. That means providing answers to common questions, using testimonials from happy customers, and proving point-specific benefits of why your club deserves the business rather than your competition. Include photos of attendees having a good time.

2 It is not uncommon that the person in charge of finding a venue, for instance, a secretary, does not know that much about golf. By providing a point-specific set of reasons for holding an event at your club, that person can either make a good decision or simply print out your well thought out sales pitch and present it to whoever actually makes the decision. This is the next best thing to having you talking directly to a decision maker. Write good copy that covers all their questions and answers them!

3 People want information on meetings and events when they need information on meetings and events—which in today's world is 24 hours a day, seven days a week. I am writing this at 9:38 PM on a Friday night! I could just as easily be surfing the web looking for my next golf outing venue! Which is why it's critical to have a request form that someone can fill in and e-mail to you about their event. At one club we are averaging almost one online outing request for information a day! Every day!

4 Your web site should be programmed to tackle the most frequently cited problem by outing planners: lack of follow up! When an outing planner sends a request online, an automatic e-mail should be sent at once acknowledging the request and stating that someone will reply the next day. But it doesn't have to end there!

Your web site can also be programmed to send out a follow-up letter in a week. It might say something along the lines of "By now you should have received your information kit in the mail. If not, please let me know at once. I just wanted to let you know about a special offer we have this month that gives each of your participants a $25 tee prize at no additional cost!"

You could follow up the first note with another automatic e-mail a week later highlighting the benefits of having an event at your course and ask whether they need anything else to help with their decision. For that matter, it can go on and on, sending automatic e-mails until you switch it off or they ask you to stop. The great part of all this is that once you have a developed a good series and your customized letters are programmed into your site, they just work on automatic pilot!

LOOKING FOR OUT-OF-TOWN BUSINESS?

If you are in an area that gets a lot of convention traffic or out-of- town business, don't wait until the planners try to find you in your home state. Hit them in theirs. Recently one of our clients in Orlando told us that he booked two outings in one week, one from New Jersey and the other from Palm Beach. He was running banner ads on the AtlanticCityGolf.com site and they clicked through and booked an event.

Running banner ads in other targeted states is a great way to reach prospects before they ever look in your market! Of course they may also find your web site searching for outing providers in your area.

You can rent and use targeted e-mail or postal lists to drive out- of-state traffic to your web site as well. (Call your local list broker for list details.)

Local convention-and-visitor bureaus and Chambers of Commerce frequently have lists of booked conventions and meetings, sometimes years in advance. Sometimes this information is available online. For example, if I go to the San Francisco Convention & Visitors Bureau web site, I can see what groups have booked for the next year.

Smaller groups than are tracked by convention bureaus and Chambers often book meeting rooms and hotel rooms at the larger hotels. Both convention bureaus and hotels frequently send out information to their inquires that includes information about local attractions. If any of your local bureaus or hotels do that, see if they will include your golf outings sales piece (you might want to prepare a special one that identifies you as the golf outing specialist for out- of-town groups).

BUILDING A LARGE LIST OF NEW OUTING PROSPECTS

In any given market there are only so many charity events, business outings, and tournaments going on. You need to have in your database the name, address, and phone number (e-mail would be nice) of the principle decision maker of at least 80 percent of all events in your area. Armed with this information, you can dominate the outing market in your area.

How to build your prospect list

1 Keep a database of all past event contacts.

2 Watch the local paper. LOOK, REALLY LOOK, at all local golf events. Watch announcements, results, and feature articles. Look at local web sites, TV, radio, and cable. When you find an event, track down the organizer.

3 Ask every player who walks through your doors if their company or group holds outings!

4 Build a giant outing leads list. Build a list of at least 1000 people, organizations, and businesses that you know, or at least suspect, hold golf events each year. Use the Internet, local papers, Yellow Pages, Thomas Guide, Chamber of Commerce, and business, charity, and church directories. All can be found at your local library.

5 Telemarket everyone on your prospect list. Call every charity, fraternal organization, hospital, church, radio station, and car dealership in your area. Then add in fire stations, bars, and any other organization, company, or person you think might hold a golf event.

- ✔ Ask if they ever hold golf tournaments? If yes;

- ✔ Ask who is in charge?

- ✔ Get the name, address, and phone number of the person in charge. Try for the e-mail. (The best way to do this is to offer them something, like our booklet on "How to Run a Successful Outing."

- ✔ Ask when they hold their outing.

- ✔ Ask how many players typically play in their outing.

- ✔ Ask where they held their outing last year and whether or not they have booked it this year.

- ✔ Get the person's permission to send them information on your tournament packages.

- ✔ Ask the person if they know anyone else who holds golf outings. (You will be astonished by how many referrals you will get by tacking on that simple question.)

- ✔ Enter all the data, especially any extra info you can glean that might help you sell this prospect, into the Customer Relationship

Manager part of your website.

(Legendary Marketing can do all this for you.)

During the telemarketing effort to build your prospect list, you will uncover a number of hot leads that are ready to book an outing now! It's quite common to uncover a dozen or more really hot leads during the telemarketing effort.

Some real examples of leads from telemarketing

- ✔ John at the Post Office would like Eagle Sticks to contact him about outing options. They used to hold their outings at the country club, and most recently at Crystal Springs, with about 100 golfers attending. They haven't held an outing for two or three years but are currently discussing it and will be holding a meeting Wednesday to make some decisions. In the past they've held their outings in October, on Columbus Day.

- ✔ Donna from the Bar Association would like someone to contact her with outing options and information for their outing. Last year their outing was held at Bent Tree in August and 110 golfers attended. The outing is always held on the third Monday in August.

- ✔ Sonya at the Car Center has not yet planned this year's outing and would like Eagle Sticks to contact her. Last year the outing was held at another local club in August and 144 people attended.

Other benefits from proactive telemarketing

While the main goal of the telemarketing campaign is to build a database of outing leads, there are several other benefits that go along with the proactive nature of the campaign. You will uncover lots of informal groups such as firemen or police officers that might travel from course to course under everybody's radar but are great sources of incremental business.

You will find groups or organizations that ask you for offers or coupons that they can give out to their group. You will also be calling several thousand people who will be hearing the name of your club. This has a trickle-down effect in driving incremental play just based on top-of-the-mind awareness and suggestion.

The way we do it

For our clients, we put together an automatic follow-up campaign designed with one thing in mind—to make your life easy! That is to say, every letter, every postcard, and every promotional item is focused on getting the prospect to call you, before you have to call them!

MARKETING TO YOUR TARGET MARKET

The best way to target groups is to market your tournament packages through a combination of e-mail, direct mail letters, postcards, and promotional items. You can always end with a phone call or two thrown in for good measure towards the end of the campaign if they still haven't called. Your competitors might take one of these actions, hitting a typical prospect just once, or perhaps twice, a year.

You are going to do all these things and keep doing them all year, to ALL your prospects!

Not a single month will go by during the season when you do not send your 400+ prospects a call to action—a reminder that your course is the best choice for their business!

If you plan your campaign in advance and systemize it as described, this is not nearly as complicated or as difficult as it may seem. When you look at the potential returns versus the actual cost of marketing you will be hard pressed to spend your dollars in a better fashion for any reason. (Legendary Marketing can do all this for you, too, of course!)

NOW IT'S TIME FOR SOME THUNDERBOLT MARKETING

Thunderbolt Marketing is a strategy that Legendary Marketing designed to hit prospects in multiple ways. We send about 4-7 letters in a short period of time—a strategy designed to make a big impression. The technique works not only because of its frequency and repetition but also because of its creativity and ability to connect with and stimulate prospects on different levels, and even with different senses. Now you can do this with emails but direct mail is far more effective!

Gathering your weapons

There are many different ways to contact your prospects and hit them from different angles. Here are some suggestions for items you might want to consider as part of your Thunderbolt campaign. Remember the more different and creative ways you find to get your message in the hands of outing planners, the more effective your campaign will be!

We typically look to see what a club has on hand in the way of promotional items and first use simple items like scorecards, yardage books, and so forth.

Postcards

Postcards are cheap to print, cheap to mail, easy to produce, and, most important, effective in keeping your message in front of your prospective clients. Rather than using one design, get four done at once (it's cheaper that way). I like to run my cards in a theme so that each card stands on its own merits but also fits into an ongoing series that will highlight the specific benefits of holding an event at your club. One might talk about catering, others about the great range, or the staff's experience, or the course.

Sales letters

Everyone uses letters to get appointments or interest but the Thunderbolt letters must stand out from the ordinary. They must challenge, entertain, inform, and interest the reader. It cannot be the typical John Doe outings letter that basically says;

> Hi, I'm Bob, call me if you ever are thinking of a golf tournament! [See Chapter 11 on Legendary Direct Mail.]

Your sales letters must have at the very least:

✔ Great captivating headlines

✔ Interesting, benefit-laden copy

✔ Testimonials to back up your claims

✔ A demand for action

✔ A reason for acting now

✔ A P.S. that sums up the entire offer

These letters will work even better if you build them around a simple promo item. Enclose a tee, a plastic bag tag, a score card, or the like and not only will you insure that your letters get opened but you will find your response rate increases dramatically.

Postcards are a low-cost way to reach prospects. Notice the different headlines: the first is time sensitive; the second highlights features and benefits; and the third motivates the prospect to turn over the card to read the rest of the message.

Booklets

Booklets have always been a particularly successful approach for me. They position you or your course as an expert. They have great credibility since they shouldn't actually make a sales pitch. Rather they should lead the reader to believe that you are the answer to the specific problem that the booklet addresses. They are cost effective to produce and can be distributed in a variety of ways to add value.

Brochures

Brochures are common sales pieces and one component of an overall Thunderbolt plan. However, rather than just sending them on their own, they should be used in conjunction with a letter and personalized to your client. Pages should be folded, highlighted, key-point-circled, and referred to in the letter. Make the brochure an interactive tool, not just a hunk of sales hype. Tell the prospect in your letter what you want them to do with the material. It also goes without saying that the brochure its self must be a sales piece that focuses 100 percent on selling outings.

Specialty products

Specialty products are also ideal for the purpose of Thunderbolt marketing and come in all shapes and sizes. There are thousands of products that are available, from the sublime to the ridiculous. I suggest using ones that are neither. Instead aim for a product that is (a) out of the ordinary (which rules out calendars, note pads, and magnets) and (b) has longevity. While our goal is to elicit an instant response from each part of our Thunderbolt campaign, we know that not everyone will be won over during our initial strikes. That's why we want our clients to keep and cherish the items we send them so they will remember us when we return for the second campaign with reinforcements.

One particular product that I like for this is a poster. I have used several different types, from a blueprint of the perfect golf swing to a full-color poster of a famous golf hole. I have used cards that clap when you open them and others that actually talk to the prospect for 15 seconds. Be creative!

First wave

Once you have decided on the eight ways you will approach your key prospects, and have all the components in place, it's time to start your campaign.

KEY POINT—Before you read any further: Remember, you are not sending a random pitch to a worthless list of businesses in your community taken from the Chamber book! This is a pre-qualified targeted list of REAL people who book golf outings! They are going to book an outing this year and you are going to MAKE sure that you are first and foremost on their mind each and every month!

Depending on where your club is located, you are going to want to do one of two things. If your season is seven months or longer I would mail every month. If your season is six months or shorter, you can either cut back on a few mailings or double up in the early part of the year when people in your state are most likely to book their events, sending out letters twice a month in late winter or early spring.

I like to start the Thunderbolt with some basic reconnaissance like a postcard. This gets your proposition in front of them via first class mail in the cheapest possible way and also allows you to receive free address corrections before mailing the more expensive pieces. While you often hear it said that it takes seven times to create a good impression, I don't believe it. I have often had good response with one hit, but your chances of a positive response do increase proportionately with each subsequent mailing provided you keep the information interesting.

After a postcard, mail your outings brochure along with a tightly written and benefit-oriented cover letter.

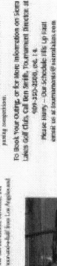

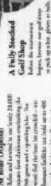

while we Do the Work, You & Your Group will Enjoy:

World-Class Golf in a Magnificent Setting

A Spacious Clubhouse At Your Disposal

Wonderful Food

Special Events Are Our Specialty

A Fully Stocked Golf Shop

An Ideal Location

All You Need to do is Relax & Enjoy a Great Round of Golf

To Book Your Outing, or for more information on Sierra Lakes Golf Club, call Ben Smith, Tournament Director at

The second wave

In the second wave you should start to use your big guns. I like the idea of allowing the collateral information to build in intensity so that the very best information hits in contacts four to seven, which is when we have found response is typically at its highest point. Send them the audio and videos in these waves. Write your cover letters so that each package builds on the previous package and highlights one to three specific benefits of doing business with you. Always refer to how the video, audio, or other collateral material backs up your point!

The third wave

The third wave starts in the sixth mailing and should be your mop-up phase. By this point you should have had the majority of your response and now you are just cleaning up the last few stragglers. At this point you can go back to postcards or use some of your specialty items with additional sales letters. End your campaign with a final appeal to try your club and the best sweetener you can possibly give.

Then it's time to sit back and enjoy the business you have already generated, which may well be more than enough, or to jump on the phone and squeeze a few more clients out of your campaign.

No more cold calls

If you follow the ideas and strategy I have just given you, Thunderbolt marketing will work for you. Even if you didn't get the response you had hoped for by mail, you can now follow up by phone. Everyone hates cold calling, but once you have Thunderbolt- mailed that prospect (one or more times), it's hardly a cold call any more. You've sent him more mail than he gets from his mother, his brother, and his best friend combined! A common response you'll get to your call is that they enjoyed your series and meant to talk with you.

When you call, you can immediately, with confidence and integrity, tell the secretary that Mr. X is expecting your call. You can do this for two reasons. First, in one of the last letters you should tell the prospect to expect a call. Second, the response I usually get from people who have resisted the temptation to call me is something along the lines of "I wondered when you were gong to call me."

Rather than being annoyed by a continual bombardment of mailing pieces, I have found just the opposite response from most people. I have even had e-mail and letters from business owners who told me that due to various other commitments and obligations they could not take advantage of my offers but they praised the high quality of the material and wished me every success. The majority of people respect the traits of persistence and tenacity, especially if backed up with quality. These traits are so rarely found that you will find people are positively disposed towards anyone who displays them.

Following up by phone can increase your Thunderbolt success significantly and you should certainly take the extra effort to do it, but the real beauty of Thunderbolt marketing remains in the in- bound response it generates. (Legendary Marketing even offers an appointment-setting service for outings and memberships on a cost- per-lead basis.)

SUMMARY

Fish for whales not minnows! Outings are big income generators and should be give special marketing attention at most clubs. Build a database of quality outing leads and follow up relentlessly with a carefully thought out Thunderbolt marketing campaign!

If you follow the plan I have outlined, you will get more in- bound leads than you have ever had before and, with proper pricing and follow up, can easily add six figures to your club's income! This outcome, of course, still depends on your staff's sales ability. (See the chapters on Sales, Promotions, and Pricing.)

CHAPTER TWENTY-TWO

Social Media for Buzz, Branding, and Profit

Social media are growing fast, with hundreds of millions of people participating. They are an important tool for the golf industry: Twitter, Facebook, LinkedIn, Instagram, Pinterest, blogging, and YouTube are just a few of the mainstays. While social media are a newer tools for marketing your golf course, lessons, realty, or other business, the general principles of marketing still apply. You need to identify your market, provide something of value, and build relationships and trust so prospects and customers will *want* to do business with you.

In This Chapter You Will Learn:

- ✔ The importance of educating, engaging and entertaining.

- ✔ How to build brand buzz.

- ✔ How to cross-promote on different platforms.

- ✔ Tips for each of the major social media platforms.

- ✔ The importance of delivering social proof.

- ✔ Why you need an integrated plan.

INFORM, ENTERTAIN, AND ENGAGE YOUR

PROSPECTS. THEN, AND ONLY THEN, TRY TO SELL THEM SOMETHING.

Whether you're selling dinner at the club, a membership, or a lesson you should form a relationship with prospects and customers and communicate with them *before* trying to sell them anything.

BUILDING BUZZ AND BRAND BY BLOGGING

Blogging is simply keeping a public "diary." You record your observations, opinions, and so on. You can also publish responses to your efforts from customers and others. I have been blogging a long time; it's easy for me because I love to write. Unfortunately, few clubs are using their blogs effectively to engage players, build brand, and produce sales. Like most things in life, getting traction takes a little time.

Many of the things I am going to share with you about blogging are equally applicable to all the other social media. There are many blogging programs out there. I use the most popular—Wordpress. It's easy to set up, easy to use, and FREE!

Your blog is important because it:

✔ Showcases your knowledge and positions you as an expert. Your club's blog gives all your key staff members a chance to connect with members and guests.

✔ A blog gives your club a human face. Many players may never have seen or heard from the chef or greenskeeper in person.

To start with, make sure your blog is easy to find on your website.

✔ A blog creates a feedback loop for members and potential customers. They can comment, ask questions, and add to your posts. (NOTE: You get to review and accept posts before they go up.)

✔ A blog starts new relationships.

✔ A blog strengthens existing relationships with members and players. Featuring them and their families on your blog or Facebook will increase their bonds with the club.

✔ A blog increases links back to your club's web site from other web sites; this increases traffic.

✔ A blog dramatically helps your search engine positioning. Google loves relevant content and inbound links.

✔ A blog builds into a large and searchable database of useful information, entertainment, and opinion that can be accessed months from now.

Write about:

✔ Things you know about that your customers want to know about.

✔ The golf professional should share golf instruction tips, travel tips, or comments on recent PGA Tour happenings.

✔ The chef should share cooking tips, food pictures, and recipes.

✔ The superintendent can educate members as to best practices, not just on the course but at home in their gardens.

✔ The club manager could blog about new wines in the clubhouse, upcoming improvements to the facility, introduce new staff, etc.

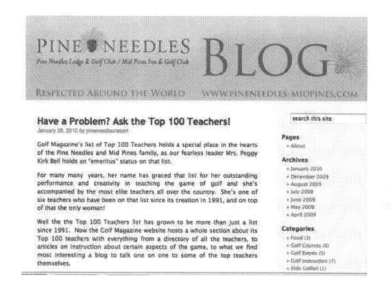

✔ Everyday events and how they tie back into your club is always good. It could be something as simple as the Rotary Club who met for lunch at your club.

✔ It could be rallying the club around a cause like prostate or breast cancer.

✔ All the staff can share pictures from the course, a deer at dawn walking across the 7th green, party pictures of members and guests, or a golf ball stuck up a tree.

✔ Topics you or your staff are passionate about that members and guests may also enjoy. Bird watching, for example.

Now here's a big secret: Your blog doesn't have to be all that original to be interesting, engaging, and entertaining to your readers.

It helps if it is BUT it doesn't have to be.

For example, September 10th is Arnold Palmer's birthday.

A simple Arnie story that week, to share with your members and guests would be a great way to celebrate the joy he brought us all with his charges. Following is one I've used.

The best-ever Arnie story!

September 10th is The King's birthday so I thought we'd celebrate in style by sharing with you, the best-ever Arnie story.

Before the 1993 Senior British Open, which was scheduled to be contested over the links of Royal Lytham & St. Anne's, Arnold Palmer received a letter from a Mr. Hans Bolton of Lancashire, England. The letter containing, as it did, the language of someone who knew nothing about the game, might have offended a superstar too full of his own importance. In Palmer's case, the handwritten letter caught his attention.

The letter, which came into the possession of a friend several years later, contains this remark in the opening paragraph: "I must admit I am not a golf fan. I realize that you must be extremely busy, being one of the 'big names' in the golfing fraternity." Bolton then talks about the importance of the upcoming Senior Open and adds, "An even more important event is taking place (at least to me anyway). You see, I am getting married to my fiancée, Sally Anne Murphy, a truly gorgeous and wonderful girl." The problem, Bolton says, is simple: Neither of the honeymoon suites at the Clifton Arms Hotel is available because, as it was explained to him, "Mr. Arnold Palmer is staying in one and Mr. Gary Player is staying in the other, and they have been booked for ages!"

He then proceeds to paint an emotional portrait. "My fiancée was, of course, distraught at this news, convinced that our big day is doomed to failure.

Something I suppose, like a triple bogey on the 1st hole." Then Bolton makes a daring suggestion. "I was just wondering if perhaps there would be any chance at all of you swapping rooms with us, just for one night. This is a shot in the dark, I really don't expect that you will, but one can only try. You see I work for the Sunblest Bread Company and Sally works as a children's nanny so this is probably the only chance we will ever have of staying anywhere as grand as the Clifton Arms."

He signs the letter "Yours hopefully," and then adds two postscripts: "P.S. You are more than welcome to join us for a drink at the reception. P.P.S. I didn't write to Gary Player because we were told you were a much nicer chap."

Palmer, of course, not only surrendered the suite but took them up on the offer of the beer where he drank a toast to the happy couple and even posed for a photograph.

Go ahead and make someone's day—share this story with a friend.

Note that at the end of the post we ask the reader to share this story with a friend; this drives additional traffic back to your club's web site. Even though this is a stock post you could easily customize it by adding a short personal intro or ending. Perhaps about a time you saw Arnie. Even just telling your readers that Arnie was your favorite player will no doubt create a small bond with many who feel the same way.

Use humor in your blog posts

Another easy way to spice up your blog is to share some golf humor. Fifteen minutes on Google will provide you with a year's supply of clean and entertaining golf jokes.

Then you can add an invitation that gathers more content for you: "Post your favorite joke on our blog—the best joke gets a free round."

Use quotes in your blog, your tweets, and Facebook

Golf is a very quotable game with lots of colorful characters. A few of your favorite quotes can be enough to engage your readers, make them smile, and perhaps pass on a link to your blog to a friend or two (viral marketing).

Here are a few of our favorites:

✔ "The more you practice, the luckier you get."

—Gary Player

✔ "99% of all putts you leave short don't go in."

—Hubert Green

✔ "Golf is a game whose aim is to hit a very small ball into an even smaller hole, with weapons singularly ill- designed for the purpose."

—Winston Churchill

✔ "Golf is a good walk spoiled."

—Mark Twain

Solicit engagement by asking readers to vote on their favorite quote. Or get them to post by asking, "Do you have a better quote?"

While we have a large library of content for our partners to use, finding this content online is as quick and easy as a Google search for "golf quotes." From search to blog post in about two minutes flat.

FUNNY VIDEOS

I shared this "redneck skeet shooting" video through all of my social media and people just loved it. They re-tweeted it, gave it the "I Like" vote on Facebook, and passed it around via e-mail. Exactly the type of response you ideally want from your posts, something so engaging and entertaining it goes viral.

This post went viral quickly because people LOVE the video.
(http://www.youtube.com/watch?v=v8z0hyIx3fE)

USE SOCIAL MEDIA TO INCREASE DOWNLOADS OF YOUR INFORMATION

The following text entices golfers to download a 20-page pdf product from their golf club.

Improve your putting under pressure

Impressed by the way the tour pros were rolling in the putts under pressure at last week's PGA Championship?

You can do exactly the same thing with **David Frost's Guide To Superior Putting Under Pressure.**

Winner of 10 events on the PGA Tour and a start on the Champions Tour, Frosty holds the PGA Tour record for the least number of putts in a 72-hole event!

Frosty's booklet is a $19.95 value but is complimentary to you. Ready to make a bunch more putts? Then grab your booklet and come on down to the course.

Offering a publication like this one that provides value to your customers is a great way to build your opt-in e-mail database.

USE BLOGS, TWITTER, AND FACEBOOK TO PROMOTE YOUR CONTESTS

Contests are a great way to get people involved with your social media. Give away clubs, balls, green fees, vacations, and memberships. The bigger the prize, the bigger the response, and once again you will be building your database.

For example:

- ✔ 1st   A fully matched set of 3 V-SOLE wedges, custom built to your specs

- ✔ 2nd   A matched pair of V-SOLE wedges, custom built to your specs (3 winners)

- ✔ 3rd   One V-SOLE wedge, custom built to your specs (5 winners)

Enter here to win your Eidolon clubs and discover what backspin really looks like!

DON'T WORRY TOO MUCH ABOUT GRAMMAR, SPELLING, PERFECT ENGLISH, OR EMULATING MARK

TWAIN WITH YOUR WRITING SKILL

In fact, I don't worry about it at all!

Now I know this drives some people nuts but at least it makes all those members who are great at English feel good when they can point out your mistakes!

Social media are informal; you don't need to be Ernest Hemingway or Mark Twain to get your message across. People are looking for content, ideas, entertainment, and education, not an English lesson.

Be yourself; let your personality shine through. It's your club's blog, your opinion, so don't water stuff down too much just to be politically correct.

Blog consistently, at least weekly, more often if possible.

As in most things, setting goals at the start produces better results than a haphazard effort. Decide how often you are going to blog, who will post, and when.

DON'T EXPECT TONS OF FEEDBACK RIGHT AWAY

You will get feedback, but it takes time. Interestingly enough, in the hundreds of useful golf marketing posts I make a year it's the two or three controversial ones that always produce the biggest response, both positively and negatively.

Sometimes to get the discussion going, you need to use plant posts, feedback, or questions to stimulate activity.

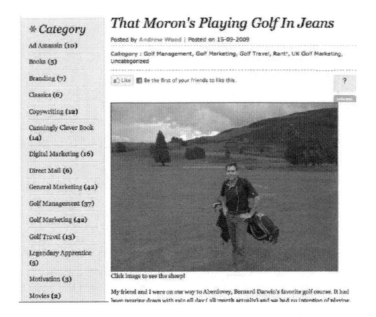

That Moron's Playing Golf In Jeans

Posted by Andrew Wood | Posted on 15-09-2009

Category : Golf Management, Golf Marketing, Golf Travel, Rant!, UK Golf Marketing, Uncategorized

Like Be the first of your friends to like this. ?

Click image to see the sheep!

My friend and I were on our way to Aberdovey, Bernard Darwin's favorite golf course. It had

**My blog on dress codes created a firestorm of
response both for and against relaxing dress codes.**

The fastest way to create a buzz is to stir something up!

Hot topics include club rules, speed of play, cell phones, dress codes, growing the game, technology, and current events.

DO NOT expect all the comments to be positive; you have to be thick skinned when using social media. Remember the idea of social media is to create dialogue, to educate, engage, and entertain.

Also remember that this sort of discussion is going on within your club whether you listen to it and address it or not! Many clubs are scared of what people might post but burying your head in the sand is not a good idea. You always maintain moderator control over your blog so can choose not to approve distasteful comments.

PRACTICAL BLOG TIPS

Add a favorite icon to your browser bar

A favicon (short for "favorite icon") is that small icon displayed on the browser URL bar, on the bookmark lists and, for certain browsers, on the navigation tabs. While a favicon will not drastically change your traffic, it will certainly improve the look of your blog. Adding a unique icon ensures that readers are able to recognize your site inside bookmark lists easily. Normally you would use your club logo for this.

Offer your readers categories

1 **The categories tell a lot about your blog.** When readers cannot figure what is going on it is very likely that they will just skip your blog altogether.

2 **Limit the total number of categories.** Every blog should have a defined structure and a set of categories to support the topics of the posts. Once you have that basic structure in place just fill the posts inside the existing categories.

3 **Make sure your list of categories fits in one screen if possible.**

4 **Try to put posts inside one category only.** If you place posts inside multiple categories the reader will find the same posts over and over again.

5 **Display the number of posts inside each category.** This feature will make sure that the reader knows what to expect when he clicks a certain category, and it also gives a general orientation about the most discussed topics on your blog.

Blogging takes a commitment but it's a commitment that will build your brand and help you increase business.

TEN WAYS TO USE TWITTER EFFECTIVELY FOR YOUR CLUB

Twitter is a communication and engagement tool. On Twitter you "tweet" your comments, limited to 140 characters. These brief comments from you can be turned into a powerful marketing and relationship tool.

Too many clubs are either not using Twitter (and other social media), not using it effectively, or using it and giving up because they can't see the point.

There are many benefits to tweeting on Twitter for all kinds of clubs, primarily daily fee and resorts:

1. Connecting and engaging with your players and members. This is the main reason why you should use Twitter for your club. The critical factor is to create compelling and interesting content to share with your players and members, content that adds value to the relationship. The more personalized you can make that communication the better.

2. Branding and building your authority. You don't have to be a big brand-name club like Doral or a top 100 instructor like Charlie King to brand yourself on Twitter. You can be an "average Joe" and build awareness, trust, and loyalty. Common ways to build your authority on Twitter are to send out links to useful resources, provide useful tips to your followers, give insight into relevant topics, answer questions, and engage in discussions with your followers.

3. Marketing. Perhaps the most obvious benefit of Twitter is generating traffic to your web site, making the phone ring, and making money:

- ✔ You can tweet special offers and provide coupons codes to give your course a traffic boost (as below).

- ✔ Invite participation in contests or give away free booklets packed with your best advice.

4. Member and guest feedback. Once you have connected with your members or guests, you will get feedback. Listening will help you provide better service in the future.

People often use Twitter to express dissatisfaction:

Playing golf at XYZ golf club, three groups on every tee this sucks!

Of course they can also use it to spread your message virally and bring you business:

Playing golf, XYZ best greens in South County!

Either way, follow the people who are following you or look at your mention tab to see what is being said about your course.

5. Learn inside-industry news first. One of the best things about Twitter is that it keeps you up to date with all the news that's important to your business. By following the right people in your industry, you can always have the latest niche news that you can't get anywhere else.

6. Spying on your competition. Twitter is a great way to spy on competition. Track what competitors are doing and thinking (watch their tweets, who they're conversing with, and so forth). You can also read what customers are saying about your competition. Find out about issues and problems people are having with your competitors so you can capitalize on them, and perhaps even gain market share.

Just monitor the profiles and set alerts on the profiles of your competitors.

7. Reputation management. Track your name to keep tabs on what people are saying about your club at any given time. If it's a positive comment, you can re-tweet it as a third party endorsement. If it's negative, this information can be useful for fixing in-house problems, and it can also help you eliminate any untrue rumors that might be spreading around. I'm a firm advocate that every problem is an opportunity when viewed from the right perspective.

8. Market research. Twitter is an ideal place to perform quick polls and research that will help you plan or implement your business strategy. Just tweet your simple question and tally up the results.

Even a simple question like, "What's your a favorite hole or favorite beer?" can get players interacting with you. Questions like, "What other courses do you play at?" can give you real marketing insight.

Be sure to offer rewards or a chance to win a prize for those who answer.

9. Solve problems quickly. Twitter provides you with a valuable resource when it comes to solving problems quickly. Simply pose your question to the community and within minutes you'll have an array of responses from your followers. It could even spark a larger discussion that gets you some attention.

10. Building customer loyalty. Communicate with your connections in a direct and informative manner. Simply participating in conversations will "push the needle" of trust in your direction, but it is more than that. Suggest resources others would be interested in following as potential customers, employees, advisors, or friends.

Simply telling people where you are at a given time can create new relationships. Recently when in France, I tweeted I was there. I immediately I got an invitation to visit a golf course near Paris from a golf professional who had bought one of my books. This started a new and interesting relationship full of possibilities, all from a single tweet!

Always invite others to follow your tweets. You can follow mine at www.twitter.com/CunninglyClever.

Build your Twitter strategy around these key points and you will find it a very worthwhile tool.

Twitter is fast, free, and powerful…just do it!

THIRTEEN WAYS TO USE LINKEDIN PRODUCTIVELY

With over 60 million users, including just about all the world's top companies and decision makers, LinkedIn has developed critical mass.

Profiles on LinkedIn include all types of business people: top executives, middle management, salespeople, business owners, consultants, entrepreneurs, and micro businesses. They are the people most likely to join clubs, book golf outings, travel, or hold meetings. In other words, they are your perfect prospects.

Understanding the importance of LinkedIn and how it can help you grow your business is an important part of your social media strategy.

1. Boost your club's business. If you want to generate more customers, LinkedIn is the perfect place to start looking. The chances are very good that your next big outing, event, or member is already on LinkedIn. Who are you trying to find? What company do you really want to land as a customer? Are you searching for a way in? LinkedIn is the answer. By using LinkedIn correctly, you can be introduced to the person you need to meet and turn a prospect into a customer.

2. Improve your Google ranking. Your LinkedIn profile will have a fairly high Google page rank. It should come up when people are looking for you by name on Google. So be sure and fill your profile with all the key information you want people to see.

3. Finding new employees or finding a job yourself. LinkedIn is a fantastic place to look for new employees for just about any position. Unlike all the other major job search sites, it's free. When you post jobs you can attract both people actively looking for a job and people who are passively looking for a job. Often times LinkedIn job postings are forwarded by contacts because they think it might be a good fit. This creates a viral effect. LinkedIn is equally useful in finding suppliers and in finding a job when you are looking. The key is to have your network well in place before you ever need a job.

4. Checking references of potential hires or suppliers. Trying to hire the perfect chef, golf professional, or manager? You're not likely to find out about an applicant's past mistakes by calling the references on their application. Do a search for others who worked at the same company at the same time and get a better background check in minutes for free.

Let's say you have a course in Cincinnati and want to get the local BMW dealership's outing business. A quick search delivers Ric, who's also in charge or advertising; perhaps a tee sponsor or GPS opportunity as well?

5. Research companies and business opportunities. LinkedIn makes it easy to do extensive, business-related research. You'll have no trouble finding information about companies you may be considering dealing with or competing with. Through LinkedIn networking you can even learn of business opportunities of which you may have been previously unaware. Talk to employees or former employees of other clubs, or competitors. Former employees usually give more candid opinions about a club's prospects than someone who's still on board. You can also track new or start-up businesses to find the new opportunities for your club first.

6. Get and give professional advice. LinkedIn Answers is a powerful resource you can use to get answers to your own business- related questions, while at the same time responding to others' questions based on your own areas of expertise. What do you need help with? Are you deciding between two POS software products for your club? Are you looking for the best marketing company for your business? Need a graphic designer in London? A golf photographer in Leeds? All of these questions can be asked on LinkedIn and within minutes you will start receiving answers to help you make a good decision or direct you to a solution.

7. Build your personal network. Although I have my own CRM, iPhone, and *Salesforce* to keep all my information in "one" place, LinkedIn offers a clear advantage over all of them. When people move, change jobs, or start new ventures, they update their own contact information. This alone is worth the price of admission, saving the cost and hassle of updating your files yourself and always giving you current contact information.

8. Increase your credibility and build your brand. If you're trying to market yourself as an expert, or develop credibility in your field, it looks good to have a strong presence with lots of connections on a network such as LinkedIn. If you answer questions with the knowledge of an expert in the Answers section, even better. Get active in club manager, golf professional, superintendent, or F&B communities, groups, and forums within LinkedIn.

9. Find people. Looking for old friends or business associates with whom you want to re-establish relationships? How about former employers or employees or people you met at a cocktail party but can't find their cards? Do a LinkedIn search.

Make it a point to find three new connections per day to build a large and targeted list of meeting, event, and membership prospects in your area. If you don't know the contact directly, ask to be introduced from one of your existing contacts. Remember he with the biggest and best database wins. And nothing is better than a handcrafted one.

10. Help others. The best way to network is to help others succeed in their businesses or careers. This very often is the start of them trying to help you or your club. Use LinkedIn to help others: Promote them, link to them, connect with them, recommend them, answer their questions.

11. Get publicity. It can be hard to contact media or top bloggers. But many of them have LinkedIn profiles where you can contact them. I highly advise you not to spam them, but a press release or a polite e-mail letting them know about something newsworthy will at least be noticed.

12. Build business referrals. People with whom you've done business in the past will be able to recommend you right on LinkedIn, and for those who don't you can politely solicit referrals from them. Getting people saying how great your course, memberships, banquets, weddings, lessons, or community is will attract more people to your cause.

13. Set LinkedIn goals. Having a few goals for LinkedIn is essential to insure you receive what you are looking for. On LinkedIn your goals might be to connect with 10 more people per month, to recommend three people in your network, to receive five recommendations, or simply to meet with four connections this month on the phone or in person.

LinkedIn is an excellent tool for clubs and personal networking, but you have to use it to get results.

YOU CAN CREATE YOUR OWN TV CHANNEL ON YOUTUBE

YouTube is an amazingly cheap and powerful tool to create buzz that basically gives you the ability to create your own TV shows. If used correctly, that's not just power, that's serious power.

Once you are on a video, DVD, or YouTube, you are on TV

One important fact to remember in marketing is that once you have produced a DVD and someone puts it in a machine and hits play, you are now on TV. The same is true of YouTube. It doesn't matter what it cost you to film it, you are up there just like Tom Cruise.

Being on that screen is an incredibly powerful tool in self- branding.

In the late Nineties, I was able to produce a pretty decent 30- minute show called *Martial Arts Business Magazine* for just $1,500 a month. The show was quick paced and patterned after *PM Magazine*. Videos were mailed out to paying customers as part of our monthly program, but were also used to solicit new business.

Film your course, your teaching, your membership sales pitch, or get someone to interview you with a series of questions that position you as an authority. Then edit it all into your own show.

The celebrity power of being on someone's TV screen cannot be overstated, even if you got there via a self-produced YouTube clip.

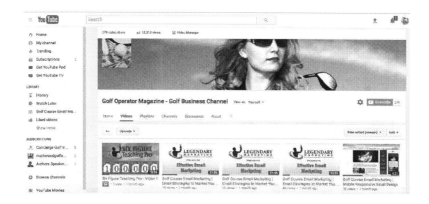

Exploit the power of YouTube to make yourself, your course, resort, or golf school a TV star

YouTube is the ideal place to share your expertise, highlight your products, and showcase your customers and results while you attract and entertain your existing and future clients. It's also a great way to go viral. It aids in generating web traffic and helps you climb up the search engine rankings.

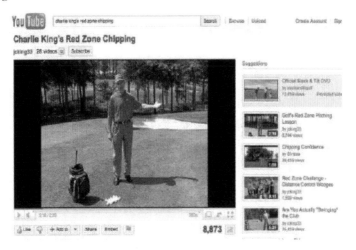

**Charlie King does a great job of building his brand
with his content-rich
teaching clips on YouTube.**

I use YouTube to showcase my sales and marketing expertise. Go to www.golfbusinesstv.com. The free shows in effect drive people back to my web site, a percentage of whom then become customers.

Many of the resorts I consult with use YouTube to showcase their golf courses, spaces, rooms, and other activities. Several restaurants I work with use YouTube to showcase different dishes they serve in the restaurant. Golf, karate, fitness, and instructors of all kinds use it to showcase their skills.

Then of course there are those businesses that put together funny skits that can quickly go viral. I did one such three-minute spot for a resort that featured Elvis playing golf with Ozzy Osborne as his caddie and Donald Trump playing through. It was watched by over 10,000 people in a single week. Just remember, if you do "funny," make sure it somehow ties back into what you offer in order to be truly effective at building business as well as brand.

Don't wait for your chance at stardom—make yourself a star on YouTube.

DELIVERING SOCIAL PROOF

No matter what *you* say about yourself and your services or products, people will be skeptical. But when *other* people say nice things about you, they are more trusted because they have no bias to promote you.

Two Guys Who Golf have a big following in the Midwest for their course reviews.

As I was traveling round France last summer I used Hotels.com, Vernere.com, TripAdvisor.com, and Bookings.com to locate and book rooms. Often when no clear choice was obvious from the limited information and photos provided, I was drawn to the reader reviews to help make my decision. Of course people's opinions can be different even of the same experience. Nonetheless, I read them and was no doubt more influenced by them than I even know.

EBay's reputation for safety was built in large part by customer ratings of the sellers. The same thing is true of buying a book on

Amazon. Before they part with their hard earned money, people want social proof that the book will deliver the benefits or entertainment it promises. I'm proud of the quality of the readers' comments I have gotten for my recent books, *Cunningly Clever Marketing, Cunningly Clever Selling,* and *The Golf Marketing Bible.* I am sure they help sales stay strong.

What are people saying about your course?

Most people don't know what others are saying, but it's something you should check regularly. There may be one or two vocal people out there who could be badly damaging your online reputation.

People do look at and read these comments. They provide the social proof that your offer is what you say it is. Very often the negative comments about your business are unfair, but that doesn't make them any less harmful. They must be countered with a response or with a stream of positive comments that relegates the negative ones to the dungeons of page ten.

Clients, staff, family, and friends MUST be ENCOURAGED to provide feedback on Facebook, Twitter, LinkedIn, Fast Pitch, and MySpace to name just a handful. If others are saying good things about you, they must be true!

Monitor and encourage, online and off line, the social proof that tells the world your business is a winner.

CROSS-MARKETING YOUR SOCIAL MEDIA

The more active you are on social media, the more people you will connect with. Make sure you integrate your marketing at every opportunity: Tell people on one service about your material on others. Everyone has their own favorite social media and they may not be the one you are most comfortable using.

Remember there are a number of free apps you can use to make sure one social media posts seamlessly with another. Take advantage of them, they will save you tons of time. That way when you tweet it will automatically post to your blog, LinkedIn, and Facebook accounts, and vice versa. Also take advantage of smartphone tools like Echofon that allow you to tweet and Facebook from your iPhone.

YOU NEED AN INTEGRATED PLAN

I try very hard to get my clients working on 90-day digital and social media plans. With so much going on you really need to coordinate your e-mail campaigns, your tweets, blogs, and Facebook campaigns. Your weekly e-mails and monthly newsletters should also coordinate and co-promote what's going on in your social media pages. Too often I see clubs working in the dark with the left hand not knowing what the right hand is doing. It takes less than four hours to map out a comprehensive 90-day plan...Just do it!

EXPLORE THE SOCIAL WORLD

While I have covered the main social media sites the fact is there are thousands out there, some of which may deserve your attention like Pinterest, Instagram my rule of thumb is simple, ACE Facebook first before you worry about the rest!

While the ones I have mentioned are getting the bulk of the action now, a smaller niche site like the following, local to your area, may actually give you more bang for the buck.

SUMMARY AND QUICK-START ACTION PLAN

I have heard every excuse in the book why clubs don't use social media, or if they start why they stop almost at once because they find it overwhelming. The truth of the matter is it's really not that hard. Like most things, it's just a matter of putting a plan together, making execution a priority, and having the discipline to stick with it.

Here is a simple plan you can use to get started:

1. Connect with me, Andrew Wood on Facebook, Twitter, and LinkedIn. Watch my posts.

2. Spend some time looking at other people's social media. Follow at least one or two other clubs in each medium so you can see what they are doing.

3. Start tweeting. Tweet at least once a day—it takes 15 seconds.

4. Join Facebook. Update it once a day; it only takes a couple of minutes.

5. Join LinkedIn. Update it once a week.

6. Register on YouTube. Upload new videos at least once a month. Film several clips in one day but spread out uploading

7. Blog at least once a week. Two to three times a week is better though.

8. Consider Fast Pitch Networking. It's another option, especially if you are in a metro market or do a lot of corporate business.

9. Set up stock content in advance. Then if you are short on time you still have something to post. Easy targets are famous players birthdays and major championship weeks. Use quotes, jokes, or anecdotes that coincide with a player's birthday or championship and you are suddenly topical even through the content was posted six months ago.

10. Get others on staff to help. Asking the pro or chef to post once a month is hardly going to kill them! Even if you don't get help, you can still post recipes from the chef or tips from the pro.

11. Repeat your core message, your unique selling proposition, often.

12. Make sure your social media is easy to find on your club's main web site.

13. Make sure all your e-mail signatures invite people to interact with your social media site.

14. Make sure all your print materials invite readers to interact with your social media sites.

15. Set up a schedule for posting across all sites and stick with it! Social media is just as important, perhaps even more so, as sending your weekly e-mail or monthly club newsletter.

16. Set goals for connections, followers, and fans. What gets measured gets done. What doesn't, gets forgotten.

17. Have at least three times more great content than pure promotion. More content is always better.

18. Work to continuously improve your social media efforts. Once you have everything started, make an effort to go back monthly and improve your profile, pictures, and additional info on each site as you gain experience.

19. Ask for input. Constantly ask for feedback, comments, testimonials, opinions, reviews, recommendations, and questions. Interaction is the KEY to successful social media.

20. Things change fast! Schedule 30 minutes a month to review other social media sites. Make sure you check out our resource sites for frequent updates on the latest trends in social media **www.GolfOperatorMagazine.com**

21. Too much work? Not enough time or resources?. Legendary Marketing can run your social media program for you. Call us 800-827-1663 or me directly at 352-266-2099.

To use social media to your advantage, pick something and get started!

CHAPTER TWENTY-THREE

Building Buzz and Brand with Facebook

F acebook was the last of the social media I adopted after blogging, Linkedin, and Twitter, yet it most likely should have been the first. Its reach is long, its power for growing your club's business undeniable, and its growth around the world truly staggering!

Almost all of the points I have made about the value of blogging, Twitter, LinkedIn, and even YouTube hold true for Facebook so I won't repeat all of them in detail. Instead I will provide practical examples to stimulate ideas for your club. Facebook allows you to find people, network, join groups, send updates, upload pictures and video, solicit feedback, make new friends, and more, all in one place. It's like all the benefits of the other social sites rolled into one.

In This Chapter You Will Learn:

✔ How to build awareness of your Facebook.

✔ How to educate your visitors.

✔ How to engage with your fans.

✔ How to convert your fans to action.

✔ How to keep your fans engaged.

✔ What you should be posting on your Facebook page.

The power of Facebook was clearly demonstrated to me when after speaking at a martial arts convention for the first time in ten years I hooked up with a few old clients and friends. One offered to help me grow my martial arts business following on Facebook. He recommended people "send a friend request" to me. Within a week I had over 1,000 professional martial arts instructors hooked up with me!

Imagine how long it would have taken in the old days (10 years ago!) to build a targeted list of customers that large. That's the power of Facebook—the power to connect with a target audience and to get that audience helping you reach large numbers of other people quickly, easily, and at no cost!

Facebook can be used in multiple ways to attract potential customers. Through joining communities on Facebook and by inviting users to link to your page, you potentially can reach large numbers of prospects and customers. Just how large? Well, let's look at the facts.

Facts

✔ Facebook has more than 1.8 billion active monthly users and over 1.2 billion log in every day.

✔ That means that 65% of Facebook's active users log on to Facebook in any given day.

✔ The average user has 155 friends.

✔ People spend over 700 billion minutes per month on Facebook.

Activity on Facebook

✔ There are over 900 million objects (pages, groups, events, and community pages) that people interact with.

✔ The average user is connected to 80 community pages, groups, and events.

✔ The average user creates 90 pieces of content each month.

✔ More than 30 billion pieces of content (web links, news stories, blog posts, notes, photo albums, etc.) are shared each month.

Global Reach

✔ More than 70 translations are available on the site.

✔ About 70% of Facebook users are outside the United States.

✔ Over 300,000 users helped translate the site through the translations application.

Mobile

✔ There are more than 1.7 billon active users currently accessing Facebook through their mobile devices.

✔ People who use Facebook on their mobile devices are twice as active on Facebook as non mobile users.

✔ There are more than 200 mobile operators in 60 countries working to deploy and promote Facebook mobile products.

PROFITING FROM FACEBOOK

The first question to ask is "What's your club's goal for being on Facebook?" Ultimately the goal of most clubs will be to increase retention of existing players and to find new players. Like most marketing on the Internet, this will happen over a period of time and involve a number of phases.

STEP 1:BUILD AWARENESS FOR YOUR CLUB AND ITS

FACEBOOK PAGE

The first step of your Facebook marketing campaign is to build brand awareness for your club and your page. People must know the general services your club offers and that they can find you on Facebook and learn more by visiting your Facebook page.

HOW DO YOU BUILD AWARENESS OF YOUR FACEBOOK PRESENCE?

Your existing website

Make sure you highlight your Facebook page on your existing web site and let people know you are there as well as promoting all of your other social media.

Your existing e-mail or snail mail database

Use your existing e-mail and snail mail databases to let people know about your Facebook page. End every e-mail with a promotion for your social media and make sure that all your ads and brochures carry your social media logos and addresses. It's Marketing 101, but you'd be amazed how many clubs forget to do this simple but powerful step!

Search engine optimization

As you develop more content and links on your page, this will also help you develop better search engine rankings among local golf clubs. This means that your web pages will appear higher than others when users search.

Targeted ads

Taking advantage of the Facebook advertising platform is also an option. The standard cost of acquiring a new fan on your Facebook page through Facebook advertising is about $0.50. (I get a lot of exotic car-related ads. Why? Because through using the site, Facebook knows I like golf, cars, and marketing. It's very targeted!)

Organic growth

The very best way to grow your Facebook presence is organically. The golden rule of viral/organic growth online is: *Create great content that people will share*. It's honestly as simple as that. (See examples of great content in the blog section and on the following pages.)

STEP 2: EDUCATE YOUR VISITORS

For those visitors who already know your club, you may not need to do much education. For the rest who are just learning about your club or who are new to showing an interest in it, the education process entails answering the following questions:

Who are you?

When I say "Who are you" I will repeat what I said before because it's so important. I'm not just referencing your club as a faceless organization. As I tell people on a regular basis, you need to *humanize* your organization. Who are the manager, pro, chef, superintendent, and staff? Who are the members? By connecting with individuals on a personal level and letting them know that there are REAL PEOPLE behind your computer on the other end, you'll build a strong connection that will help the individual associate positive feelings with your club. Yes, you also need to let them know what your organization is, but the personal touch is much more important.

What does your club sell?

This could be as simple as something within the information tab in your Facebook page that describes what your club offers in the way of memberships, annual passes, outings, and events. You could also create an entire tab dedicated to describing your unique sales proposition (USP).

Who's in your community?

When a new visitor lands on your Facebook page, one of the first things they'll look at is the number of fans you have. You'll notice that as Facebook pages grow in size, they also tend to increase in the volume of new fans per day. This is because having a large number of fans turns you into a trusted authority.

Users will also browse through the members on your Facebook page to see who else is part of the community. They'll also view the comments people are posting to see if your content is something they are interested in hearing about. Do you have brand advocates who are speaking up for you when you aren't around? Do you have people who have something valuable to add to the conversation?

They say that you are who your friends are, and on Facebook you are who your community is. Foster a valuable community and there's a greater chance you'll convert new visitors into fans.

Why do I want to join?

Finally, before becoming a fan, the user will try to figure what benefit they are going to get from becoming a fan of your Facebook page. The benefit could simply be an opportunity to express their affiliation with your brand. Another benefit could be ongoing access to valuable content. If your Facebook page has nothing to offer the visitor, the only people who will become fans are those who are already your fans or those who are interested in existing community members.

If your goal is to reach new customers, you'll need to present significant value through your Facebook page.

STEP 3: ENGAGEMENT WITH YOUR FANS

"Engagement" has become the cornerstone of social network marketing. While many marketers criticize engagement for the inability to quantify it, every online marketer knows that engaging your customers is the new form of marketing. Rather than speaking *at* your customers, marketing has now become a two-way dialogue, leaving many traditional advertisers feeling powerless and confused.

You aren't completely powerless though since you can control the environment in which much of the conversation takes place. While there are many other platforms for engaging your customer base, Facebook pages are a great environment for directly interacting with a large portion of your customers and fans.

The engagement process is also critical to building a relationship with your fans and strengthening their personal brand affiliation. One thing to keep in mind is the impact that various forms of engagement have on the relationship with your customer:

- ✔ Low-impact activities—There are a lot of low-impact activities that a consumer can engage in. One example would be "liking" a status update in Facebook. (For those who may be confused, "liking" is the feature in Facebook that lets you click "Like" under a feed story.)

- ✔ Medium-impact activities—Commenting on a status could be one example of a medium-impact activity.

- ✔ High-impact activities—An individual or brand could turn a medium impact activity into a high-impact experience by providing one-on-one dialogue to turn the experience from a single comment to an ongoing conversation.

For daily fee, private clubs, resorts, and different people, the impact of your efforts will differ, which is why it's best to provide as many engagement opportunities as possible.

STEP 4: CONVERTING FANS TO ACTION

In contrast to search engine advertising, which involves clicking on an ad and then taking some sort of action (for example, filling out a form or purchasing a product), Facebook sales normally involve building a relationship and presenting multiple opportunities to take an action. At this point you've already converted new visitors and, in the engagement phase, you built the relationship. Now it's time to present opportunities to make a purchase, attend an event, book a tee time, join the club, or take some other form of measurable action.

Most Facebook users are not ready to buy when they initially become a fan, which is why you need to present calls to action on a regular basis. One example would be instant discounts. For example, you may want to provide a twilight-special today only, or free cart for the next four hours only. Another example is entering their names and e-mails into a newsletter list.

STEP 5: CONTINUE ENGAGEMENT

Now that you've presented a call to action and some of your users have taken that action, you need to continue to engage them. If you use the relationship-marketing model on Facebook, you'll end up a winner.

Relationship marketing is not about a one-time sale or action. Instead, we are in the business of building relationships and Facebook provides a good environment for doing just that.

You've already subtly introduced calls to action and now that some users have taken those calls to action, you need to keep doing what you did in step 3: Engage them and keep engaging them.

WHAT SHOULD YOU DO ON FACEBOOK?

- ✔ Invite your friends to like your business page.

- ✔ Upload your email database – it will match the emails with profiles and invite them to like your page.

- ✔ Invite your players and members.

- ✔ Then start looking at who they know and ask them to recommend you to their friends.

Post special events

Create events to promote upcoming club events, tournaments, dining events, live music, etc. When you create an event, it gets a fully featured page, much like a group, that includes a discussion, photos, videos and links. Facebook Events makes it easy to get the word out to hundreds of people, manage your guest list, and build community around your upcoming event.

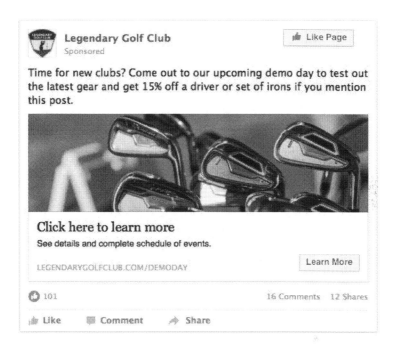

Highlight specific services or promotions within your club

Most clubs have a huge range of ongoing services and activities that should be constantly highlighted on their Facebook pages: social events, tournaments, clinics, lessons, new inventory, seafood night, happy hour. Meeting space, tennis lessons, fashion shows, book clubs, and investment clubs are all things you should consider posting on your page.

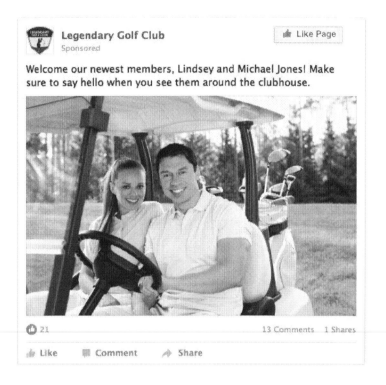

Post pictures of people enjoying your club

They say a picture is worth a thousand words and when it comes to pictures of people enjoying your course and events they could be right. Make sure there are lots of pictures of every club event and get them up fast so members and guests can in turn share them with their friends while the event is still newsworthy.

Post videos

The more multimedia you can add to your Facebook page, the more different people you are likely to attract. Post videos, audios, webinars, and slide shows. Some people like to read, others like to watch, so cater to both. Plus videos are more likely to go viral.

Post coupons and ads

Intersperse regular promotions and a special in between your news, events photos, and links. You can do monthly, weekly, or even daily promotions, provided that's not the only thing you do. Be sure to work real content in between your promotions and you will not risk offending your fans.

Remember the real beauty here is there are no spam filters, or bad addresses. EVERYTHING you post will make it on to your fans news feed!

Use this power wisely!

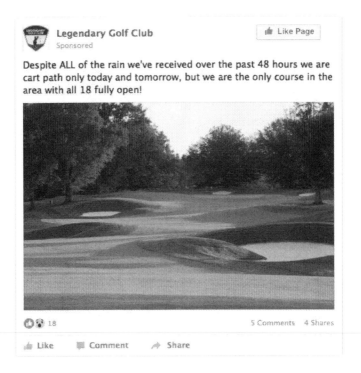

Post course updates

Facebook is a great way to get out info about changing course conditions. People will appreciate knowing that your course is closed before getting in their car and driving twenty miles. Likewise it could be raining hard in Philly but sunny on the other side of the bridge in Jersey, thus giving you a great opportunity to get people to come out and play if you tell them.

You can also post routine maintenance updates, explain why certain things are being done, and generally educate members and players about what it takes to get the course in great shape.

Share your club's history

Facebook is the place you can share you club's rich history. Pictures and stories from the past help to communicate the tradition and brand that your clubs has. You can show past and present pictures, discuss remodeling through the years, or offer bios of the architect and prominent members.

Promote gift certificates

Facebook is a great place to promote gift certificates, especially when your club may be closed for the winter. The clubhouse may be closed but your virtual clubhouse on Facebook is always open. Keep your buzz going while your competitor's hibernate!

Discovery tours and real estate

If you have real estate, frequent mentions of your discovery tours, models, and special offers are appropriate.

Post interesting facts and testimonials

Facebook is the ideal place to solicit testimonials or re-post testimonials that have come in via e-mail or snail mail. Repost your recommendations from LinkedIn, and stream video or audio testimonials. This gives your club and its events great third party endorsements that are proven to significantly increase response in prospective members.

Legendary Golf Club
Sponsored

23 problems only golfers will understand:
https://www.buzzfeed.com/awesomer/problems-every-golfer-will-understand

👍 Like Page

119   19 Comments   23 Shares

👍 Like   💬 Comment   ➵ Share

Post links to interesting articles, sites, or videos

Use Facebook to bring attention to articles or reviews in other publications about your facility. Use it to bring attention to other news and blogs on the Internet that you think your members and guests will find interesting or entertaining. While you may think it defeats the purpose to send your fans to another site, the reverse is actually true. Providing your fans with quality content makes you a trusted authority and a trusted source.

Run simple quizzes to encourage engagement

Quizzes are a quick easy way to get people interacting with your club's

Facebook page, and interaction is the KEY to building trust and business.

Do a Facebook Live video

Do a quick live video of the first group of the day teeing off, a shotgun event, happy hour, etc.

These are just a few ideas for what you can post on Facebook. The possibilities for a post are nearly endless. Just remember to engage, educate and entertain.

INCORPORATE THE TOOLS YOU'RE ALREADY USING ONTO YOUR PAGE

Do you blog? Do you tweet? Let's hope so after reading this book. Do you read feeds? There are Facebook apps available for all these services. After you add the respective app, you simply do what you were already doing and let the app do the work. You can have your Tweets post to your Facebook page and vice versa. If your blog is on WordPress, you can add the WordPress app and your posts will automatically be pushed to your Facebook page.

JOIN GROUPS RELATED TO YOUR BUSINESS INTERESTS

Many groups on Facebook are nonsense, but there are quite a few that can provide useful information and professional connections. Rather than trying to search for groups, watch the groups that your friends are joining, as often you will find them of interest for yourself. After all, they're in your contact list because you have something in common, right?

LIMIT WASTED TIME ON FACEBOOK

Facebook can easily suck you in; it's very addictive once you get going - just ask any teenager! You, however, have important club work to do. You won't help your club or career if you fall behind on projects because you were too busy playing on Facebook. If you find that you're spending too much time reading Facebook message boards or reading about your friends' favorite book selections, then set limits for yourself. Check it only once or twice a day, switch off all the e-mail notifications and ignore all the game requests!

Facebook can be a black hole. Use it wisely or you might get lost.

SUMMARY

Used correctly, Facebook can be one of the most powerful tools in your marketing arsenal. However, you have to remember that people are not going on Facebook to book a tee time or buy into one of your events so everything you post should not be sales-based, that's a sure recipe for failure. You must first build a relationship by engaging, educating and entertaining, then you can go about collecting their email for your database or trying to sell a tee time.

CHAPTER TWENTY-FOUR

Facebook Ads

I n the last chapter Facebook we learned that almost 2 billion people use Facebook every month and 65% of them access it every day! It is far too big of a marketing platform for you to be ignoring!

In This Chapter You Will Learn:

✔ Why Facebook ads are so important.

✔ What type of results you can expect.

✔ The various ad options (at this time).

✔ The anatomy of a Facebook ad.

✔ The Facebook Ads Checklist

✔ 15 ways you can get started.

What makes Facebook such an effective advertising platform?

The user base is continually growing and doesn't show any signs of slowing down as the number of daily monthly users represents a 17% increase year over year and the number of daily active users represents and 18% year over year increase.

There are 218,419,100 profiles with "golf" interests on Facebook in the United States just waiting for you to reach them! This number increases if you begin to add other golf keywords. Obviously you aren't going to target an area this broad when running your own ads, but you get the picture, **golfers are out there and not many businesses are targeting them!**

Facebook has made it harder and harder to reach even your own fans with organic posts.

The wealth of user information that Facebook has makes it possible (and easy) to create incredibly targeted ads that your specific prospects can relate to and will take action on!

Lookalike Audiences make it easy to reach people similar to your ideal targets.

It's easy to create brand awareness through Facebook – especially when the majority of your competitors are not taking advantage of it!

What type of results can you expect?

Leads

Driving conversions and leads is nearly everyone's top goal of online marketing. You can drive conversions straight from your ads using website conversion ads and boosted posts. One feature of Facebook ads is a call to action button that invokes people to take an action that is specific to your ad.

Visitors

Driving traffic to your website or landing page is another way to generate conversions from your Facebook ads. You can target relevan--t audiences and attract valuable visitors to your website by promoting offers, contests, downloads, and more. Use website click ads or boosted posts to drive your prospects to a landing page where they can enter a contest, sign up for a service, make an appointment, or download a coupon.

Engagement

You can also use Facebook ads to generate engagement on your page with your current fans and targeted audiences. Boosting posts increases Likes, comments and shares which actually helps to increase your organic reach (that Facebook has made harder and harder to obtain).

Ad Options

There are currently 13 different objectives you can choose from:

Clicks to Website – *Get more site visits*

> "Clicks to Website" ads drive traffic to a particular page on your website. They are automatically optimized to reach people who are likely to click.

Retargeting – Target people who have already been to your website or landing page

> If someone visits your site but doesn't take the next step, you can retarget them on Facebook.

Website Conversions – Increase website conversions

> Website conversion ads encourage people to take a specific action on your website or landing page. These ads feature a selection of calls to action such as "Sign Up" that urges the user to take a specific action rather than just liking or commenting.

Product Catalog Sales: Dynamic Product Ads – *Promote your online products*

> Dynamic Product ads are Facebook's version of Google's Dynamic Remarketing Display ads, these ads retarget users who have already visited your online or in-app store.

Page Post Engagement – *Promote your posts*

Promoting page posts increase interaction and engagement. You can promote any of your page posts – photos, video, text – via the Boost Post button on your timeline or using the Ads Manager. You can target current fans, current fans and their friends or people you choose through targeting if you're going after new blood.

Page Likes – Increase Likes on your page

One strategy that we employ is using Page Likes ads to increase the number of Likes on a page, THEN going after these new people with Page Post Engagement ads targeted towards people who like the page.

App Installs – Get more app installs

Target people who are most likely to install and use your app.

App Engagement – Increase engagement on your app

Drive more traffic to a specific area of your app such as the store section of a freemium app.

Offer Claims – Get people to take advantage of a special offer

Promote exclusive offers that are available only to your Facebook fans. A great way to get more people engaging with your page.

Local Awareness – Reach people near you

Target people who are near you to increase awareness, promote an in-store sale that you're running or another special offer.

Event Responses – Increase event attendance

Have an event that you want to sell out? Use Event Response ads to promote it. People who click that they are interested will receive reminders and updates about your event as it approaches.

Video Views – Get your videos watched

Encourage people to watch a video about your company, a new product offering, positive testimonials, etc.

Lead Generation – *Grow your database*

Obtain an email address without sending someone to a landing page. These ads pre-populate a form using the person's Facebook information so they don't have to do anything!

The anatomy of a Facebook Ad

Design

Every Facebook ad includes the following: a powerful main image or video, a small amount of headline text above the image, a heading below the image with teaser text, a 'Like Page' button in the upper right and a call-to-action button in the bottom right.

On Facebook people *will* judge a book by its cover, so using attention grabbing photos or illustrations will help your ad to stand out (and get clicked on!) as people are scrolling through their news feed. Your prospects are going to look at the image before they read the text, so make it count!

Facebook recently removed the much-maligned "20% text " image requirement, meaning that the image you chose for your ad could not include more than 20% text. However, although this rule is "gone," images with too much text will either be shown to very few people or not be shown at all. A general rule of thumb is to make sure your image doesn't rely too much on text and is more about illustrating your product or service.

The headline and teaser text must be compelling enough to force an action to be taken – whether it be a page Like, website click or app install. The message in your headline *must* match what is presented on your landing page and ideally be the first thing that they see when they click through, or they will feel like they were tricked into clicking your ad!

Ad placement

Ad placement is an important when part of advertising on Facebook. Ads can be placed on desktop newsfeed, mobile newsfeed, right-hand column, the Facebook audience network and on Instagram (ads are run through Facebook) – which caters to a different demographic than Facebook and is a valuable part of your Facebook ad strategy.

Targeting

One of the reasons Facebook is so powerful is its targeting capabilities. It allows you to target users based on criteria like:

Geographic Area

Local (Radius or City up to 50 miles out)

Designated Market Area

National Demographics

Age

Gender

Level of Education

Income Level

Relationship Status: Married, single, engaged, etc.

Family Demographics: Have children (specific ages), expectant mothers, grandparents, etc.

Interests & Hobbies

Behavioral Traits

Custom List Uploads

Employment & Employer Information

Other targeting options are:

Lists you upload: People you already have in your database that you can target through Facebook

Lookalike Audiences: Users who are similar to those you're already targeting

Engagement on Facebook: People who have engaged with your content on Facebook

Website Traffic: Create a list of people who visit your website or landing page

Budgeting

There is no set amount of money you need to spend to achieve success in Facebook advertising. You can achieve good results with a small budget, but one thing to consider is that the more niche you go, the more expensive your cost per click will be. If your budget is limited, it's better to start more broad before deciding to narrow down your targeting.

To test out how your ad will perform, start out with a small amount of money – it can be as little as $5 – to see if it's worthwhile to devote more money towards it.

When I run ads, I will runs 5-10 different ads targeting different areas, demographics and interests at $20 each and increase the budget only on the highest-performing ads. 9 times out of 10, the initial test is entirely indicative of how your ads will perform overall.

That's great, but how much do Facebook Ads cost?

It's a fair question, because when you have a limited ad budget you want to know how much you're going to get for your money. The true is, it depends on a lot of factors.

Facebook ads work like an auction, you're effectively bidding against other advertisers for that ad space. So, the more competitive the space the more you will have to pay per click or impression.

Some of the biggest factors that affect how much Facebook ads cost are your audience, the quality of your ad and the time of year.

You must remember that when someone has skiing listed as an interest on their profile and you're a ski resort, you're also competing against the companies that are targeting that person's interests in fine dining, football, mountain biking and whatever else they are interested in. You're not just competing against people in your industry, you're competing against EVERYONE trying to market to these people, and Facebook limits the number of ads a person can see. Luckily, for the majority of keywords that a hotel and resort will target you aren't going to have extreme overlap with more mainstream companies.

So how do you stand out from the competition? You create high quality ads. With high quality ads you could pay significantly less than your competition to the same exact user. The quality of an ad is determined by two factors, relevance score and click through rate. Your relevance score measures how relevant your ad is to the audience you're targeting. The higher the score, the lower the cost of your ad. The second factor is click through rate which is your number of clicks/impressions. If you have a high click through rate, your ad will cost less. Now isn't that motivation to create a great ad!

The final big factor is time of year. You can bet on holidays, the holiday season as a whole and Black Friday to have higher ad costs because everyone will be advertising during those times.

In the end it's really all about ROI (return on investment). As long as you're getting a positive ROI on your Facebook ads, they're worth running.

Set yourself up for success

Use the Facebook ads manager to track your ad performance. See how much you've spent, how many you have reached, your ad relevancy score (very important in determining how often your ad will be shown), how many clicks, your cost per click, and many other important statistics. Checking this will enable you to tweak your ad so that you maximize performance to get the best possible results.

Facebook Ad Checklist

Getting Started

      Create a business page (if you don't already have one)

      Add or review business information

      Add a profile picture & cover photo

      Post frequently – engage, educate, entertain

      Respond to comments and messages

Creating Your Ad

      Determine your advertising goals

Determine your budget

Determine your target audience

Choose your ad formats

Create your landing page or dedicated page on your website

Craft your ads – image, headline, description, call to action

Create multiple ads with small budgets to test different target markets

Set your campaign live!

After Your Ad is Live

Check Ad Performance in Facebook Insights

Determine which of your test ads are high-performing. Put more money towards them, deactivate the ads that are not performing well

Respond to comments on the ads

Track all relative KPI's

Tweak your ads to achieve maximum results!

What type of results can you expect from Facebook Ads?

Here are two case studies that prove the effectiveness of Facebook ads-:

Pine Needles Resort

Southern Pines, North Carolina

4 day / 3 night golf trip giveaway

Goals: Increase Pine Needles Resort's email database through the use of Facebook ads.

Approach: A dedicated landing page was created which provided a contest and information about the resort. Facebook posts and Facebook ads were the only means used to drive traffic for this campaign.

Results:

164,137 people reached

1,800 likes

267 shares

9,621 total clicks

$0.17 cost per click

7,553 unique visitors

3,717 unique emails obtained

49.2% conversion rate

$1,000 ad spend

Treetops Resort

Gaylord, Michigan

$10,000 Wedding Giveaway

Goals: Generate wedding leads and increase awareness of Treetops Resort as a wedding destination that's "closer than you think."

Approach: Facebook boosted posts were created and used to generate leads for this campaign. We targeted people who were engaged within the last 3 months that gave us an extremely targeted and motivated target market.

Results:

162,426 reach

755 likes

519 shares

$0.32 cost per click

9,294 unique visitors

2,993 wedding leads

38% conversion rate

$2,500 total spend

Looking for some ideas on how you can get started with Facebook ads? Here are 15 things you can do:

Gather email newsletter sign-ups

Promote upcoming events

Advertise services or sales and get clicks straight to your site

Promote a new Facebook group you started

Announce a Giveaway and get more entries

Promote the launch of a new program

Increase your followers on other social networks

Big on blogging? Send people directly to your latest blog post

Teach an online course? Find some new students

Have a daily special or sale? Promote it to your current fans or target a new audience!

Get presales on a new offering you're promoting

Attending a trade show? Let prospects know where you'll be

Promote a class, workshop or group coaching lesson coming up

Have an awesome tip or trick? Use it to drive traffic to your site (or newsletter.

Promote an e-book download

SUMMARY

Facebook ads are one of the cheapest ways to reach golfers in your market, and most golf courses are not using them! Since most courses are not using them, targeting golfers will be extremely cheap due to lack of competition. If you are unsure how to use them or want my team to handle your Facebook advertising, call me at 352-266-2099.

AFTERWORD

I sincerely hope you have enjoyed and profited from *The Golf Marketing Bible*. I have tried hard to pack as many Legendary ideas and strategies as possible into one book. These strategies are current. They have been tried and tested in the tough conditions of the last five years and they will work for you.

Even the best ideas only work when they're applied! That part is up to you. Start with some bite-sized steps. While instant results are possible, it generally takes two years to get everything you need in place. And it only works cumulatively if you are committed to a real marketing system, either mine or one you devise yourself.

You must have a plan, a calendar, and a central point like our Legendary websites where you can manage all of your marketing information. Your online and offline strategies should be seamless and your staff must be trained in how to handle the leads you generate.

I'm sure this book has taken your thinking in many different directions and I'm sure it has stimulated you to come up with many ideas of your own. If you have any questions or would like to share your ideas, please don't hesitate to call one of my Legendary Staff at **800-827-1663.**

All the best,
Andrew Wood
Marketing Legend
Andrew@LegendaryMarketing.com

P.S. Knowledge is power; be sure to pass this book along to others in your organization

BONUS CHAPTER

How to <u>Really</u> Grow the Game!

INTRODUCTION

According to the National Golf Foundation, the total number of traditional golf facilities in the U.S. fell from 16,052 in 2005 to around 15,000 in January 2017, of which 11,000 were open to the public and 4,000 were private.

According to CEO, Joe Beditz, CEO of the Foundation, the national population of golfers in the USA has declined by 5 million in the past 10 years, dropping from roughly 30 million to approximately 25.3 million. There has also been a 25 percent decline in the number of people who play golf regularly. England is another country where the number of golfers is decreasing. In 2000 the EGA counted 868,966 golfers, compared with only 761,000 in 2016.

"We've lost one out of four of our core customers, and all core customers are responsible for 90 percent of the spending and the rounds played in golf," Beditz said in a January news conference at the PGA's, Merchandise Show.

Of course the good people at the NGF were also the people who told us a decade ago to build a course a week to meet demand! Nonetheless I think we can all agree that right now golf does have a problem with play down significantly in the USA, Canada, UK, Australia, Spain and Portugal. In fact it's down in all major golf markets except France!

There are a few other countries where participation is such as Switzerland, 3,000 new players, the Czech Republic up 4.9% (2,800 new players) to 55,000 players and up in a few of those new countries in Eastern Europe. Lithuania was up nearly 50%, Bulgaria 42% and Serbia 41%, but the later were starting from nothing.

What Is the Industry Doing to Tackle This Problem?

Most of the stuff I see out there from the various industry groups is like campaign promises from politicians. It sounds good, but in reality are nothing more than a pipe dream, pandering loudly to special interest groups and the media, trying to make everyone look good!

Industry groups have little regard for the economics of running a club and even less for the disaster that is a foursome of beginners teeing off in front of you!

With all due respect for their efforts, the PGA, USGA, NGCOA and other national and regional associations are far too conservative and politically correct to embrace the out-of-the-box thinking and ACTION that is REALLY needed to tackle the problem!

"As an example, Golf 2.0 is a PGA initiative that is heavily dependent upon (and centered around) the PGA Professional. It places the responsibility of marketing and implementing on the already over-burdened PGA member. Many PGA members are incredible golfers, teachers, and operational managers but my experience (I know over 500 personally) is that many do not have strong enthusiasm or training for marketing (especially social media).

They are afraid they will do or say something on social media that will have negative repercussions. Course owners are asking them to do more and more for less and less. They, too, are confined by "Codes of Conduct" and risky initiatives could have negative impact on their membership status." - **Excerpt from an excellent article by Kevin**

Unterreiner, *Twin Cities Golf*

None of these programs like Golf 2.0 even mention the three largest obstacles to growth simply because they are not in their expertise!

On top of that, the actual results of the associations existing programs are marginal at best.

Let me give you an unwelcome dose of harsh reality regarding the general message from these various, well-meaning groups;

You know the drill…..

"Get More Women Involved in the Game"

Okay, sounds good, Women generally make up about 25% of the players worldwide except in the UK where they represent only 14%, so you would think logically it would be a good market for growth right?

Maybe, why? Because the game is not and perhaps never will be set up for women. Forget all the male bias for a moment. Firstly courses are set up way too long for 95% of women (even with different tees). Yes, I know there are lots of great women players at the tip of the talent iceberg, who can hit it further than me, but there is not one women at my previous club, that can hit it further than my 5 iron. And perhaps only one or two at most at my previous four clubs!

This is a fact, not male basis and it's a fact that stunts the growth participation among women.

For example:

A 60 year old guy playing a 500 yard par four hits his drive 220 and hits his 3 wood 180 and has 100 yard wedge left.

A 60 year old woman has a 50 yard head-start hits it 150-175 (maybe) and then hits wood, wood, wood and perhaps gets there. Tees should be set up so the average lady has the same club in her hand as her male counterpart for her second shot not her 3rd or 4th!

To quote Barney Adams founder of Adams Golf, who recently wrote an interesting series on the state of the game:

"In fact, if you adjust course yardages for a tour professional's length, you'll find that average male golfers routinely play the equivalent of 8500-yard courses, and women play courses that are equivalent to a 9000-yard course."

So to start with the fact that the playing field for women is not fair; they have to hit the ball far more times to accomplish the same result as their spouses. This leads to higher scores, longer rounds and greater frustration. More on this later but that's just strike one!

Women also spend a fraction of their male counterparts (I know this is hard to believe guys but its true when it comes to golf) It also costs far more money to reach them and you convert far less of them to long-term customers. These are simple economic facts. If you are a women you don't have to like it or agree, but it won't change the facts. I have been in the marketing business 25 years and can tell you women cost more to reach and return far less than males when you are selling the vast majority of sports!

If You Own a Business, Return on Investment Actually Matters

Long ago, when I was in the karate business, I learned a very important business lesson. If I spent $3,000 of my hard-earned money in the local Penny Saver and ran three different ads, one aimed at women, one aimed at men and the other at children this was my return:

The ad aimed at women would get a $100 return on my $1,000

The ad aimed at men would get a $400 return on my $1,000

While the ad aimed at kids would get a $4,000 on my $1,000

Now trust me I wanted women in my school. Women between 14-40 are the number one victims of violence and sexual abuse and are the people who can benefit the most from karate!

Women also attract men to the school and they are often more fun to teach!

Of course I also wanted adult men also so I could spar with them and bond with them but it does not take a rocket scientist to figure out where I started spending ALL of my advertising dollars. Dollars that came right out of my pocket!

As the world's leading expert in golf marketing (say I modestly) it's my job to monitor response rates from the thousands of campaigns we have executed. I can assure you that with one exception I can think of from a client who specialized in women they are far harder and far more costly to reach for far less revenue than white middle-aged males. Which by the way, despite all the BS you hear about golf having too many of them, is the very market you should try to re-energize first!

Much more on this later!

Of course we must do everything we can to attract more women to the game. BUT, if the money is coming out of your wallet, you want quick growth and making a profit actually matters to you, it's not the first market, the second or even the third market segment you are going to target, no matter how appealing an opportunity it looks on the surface!

"Get More Minorities Involved in the Game"

"We need more Blacks, Hispanics and Native Americans playing golf" they say....

You might as well say we need more Arabs, a group badly underserved by the golfing world! They have tons of money but as a percentage of the population very few of them play golf so that's not a very good market either, it's just not part of their culture!

Morocco for example has 42 golf courses and just 7,000 native players.

Loredo, Texas has 300 registered golfers in a town of 250,000 people.

It's not racist, it is just a fact. Arabs are not likely to be a core market worth going after any time soon. Not because we don't want more of these groups but because the cost-return ratio is simply not there!

Preach to the choir, don't try to convert the Muslims if you want to survive financially!

"We Need to Attract More Kids to the Game"

Yes we do! But, if you are running a golf course, trying to stay afloat betting on the come line for a 20 year pay off can't possibly at the top of your agenda. (Although there is a good case for kids attracting their parents.)

Remember I am not writing this manual as a politician or the PGA, NGCOA, NGF, USGA, a major manufacture or 1st tee member but as someone trying to help the golf course owner, manger or golf pro make it through the decade and grow their business while growing the game. These groups are NOT going to give you the answers you need!

Not that you wouldn't welcome every single kid you can get, but like women and minorities the cost-return ratio is just not there any time soon! That may change in the future but it's not there now. Yes, we must plan for the future and attract children, and I'll share lots of way to accomplish this, but we must also survive in the present!

How About 15-inch Holes, Foot Golf, Frisbee Golf or Adventure Golf?

Recently Taylor Made Golf funded an organization called HackGolf, which is trying to get more people to play golf by, among other things, introducing the 15-inch golf hole. So what happens when you change the size of the hole from 4.25 inches so something about the size of a large pizza?

At the venues that tried it, the average length of an 18-hole round was reduced by nearly an hour, and golfers saw a 10-stroke improvement on their scores.

Sounds promising?

Not really. I met Mark King (CEO, of Taylor Made) once. Smart guy, but with all due respect 15-inch holes is great for a laugh but it's not golf as we know it. Nor is it the magnet that brings anyone to the game!

And why stop at 15-inch holes? Maybe we should try 20-inch holes or 30 inch holes?

I played Foot Golf recently. It was fun, a laugh but it's basically playing soccer on a golf course, nothing more or less. It generates income, brings in new faces and at the same time alienates traditional golfers, not just on the course but in the bar afterwards! One of my clients has had to break up three fights already in the first month!

In short it's a double-edged sword. There is no doubt you can make money with new golf "alternatives", but at what cost to your core business?

I have a couple of client's who put in adventure golf courses, one in his parking lot and he is killing it in the summer. He's doing so well he'd rather close down his course and stick to adventure golf. While that's well and good it's still not golf.

Let's be serious, all of these things can increase income but they're not real golf as we know it! I think the game is a great enough game to survive and thrive in a very similar form to what it is now, not as a totally different game. There are still around 50 million people teeing it up across the globe!

So What Are My Solutions…?

Well Play Golf America, Get Golf Ready For Golf, Golf 2.0 and the like are all well intentioned and may have a small positive impact in the long term, but the first order of business is not to get new people playing; that's too hard and too expensive. The first key is to get existing people playing more and lapsed people playing again.

To quote Barney Adams again, "Golf has 7.6 million golfers who play more than 8 times per year and another 11.3 million golfers who play once annually. They play, but not enough to be considered avid golfers. So we have a pool of 19 million who have shown enough interest to try the game, own clubs and fondly look at courses as they drive by. Our goal is convert 10 percent of these golfers to the avid category, and between us we'd settle for 5 percent and let momentum do the rest."

Start with the low hanging fruit, the lapsed,
white, middle-aged male, then expand out
for the future....

Is golf too expensive? If so compared to what?

Before we get in to details of how to grow the game, let's look at the many factors that have contributed to its decline, some well documented, some erroneous and others of great significance but rarely mention.

The three reasons cited in the hundreds of articles I have read about the decline in rounds pretty much all say the same thing.

1.   Too long to play

2.   Too hard

3.   Too expensive

Actually I think they all quote the same article because the entire media industry repeats it like a Pavlovian dog.... And while the first two are true, the third is not. While the <u>real reason for poor participation is never ever mentioned..!</u>

Golf is not too expensive when compared to other
forms of entertainment. In fact, golf is not only
cheap, it's ridiculously cheap!

Let's look at the average cost of an NFL ticket 2017
season:

Philadelphia Eagles Average ticket price: $203.20

Dallas Cowboys Average ticket price: $210.22

Green Bay Packers Average ticket price: $229.5

Chicago Bears Average ticket price: $233.66

New England Patriots Average ticket price: $260.94

Club seats at Tampa Bay start $325, in Dallas $650 a game!!!

Let's take a look at hockey:

Toronto Maple Leafs average ticket at $124.69 (converted to U.S. dollars)

Winnipeg Jets at $97.84

Vancouver Canucks at $87.38

Edmonton Oilers $79.27

Montreal Canadiens at $78.56.

The Washington Capitals $79.25

New York Rangers $72.04

Philadelphia Flyers $71.59

Match day tickets for the Premier League soccer teams in the UK average around $90 a game.

My last three dinners for two out ranged from $80-$150 per meal.

My cable bill is $210 a month and I hardly watch TV.

We could go on comparing other sports, concerts or events and none would offer even close to the value that is provided by most golf courses!

According to *Golf Digest*, the average national green fee in the US, including cart, is $48 but there are thousands of places you can play

for less!

So let's stop pretending that golf is too expensive because in every city there are multiple places people can play or join affordably. There is very little entertainment to be had for under $12.50 an hour!

Is This True Outside America?

Let's take a look. In The London, UK a Lacoste polo shirt with a nice alligator on the breast costs 65 pounds. In Orlando the exact same shirt costs just 55 dollars or about 28 pounds. A meal in England costs almost exactly the same in dollars as it does in pounds and so is 40% more expensive. Hotels too are exactly double and usually for far less amenities. In fact as far as I can tell in my last 8 weeks in Europe, everything is 50 to 100% more expensive than in the USA. Everything that is, except one thing.

The price of golf memberships!

I find this very interesting.

Well-known and seemingly affluent clubs are forced to drive guest and society play just to pay the bills! Why not just raise the dues???

SHOCK HORROR!

But, you say, the economy is bad. All the members already complain about the prices. There are plenty of other places they can go that are cheaper! Yes, both arguments are no doubt true. People the world over complain about prices, whatever they are and yes they could go somewhere cheaper. BUT, And it's a BIG BUT, They could also buy cars that are cheaper; meanwhile the parking lot is comprised in large part of BMWs, Mercedes, Lexus and Jags…!

The situation at UK clubs is not unlike the situation I found in businesses 20 years ago. Clubs starving for members, hoping nothing goes wrong because if it does, a drought, a fire, an infestation of bo weevil bugs, they simply won't survive.

On a visit to a club in Manchester, UK, charging around 500 pounds a year for membership, a committee member told me that there was no way they could put the fees up. I asked whether or not any of the members ever went to a Man United game, he said yes and admitted that the last time he had taken a couple of clients to a match the day (DAY!) had cost him 460 pounds or just about what he pays for a year of golf! So with that myth slain let's look at the real problems and solutions

1. Increase the Speed of Play

When describing the length of the Sunday round at the 1983 Kemper Open, former CBS announcer Ben Wright said "See those ducks? They were mere eggs at the beginning of today."

Things have only gotten worse in the three decades since then and while the USGA and PGA have frequent meeting on the subject they are as much of the problem as anyone.

Talk is cheap!

Ironically, given the fact the USGA has now hosted back-to-back symposiums on slow play one would wonder how many times the association has ever penalized players for slow play in its biggest event— the U.S. Open?

It has done so just twice. Both players who fell foul are not exactly household names—Robert Impaglia for two strokes at the 1978 Open at Cherry Hills and Edward Fryatt at the 2007 Open at Congressional.

The last time a PGA Tour event slapped a two-stroke penalty for slow play was back in 1995 at Honda Classic when Glen Day— nicknamed "all day" because of his tortoise movements—was penalized. Playing on perfectly manicured courses, with hundreds of people to help find their ball, how can it take the world's best players five hours or more to complete a round in a threesome?

For me speed of play has always been an issue; golf has always been too slow. I like to play fast. In fact, I once played a tournament round, walking, in one hour fifty nine minutes and shot 71, going through 6 groups in the process!

As recently as 2008 playing in the English amateur my group had a run in with an official who told us on the 12th tee that we were a hole behind the group in front who had just left the 13th green and would be penalized. My playing partner a short, tattooed, Popeye-armed guy from the East end of London, none too happy after losing a ball on the previous hole, got about an inch from the officials face and pointed out in no uncertain terms that "We had already played through 5 groups and he ought to look at his $#%& sheet before threatening players with penalties!"

We went through the group in front two holes later, but fast rounds are the exception not the rule!

Time is a huge issue for today's players and you have to be brutal about how to manage it at your club. The vast majority of members or players who pay rack rate don't want to be out there for five or even four hours.

Meanwhile the seniors group may well enjoy their day more the longer they stay on the course, as it keeps them out of the house.

I hate seeing signs that say, "We are a 4.15 golf course. "My last private club was a "4.20 club"

What the hell is wrong with playing golf in 3 hours? There is just no reason not to play in three hours in a golf cart, none!

But You Have to Set the Expectation!

The vast majority of golf clubs are far too timid about slow play, as are the PGA Tour, USGA and the R & A. So afraid of offending the offenders they choose instead to talk about the issue without doing anything other than the VERY occasional penalty on a C named player!

It takes balls, brass balls, but clubs need to be much more up front about their pace of play policy and guarantee rounds in under four hours. It can be done. Not everywhere but most places!

Set the expectation in your marketing message: Play in under 4 hours!

Set up the expectation with your auto reply to a tee time booking: Send an auto responder that outlines your speed of play policy and offers tips for its successful accomplishment!

"Thanks for booking your tee time at beautiful Legendary Country Club

"We are looking forward to seeing you and you getting round in less than four hours so you can play more holes, drink more beer or catch up with the family!

"We guarantee all our players a round in under four hours. In order to help with this please review the following and pass it along to those in your group who might need a little pre-round prod!"

16 Tips to Speed up Play

1. **Be early for your tee time.** Proper pace of play begins with tee-ing off at the appointed time. Allow time for unloading your equipment, putting on your golf shoes, any desired practice or warm-up, purchasing any refreshments or balls and driving your cart to the first tee.

2. **"Tee It Forward" unless you are consistently able to reach greens in regulation from the back tees.** In other words, play from a set of tees that is comfortable for you – one where you are more likely to hit lofted irons into greens instead of hybrids or fairway woods. It is acceptable for players in the same group

527

to play from different tees. (The USGA Handicap System provides a formula for adjusting handicaps from different tees.)

3. **Be helpful to others in your group.** Follow the flight of all tee shots, not just your own. Once in the fairway, help others look for their ball if you already know the location of yours. Volunteer to fill in a divot or rake a bunker for another player if needed. Be ready to attend the flagstick for others.

4. **Plan your shot while walking to your ball** or while others are playing. Carry extra tees, ball markers and an extra ball in your pockets so you never have to return to your bag to find one when needed.

5. **Line up your putt when others are putting** and be ready to play when it is your turn.

6. **Play ready golf** first on the tee hits, not first in the hole!

7. **Walk directly to your golf ball;** don't follow others unless assisting in search.

8. **When two players are riding in a cart, drive the cart to the first ball and drop off the first player** with his choice of several clubs. The second player should proceed in the cart to his ball. After the first player hits his stroke, he should begin walking toward the cart as the second golfer is playing.

9. **Don't step off or measure yardage for every single golf shot,** develop an "eye" for distance.

10. **Be efficient with your pre-shot routine.** Take only one practice swing.

11. Play a provisional ball if you think the original might be lost outside a water hazard or out of bounds.

12. **When hitting a shot from the bunker, make sure you put the rake next to you.** That way you'll be ready to rake right after you nestle your shot next to the cup

13. **Park the cart at greenside as near as possible to where you expect to exit** the green after holing out or if walking leave your clubs on the side of the putting green towards to next tee. This avoids backtracking.

14. **Exit putting green promptly after holing out.** Wait until you're on the next tee to start writing down scores

15. **Don't ask your playing partners to help you search for a lost ball** - unless you are absolutely certain there is time for them to do so (e.g., there is no group behind waiting). If the course is crowded, your partners should continue moving forward, not slow things down further by stopping to help your search.

16. **Let them play through:** If the group behind you is faster, it's okay to let them play through. Finish your hole and then let them tee off ahead of you. It's not a sign of weakness.

We look forward to seeing you, remember to forward this to your group so we are all working out of the same playbook.

Your Friendly
4 hours or less PGA pro

Obviously you could edit this down to suit your specific needs but it covers most of the bases.

Set the expectation at check in: "Sir, we promise our customers a round in under four hours and most like to finish in 3.30 is that a pace you are comfortable playing at?"

If not suggest they don't play!

Set the expectation on the first tee: "Ok, gentlemen as I am sure you know speed of play is something we pride ourselves on here. If for any reason you fall behind you should immediately call the group behind through, or you will be asked to pick up and skip a hole."

Set the expectation with your superintendent: He's the guy that sets up the course.

Set the expectation with your ranger: "Gentlemen just want to let you know you are a little behind is there anything I can do to help?"

If that doesn't work ask them to let the group through or pick up and go to the next hole.

If that and polite encouragement doesn't work throw some people off your course to show them you mean business!

Sign on the 10th Tee at Llanymench Golf Club, UK, although it would be better on the 13th tee ☺

No I really mean it, become known, as a three and a half hour course and you'll lose a handful and gain an army! Not to mention how many more players you will be able to put on the course, earning you more *money!* Offer the first groups out a bonus for finishing in a specific time, free cart, free replay round, free beer, etc. Or let proven fast players book their tee times ahead of everyone else!

Here are some ideas from others:

Kiawah Island Golf Resort in South Carolina, one of the toughest in the world, tested a program this summer aimed at having golfers play a round in three hours or less. The resort set aside tee times in the morning and mid afternoon for singles, twosomes and threesomes who wanted to play a quick round before returning to work. Instead of sending off groups in 10-minute intervals, groups were sent off every seven minutes. The only restriction was that golfers must be able to keep pace in order to use these tee times.

"At Castle Pines in Colorado, a high end private club, a pace-of-play board is on display at the clubhouse, which shows the names of players in the group, the start time, finish time, and number of minutes behind the previous group. If the finish time of a group is more than 10 minutes slower than the time of the preceding group, the golf committee sends a slow-play warning letter to each member of the slow group. If a player receives a second warning letter, eligibility for morning rounds on weekends is suspended for one month.

"Groups receiving a warning letter can ask for a review. A small percentage of members are offended by receiving a warning letter; the great majority endorses the program. The fact is, a golf course has to implement -- and enforce -- a pace-of-play management program, or else nothing will change. If your course is wary of offending slow players, keep this in mind: Slow players are ruining the day's play for all the groups stacked up behind them.

"After the first year of the Castle Pines program, the number of first-warning letters was down 40 to 45 percent. The number of second-warning letters was down from seven to one." **Dean Knuth,** *Golf Digest*

For the record, one hour, 24 minutes is the fastest round in a PGA Tour event. Greg Norman and Mark O'Meara played the final round of the Nabisco Championship at Pebble Beach in 1998 quicker than usual because weather threatened to cancel Norman's flight to Australia. Both players shot a 79, and yes they were walking!

2. One Rule Change Much Needed to Speed Up Play and Increase Enjoyment

Why is it that a ball lost in a water hazard is just one shot whereas the same ball lost in a bush or over the fence out of bounds is two? It really never made any sense it slows down the game and hurts the enjoyment for players.

Change the lost ball or out of bounds rule to same as the red stakes rule for amateurs.

Jack Nicklaus has been campaigning for this important change for decades and he's right!

Noted instructor and commentator, Peter Kostis, writing for *Golf Magazine* called the OB rule one of the five dumbest rules in golf.

> *"You are penalized less for whiffing your tee shot than you are for making contact and hitting it out of play. Out of bounds should be played as a lateral hazard rather than stroke-and-distance. The current penalty is too severe. Also, playing OB areas as lateral hazards would speed up play!"*

If the USGA won't do it for you make it a local rule or just red line the entire course. Bingo you just speeded up play and enjoyment with a few cans of spray paint!

Who'd have thought?

3. Make Your Course Easier

Pete Dye started it thirty years ago and the concept became a monster. Longer, tougher courses that at one point in the early days of TPC, even the world's best couldn't play! Phil Mickelson wasn't whining. He was just stating the obvious. Many of today's golf courses are too difficult for those trying to play them.

Phil Mickelson took shots at architect Rees Jones for his redesign of the Atlantic Athletic Club during the PGA Championship and the BMW Championship at Cog Hill in Chicago. Of the Atlantic Athletic Club course, Mickelson said, "It's a perfect example of how modern architecture is killing the game, because these holes are unplayable for the members. It's a good reason why the number of rounds is down on this course."

When I lived in California my home course was Coto De Caza, (North). The 1st was almost 600 yards with a 220 carry over a ravine, which ran down the entire length right, OB left and several 10 feet deep traps also guarded the hole.

I was in that bunker, 224 from there, par 4, and
I hit a good drive, bad bounce… really ☺

From the member tees the average score was 9.7. In the decade I was a member I had a standing bet that no one could get round in less than 40 putts first time out. Not only did I never lose the bet, no one even got close. I think 43 was the record! As membership grew rounds went from 4 hours to 5.45. My last round there a few years ago as a guest I walked in after 5.20 hrs with three holes to go and that's at a private club! I was pretty good player at the time; how much fun can that be for the average hack?

I was working with a club in Europe this year when a guy came into the pro shop where I was working on my computer.

"How did you do?" I asked.

"Oh good day." he said "I only lost two!"

"Wow, that pretty good just two balls on a windy day like this" I said.

"No not two balls" he said cheerfully "Two bags!" (24 balls). Not everyone is quite so accepting of 24, $3 swings.

It's not just the length of courses either:

- ✔ You know that bunker out there 150 off the white tees, get rid of it and every other bunker that no single digit has ever played from!

- ✔ Clean out the woods so you can find your ball (get volunteers to help they can keep all the balls they find).

- ✔ Green speeds are often faster than the architect intended, fine for events not great for everyday play when someone in your group putts off every green.

- ✔ Pins cut in Sunday positions on Tuesday.

- ✔ Crowned greens that feed into a run-off area where weekend players can hack back and forth like a hockey game.

- ✔ Not enough rough or bunkers in place to stop balls bouncing off raised greens into the woods or water.

- ✔ Too many forced carries.

- ✔ Eliminate as much as possible hidden bunkers, streams and water hazards. They slow play down and annoy players when they lose a ball!

- ✔ Put up markers to guide players where to hit their ball.

✔ Consider re-routing the course to use the easier 9 holes first so play moves and players are warmed up by the time they get to the harder nine.

✔ Have the yardages on all the sprinkler heads along with disks every 25 yards from 100 yards to speed up decision-making and help with clubbing.

✔ **Set the expectation with your greens keeper:** Keep the Sunday pins for Sunday, tee it forward, keep the rough down, mark everything you can in red to speed up play.

4. Offer Child Care

It works in gyms, hotels and health clubs; why not golf clubs?

Try it out Saturday morning, FREE Child Care with a paid round!

Take the kids to the back of the range and get em' started, play movies and video games, draw pictures and let mom or dad, or both, go out and enjoy a game!

Unless you have a great database it takes time to get the word out so don't give up after a week. Give it a real shot and expand it to Sunday if you like what you see. You might want to try it Thursday as well for *Ladies Day*!

In the summer offer junior camps. Not only can these be very profitable just from the kids ,but it brings the parents to the club everyday as well.

5. Have More Events - People Love a Reason to Come Out and Play!

Create a reason to be at YOUR club events, golf or social. Almost any event creates a reason to act. No event and it's just another day!

When I lived in California I ran the Orange County Amateur Championship simply because there was no amateur tournament and I wanted an event to play in. It was a 36-hole scratch event, not affiliated with anyone but me, that attracted over 100 players a year who each paid an entry fee of $150! (1992 $$$)

I got a sponsor for the prizes, so the three private clubs all made money and I made money. Any one of those three clubs could have done what I did and made the event their own, perhaps even quickly turning it into a prestige event. It always got good press coverage in the Orange County Register…But none of them did.

Even though it was a $10,000 plus day for them on a Monday!

There is little to no profit in running golf events with your local golf association — there's plenty of money and increased participation in running your own!

Create an Active Calendar of Events that Appeal to Different Interest Groups

- o Couples events -Pine Needles attracts 60 plus couples for their annual Couple Carousel three-day event, and it's a *high-end* event.

- o Meanwhile their Golfari Golf School attracts over 600 women at over $2,000 a head! And they do it in their shoulder season!

- o They do another one for kids in the summer!

- o Open four ball events are something that UK clubs do a great job of promoting. Just about every club in the UK has one and they fill them up every time. Often they play like the Ryder cup, four ball in the morning and foursome in the afternoon. That format tests some friendships ☺

- o Open stroke play event with a handicap and scratch division. If you are a private club, it's a great way to showcase your club to the public at large.

o Palma Ceia Golf Club, in Tampa, Florida, runs a three-day event in conjunction with the Gasparilla Festival It's a full field shotgun, three-day event with plenty of eating and drinking and fun. From my personal experience, the bar receipts those three days may well rival a normal months'!

o Many clubs in the UK, especially in holiday areas, host an entire Golf Week with multiple events each day for an entire week. Some people play them all!

o Member Guest, Member-Member and one day Member and three guests.

o Hospitality tournament – Invite all of the local hotel concierges, bellmen, front desk folks for a day of golf with lunch and prizes. Great for boosting business in the form of referrals. ☺

o Affinity tournament – Target a special group such as lawyers, doctors, car dealers, etc., and have a tournament or play day just for them.

o Partner with the Chamber of Commerce or local newspapers and run a business golf challenge.

o Monster event around Halloween; make the course crazy tough!

o Father/son, mother/daughter even if it brings only a dozen people out it's a start to build on and make it a must-play event!

o Put on your own BIG Break or Golf Olympics with various challenges to test players' skills.

o Run Golf Leagues. It's interesting to me that golf leagues are huge in many parts of the country like Michigan, Ohio and Wisconsin and seem to be non existent other places. Golf leagues are a great way to get occasional players playing more often.

- o Demo days. Golfers love to try new equipment but most clubs only do one a year. Try adding a second or third to increase activity!

- o Open house. Invite the public to come try golf for free!

- o Hump Day Skins Game. 9 holes every Wednesday with a 5-6 pm tee off!

- o Sunday evening nine and wine couples event.

- o Three club event, hickory event, 15-inch hole event, Nite Golf —

The possibilities for events that target specific groups are endless. You just have to put them on a calendar and put some marketing muscle behind them!

6. Increase the Number of Social Events You Hold to Increase Bonding!

For many people especially in the US, and especially among women and a large majority of seniors, golf is not a competitive sport, it's a social pastime. The social aspect of golf is in many cases just as important to your long-term success as cutting the grass. The social aspect of golf is often overlooked in the discussion about growing the game yet it's often the glue that holds a good club together. The more you can get people interacting with each other and developing true friendships beyond the course, the more likely they are to stay involved in the "club" and play!

Just as on the golf side of things, the social side of things will create a whole lot more income if you create an event to attend. No event, no motivation!

"Let's go out for dinner" is not as strong as "Let's go to the club — they are have a wine night!" Obviously the possibilities are endless, but if you look at the massive rise in theme restaurants, it's easy to see why this concept resonates with people. They want to escape "normal life." They want a reason to dress up, dress down, dance and party!

- ✔ Wine Tasting
- ✔ Whiskey Tasting
- ✔ Beer Tasting
- ✔ Hawaii Night
- ✔ Casino Night
- ✔ Hollywood Night
- ✔ Gangster Night
- ✔ Gourmet Night
- ✔ Steak and Ale Night
- ✔ Italian night
- ✔ 20's, 50's,70s, 80's 90's Night
- ✔ Pig Roast
- ✔ Fish Fry
- ✔ Cigar Night
- ✔ Toga Party
- ✔ Caribbean Night
- ✔ Movie Night
- ✔ Oscar Night
- ✔ Octoberfest
- ✔ Western

✔ Luau

✔ NFL Kick Off

✔ Mardi Gras

If you want more income, plan more theme nights to give people the reason they need to say YES!

7. Emphasize the Health Benefits of Golf

Push the health benefits of golf, especially walking. No matter how good or bad your play, if you walk you can at least get some exercise and calorie burn out of your round!

A study done by Reebok showed that golfers who walk and carry burn approximately 55 percent more calories than those who ride in a cart.

The number of calories varies by distance walked and also the metabolic rate of the golfer. But fitness experts estimate you'll burn roughly 1,500 calories during a four-hour round. That's 825 calories more than if you ride in a cart. A round of golf is 10,000 steps or about a 5 mile walk. It's not just the calories either; golf reduces stress and golfers live longer!

According to a new study from the Swedish medical university Karolinska Institute the death rate for golfers is 40 percent lower than for other people of the same sex, age and socioeconomic status. This corresponds to a 5 year increase in life expectancy. Golfers with a low handicap are the safest. Another good reason to sell lessons!

The study, which was published in *Scandinavian Journal of Medicine & Science in Sports*, is based on data from 300,000 Swedish golfers and shows that golf has beneficial health effects. Professor Anders Ahlbom, who has led the study with Bahman Farahmand is not surprised at the result, as he believes that there are several aspects of the game that are proved to be good for the health.

"A round of golf means being outside for four or five hours, walking at a fast pace for six to seven kilometres, something which is known to be good for the health," he says. "People play golf into old age, and there are also positive social and psychological aspects to the game that can be of help."

The study does not rule out that other factors besides the actual playing, contribute to the lower death rate observed amongst golfers. However, the researchers believe it is likely that the playing of the game itself has a significant impact on health.

Golf players have a lower death rate regardless of sex, age and social group. The effect is greater for golfers from blue-collar professions than for those from white-collar professions. The lowest rates are found in the group of players with the lowest handicap (i.e. the best golfers). "Maintaining a low handicap involves playing a lot, so this supports the idea that it is largely the game itself that is good for the health," says Professor Ahlbom.

REPRINTED WITH PERMISSION; Red Orbit. license

The golf industry does a poor job of communicating this important aspect of the game. Encouraging players to ride nine and walk nine by appealing to fitness may be a good start. For instance:

Golfers Live Five Years Longer!
Make Friends - Lose 1500 calories – Play Golf!

Golf - More fun Than the Gym and You Burn More Calories!
Lose Weight. Make Friends. Play Golf!
Increase Your Business While You Decrease Your Waistline – Play Golf

Develop educational ads, website copy and e-mails focused on the health benefits golf offers; See www.golfoperatorassocition.com for hundreds of examples done for you

8. Emphasis the Business Aspects of Golf – Create Networking Value!

Everyone knows that playing golf is good for their business and career, or do they?

Certainly in the past there where countless articles on the benefits of business golf but if people are in their 20's or 30's they may have missed them. All you see in the press now is how the game is declining and courses everywhere are closing. If you were a young 28-year-old executive, you may well be forgiven for not knowing or understanding the amazing value of golf to business.

Street Directory reports that: "Executives who play golf experience an 85% better chance of securing a business deal on the golf course than through conventional methods of marketing." This makes sense – as a golf course is an extended boardroom of sorts, with the added bonus of being both more relaxed and comfortable.

In her latest book *Two Good Rounds TITANS--Leaders in Industry & Golf,* author Elisa Gaudet explores how the game of golf helped pave the way to success for some of the most prominent global business leaders.

"There is a special connection that exists between the worlds of golf and business, and it's a reason why many of today's business leaders have achieved success," says Gaudet, who is highly regarded for her work as founder of the strategic golf marketing firm Executive Golf International (EGI).

TITANS--Leaders in Industry & Golf, offers candid personal accounts from thirty three global business leaders about their success in business and paths to owning a golf course including Donald Trump, Julian Robertson, Gilberto Benetton, Herb Kohler, Paul Fireman, Peter Ueberroth, Peter Hill, Hans Peter Porsche, Ken Chu and Tom Cousins.

"In the book, each of these individuals reveals how golf enhanced their businesses and ultimately inspired them to own a golf course," Gaudet says.

Paul Fireman, founder of Reebok and owner of Liberty National Golf course, offers readers this advice, "When you go on a golf course with a person for four hours, you build a relationship in four hours that could otherwise take you 40 years to get. You have an understanding of the person. Golf teaches you a great deal: integrity, patience, perseverance."

Excite Potential Players about the Business Opportunities!

Clubs in general do an awful job of communicating this important aspect of the game to prospective players and members. If you can't excite them about the game excite them about the positive effect the game will have on their pocket book!

Think about it: if you are a chiropractor, accountant, financial advisor, car dealer, realtor or hairdresser to name just a few professions, where could you possibly find more clients faster than a golf club?

I can't think of anywhere!

This needs to be stressed in club marketing, on your website, on your blog, in your social media, in your membership literature and sales pitch. But stressing it is not enough you must go out of your way to create business opportunities for your members or frequent players. Let everyone know that the place to look first for any product or service is within the "Club family!"

Be proactive in making the club a business friendly club:

- ✔ Free meeting rooms

- ✔ Free Wi-fi

- ✔ Cell phones are not banned

- ✔ Dress codes are casual and do not single out blue jeans

- ✔ Inquire what business people are in and ask how you might help.

Help promote business within the club:

- ✔ Have a networking group

- ✔ Business card board

- ✔ Webpage listing services available through members

- ✔ Feature a business each week on your webpage or in your newsletter

- ✔ Run a banner ad in your e blasts for a business

- ✔ Have a member services table, binder or booth

- ✔ Educate your pro, bar and wait staff as to what products and services individual members may offer so they can alert other members to the opportunity.

When people can justify the cost of playing in time or money with the return to their businesses, playing more golf is an easy choice!

This may also be your best chance of attracting more women.

Some Business Golf Networking Groups:

http://www.businessgolfnetwork.co.uk

http://www.businessgolfersnetwork.com

http://www.vipbusinessgolfnetwork.com

http://www.fore-business.com

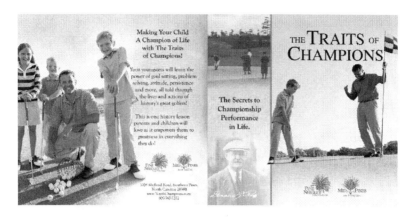

9. Emphasize Life Skills For Kids

My karate business made millions for one simple reason -- because parents wanted their kids to have confidence, self-esteem, discipline and persistence!

While organizations like the First Tee are promoting life skills in the golf industry I never see it promoted at regular clubs. This is a huge opportunity to connect with parents and encourage them to get their kids into golf! (Then the parents will golf more too.)

Start the conversation on your social media channels:

✔ Safe positive environment

✔ Develop social skills

✔ Make friends for life

✔ Increased self confidence, persistence and respect for others

✔ Improved health and motor skills

Combine these positive messages with promotions for parent-kid days, junior clinics, after school programs and summer camps.

Additional Resource: Check out this amazing life skills curriculum called *The Traits of Champions* which is a book and audio program I co-wrote with world famous motivational coach, Brian Tracy.

http://traitsofchampions.com

10. Change an Element to Increase Interest from Fringe Players

For the most part we focus on the actual golf experience but what if there were other ways to interest people in the game. What if golf is mildly interesting but golf plus a cool ride is much more interesting? That might be a good way of connecting with a younger generation!

Think about how snowboarding saved the ski industry!

Three products look to me to create more interest. The first is Golfboard and I quote directly from the company website, although I saw the product first hand and loved it! [Golfboard is like a big electric skateboard that you do your round on.]

The GolfBoard is the most innovative creation for the golf industry since the softspike.

"In harnessing the newest technology in electric power, the GolfBoard will give your members and guests an option to experience your course like never before. Players can carry their bag just like they would if they were walking, or they can opt for the handlebar bag mount which allows players to use the GolfBoard like a stand-up personal golf cart.

GolfBoarding Appeals to Everyone

"This extraordinary new way to traverse the golf course is sure to excite your membership, while at the same time generating new interest in golf to the next generation of golfers. The GolfBoard will provide players the feeling of golfing freedom that walking gives, while at the same time speeding up pace of play - a big problem at many courses today.

"Aside from having less impact on your turf than a standard golf cart, the GolfBoard will require considerably less maintenance. Utilizing the latest in lithium-ion battery technology, the self-contained GolfBoard has fewer moving parts to break or wear out, resulting in more time carrying players on the course and increased revenue for you.

Reduced Course Wear and Tear

"Golf Professionals and Golf Course Superintendents will love the GolfBoard too. We have made sure to make the GolfBoard as sustainable as possible to the environment they ride on. We incorporated 4WD technology to evenly distribute power to the GolfBoard's 9-inch turf tires, virtually eliminating 'tire-spin' and torn up turf - even on dewy mornings or damp conditions. And with sleek fenders covering all four wheels, golfing riders can play those wet-weather rounds without fear of mud or water splattering their clothes."

> *"GolfBoard is the most significant product introduced to golf in a long time. It will add a new and exciting element of fun and fitness, and as an operator will help my facility drive rounds."*

TJ Baggett/General Manager Princeville Golf Club Princeville, Hawaii

The second is the golf Segway

I have always thought that riding on a Segway tended to look a bit like a goofy stand-up motor scooter, but I actually think Segway may be onto something with the X2 Golf. Let's face it, golfers already look a tad bit goofy, so riding on the Segway X2 Golf may actually be fitting... and fun. The X2 Golf goes 12.5 miles, carries your golf bag, has a handle bar mounted scorecard holder, and beefy all-terrain tires.

Kierland Golf Club in Arizona, was the first golf resort in the country to offer a fleet of Segways for golfers to use. They also purchased two specially-built bicycles that cause minimal damage to fairways. This allows golfers to cycle round the course as if they were using a cart. The result is faster rounds but also golfers who feel that they have had an active workout.

The third is the good old-fashioned but slightly modified bicycle

Cycling has surged in popularity over the last five years and I know many golfers who now give up golf time for road time. Perhaps combining biking with golfing is the answer.

Quoting once again from the company's website:

"My inspiration for The Golf Bike was to combine two of my favorite passions: golf and cycling. In recent years I found it difficult to make the time to experience both activities on a regular basis. With The Golf Bike, I have combined the benefits of each, bringing the elements of fun, fitness and speed of play to the greatest game ever played. This new spin on an old tradition will provide the avid golfer with the ability to play at the speed of a cart while getting paid back with fun and fitness. It will also introduce the game to cyclists by combining a great outdoor experience with a fun, new way to exercise. And let's not forget the future. The Golf Bike will help make the game cool and exciting to the younger generations, hopefully making golf's future as bright as its storied past." Todd May, http://www.thegolfbike.com/

And a related product:

Clubhouse so close that driving is overkill but far enough that lugging your bag seems like a death sentence? The TowCaddy is for you! Pull it behind any bicycle, then detach it at the course for a smooth-rolling pushcart. So for the young...and young at heart, the only driver you will be using is on that long par 5.

http://towcaddy.com/index.html

11. Innovative Memberships that Suit Today's Players

How memberships are packaged can lead to a large increase in interest and a corresponding increase in play. The days of people collecting clubs as they did in the 90's and early 2000's are gone. While many snowbirds may still have two memberships there is increasing demand for non-traditional categories of membership.

Range Membership

In Morocco, a country with very few golfers and 42 new courses, Braemar Golf offered a family range membership for $199 that attracted over 300 families. For that they got unlimited range balls and the kids got free rental clubs and free coaching for a couple of hours a day. In addition to an excellent increase in F & B revenues, 15 of the range memberships turned into full playing members.

Five-day Memberships

Popular in the UK but not used much in the USA this is often an ideal membership for seniors or those on a budget with flexibility in when they play. They are typically priced at 50%-60% less than full membership.

Seasonal Memberships

Clubs fought this for a long time but there is a growing trend in offering snowbirds or summer guests an option other than full membership: usually priced at about two thirds of the regular fee.

Weekly Memberships

These are quite popular in the holiday markets in the UK and are typically priced at 3-4 times the green fee. While a visitor may be unwilling to pay $75 a day, $199 for a week might seem a great deal!

Monday & Tuesday Memberships

Most private clubs close on Monday and some on Tuesday. Yet some players may still want a place to play. Most daily fees are dead on Monday and Tuesday creating the perfect opportunity for a demand to meet a market! Priced right this can attract second memberships, seniors, college students and others with flexible schedules but low budgets!

Afternoon Memberships

This is a new trend I have seen cropping up to fill the largely unused afternoon weekday tee times. Clubs offer a membership good only after 2pm.

Temp Memberships

For the many people who travel and work out of town, a temporary membership at a private club might be the ideal opportunity that keeps them playing!

Review your current membership options and see if adding new ones might encourage players to commit and therefore play more golf.

12. Set the Expectation that New Members Bring in More Members

Most people are shocked when I suggest this but it is common practice in many businesses and it could be common practice in the golf business. All people rise to the expectations that are set when they first join any type of club. We make it an expectation that for the good of the club the new member would agree to introduce a minimum of two new members to the club! We even put it in writing!

You simply explain to the new member that the club is made up of good people like him and that the club depends on good people like him recommending the club to others at work, church or play for its long term sustainability. Then you simply ask the person to commit to bringing you some new blood.

No one will refuse!

13. Free Lessons and Clubs

The best way to market any business is with free samples as it removes all the obstacles. The old puppy dog close 101, take Fido home and see how he likes it "just for the weekend" or the free taste samples at the grocery store. Then there are toothpaste samples in the mail or a Free 30 day trial of software online.

One way to apply this to the golf business and help tackle much quoted objection #2 "the game is too hard" is to offer FREE lessons on the range every day for a couple of hours after school or work.

A study by the NGF showed that 83% of people would play more golf, buy more clubs, eat and drink more at the bar if what?

They had more money?

They had more time?

No, the correct answer is if they played better!

Yet only 13% of players have EVER taken a lesson!

Ladies and gentlemen if you don't hear the sweet sound of opportunity knocking you are not listening!

Why not employ a pro or even assistant pro to walk the range coaching for free, 2-3 hours a day!

It's a great way to get a beginner started on the right foot. Offer free clubs as well. You could really kill it and offer the first bucket of balls free or you can use that to generate income.

For established players the benefits are equally clear as better golf means more golf. I know a few years ago I went through a dark patch and almost stopped playing when my handicap went from plus 2 to could not break 90! My interest only returned when I started working with a great coach, who helped me rebuild my swing.

Big "Thank You" Mark Wood!

The more people you can help play better, the more people will help you by referring others to your coaching program and playing more!

This is a concept you should clearly put into action and test!

14. Offer a Year Round "Golf Starter" Program

Why "Get ready for golf" a few weeks a year rather than all the time?

If Free sounds too cheap put together and ongoing "grow the game" program like the folks at Foresight Golf have successfully done in Texas. Here's their description:

Join your favorite participating Foresight Golf course's Men's Golf Association or Women's Golf Association! These associations have been developed to encourage you to work on your game, meet new golfers, enjoy the camaraderie of friendly competition all adding up to enjoying golf more! The association memberships include:

USGA Handicap Service - you have to have a handicap to play in most tournaments and getting a handicap is one of the best ways to track your improvement!

$10 Individual 30-minute lessons - providing you affordable instruction from qualified instructors is the driving force behind our Play Better Golf program. One-on-one teaching allows you to focus on what you need to do in order to play better.

$5/person Group lessons - learning together is fun and can be quite rewarding! You glean the benefits of other golfers questions and input and have fun doing it!

Designated Weekly and Evening Association Group Play Dates with Hospitality and Prizes - a chance to take what you've learned to the course and enjoy friendly competition as a team. Add a nice food & beverage special after play along with prizes and you've got yourself a fun evening enjoying golf!

10% off Non-Sale Golf Shop Merchandise or Special Order Merchandise - once you start playing better you'll probably want to dress the part! Look good and swing away!!

Free Junior Clinics for Kids on Saturday Afternoons - all sports are easier to learn when you're young, and starting your little golfer with the right grip, stance and swing is the best foundation they can have. And it gives you time to work on your swing while they're learning theirs!

Free Green Fee When You Refer A New Member - have a friend that keeps threatening to learn to play? Now's the chance to help them start on the right foot and get a little benefit yourself!

**The Annual Association Fee is only $49.99 - about the price of one lesson from your usual instructor. To sign-up, you can stop in the Pro Shop and fill out a form, or download the form below. Once you've signed up you'll then be presented a MGA or WGA Membership Card and are well on your way to playing better golf!

Remember the better they play the more they play so whether you give it away or sell it cheap it still helps drive participation in both the short run and the long run

15. Turn the Range into a Three-hole Course a Few Afternoons a Week

Putting rank beginners out on your course is a horrible idea unless there is no one else on the course. I trust I don't need to explain that. Instead what I have seen as a great alternative is to turn the range into a short course with 4 – 6 par threes at set times during the week and let beginners get a taste for golf beyond the range markers.

While some go all out, you don't need regulation greens for most beginners to be successful with this concept. Winter greens will do, all you need is to create enough extra fun to get them interested in actually holing out and taking golf to the next level. Let people play for $5 or $3 or even free to increase their skills and get them excited about moving up to the real course when they are ready!

AK-Chin S. Dunes Club has just opened Mini Dunes. A driving range during the day, but in the late afternoons will transform to a professionally maintained short course with fully manicured greens.

Building Your Client Base Young

In my area, Home Depot was giving FREE workshops to kids on Saturday mornings. My son made a model plane, a boat, a birdhouse, and a fire engine out of wood. While the kids were busy building, parents had an hour to kill wandering about the store.

Do you think they bought anything?

Talk about positive branding! Every time I look at that bi-winged red plane, guess what company I think of? On top of that, where do you think these kids are going to tell their parents to shop? Where do you think these kids are going to shop when they grow up?

Barnes and Noble Offers Free Story Time

Saturday afternoons, my local Barnes and Noble bookstore offers children's story time. Just as with the Home Depot program, the parents linger in the store. They browse the aisles, drink expensive coffee, and buy into the brand in a bigger way than they otherwise would because now Barnes and Noble is not only entertaining their children, but they are encouraging the children to read and setting up their next generation of customers.

The Golf Industry Needs To Do Something Similar

Gone are the days where Dad spends his entire Saturday and Sunday at the club. If every club is looking for the 30-40 something demographic, here's where you'll find them: the soccer field. They are there every weekend – for hours on end.

Find a way to attract the kids, and you'll get the parents!

16. Introduce Snag Golf

The SNAG® Golf Coaching System is the best first touch program to effectively teach the game of golf to people of all ages and ability levels. SNAG® Golf offers the versatility to teach or play in almost any environment you choose.

Over the past 12 years, SNAG® Golf has built a premier first-touch learning system recognized by industry leaders around the world as the superior method to teach golf fundamentals in a fun and easy way. SNAG® Golf provides cutting edge learning techniques never before seen in the world of golf. SNAG® Golf is all about having FUN while learning the basics.

SNAG® Golf incorporates developmentally appropriate equipment that will allow golf to be learned and played in non-traditional venues, such as on a soccer field, in a gym, or on the beach. The program builds on strong fundamentals of the different strokes and swings and develops playing ability quickly and effectively. SNAG® Golf can be taught and played almost anywhere with immediate, positive results. This immediate success keeps new learners wanting to be further involved with golf.

http://www.snagpros.com/home.html

17. Juniors Play Free, on Scholarship or at Least Really Cheap

I am really lucky in that both the clubs I belonged to as a junior, Lilleshall Hall and Shifinal treated juniors really well and with no restrictions on play. I was also somewhat unusual perhaps in that I joined the club even through my parents did not play golf. (My dad took the game up soon after I did). Between 1978 and 1980 I played over 700 rounds a year, yes 700, and the combined cost of both memberships was less than $50. I played from sun up until sundown, seven days a week making my membership the best value purchase I have ever made and ever will make!

A sincere thanks, to both clubs for an amazing time as a member. But that's not how it is everywhere.

"Many country clubs still treat juniors like second-class citizens. It is funny how in marketing, 16-21 year olds are **a huge target audience** while at clubs, there are many restrictions on what they can do and when they can play. It sounds cliché, but kids are the future of the game. Getting more kids involved by giving them more opportunities to play everywhere is vital for short-term and long-term growth of the game." **Brett Packee, PGA, Teaching Professional, IL**

While the future might seem a long way off when you're paying the bills today, clubs must make a serious investment in their junior programs not just for the future but for the opportunity to get the children's parents involved. My dad didn't play golf when I started but not long afterwards he decided to join the club. Score one for the junior member!

Crown Golf said that anyone under 14 can join any of its 25 golf clubs for free, if at least one parent, grandparent or guardian is a seven-day or five-day member at that golf club.

St Mellion International Resort, the group's flagship property, introduced a 'Junior Golf Scholarship' for 25 young golfers aged between 12 and 18. Each junior on a St Mellion Junior Golf Scholarship receives free golf and coaching at the club, with scholarships being re-assessed on an annual basis. "We are serious about playing our part in safeguarding the future of the sport" said Crown Golf's outgoing chief executive officer, Stephen Lewis, "and Juniors Go Free is the strongest possible statement we can make.

"Juniors Go Free means that many existing members will now enroll their children at the club for the first time," he continued. "Far more families will get fully involved at a Crown Golf club in 2014: we're sending a clear message out, that golf is not just for the parents. – Source Club Management .Net

Every club should offer:

✔ 50 junior memberships at a very low cost $199 -$499 a year

✔ 4 junior scholarships

✔ A series of free coaching clinics

✔ A decent series of competitions

18. Show & Tell, Take It to the Schools!

OK, this is another long-term investment but we must have both short-term cash solutions and long term sow and reap efforts for a perfect balance. Back in the eighties Apple started giving schools free computers. When those kids who learned on Apples grew up guess whose computers they bought!

One tactic that worked amazingly well for me in the karate business was to invite all my students to bring in one of our instructors to "Show and tell." Everyone of course got a FREE pass to try karate out for real at my studio. You can do the very same thing with golf and invite all the students to come down and try golf at your facility for free!

Corporations also often have guest speakers come in and do a demonstration. Contact the major employers in your area and offer to do a clinic. Use the angle of golf being a healthy outdoor sport that will cut their health care costs over the long term. Hand out promotions for lessons, range balls, free rental clubs and rounds!

19. Start an After-School Program

This is not only a staggering opportunity for you to sow the seeds of future participation at your club, it's a huge moneymaker. With both parents working and a huge amount of single moms too, kids need somewhere to hang out between 3 and 6 pm when their parents get home from work!

An after school program done right can add tens of thousands of dollars to your club's income. Provide a useful service to the community and generate addition play income and memberships from the parents.

Yes, it takes some effort but it's worth it!

✔ Contract with a bus company to pick the kids up directly from school and drop them off at the club.

✔ Provide a beverage and small snack

✔ Take them to the back of the range to hit balls

✔ Have them do homework

✔ Watch TV or play video games

✔ Read, draw

20. Summer Camps

You can take after school programs to the next level and also organize golf summer camps. This is another great way to get fringe players or new players who are friends of existing players into the game. This too can be very lucrative and provides a safe environment that parents love!

Camps could be week-long 9-5pm so the parents can use it as break, or you could run it for the entire summer 6-8 weeks so parents can use it as a babysitting service. Assistant pros, school teachers and inters from golf collages can be a great source of temporary help if you decide to gear up. You might also look to partner with local collages for dorm accommodations and draw people from the entire state if not overseas.

Pine Needles in North Carolina runs one of the best and most lucrative kids golf camps, see above but there are lots of examples to model.

21. Hit the Community Colleges

Almost every community college offers golf as an option and a number of Pro's do really well teaching at community colleges. The pay may or may not be great, but the endless number of converts coming from their college classes to your course can more than compensate. The thing to remember about community colleges is you won't just get young men and women but many adults looking for further education as well.

In addition the amount of exposure provided each semester by liberal distribution of catalogs and/or brochures (often to every household in your county), can really benefit the local instructor in terms of community prestige and recognition, as well as reminding your existing golfers to come to your club. Depending on your location, it may make sense to do this at more than one school for extra impact.

22. Appoint Some Ambassadors to Help Attract Players/Members and Shepherd Beginners Around the Course.

One of the best ways to learn something is to teach it. You can harness the energy of some of your members for free with an Ambassador

Program. In addition to making new member or players feel welcome, you can also encourage referrals for both members/players and other Ambassadors you're your Ambassadors. They can also do show-and-tell at schools and other community outreach.

The one thing that is always in great supply at golf courses around the world is free advice. There are lots of retired people, many with nothing much to do. Take advantage of these two facts and create an ambassador corps to help attract new players and help beginners around the course by introducing them to the basic tenets of the game!

Setting Up an Ambassador Program

Why take care generating all the new business yourself when you can enlist the help of others? You can develop your own Ambassador Program. This very well could be the most important program that you ever set up at your club since it deals with the lifeblood of your club – *Membership*!

In short, your goal is to have a select group of members dedicated to reaching out to the community on your behalf to find new members. Their role is to help ensure continued growth at the club for the final goal of a full roster at the club. The ultimate (albeit mighty) goal for a private club is to reach its membership cap and have a waiting list of people to join.

Look for people who want to have an official role in your success. Identify members that are influential movers and shakers of your community. Find respected members who are in touch with your market. Maybe they are in fields like insurance or real estate, where they want a reason to meet more people. They are likely to be naturally outgoing, personable and persuasive people. Maybe they are retired and have time and want to be involved.

All members of the club should be involved in the process of referring others. Even the most connected of members will eventually run out of friends, associates, contacts, etc. to refer so a key purpose of the Ambassador Program is to develop an ongoing plan to educate and involve all club members in the referral process. They can help identify pockets of opportunity and new markets to tap for potential prospects.

The Ambassadors will host prospective members and be rewarded on a structured program based on their success in attracting new members. They are the eyes and ears of the membership and can make recommendations to the club about the creation of new programs, services, etc. that the club might offer to increase member involvement and thus satisfaction, resulting in higher retention. They should be looking for ways to get all members, especially new ones, involved and connected to the club, its members, and its activities. Happy, satisfied, and involved members will refer the club to their circle of influence.

Have regular meetings with an agenda, create a mission statement, set goals, and reward efforts. Make the meetings fun. Have guest speakers and run contests to see who can bring in the most referrals among the Ambassadors. Do something unexpected and surprise the group each meeting in appreciation for the arduous task they have committed to, such as having ice cream sundaes or flaming coffees served by the chef, giving them a special trinkets from the golf professional, having a masseuse give each a five minute foot rub. Present flowers to the ladies and cigars to the men or a bottle of wine to all. Be creative as your Ambassadors can be your most valuable resource. Have an annual appreciation dinner with "no holds barred" for this special (and valuable) group.

Appoint or elect a president. Let him send a referral reminder letter to the general membership on his behalf (not the clubs) at least once a year along with the new welcome letter to all new members. (And yes, there needs to be a paragraph in the new member welcome letter about the honor and privilege of giving referrals.)

The Ambassadors should also be present at any membership prospect function and be willing to serve as a sponsor if needed for either a golf game, or for membership (if needed at your club).

If you are not a private club Ambassadors can still perform a valuable function in attracting new players and helping them on the range and on the course. This can be formal or informal but you should advertise that you have these ambassadors available for free to play with people who would like to learn more about the game. Many people are freighted by golf and golf club rules and having a designated "friend" in the form of an Ambassador can be a huge help.

Offer Ambassadors free perks like:

✔ Free carts

✔ Free range balls

✔ Or some free guest passes

Make them compete in a contest to see who introduces the most players with a cool prize like a weekend in Las Vegas or Spain. There are a dozen people at your club right now chomping at the bit for this opportunity, give it to them!

23. Start a Caddie Program

The number of facilities that readily employ caddies has shrunk dramatically over the last two decades. That talent-rich door through which many of modest means entered the game has virtually closed. Gene Sarazen, Sam Snead, Ben Hogan and Byron Nelson -- four the best ever -- were all poor kids who started as caddies.

It the idea of free golf doesn't get kids initially excited, the idea of making money should. There is also the possibility of caddies earning a scholarship through the the **Evans Scholars Foundation.** It is a nonprofit organization based in Golf, Illinois that provides college scholarships to golf caddies. Sponsored by the Western Golf Association, the Evans Scholars Foundation has helped more than 10,600 caddies attend college since its creation in 1930.

Here is how to start one ....

http://www.wgaesf.org/site/c.dwJTKiO0JgI8G/b.6181555/k.70AF /Starting_a_Caddie_Program.htm

Take Advantage of ALL the Existing Golf Programs & the PR They Generate

We have already discussed that the programs produced to promote golf by the PGA and other big groups have minimal effects, but that's no excuse not to hitch a ride on their PR bandwagon, which can be huge. Take advantage of every one of these programs and the traffic they can generate from their TV advertising by signing up for all of them. Less than 50% of clubs engage with these efforts, which is just foolish. No matter how incremental the impact, it is a *positive* impact. Like the journey of 1,000 miles, growing the game must be done one step at a time!

24. Generate Your Own Positive Media to Drive Awareness & Participation

Unless you have been living under a rock for the last five years you will know that almost every article in the newspaper or segment on television about golf has been overwhelmingly negative.

Local Course Closing Down After Fifty Years
Participation in Golf Down 10%
Golf Losing Its Players
Local Course Being Sold to a Housing Developer
Private Course Opens to Public in an Effort to

Generate More Business
Local Club Dropping Membership Fees to Attract
More Players in a Shrinking Market!

The message the media is delivering is simple:

"Golf is out of favor and no one is playing the game
anymore therefore you shouldn't feel bad if you
have quit or don't want to start!"

IT DOESN'T HAVE TO BE THAT WAY!

After leaving office, Winston Churchill was asked by a young reporter how he expected history to view him in light of his many failures. Churchill replied that he expected history to view him very favorably. The reporter asked why? Churchill, already several volumes into a definitive history of World War II, cheerfully replied,

"Because that's the way I intend to write it."

He went on to write 93 books and surprisingly enough was viewed very favorable in all ☺ Indeed, there are constant opportunities for leaders at all levels to influence the way people think about them, their business or cause! The golf industry has done a shockingly poor job of managing their story in the media!

It used to be you would read articles in *Forbes*, *In Magazine*, airline magazines' or the *Times* about the benefits of business golf on a regular basis. When was the last time you saw one of those articles?

I monitor hundreds of newspapers and magazines and I can tell you that I have seen just one article on business golf in the last two years! Has the value of doing business somehow diminished in the last few years?

No, not one bit. Business golf is every bit the powerful tool it always had been it's just no one writes about it anymore!

No one that is until you!

You don't have to be a national organization to generate public relations in your own town. Generate your own PR by sending your local media positive golf stories. You'd be surprised how easy it is to start a positive trend among people who read the right articles.

Start with Your Own Mini Media Company

You can reach far more people than perhaps you realize through your own mini media company. In fact add up the number of people you can reach with your positive message through your:

- ✔ Website

- ✔ Blog

- ✔ Email list

- ✔ Facebook fans

- ✔ YouTube subscribers

- ✔ Linkedin connections

- ✔ Twitter followers

- ✔ Google plus

- ✔ Your snail mail list

- ✔ And whatever other media you may employ.

You might be surprised to find just how big an audience you have for your PRO GOLF articles if you combine all the numbers. You cannot rely on anyone else to do this critically important task by mere chance. You must continually educate your existing market and your potential market as to the wide and wonder array of benefits that result from golf participation.

Don't Forget to Constantly Re-sell Your Existing Clients as to the Many Benefits of Golf

In one past business, I ran one article a month in my newsletter re-selling existing members on the benefits of continuing with their programs. Many people make the mistake of thinking that people will figure it out from themselves. It never hurts to remind people of your benefits. Not everyone needs to be told, but we all need to be reminded.

Send Stories to Your Local Media

If you are lucky, your articles might get picked up from your website, blog or emails and republished by others such as a local newspaper, parenting magazine or the Chamber blog. But you cannot afford to leave it to luck. You must solicit their help. Most in the publishing business, short on staff and resources will be more than happy to take your well written piece and run it for free. And don't forget to submit your articles to other websites, blogs, and online outlets. They reprint a lot of material.

Send your stories to local newspapers, magazines and websites with a short cover letter explaining that you are telling the other side of the story that the mainstream media is missing!

Here as some examples

If you like them you can use these as a model for writing your own or click here to license mine. If you choose to license them you can quickly and easily edit these to benefit your own club by customizing the part where it refers a club and sending them in to your local media, newspaper, magazines, TV and radio. Add in your specific programs and results and the local media will eat it up!

Just like most people if someone else does the work for them they are more than happy to run with the results…

- ✔ Ten Reasons Why You Should Get Your Children Into Golf

- ✔ Ten Why Reasons Golf is Great for Your Business

- ✔ Ten Reasons You Should Play Golf

✔ Ten Reasons Seniors Should Play Golf

✔ Ten Reasons Women Should Play Golf

Attracting new players and indeed keeping existing players involved is a full-time effort in the sales and marketing department! You must constantly spell out the specific benefits players can derive from the game and constantly reiterate them using all the channels at your disposal.

Seek out personal stories from your club of:

✔ Business won at the club

✔ People finding health and love at the club

✔ Kids being drawn away from video games to the healthy atmosphere of the course

✔ Families bonding through the decades

The more personal the stories you have, the more often you share, the more they will positively impact the future of your club!

ABOUT ANDREW WOOD

Andrew Wood's Passion in Life is Helping Businesses Maximize Their Sales, Marketing and Growth Potential! He founded Legendary Marketing, a business designed to combine his passion for golf and travel with his marketing expertise. Legendary quickly built a name for itself in the golf industry with innovative websites, social media and online campaigns.

Born in Oxford, England and growing up in the Midlands near Shrewsbury, Andrew Wood immigrated to America in 1980 to pursue a career as a professional golfer. Unfortunately, lack of talent held him back and he accidentally found himself running a small karate school in Southern California. After struggling to survive for 18 months as a small business owner he decided to focus all his attention on marketing. This focus soon paid off and he quickly increased his income to six figures while still in his twenties.

His initial interest in marketing turned into a passion and he quickly turned the single school into a national franchise of over 400 units. After selling out of the karate business in the late 90's he move to Florida where he founded Legendary Marketing. Now their clients extend far beyond that industry. and indeed far beyond the USA with clients in Canada, the UK, Spain, Russia and Morocco to name just a few.

Author of over 40 sales, marketing and personal development books including; Legendary Advice, Making Your Business the One They Choose, **Cunningly Clever Marketing, Legendary Selling, Cunningly Clever Entrepreneur** and **The Golf Sales Bible.** He is considered the world's leading expert in golf, resort and real estate marketing and spoken to thousands of audiences worldwide on this and other topics from his books. A pioneer in internet marketing his creative talent, out of the box ideas and copywriting skills are at the core of his expertise. Regarded as one of the top marketing minds in the world his ability to generate leads and increase income are the key to his client's successes!

In his spare time he travels the world, plays golf & tennis, writes books and occasionally races cars!

Contact: Andrew Wood, Directly @ 352-266-2099 | Andrew@LegendaryMarketing.com

OTHER BOOKS
BY THE AUTHOR...

Other Books by Andrew Wood

Legendary Advice—101 Proven Strategies to Increase Your Income, Wealth &
Lifestyle
Legendary Achievement—How to Maximize Your True Potential & Live the
Life of Your Dreams
Cunningly Clever Marketing
Cunningly Clever Entrepreneur
Legendary Selling
Legendary Leadership
Making Your Business the One They Choose
The Traits of Champions (with Brian Tracy)
The Joy of Golf
The Golf Marketing Bible
The Hotel & Resort Marketing Bible
The Golf Sales Bible
How to Make $150,000 a Year Teaching Golf
Desperately Seeking Members (as Harvey S. McKlintock)

Micro Books 30—Minutes to
Legendary Leadership Series

Legendary Vision
Legendary Passion
Legendary Confidence—How to Build It in Yourself and Others
Legendary Trust
Legendary Strategy
Legendary Action
Legendary Communication
Legendary Charisma—How to Get It!
Legendary Problem Solving & Creativity—How to Remove Any Obstacle
Legendary Motivation
Legendary Courage
Legendary Persistence

Legendary Entrepreneur Series

Legendary Service—How to Give It!
Legendary Innovation—How to Unleash It!
Legendary Problem Solving—How to Remove Any Obstacle
Legendary Management—How to Deliver Fast Results!
Legendary Start-Ups—How to Start & Grow a New Busines

"Our membership director started using sales closing techniques from The Golf Marketing Bible and closed 4 of the first 5 prospects and transacted 7 membership sales in November and December We are in the metro Detroit area so closing ANY membership sales (let alone 7) at that time of the year is a huge bonus. Thanks!"

**– Brian Bach, GM,
Edgewood CC, member-owned private club,
Commerce, MI**

**"Every PGA member could benefit by reading
The Golf Marketing Bible..."**

– John Reger, Jr., PGA, Briefcase Golf, Inc.

"This book is the most complete 'how to really get it done' of any marketing book I've seen. I've also seen Andrew speak. you can hear him in this book inspiring and pushing you to market more effectively. Anyone who follows his systematic advice is bound to have big increases in business."

**– Dr. Rick Crandall, Author,
Marketing Your Services: For People Who Hate To
Sell**

"I purchased The Golf Marketing Bible last year and Cunningly Clever Marketing this year. I couldn't wait to start reading it after listening to your wisdom during the PGA Show seminars. Once I started reading it I couldn't put it down. I read almost the entire book during my flights back to North Dakota. It is truly jam-packed with all sorts of great marketing ideas. Thanks so much for these great books."

– David Solga, CGCS/PGA
Director of Golf, Bully Pulpit GC, Medora ND